"Gentlemen, meet DataBase. DataBase is merely a symbol of what I became ... See these strings here? Watch what happens when I pull on one of them. The marionette responds to my slightest hand movement. That's what happened to me. IBM wanted me to produce a certain image at its business meetings with an impossible budget, pulling my 'figure-it-out' string to do it. Now, in the middle of my career with IBM, before I got all strung up, I developed a program called Operation 30/30 that is helping pay for your hefty retirement. A retirement denied me."

Five pairs of eyes were riveted on me. Still crazy, they seemed to ask?

"So, DataBase, here, represents thousands of other IBMers out there who either need IBM's strings to hold them up or hate the strings because they hold them back or, like in my case, get entangled in them. DataBase symbolizes an International Business Marionette – an IBMer."

I kept going. IBM would hear me out and it would handle the problem I posed to them. "Now, you gentlemen have had several months to ponder my Open Door. From your dour expression ... you either don't believe me or you do believe me and have a 'so-what' attitude about it. Well, after enduring three mental institutions I've learned to be patient. I can wait on a court of law. I know what my witnesses will say."

I stuck my hand in an inner suitcoat pocket, hauled out a cigar, tapped the middle string on DataBase's head and plopped the cigar into his open mouth, releasing the string and watching it clamp down.

"All that's been discussed here, today, is over a box of these." I pointed at the cigar in DataBase's mouth. "Incredible when you think about it.

"Have a nice day, gentlemen."

With a flip of my wrist I had DataBase sitting on my shoulder as I sauntered out of the boardroom.

Twenty minutes later my lawyer approached me. Smiling, he said, "You did well. They don't know what to make of you, and that's probably good. They asked for ninety days to receive IBM's final position. I think we'll be getting an offer of settlement. After that it's a question of how much."

International Business Marionettes

*An IBM Executive Struggles
to Regain His Sanity after a Brutal Firing*

Max Beardslee

Lucky Press, LLC
Lancaster, Ohio

Lucky Press, LLC
126 S. Maple St.
Lancaster, OH 43130
www.luckypress.com/internationalbusinessmarionettes

Jacket and illustrations by Janice Phelps
PRINTED IN THE UNITED STATES OF AMERICA

Publisher's Cataloging-in-Publication
(Prepared by Quality Books Inc.)

Beardslee, Max
     International business marionettes : an IBM executive struggles to regain his sanity after a brutal firing / Max Beardslee. -- 1st ed.
     p.cm.
     ISBN 0-9706377-0-5
     LCCN: 2001088096

     1. Beardslee, Max.   2. International Business Machines Corporations--History. 3. Businessmen--United States--Biography. 4. Computer industry--United States--History. I. Title.

HD9696.C62B43   2001   338.7'61004'092
                                             QBI00-908

This book is dedicated to the millions of people enduring mental afflictions. Life can get better.

Also, in memory of Ralph Pennington, who passed early in life but gave so much while he was here.

*"There is no greater agony
than that of bearing an untold story."*

Introduction

This book reflects what happened to me in a twelve-year career at IBM. Some of it great, some of it bizarre, I believe it to be a good story and capable of helping others avoid the pitfalls of big business — and few represent big business more than the International Business Machines Corporation.

The writing style is novelized: the truth, as we have often heard, *can* be more interesting than fiction.

International Business Marionettes covers the gamut from a high of pioneering a worldwide marketing program at IBM to the low of insanity, buried away in the back ward of a mental institution, unable to deal with being summarily fired. It does have a very happy ending, however.

IBM came with plenty of structure and therein laid the incompatibility. My right-brained creativity was ultimately no match for IBM's left-brained layers of conformity. Those strings of structure blurred individual contributions by holding back the achievers albeit propping up those who just wanted a ride. My wife told me at the fateful end of my career I was not an IBMer, but an "International Business Marionette." She was right.

Prologue

Thursday – June 19, 1981

AT THE TOP OF HIS PROFESSION, THAT'S HOW THE OLD MAN HAD BEEN billed. Working deep in the alleys of lower Manhattan, hard to find and harder yet to meet, he had at first seemed reluctant to fill my order, but I had insisted.

"This is one time in my life when I need the very best," I had told him. Finally, after three weeks of nervous anticipation, the job was done.

I counted out the hundred dollar bills, thirty in all, and stacked them on the workbench. He bent over and scooped them up. Then the craftsman's recount began. He thumbed meticulously through the bills as I watched.

"As agreed," he finally said, carefully folding the bills and slipping them into his pocket. There would be no receipt. He reached for the black carrying case and handed it to me. "Hope this does the job."

"So do I," I replied.

With a tight grip on the case, I turned to leave the shadowy room. Remembering my manners, I stopped, looked back over my shoulder and added, "Thank you."

"Not at all," came the faint reply from the slight body already stooped over the workbench again.

Walking into the murky alley, I hastened my pace, anxious to find a sunlit boulevard and a cab. In minutes I had secured both.

"LaGuardia Airport, cabby."

During the cab ride to LaGuardia, I kept the black case tightly beside me. It worried me, now. I wondered about carrying it on board the flight to Detroit and if it would pass through security without a problem. Would it fit beneath the seat once I was on board? I wanted to avoid an argument with a security guard or a flight attendant. Certainly, I didn't want to have to explain or show why the object in the case required special care. Its unique construction; its special purpose; that knowledge belonged to me and me alone.

The driver expertly drove to the airport. After dodging in and out of the clogged New York traffic, he dropped me off at the American Airlines terminal. A generous tip reflecting pleasure with my purchase and an uneventful ride accompanied the fare.

Approaching the security check, I took a deep breath, placed my case on the conveyor and walked through the detector. The security attendant looked up from her scope to give me the once over. Her squinting eyes seemingly bore a question, but none was asked, and she let the case and me pass.

Good, I thought. *The last thing I need is to be stopped and questioned.* Picking up the case, I moved toward to the airline's departure gate. Minutes dragged by as I impatiently awaited the call for boarding, the case resting in my lap, my fingers drumming upon it.

Hearing the boarding announcement, I carefully lifted the case up before rising. Once past the stewardess who took my ticket, I thought, now just to get on and get this thing safely under the seat.

I walked down the narrow aisle, the case held stiffly in front of me so it wouldn't bang into the seats on either side and jostle the contents. Squeezing into my seat, I pulled it up to my chest with one arm and held it against my body with the other. I wanted to be sure not to hit some passenger in the head and call attention to myself. Sliding down into my seat, I leaned forward and carefully maneuvered the case between my legs, then onto the floor and gently eased it below the seat in front of mine. Just barely, the case fit.

I could relax a bit — at least until I got to Detroit, where I would have to change planes and catch a flight for Grand Rapids.

I sat with my eyes closed during the take off, relieved to be heading home. When the attendant came along for drink orders, I opened my eyes and asked for two. As I poured the scotch into the soda I imagined just how and when I would use my newly acquired weapon. I chuckled. Yes, it served as a weapon. Quite a formidable weapon.

I made the connection to Grand Rapids, going through the same motions and fears with the case once again, but by early afternoon arrived back at my apartment with my precious baggage safe and sound. I frowned as I entered the small austere living room. How unsuitable the place looked for a man who'd enjoyed a dozen years of the first class accommodations offered by big business; its only attraction came from the low rent.

"And that should not be a consideration much longer," I told myself in a loud, firm voice.

I carefully put the black case down on the sofa, poured myself a generous drink, and settled down beside my new acquisition. I wanted to unzip it, examine the contents, maybe run a test of sorts. Yet, keeping it closed and letting my imagination run wild felt more gratifying.

Patting the case, I looked out the window and said, again in a bold and determined voice, "Yes, you bastards. This oughta do it."

The plan for vengeance that I had in mind would soon be set in motion. Risk loomed large as a factor, casting its shadow over me, but I just shrugged. *No matter.* I had my priorities.

Expose IBM. My desire to uncover the inner workings of the corporate giant had begun gestating thirteen months earlier. I'd never forget that ugly Friday...

One

THE FLASHING BLUE LIGHT APPEARED BEHIND ME SUDDENLY. I PULLED my new high-performance Olds' to the curb and rolled down my window. "What's the trouble, officer?"

He stood tall and solidly built, his creosol shoes permanently glazed. "You were driving erratically, sir. May I see your drivers license and registration?"

Numbly, I obliged.

"Mr. Beardslee, I'm going to ask you to step out of your vehicle."

I leaned forward and reached for the doorknob, but my shirt stuck to the leather seat, the dampness acting like glue and rendering my effort useless. I didn't have the energy to break its hold and leaned back against the seat once again.

"Step out, Mr. Beardslee."

A day for losers. As I had already been once marked, I knew arguing would be futile. Slowly, I obeyed the officer, this time exerting a bit more effort. My shirt pulled away from my back before its hold on the seat gave way and then settled clammily against my skin.

"Now walk toward me."

I followed his command, meekly trying to clear up what seemed to be a misunderstanding. "I haven't been drinking, if that's what—"

"Stand in place, close your eyes, tip your head back, and touch your nose with your first finger."

With a sigh of resignation, I did what he asked.

"Try again."

Next came the Breathalyzer. I inflated the balloon, and the officer performed a quick test with a small instrument. Frowning, he said, more to himself than to me, "Tests out zero: no alcohol."

"Of course not. It's barely noon and I never..."

"You were weaving all over the road, Mr. Beardslee," he said before I could finish. Looking at me closely, he added, "And your eyes don't seem normal."

I stared back at him; not about to admit that the red rims surrounding bloodshot eyes were a by-product of my earlier tears.

"Are you taking any medication or — "

"I'm *not* on drugs."

He gave me another once over and then said, "Stay right where you are."

I watched as he walked purposely to my car and spent several long minutes searching the interior. He returned rubbing the creases on his forehead, and I wondered if he was going to ask me to assume the position and frisk me. Rather than endure that ordeal as well, I blurted out, "I've lost my job. It happened this morning. I'm shook up about it. I've been driving around trying to figure out what to tell my wife."

"A lay off?" he inquired, his stance getting a bit less stiff, less intimidating.

"No. Fired. I got canned because of a lousy box of cigars."

"Cigars? What kind of a job did you have?"

I took him through a portion of the dark tunnel I'd experienced. I'd worked twelve years for IBM, rising from lowly trainee to head honcho in the Western Michigan area. As I fed this officer the bare basics, my mind raced through the intricate details.

Yes, I'd started with IBM, outwardly one of the world's most glamorous business operations, right here in Grand Rapids. Eighty-hour weeks sapped me in the beginning as I struggled to master computer technology, a field foreign to me at the time. From there I fought the sales quota wars, starting fresh each year with new goals, larger hurdles to jump over to prove my worth to management.

In the past six years, my good-natured wife, Pat, and I had moved four times. Each time she had to cope with setting up camp in a new city and then tearing it down and starting over again somewhere else. While not enjoying these disruptions, she handled them without complaint, knowing each move brought her husband closer to what he wanted. Or thought he wanted. All the while I kept my sights set on achieving the very opportunity I'd gained just five months prior — my own sales organization.

Sales branch manager: the most sought after job at IBM and the springboard every high-powered exec in IBM had used to move up. To come back to Grand Rapids, where my IBM career had started, well ... that made the new job even sweeter. It also made it easier to visualize the comparison between the Spartan desk in the trainees' "bullpen" that I had occupied twelve years earlier to the ornate, polished-mahogany one in the corner-pocket office I'd commanded until a few hours before.

Along the way, Pat and I had started a family that now included three boys, put some money in the bank and looked forward to the security and prestige this promotion would bring with it. *An IBMer for life*, I'd thought.

Strong business friendships dominated those twelve years. I'd bonded with successful men and women from all over the United States. Talented executives had made investments in my training, shaping a raw stone into a many-faceted gem. I'd grown from a green recruit to an experienced sales executive with confidence and responsibility. My latest position meant that I served as the IBM representative for the several million people living in Western Michigan — and that the IBM execs on the rungs above mine believed I was the right person to do so.

"I was responsible for a forty-million-dollar operation and thought I had done a damn good job," I told the officer with indignation. "Then, a guy who'd been climbing the ladder in front of me

— someone I'd always thought I could count on to speak up for me — flew in this morning to tell me I was suddenly beyond saving." I shook my head, and the anger left my body as confusion filled its place. I could hear the words he had used as clearly now as when he first spoke them aloud.

"They're forcing me to let you go, Max," said Len Fillmore matter-of-factly. My giant-sized and intimidating regional manager, a person who could freeze people in their tracks with an icy stare, was a man I'd grown to admire. He had plenty of candidates to pick from in filling the prestigious job of sales branch manager, and five months ago he had picked me. While his own considerable talents stayed taxed to manage a four-hundred-million-dollar-per-year sales operation for IBM, I'd served as his assistant in the final grooming stage before gaining the job.

"Because of some cigars, eh? Weren't supposed to smoke 'em in the office, eh?" the officer joked.

The sarcastic smile fell away from the policeman's face as I stared at him, wondering whether he'd even begin to understand if I tried to explain. I decided he probably wouldn't. Who would?

"I don't know much about IBM, Mr. Beardslee," he broke the silence. "Typewriters?"

"I was in computers ... the sales end. Gave it everything I had. Went wherever they sent me, six promotions, four moves in just the last six years. My family and I just recently came back to Grand Rapids. It's home. We'd hoped to stay a while."

I could feel my eyes filling with tears again. *God, I don't want to have to move my family and myself again*, I thought. *I don't want to work for someone else somewhere else.* I hung my head and kicked a small stone across the tarmac.

The officer put his hand on my shoulder. "The cigar deal doesn't sound like enough to get anyone fired. If I had a beef like yours, I'd go to my union for help."

"I was management, and management doesn't have that advantage. Besides, IBM doesn't have any unions."

I could have gone on to tell him how, over a sixty-odd-year existence, IBM prided itself on the fact that few of its three hundred and forty thousand employees had ever seen the need for a union. I'd been proud of that myself and shared the position that unions existed mainly for those workers who couldn't trust management. But now ... I wished I had such clear recourse.

"Then maybe you oughta see a lawyer," he suggested.

"Yes, maybe I should. Well, thanks officer. May I go now?"

He nodded. "You seem to have settled down. I'm not going to write you up. Just be sure you pay more attention to the road. And good luck to you, Mr. Beardslee."

I figured I needed it; but the idea of good fortune coming my way from any direction just didn't compute. Getting back into my car, I collapsed against the seat. Again Fillmore's words resounded in my head as if he were sitting beside me. I'd asked him for the real reason I'd been fired.

"They're calling it 'premeditated intent to obligate IBM funds,' " he had replied. "It's considered a serious breech of conduct. Twenty-one people were let go for the same reason last year."

Premeditated. The word sounded so sinister, like I had performed some criminal act for Crissakes.

I glanced in the rearview mirror. The officer was waiting for me to do something. I pulled away from the police car as quickly as I dared.

I drove gloomily on without a destination until a thought, followed by a snicker, momentarily pushed my depression away. *How silly,* the way I had let the events of the day play tricks with my mind and get me down. I laughed and shook my head at myself. *I'm too strong for that,* I thought, jutting my chin forward. *I've always been able to overcome even the largest of hurdles. Anyway, it's just a job. I can get another.*

As quickly as the mirth arrived, tears pushed it aside. I put my left elbow on the window ledge and leaned my heavy head against my hand as they rolled slowly down my cheeks.

"Damn, how could they do it to me?"

Fired. Terminated. Tossed out and discarded like some obsolete circuit board. However I chose to say it, I was through at IBM, and I had never even considered that a possibility. In fact, I had based every hope and dream for my future around my career with the company.

I pondered one of IBM's founding principles: Respect for the individual. None had shown here. Or maybe my actions didn't entitle me to respectful treatment.

"Damn, how could I ever have let it happen?" I said aloud as my mind flip-flopped from blame to self-criticism. IBM's internal tie line phone network would be glowing by now. "Beardslee got the axe. Shot." That's what they'd all be saying.

Others would put it together another way. Fillmore was the real target. When they couldn't get him, the rogue elephant in the center of the herd, they'd gunned Beardslee down instead. Yeah, I was easier to site-in on, less able to withstand a bullet.

I drove on, moving aimlessly from one end of the city to the other, although paying better attention to my driving than I had earlier. Hours passed, each one representing one more mental review of my years with IBM. As the day faded, lengthening shadows enveloping the road, and I turned the car toward home.

I dreaded telling my wife the news but tried formulating words in my head that would break it gently. The words didn't want to come together into coherent sentences. *Best to get it out fast, though,* I told myself. *She needs to know.*

Pulling into the U-shaped driveway, I thought, *home, but for how much longer?* Uncertainties crept into my previously secure life: *Would the family be uprooted from our prized surroundings? Would shame extinguish our connection with newly found friends? Our financial status definitely would erode without my paycheck, but how far – and for how long?*

I sat in the car for a minute feeling my stomach clench like a fist before I slowly opened the car door, heaved myself out of the seat and headed for the front door. Pat had put up with a lot as my wife for most of my dozen IBM years: late hours, the uncertainties of an income tied to sales performance, a heavy travel schedule. I hated to have to put her through one more ordeal ... just when we thought most of them were over.

She'd know my arrival home early bore bad news. I thought about whether to ease into it or just blurt it out when I opened the door. Before I got that far, however, the door opened and Pat stepped out onto the porch, her pony tail bobbing. From beneath her blonde bangs her large blue eyes looked up at me from a chassis a shade over five-feet tall. Her apprehensive and questioning look turned into a worried frown as she saw the dejection stamped on my face. I walked past her and into the house.

Taking in the expanse of the living room, I tried to focus on the thrill she'd felt as we moved in just months before. She'd loved this house from the moment she saw it and was eager to make it a home and get our school-aged kids adjusted and comfortable.

I tried to remember the carefully chosen words I'd planned to use to make the news more palatable to her, but my rehearsals proved useless. "Honey, IBM let me go. I'm out," I blurted.

That morning I'd tried to condition her to expect the worst, but I could see the shock waves of surprise flash in her eyes. She took my hand and motioned for me to follow. "Let's go into the kitchen," she said in a quiet voice, "where you can tell me about it."

Pat knew almost as much as I did. In the past two weeks I had been ordered on two different occasions to fly to Atlanta, meeting there with the divisional director of personnel and the vice president of finance to discuss my role in the Fillmore regime. On both occasions these guys had bobbed and weaved before zeroing in on one subject — the business meetings held for Fillmore's key people, his branch managers.

These two execs had taken the position that Fillmore spent extravagant amounts on these meetings. They showed and discussed with me vouchers from first-class hotels, chartered airplanes, and expensive awards — obvious proof of his expensive tastes and spending habits. They even got hold of vouchers never submitted to IBM but paid for outside the company for things like liquor and cigars.

What they really wanted to know, however, was what went on in the meetings themselves. Not much leaked out as to how Fillmore conducted his off-site sales meetings. Few outsiders got invited, and Fillmore's guys never breathed a word of the goings on to anyone not part of the exclusive sales force. What these investigators hoped to gain through my interrogation was something juicy they could blow up — like a story about sales execs drinking at the elaborate dinners scheduled during the meetings.

And they had good reason, at least in their minds, for wanting to pin something on Fillmore. Fillmore's chilly stares and booming voice backed up by the physique that helped him in his former career as an NFL defensive tackle, had won more enemies than friends. And Fillmore obviously managed to bend most of IBM's strict rules about expenditures and appropriate conduct for company-sponsored meetings — but no one could prove it. Like a crafty accountant, he always managed to stay just a hair within the law. They would want to catch him "cheating on his taxes" as it were, and that was why they kept hauling me, one of his lieutenants, in for questioning.

The first time I got ordered to Atlanta, John Paulos, the divisional director of personnel, hauled out invoice after invoice showing a dozen quarts of booze and wine consumed at the Hyatt Regency in Detroit where a recent meeting had been held. IBM acted like a sonovabitch about booze and everybody knew it. From the day when Tom Watson, Sr., IBM's founder, dismissed a key executive when he smelled liquor on his breath, IBM frowned on liquor consumption — or, more accurately, pretended it did not exist — at any type of company event be it luncheon meetings or awards dinners. Even at the IBM recognition events, also attended by spouses, no booze was allowed, not even a glass of wine before a sumptuous meal.

As the company shut its eyes, however, IBMers drank their share, particularly those in sales. While sales meetings were notorious for being as much party as they were business, we made sure that as far as corporate headquarters and the divisional staff bloodhounds surrounding Fillmore's boss were concerned, it appeared that we consumed no booze at all.

"Beardslee, these guys must have been drunk! How about it?"

Then, I'd almost laughed. Paulos assumed all that liquor had been lapped up by thirteen people: Fillmore and his twelve area managers. In truth, including Fillmore's staff over forty people attended that meeting, and the billing of the booze had been correct, except for one fact: the liquor got paid for by me or the attendees, not by IBM.

To get around IBM's rules, we all chipped in for liquor; thus insuring that IBM never even saw an invoice for booze. This time, however, the personnel people had commanded the hotel to release figures showing how much liquor we'd purchased. IBM hadn't paid for any of it, but they still wanted to know what we'd consumed.

Feigning a confidence I didn't feel, I'd corrected Paulos. "You are assuming only a dozen people or so attended the meeting. Roughly forty people were there. I'd be happy to provide you with a list."

When Paulos found out his attendance figures needed revamping, he clenched his fists and stared at the ceiling. Then, sweeping his hand over his thinning hair combed upward from the sides to delay the inevitable, he took a new tact. He opened a folder with my name on it, his lips turning slightly upward as he handed me the top document.

"This invoice ... look at it."

I did. The sound of my heart beating in my ears created an almost unbearable pressure in the drum. I swallowed as if I was on an airplane to clear them so I could hear once again.

"Coppies: $77," was scrawled in the misspelled handwriting of the Hyatt Regency's Italian headwaiter.

"This invoice for photocopies ... did you make photocopies?" Paulos knew the answer to his own question. His smug look gave this fact away. Besides, I had already told an auditor of my plan to bill IBM for a box of cigars by calling it copies so that I wouldn't have to pay for them out of my pocket.

IBM wouldn't pay for cigars smoked at meetings — and required by Fillmore — any more than it would pay for the liquor. (My boss wouldn't allow me to collect more than twenty dollars from attendees, which was not enough to cover all the expenses IBM refused to pay.) Therefore, I faced two unattractive alternatives: either I pay for the cigars out of my own pocket or cover them up as something else that IBM considered an acceptable meeting expenditure.

Anticipating that the monkeyed invoice would come up, I looked Paulos straight in the eye, and evenly replied, "No John, I didn't. I bought cigars." My damp hand hauled out of the inside breast pocket of my suit jacket a cancelled seventy-seven dollar check written against my personal account. "But, IBM never paid for them. I did. And here's the check to prove it."

Solid evidence that I paid for the stogies. Counter Paulos' ace with my own. *That oughta derail him,* I thought.

Paulos picked up the check, looked at it and quickly set it down, brushing it aside like a piece of third-class mail. Then he looked right at me, the corners of his mouth turned downward. "But you set this invoice up for IBM to pay, is that right?"

You're damned right I did, I thought. Was I supposed to not only handle all of Fillmore's dirty linen but pay the laundry bill, too? Forget it.

"Yeah, at one time I planned to have IBM pay the invoice...," I paused for effect, "but I never followed through."

My conversation with Paulos plowed downhill from there, any pretense of respect leaving the conversation. But that was then, and here was now with my wife in our new house and the bad news as our new roommate.

Pat quietly listened to me relay the mornings events, but when I told her, "Honey, when Fillmore dropped the bomb, I even called Hampstead," she looked at me in surprise, and replied, "You're kidding."

Bruce P. Hampstead had arrived in January as the president of my division, a relatively new one called the General Systems Division formulated to sell smaller computers to all-sized companies across America. Hampstead had emerged from a laboratory assignment, where he had headed up some computer development effort; rumors preceding his arrival implied that he lacked sales experience. At that time, IBM had six selling divisions worldwide. With the exception of Hampstead, all of the execs who presided over those divisions had been sales leaders.

Since Hampstead had seen little of the workings of a sales organization, I figured the lab man to be neutral at best about the hoopla most divisions of IBM used to keep the sales force whipped up. Maybe the corporation wanted that kind of stuff toned down, I thought, and he was the first of a new breed. No, I thought, they were smarter than that. Personalities like Hampstead's would breed discontent. IBM wanted harmony. He was just an anomaly soon to pass over the horizon.

I had felt apprehensive about calling Hampstead, but I was out of options. I knew getting any type of help from him would require translating Fillmore's brand of meetings into terms that would seem acceptable based on his more conservative perspective. From the airport where I'd met Fillmore I picked up a pay phone and dialed. Fillmore sat just a few feet away straining to hear — his massive bulk looking to collapse his small chair. I turned my back to him as I raised the receiver to my ear.

"Bruce Hampstead." The voice sounded cold.

I fumbled for words to muster honor in my position, to somehow find a way to convince him I should be allowed to stay in the company. *Don't mention the hundreds of dollars of expense you paid out of your own pocket,* I cautioned myself. *Don't whine, Beardslee. Suck it up. Yes, altering an invoice proved to be a mistake but you admitted your error months before the audit and wrote a personal check to rectify that blunder. And, the cigars got doled out not for personal use but for others' pleasure. It's not like you bought them for yourself and then tried to get the company to pay for your good smoke.*

"Yes sir. This is Max Beardslee ... calling you from Grand Rapids. Len Fillmore is here with me. He's just finished telling me that you're firing me for calling cigars photocopies instead. I don't want to believe you are firing me over this, especially when your man, Paulos, knows I paid for the cigars. I showed him my cancelled check."

Hampstead remained chilly, saying something about "mitigating circumstances" that I didn't understand, followed by an icy, "The decision has been made, I wish you well." Click. Silence.

Hampstead had spent just seconds considering a career spanning a dozen years with the company he represented. Stunned and angered by the finality of this rejection, I slammed the pay phone back into its holder, barely noticing Fillmore's startled expression.

"Damn," Pat said as she banged her fist on the counter. "That's awful that the bastard wouldn't even talk to you." She hesitated, her anger turning to sorrow, then dabbed at her eyes with a Kleenex as she continued. "Look, honey, I know you've told me all about this, but was there more? What Hampstead said — the 'mitigating circumstances' — did he have other stuff on you?"

I looked at my red-eyed wife and said, "Not that I know of. Besides, I thought mitigating meant pro-defendant, but Hampstead used the word in the opposite context, which I thought was odd. Right after I hung up with Hampstead, I asked Fillmore what the other circumstances were; he said he didn't know. The only thing Fillmore had heard, other than about the cigars, he said, was something about a bottle of brandy that got billed to IBM."

I had been quite surprised at Fillmore's comment about the brandy. "What brandy?" I had yelled, the words seemingly thundering out of my mouth. I had never shouted at a powerful IBM executive before. I would have been afraid I'd get called on it — even fired — but what did I have to lose now?

No brandy had been bought for this sales meeting. It was impossible. And even if it *had* been bought, it wouldn't have been billed to IBM, of that I was certain. I knew that calling booze anything else and submitting the invoice for payment could result in a firing. IBM flatly refused to pay for booze. A branch manager I'd worked for had been let go for creative invoicing of liquor. I had, however, foolishly applied a double standard to the company's view of other unnecessary meeting expenditures and how they were covered: liquor verses everything else. IBM, I thought, would have patience for creatively calling cigars, gum or mints something like photocopies to gain proper expense reimbursement.

But no brandy was ... *wait a minute.* I caught my breath. We'd been served crepe suzettes that night ... something had been used to make them flame dramatically. *Probably brandy,* I thought, shaking my head at the absurdity of the situation.

Fillmore and I had aimlessly walked together down the airport hallway. The big man put his arm around me, the discomfort of the gesture providing a clear sense of how out of character it was for him to act in that manner. Tough mail for him to deliver; tougher yet for me to receive.

"No, honey. There was nothing else. Believe me," I concluded my saga.

Pat's face looked pale. Damn, why did I go and screw everything up after all that I'd put her through? A woman of strong Scottish-Irish stock, I'd taken her out of a happy home in Maine, put her on the "I've Been Moved" circuit and left her at home as I pursued the long hours required for advancement up the corporate ladder. After a decade of struggle, we'd turned the corner to Easy Street. The last three years had been heady stuff as my career picked up momentum, but it had looked like she was finally going to get to settle down as I got what I'd been waiting for as well. And now, a twelve-year flight soaring to higher and higher levels, the view reaching to wider and wider horizons, crashed to smithereens by a box of cigars acting as the errant missile.

I reached over and picked up the coffeepot. As I filled my cup with shaky hands, about a third of it splashed on the kitchen table. I moved to look for a sponge, but Pat jumped to her feet before I got far and put her hand on my shoulder. "You sit."

While Pat mopped up, I continued. "A cop pulled me over while driving home. He thought I had been drinking, because I was paying so little attention to my driving." She looked up, sponge in hand, with a wrinkled brow then sat down. I shrugged my shoulders sheepishly. "He let me off because of what happened earlier and suggested I see a lawyer."

Pat looked at me and burst into tears. I listened to her sobs muffled by shaking hands covering her face. Her small frame sat hunched on the kitchen stool. *God,* I thought, *this is gonna be awful.*

Two

INNER WAS SOMBER. JUST THE SOUNDS OF DISHES AND SILVERWARE could be heard, unusual in my noisy family. I sat in silence, hearing Pat's voice crack as she tried to make normal family conversation without her usual enthusiasm. She got no response from any of us; our three boys picked at their food, grumpily responding to the stress they felt in the air.

John, dark-haired and quietly thoughtful, our oldest at nine years and a straight-A student, brought the situation into concrete terms. Fussing over a piece of salad he hoped he wouldn't be forced to eat, he asked, "Dad, does this mean we'll have to move?"

A good question, I thought, and one I had briefly confronted earlier in the day. *Could I get a decent job in Grand Rapids or would we have to move once more?* The city, known for its Dutch furniture craftsmen, stable economy and good schools, had become a highly sought after place to settle in the Midwest.

Little Chris, too young at three to know what had happened, wrinkled his nose at his salad, a sign that he remained unaffected by the day's events, while our middle son, Steve, muscular, towheaded, and boisterous at not-quite-seven, understood the basics: Dad didn't work for IBM anymore. He didn't seem upset, just uncomfortable in the heavy home environment the day's events had created.

I left the table, my plate untouched after murmuring an answer to John's question. "I don't think so, Son. We'll be all right." As I walked away, some chatter emanated from the table. Maybe my presence had affected everybody's mood. *If so,* I thought, *hopefully my gloom moves when I move. I don't need the whole family down about this.*

The phone rang so often that evening that Pat began a log in which she recorded about a hundred calls over the next few days. The well-intentioned callers, perhaps a testimonial to the number of friendships I'd built up over my years at IBM, actually served only as a painful reminder — they're in and I'm out — rather than as a consolation.

Bill Fleming called first. Fleming, whose immense height required stooping for doorways, had worked for me for a short time the previous year. "Too Tall," as many called him, spoke from a phone booth at an IBM promotion party in Detroit. I could hear the din in the background. It didn't seem fair that somebody there was feeling the pleasure of his or her recent job promotion while I was enduring the immense pain of having just lost mine.

"Beardslee, you sure know how to ruin a good party. This joint is like a tomb."

It sure doesn't sound like one, I thought.

"I called to offer my regrets at what happened today. Plenty of other people feel the same way. In fact, I polled the troops asking them what they thought about your getting the axe. The vote is running about forty to one in your favor. One asshole, however, figures you got what you deserved."

I'd forced a small laugh knowing my unstructured style had not been to everyone's liking. I'd broken every code of dress and conduct and my lack of conformity had gone against the IBM grain. Most men wore blue or gray suits, plain or striped, with all-cotton white buttoned-down collar shirts and black laced wingtip shoes with socks to the knee. Less conservative in dress than most IBMers, I'd worn light suits, an occasional colored shirt, and bright printed ties.

Most employees focused on the rules of conduct in hopes of getting approval for doing so: "Don't get shit-faced at parties"; "Don't disparage the competition"; "Don't talk negatively about shortcomings in IBM's product line"; "Don't stand out." None of that had mattered much to me. I had broken the rules often enough to be noticed but not branded as a misfit. I noticed too, and acknowledged to myself when I did conform that I operated unnaturally, but I did so more and more often as I climbed higher up the corporate ladder.

Saturday morning I woke early covered with sweat and feeling as if I'd tied one on. My head ached, a dry mouth, but I hadn't even had one drink the night before. The room felt cool, an overhead fan quietly humming away creating a gentle breeze that didn't seem strong enough to dry my damp skin. Crawling out of bed, I discarded my pajamas and walked into the master bath.

I stared at my face in the mirror. Normally, I carried the sun with me year round since my skin tanned easily and I spent as much of my free time outdoors as possible. Today, I looked pale, almost milky white. *Not good,* I thought.

Cold tiles greeted my feet sending a chill upward through my body as I stepped into the shower. The jets of water bouncing off my chest energized me and seemed to wash away the pounding in my head. I filled my mouth with water and spat it downward at the drain, rinsing the dry stale taste from my mouth. *The shower: a good place to think,* I figured. I hadn't allowed thoughts of anything to do with my firing enter my head clearly since I had awoken, letting them instead reside in the background, present and accounted for but not consciously acknowledged. Now I allowed them to flood my mind, which actually cleared my head all the more. The effort of holding them back seemed to make my brain foggy and lethargic.

I tried to turn my thoughts to the future, even just toward today, wanting to come up with a game plan. But each effort proved futile, my thoughts of job searches and new careers consistently pushed out by thoughts of the sacking I had experienced the day before. Dwelling on the past seemed unhealthy, but I couldn't help myself.

All of my thoughts focused on the negatives of yesterday; nothing else would fit into my cramped brain. *A feeling of normalcy is bound to creep back in,* I reassured myself, *probably just a slow process. After all, the firing only happened yesterday, for Chrissake. Give yourself a break. It is impossible to know where this will lead now or to expect yourself to get up and be cheerful and ready to find out.*

Over the next few days I kept trying to focus on finding a new job. It was nearly impossible. My logic kept telling me that should be my next step, however, the only future-oriented thought that I could conjure up revolved around getting my old job back.

I wanted justice. I had been wrongly relieved of my duties with IBM; the right thing to do would be for the company to reinstate me. But how would I get them to do that? IBM never let anybody back in. And all that talk about premeditation, whatever it meant, insured that I, too, would remain outcast. They would never let someone back in who had seemingly tried to hurt "Big Blue," the nickname the company had gotten from its corporate colors and logo. IBM's lawyers had signed off on my sacking, which meant they felt the action was justified with no reason for the backlash of a lawsuit initiated by me. I could count on IBM being thorough there. I'd known of perhaps fifty "whack jobs" in the dozen years I'd been with IBM, and not one had been reversed.

Beneath this train of thought — or any other that entered my head — lay yet another. No matter what else I thought, always present, like a computer running two or more programs at once, were the cigars and that little piece of incriminating paper ... C-O-P-P-I-E-S. An uncomfortable feeling of guilt arrived. I knew I had done something wrong, I knew it when I did it. *But I paid for the damn stogies,* I thought. *Why had they fired me over such a miniscule deal? I had righted my wrong, and yet they still fired me? Why?*

Stop it, I told myself angrily. *Going over and over this crap isn't going to help and neither is longing for your old job. Maybe,* I thought, *this grinding over the past is normal. Hell, yes, it is. People have to resolve events like this in their minds before they move on. And anybody in my shoes would want to get their dream executive job back, too.*

My mulling returned to ways of accomplishing this goal. *Maybe if*

I pieced this thing together more carefully, I could dig up something. I needed a logical place to start, like who ... what ... where?

I settled on who: an enemy. That seemed a tangible place to start. I had a few, but which one did me in? *Who in hell got the goddamn auditors alerted in the first place?*

Adjusting the showerhead's spray, I moved the lever to maximum cold, icy water forcing my numbed brain into action. Regional staff people had rumored that the audit got started by an unsigned letter to IBM's chairman. Certainly, somebody had complained about the Fillmore regime to somebody else important and high up in the company. I tried to picture this type of person; a whiner who had visibility into Fillmore's expense habits, a small-minded person who believed Fillmore dragged IBM's profits down.

I stepped out of the shower, toweled down and glanced in the mirror. *Better.* Some color had crept back into my face. A little gut hung from my middle, the result of too many long hours at the office and too little exercise. Otherwise, none the worse for wear after my dozen years with IBM. Outwardly, at least.

In a flash it hit me. I jerked my shorts on so hard I could hear the fabric groan. I knew who did me in. *Dumb. Should have figured it out before this.* The accounts payable clerk, Martha, must have sent the incriminating letter.

Kind of heavyset, drives a BMW with the license plate "M-M-M-M-M." Sure. Martha knew about the C-O-P-P-I-E-S stuff and openly disliked Fillmore. She had probably penned a dazzling letter about Fillmore's meetings, which were the actual subjects of the audit that got me fired.

Why not? She sat in a perfect position to examine all the invoices mailed in. She saw the expensive artwork hanging in the halls of Fillmore's regional offices, the chartered flight bills and all the invoices from every meeting conducted. They all got funneled to her, the last stop before payment. Marry what she saw with a current corporate slow-down and delayed raises — probably her own salary impacted — and she'd want to strike back. Her level would afford few opportunities until the C-O-P-P-I-E-S invoice landed on her desk. She could surely put it together to lash out at Fillmore, her main target, and secondarily at me.

Yeah, that's who did it. Well, at least I know, I thought ... not that it would do me any good. But knowing seemed to shore up my wavy brain.

Much like last night's dinner, breakfast passed quietly. I picked at a piece of toast, my appetite as absent as my job. The house was quiet, too, the three boys out playing, Pat working on the bills, and the blasted phone finally silent. *Good,* I figured. *I didn't want to talk to anyone, not even my family.* I felt a need to crawl into a hole for a while, avoiding reality, avoiding people, avoiding pain.

Sticking my head into the den, I said, "Pat, I'm going outside to work on the lawn."

She looked up from the desk and turned to look at me. Her light mascara looked smeared; she had been crying, again. "Okay, honey," she replied.

The thick, rich, green, fescue sod had been laid down just a few days before, a tribute of sorts to what my promotion had produced. The branch manager's job meant lots of green money. I reminded myself of our first house's scruffy grass, the best I could do while throwing out overseed. Busying myself with the lawn edger, I tried straightening out the seams around the bushes. After half an hour, during which time my mind hammered away over the cigars hundreds of times until my brain felt it would explode, I examined my dismal results. More crooked than before, just like my thoughts. I lit a smoke.

Hearing the hum of a car on the street, I looked up to see a late-model Cadillac rapidly approaching. As it turned sharply into our driveway and then skidded to a halt the driver's door opened and out jumped Arnie Chance, eyes flashing anger.

Chance, a close former associate of mine, had left IBM a year earlier. Most people figured Chance had left IBM because he wanted to stay in Grand Rapids and raise a family rather than take an internal IBM promotion that meant moving to Detroit. The impeccably dressed and popular figure that had moved rapidly up the corporate ladder had implied something else to me at the time.

As I recovered from the shock of his surprise arrival and watched Arnie stride purposefully toward me, I remembered that conversation. He had informed me that his boss had privately told him what to expect when performing one of his new duties, setting up the regional meetings: He'd have to tell the people who worked for him to hustle up cigars, booze, mints, and fruit bowls, a task Chance felt fell outside what should be expected of his people.

Unwilling to delegate these duties, Chance said no way and resigned, but his peers, me included, didn't see avoiding subservience as the real reason for his decision. Rather, we thought it revolved around pressure from home to stay in Grand Rapids. After Chance's resignation, however, I noticed that meeting protocol was changed. Managers bought the booze and cigars, not their employees, thus keeping the goings on under a tighter rein with fewer people involved.

Chance, wearing matching mauve and white golfer's togs and sporting a pate with every one of his hairs perfectly blown dry into place, stopped in front of me. "Max, I got a call last night saying you've been fired from IBM, because you covered a box of cigars on your expenses. Tell me I heard it wrong."

IBM's grapevine, including alumni, worked fast, I thought. *Not only did they know I'd been blown away but what I'd done to deserve the execution as well.* "You unfortunately heard it right, Arnie. I'm out."

My voice sounded squeaky. Embarrassed, I stuck the toe of my sneaker into the sod. Watching my foot offered my eyes relief from his stare and my face a chance to drain its blush.

Chance couldn't get the words out fast enough. "I knew it. I knew it. I told my wife somebody would get fired some day over those goddamn meetings!"

He had my attention. "Why, Arnie?" I asked with fresh interest. It didn't sound like he had come over for a bury-the-dead deal.

"Well, you may not know this, but I resigned from IBM over

what went on in those sales managers' meetings. I didn't want to do all the crap that went along with them. It wasn't right."

Chance jammed his finger at me for emphasis. He looked dead serious. "Look, Max, I'm going to New York on business next week. A good buddy of mine, Doug Larue, works in the IBM chairman's office." Chance paused. "You remember Doug, don't you?"

I remembered. A graduate from Michigan State, my alma mater, rocketing through the business. I'd heard he'd been assigned to the chairman's office. And the way it worked up there, if he could cut the high-exposure staff work in Armonk, corporate headquarters, Larue would be an automatic for bigger job responsibilities.

In that job, a lot of Larue's time would be spent handling employee complaints through what IBM called its "Open Door" policy. This policy was meant to give IBM employees communication access to the chairman's office without fear of reprisal. Most of us never viewed it that way. Going to the chairman meant bucking several bureaucratic levels, and none of the people bypassed would be happy about somebody writing to the chairman with a complaint. Therefore, reprisals seemed inevitable. I had viewed the "open" part of the policy, at least, as an illusion.

"Look, damn it, I'll go see him and tell him what I know," said Chance angrily. He continued, "I saved the lists of the stuff we had to get for the meetings. I've got 'em at home. Typewritten lists of items that we, as so-called managers, had to serve the king ... Fillmore. Booze in pint bottles to make it appear like we didn't have a lot in stock, the brands of cigars we had to have, even the butterscotch mints we had to have for that one guy...Gonzo'.

"Let's get you back your branch. Together, you and I can do it. What do you say?"

I reached down and pulled out a weed. *An amazing development*, I thought. *A former IBMer living in the same town I did knew exactly why I screwed around with the lousy cigars. He even seemed to know better than I did, and right here, right now, he wanted to help.*

But what did Chance have that really could help me? We had

different outlooks on those meetings, as we did on Fillmore himself. Chance never enjoyed the same relationship with the leader as I did. Also, I had to admit I liked the way Fillmore controlled those meetings. Always first class, going against the grain of IBM's Spartan approach, much the way I also liked to operate. Even as impossible as Fillmore could be at times, like turning his massive back to me when he didn't want to talk any more and flintily refusing to open his wallet to contribute to the expenses of those meetings, I very much respected him.

Fillmore could lead and make things happen, and he'd taken me under his wing, making me a key member of his small inner group, or palace guard, as I liked to call it. Heady stuff. I couldn't develop a people-management style like Fillmore; his intimidation came from his large physical stature, booming voice, and cold hard stare, and his attitude appeared unfriendly, aloof. With a physique and way of handling people too dissimilar to his, I couldn't have a management style like Fillmore's, nor did I desire one. What I wanted was his knowledge of the business and his flair for things first class.

Two guys banging on the chairman's door sure beat one, but I didn't think we could be united. Chance saw the meeting coordinator's job as being forced to grovel; I didn't. I only disliked the way the meetings got funded. What should I tell him, a decent guy trying to help? He waited for my answer with impatience, tapping his foot and staring at me with upturned brows.

I didn't have an answer. I stumbled for something with which to stall him, a response that would give me a couple of days to think about it. "Arnie, I have no major bitch with Fillmore. Hell, the guy loved me … got me this branch … treated me like a son."

I knew where my real concern lay — in running against Fillmore; I'd become a trusted member of his palace guard, and violating that trust would prove difficult if not impossible. But those words wouldn't come.

"Look, I didn't have to cover the cigars, I could have paid for them, and as a matter of fact I did."

I told Chance about the check I'd written for those stogies months before the audit. "What a sucker I was. I bitched and moaned to Rusty Langley about those expenses, and then I wrote a check. Do you know what Langley suggested to cover my shortages?" Chance didn't reply. "He said that changing invoices ran too high of an audit risk. A smarter way would have been to pad car driving mileage on the expense report."

I had thought, *Smart? Hell!*

"Damn! What a dumb asshole I've been. Nobody, including me, had the balls to confront Fillmore with a bullshit problem and get it fixed."

Stupid, stupid, stupid, I thought. *Who would believe this?*

I'd gotten myself worked up into a rage and, wanting to flush it all out, I plodded on.

"Tom Blaylock should have allowed me to collect whatever got spent from the branch managers. He didn't. Maybe Fillmore intimidated him, I don't know.

"Fillmore sometimes walked out of the meeting without paying anything. Others, as well. 'I'll send you a check, bub,' they'd say, but they didn't. I just got sick of it.

"I don't think I should have been canned because IBM didn't allow me a way to break even. Christ, I had to go around to other staff managers bumming for dough to balance the pot. I got tired of them shuffling their feet when I hit them up, so I quit doing it."

Pat came out in the yard. Chance walked over and hugged her. I filled Pat in on his strategy, then I turned to him and said, "I'm pretty sure I don't want you acting in my behalf at the chairman's office." Pat started to protest, but I waved her off.

Chance butted in, walking right up to me. Just inches away, he invaded my space making me more than a bit uncomfortable, almost panicky. I took a step backward.

"You're making a mistake by not fighting back. Don't give it up, Max."

I didn't know if he was right; I only knew I wanted out of the debate. I had a sick feeling in my stomach. My other emotions allowed little room for thoughts that said I'd have to slime Fillmore for any opportunity to retrieve my job. "Thanks for coming over," I mumbled. "Call me from New York. By then, I'll have reached a decision." A delay.

Chance shrugged his shoulders, shook my hand, his eyes failing to meet mine, and drove off. Pat stayed outside on the grass with me.

"What are you going to do?" she asked.

A damn good question, I thought. *Doing in Fillmore would be like an act of Judas. No good. If I had to go after the big man, screw it. What would come of me even if I could? Tainted meat. Beardslee couldn't handle being fired, so he tried to slime the others. No good. Where would I go from there?*

"I don't know, honey," I replied in an unusually flat voice.

Either way, I figured no long-term deal for me at IBM ... unless Blaylock dialed up the chairman's office and acknowledged that he wouldn't let me collect what I spent. Blaylock, the square-jawed, hard-working executive, safely tucked away in California, had acted as my co-mentor. He could be the white knight. Would he call? Should I call him?

Darkness brought no relief after a restless, reflective day; the cigars lay in bed beside me. I got up a dozen times during the night, each time dodging Pat's attempts to find out how I felt. A forlorn "Okay" was I all I would say.

On Sunday, in a distracted and confused state I drove the fifty miles out of Grand Rapids to see my brother. Five years younger than I, Denny lived on a ranch outside of Sheridan, a small town where the wall calendars in the dozen or so businesses occupying the two-block so-called downtown area could be counted on to say "Beardslee Oldsmobile, your dealer for XX years." The current edition said forty-four. Denny had come out of the back room of the business when Dad unexpectedly passed away. The slow but steadily progressing side effects of diabetes had weakened his system until he contracted fatal pneumonia. Now well established as the Olds' dealer, people liked doing business with my brother as much as they had with my father.

In a low voice, I told Denny about Friday's events, concluding my story with the fact that I'd been let go from IBM. My brother seemed easier to talk to than Chance. My own flesh and blood made it more comfortable to share, I guessed. As I finished, I looked at Denny's eyes for a reaction. They were filled with sadness and concern.

I'd always believed my brother to be a compassionate person. In his grade-school days more than once Denny would come home without his winter coat and with a plea of having lost it. Later, we found out he gave his coats away to kids he knew couldn't afford one. And now he took his brother's troubles personally.

Denny lived with his wife and kids in a modest home surrounded by several acres of hardwoods. State-of-the-art wood burners crammed all available space in his basement. "Come help me cut some wood," Denny said. "It'll take your mind off your problems for a while."

As we walked out back to chain-saw logs for the cold Michigan winter still months away, he explained to me that his fifteen acres matured fast enough to replenish what he chopped down. As my brother discussed the business of replenishment, I wondered how many IBMers would be vying for my job. Plenty for sure. Which "tree" would replace the one IBM had cut down?

Denny and I had different sets of values, I thought, busying myself with a twenty-foot section of oak. And, from my viewpoint, I always took for granted that I had things better than my brother did: President of the Student Council, All State football honorable mention, college, Air Force officer, overseas travel, prestigious IBM job, big-city life. Denny had not bothered with any of that. He finished high school and a short tour as a lumberjack in Idaho before going to work for Dad.

Our brotherhood looks like a tortoise and hare replay, I thought. *While I thrash and flash around, he keeps plugging away.*

Yet, for the first time, being a small town car dealer and having the freedom to handle a box of cigars any way I pleased looked really good to me. At that moment I could appreciate his down-to-earth, much-simpler values. They seemed more balanced and tangible somehow than mine did. Getting ahead professionally at any cost dominated my other values of family, friends and religion. But with the career gone ... strange how a sequence of events could change one's outlook.

After watching my distracted chain-sawing efforts, Denny called a halt to the activity. "Brother, I'm getting you back to the house before you cut a leg off." On the walk to the house, Denny placed his arm around my shoulders in an unusual display of affection. Remembering Fillmore's similar gesture, I noted it was unusual for both of them.

The smell of fresh-cut timber filled my nostrils and the natural setting instilled a long-forgotten sense of relaxation in my body. Perhaps being miles away from the site of Friday's painful event helped. Certainly this visit with my brother provided a short escape from the realities I'd be facing again in a few hours.

While I slouched into an oversized chair with a glass of iced tea prepared by his wife, Gail, Denny tried to cheer me up by reminding me of something that had happened to one of our relatives. "You know, a year ago our cousin's husband was fired from his job as the president of a small company. The way he tells it, he built the business up, and then the owners figured they didn't need him any more. So, they dumped his ass and his high salary. He got all fucked up, but he's got a good job today."

I wished I could feel anger and let it displace the growing uncertainties I felt. Mostly I felt guilt about the fake invoice. I didn't feel able to cope with interviewing for a job; my embarrassment over what I had done and over being fired in the town in which I'd started my IBM career was too large. I felt exposed.

Plus, I was aware that it was becoming increasingly difficult for me to hold a train of thought, let alone pay attention to basic things like driving a car. My head continuously held jumbled thoughts bashing from side to side, mixing like oil and water, all together one minute, then separating out into meaningless fragments the next.

Denny regained my attention when I heard him mention Fillmore. "You think he'll want to keep the car he leased from Beardslee Olds'?" Denny queried.

I had blanketed the big man with a full array of services. Researching vacation rentals, setting up leased cars, providing auto repairs. Fillmore had once introduced me to an associate as "a guy who could get anything done, anything at all." I'd beamed, then. Not now.

"I figure Fillmore will probably turn the Olds' in," I replied. "He won't want a business tie to me." That thought hurt, kinda like having your best friend suddenly not want anything to do with you.

I thought about Fillmore's attempt to comfort me at the airport. He had reminded me of the story Lou Holtz, then coach of the Arkansas Razorbacks, had shared with two hundred IBMers at a recognition event the previous year. The story was about advice Holtz' mother had given him years before when he returned home after a high school football practice session. He complained about the difficulty of the practice period to her. She consoled and then counseled him about values and ethics and finished her advice by telling the kid to always give any and all tasks his best shot. And if that didn't work, from his mom's loving lips..."Piss on it."

Holtz had brought the house down, but Fillmore's rendition of the story fell flat as any humor was squeezed out by my gloom.

Once again, Denny's voice pulled me back into the present. "Nothing like this ever happens to most of us, but I know you're a fighter. Christ, I watched you play football, you're a tenacious bastard. You'll get over this IBM deal." He shifted his generous, six-foot-plus, bib-overall-clad body on the sofa and perched his yellow "CAT" cap on the armrest.

I motioned for Denny to walk out in the yard. "I gotta head back, Bro'. Thanks for the conversation, I think it helped."

"Hey, no problem. Any time," he said as he patted me on the

back with a large hand. Feeling embarrassed and confused, I crawled into the car.

As soon as I left Denny's driveway I regretted it. The temporary escape from reality had been too short. I drove back into the thick of it with reluctance. I wasn't ready to cope. Not yet.

Pulling into the driveway at home, I realized I had no recollection of the drive itself. A total void. *How did I get here?* I asked myself.

Once inside, with a stone-like face and a somber voice Pat read from her neatly written log the latest batch of condolence calls. *A funeral. This has turned into a goddamn funeral,* I thought in disbelief.

With the kids already tucked into bed, I poured two glasses of wine and motioned for Pat to join me on the back veranda. Being with Denny clearly showed me how being close to my family could help. I was tired of the distance I'd placed between Pat and me. I felt so alone within my predicament and wanted to feel close to her and confide in her, to receive her support.

As she took the glass from my hand, I looked at her haggard face. This predicament was treating her hard, too. I needed to be more sensitive to her feelings.

I took a sip of my wine, then said, "Honey, I'm very ashamed and very embarrassed over this firing." Pat nodded her head, looking down at the decking.

"I've put you and the boys, but mostly you, through a lot of grief while I was out playing IBMer. Then, when it all seemed to be paying off, it got jerked away from you as well as from me."

As I spoke, Pat began to perk up and her face took on a more relaxed hue.

Reticent to speak before, now she murmured in a soft voice, "Hey, thanks for looking at it from my perspective as well as yours," and rested her head on my shoulder.

"Should we list the house?" she asked. I thought about that. We'd done well on the sale in Detroit, well enough to put fifty percent down on this home. "I don't think we need to, honey. Seems like we'll have enough money for quite a while, at least for several months." Money wasn't the issue, here — yet.

Well after midnight, we carried the remnants of a second bottle of wine out into the backyard, making love on the fescue mattress under a full moon, a welcome and needed release from the last forty-eight hours. I thanked God I still felt so inclined, since my other desires, like eating, seemed to be sapped since the firing. Later, I even managed to catch snatches of sleep. *Let some time go by,* I thought. *Maybe things can get back to normal.*

In the morning I drove to a public park for private headwork. The IBM building would be jammed with regular working people, the corner-pocket offices on the second floor noticeably empty.

Sitting down on the grassy bank by the side of a creek, I watched a squirrel getting ready for winter by busying himself with the droppings of an oak tree. While the little animal prepared for the months ahead, I found myself once again reliving the meeting at which I'd asked the waiter for a favor — "Just change a small invoice..."

"Cigars" wrote the auditor with the seersucker suit and flat-topped hair cut whose report initiated my downward spiral. Guilt, now my constant companion, stuck in my head and my heart. I forced myself into another level of thought.

During those dozen years there was so much action, so many highs. There was the satisfaction of achieving sales quotas, gaining confidence, and being handed promotions at a steady pace. I thought back to five months ago when I led the triumvirate into town. The biggest high of all...

◆ ◆ ◆

January 5, 1980

Fillmore and I climbed aboard a private charter in Detroit. Destination: Grand Rapids. I looked around the luxury confines of the cabin: *Wall Street Journal,* fresh juice and rolls... Just the way Fillmore liked things, first class.

"Danish, Len?"

"Don't mind if I do."

Fillmore had knocked forty pounds off his ample frame. Okay to eat a little pastry now. During the diet I had visited a clothing store with him, called The Tall Man's Shop.

"I buy my ties here even though I'm not that tall. Why do you think I come here?"

Jesus, I remembered thinking. *With this guy, you gotta be constantly alert. There's always a quiz.* "I don't know, Len. Why?"

"Because my goddamn neck takes up so much of the tie. Nineteen and a half neck." I'd had to look away so my grin would go unnoticed.

The chartered plane descended through broken gray clouds offering a view of the industrial sector below. In a few minutes my boss and I would land in Grand Rapids and in a few more, he'd announce me as the city's IBM branch manager — my latest in a series of promotions within the company.

Hearing the rush of air signaling the flaps extending, I had thought, *How can it get any better than this? Twelve years ago I'd been a lowly trainee in this same city. Now, I was approaching home – if an IBMer ever had a home – and doing so as the head honcho of the same sales operation I'd begun in.*

After a short car ride, we walked into a third-floor meeting room packed with about one hundred people. I spotted several I knew from my past stay in the city. Five relocations later, I walked back into their lives. I'd come full circle. Lowest of the low to top dog. I'd never heard of a bottom-to-top rung in the same IBM location being climbed before.

Fillmore strode to the front of the room. As usual, his presence commanded full attention. All eyes focused on him and the talking abruptly stopped.

"I want to make two major announcements today." Fillmore paused, the master at playing an audience as if it were a Stradivarius. "From your excellent sales record here in Grand

Rapids, along with Kalamazoo and Traverse City, you've grown yourselves at a very rapid rate. My records say that you've been the fastest growing area of the region. Because of this success I'm announcing Grand Rapids as the headquarters of IBM's newest branch, Western Michigan."

Whistles and applause followed the announcement. These people didn't like reporting to their smaller brethren down the road in Lansing. Now, they wouldn't have to.

Standing in the back of the room, I straightened my tie.

"And now, the second announcement: A new branch needs a new leader."

I buttoned my suitcoat.

"Your new branch manager," Fillmore grinned and adjusted his silver-framed glasses, "a guy who's done a heck of a job for me back in the region, and I understand a few of you know him around here — *Max Beardslee*."

I dog trotted to the front of the room, running my hands over the sides of my suit jacket to insure that its pocket flaps hung outside then over my unruly, curly hair. I had to work on looking sharp; it had never been a high priority. A quick flash across my mind reminded me of an awards banquet I had attended in high school. Damned hair had stuck out then as well. This time as I got up to the stage I was winning an invisible trophy, but the sense of pride and of achievement was so much greater.

Applause filtered into my senses as I walked to the front of the room ready for an acceptance speech. My face felt flushed as I tried to remember the much-rehearsed remarks given to the bathroom mirror earlier that morning.

Surveying the faces in the room, many well known to me, I thought about the task at hand and felt well equipped to manage it. I'd had the training, the dress rehearsals, and this operation had its share of high potential sales reps. I knew almost everything one could know about the branch without having actually managed it; the thick binder I had put together justifying its creation gave me all the information I needed. Remembering the dog days in the past, I now had one question I'd often asked myself: Was it all worth it? Yeah!

My first few days as a branch manager passed in a blur. Telegrams, letters and phone calls of congratulations poured into my home and office. I settled into the traditional "corner-pocket" office on the second floor with a private secretary. The transition could not have gone more smoothly. All the training from Blaylock and Fillmore had paid off. Day-to-day problems were taken care of with well-rehearsed solutions. Nothing came up that I hadn't seen before or didn't know how to handle — the sign of a good coaching job. With each passing day on the job, I felt more exhilarated and surer that this was exactly what I had been working toward and exactly what I wanted. Plus, it was exactly what my previous two years of hard work had prepared me to do.

A month into this exciting assignment, I drove to Detroit and laid out my game plan to Fillmore. Quota assignments, strategy, people strengths, and the numbers — always the numbers upon which IBM thrived. I wanted Fillmore; a master of the digits, to know his coaching had hit its mark. He was the only guy I knew who could spot in his head a one-percent error in the division of seven-digit numbers.

Fillmore smiled as he leafed through the control book as I acted as the guide for the plans and programs I'd prepared. I could tell he liked it. Looking up at me he said, "That last job I gave you helped you a lot; this control book is laid out the way it oughta be. People, business priorities, backlog management, it's all here. I figure your branch could finish in the top three of my twelve branches by year end," Fillmore told me. "With what you already got on the books and the solid sales guys up there, you could give Columbus and Indianapolis a run for their money."

My ego sucked up Fillmore's words, making me feel like a veteran branch manager as opposed to a rookie.

Branch ranking charts, which acted like a statistician during a competition, commanded a highly visible part of any IBM sales operation. Fillmore had his staff put out large posters every month showing the status of all branches in his region so each could see how they stood in comparison to the others. A series of singular measurements, such as individual product sales and revenue gained by getting a customer to buy his computer as opposed to leasing it, dotted the chart. The right-most measurement, listing each branch in sequence from best to worst, showed overall ranking. Fillmore used a lot of additional data not on the charts to look ahead and guess how the branches would finish the year. His belief that mine would be in the top three sat well with me, because the man was uncannily accurate in his predictions.

"Let's go to the Suss' after work." An invitation to share a drink with this powerful businessman at his favorite watering hole, the Sussex Inn, equaled meeting the Queen of England as far as those of us who worked under him felt. Yeah, I had finally arrived.

By the end of the first quarter, the regional rankings showed my operation as standing second out of twelve in overall performance. I attributed that to luck, solid players at most positions and, best of all, a desire by my people to get out in front and show the IBM world this new branch could bring home the bacon. The all important "Coverage" measurement, which projected future revenue from the backlog of new machines to be installed minus ones anticipated to be removed or discontinued, thus showing a branch's expected revenue over the months ahead, showed us as number one. Since coverage projections usually held true, I could expect to have a shot at the number one overall ranking by year's end.

IBM's complicated employee opinion survey, taken the year before, said the Grand Rapids and Kalamazoo people performed and got paid well but bitched a lot. However, Fillmore's two-man personnel department conducted informal studies three months after I arrived and the results showed that branch morale had gone up: important news.

Years ago I'd concluded I was more of a hands-on manager than most IBM execs. I liked the people aspect of the business, the sales contests, the action, all driven by the branch personnel, and pursued that venue more intensely than most. Some others had been critical of me. "You're buddying up to your people too much. You gotta stay separate from them, or they'll take advantage of you."

Maybe, but for me the hands on style felt more natural, distancing myself would feel contrived. In any case, judging by the morale in my branch, my usual charisma had started to work. People were happy working for me.

Blaylock, my friend and co-mentor, called from San Francisco where he now headed his own empire, the four-hundred-million-dollar-per-year Western region, equivalent to that of Fillmore's. "Fillmore is pleased about your smooth take-over, Max. He's calling it the best he's ever seen."

I acknowledged this as an exceptional compliment since Fillmore had been present at Blaylock's Cincinnati branch coronation three years prior, and that had gone pretty smoothly. "Keep it up, and you'll have my job. The people skills are a natural for you, and you've got the smarts. It looks like you're becoming a good businessman as well."

I hung up the phone and took stock. High marks from Blaylock and Fillmore. One couldn't find a pair any more demanding. They knew their stuff. The big surprise to me clearly lay in the way I fit into this job. I hadn't expected it to be this easy, because I thought the higher one went the harder it got. *Au contraire,* here. If I kept things going the way they'd started, I knew that in a couple of years I'd get another promotion. I had enjoyed the finest training and experiences available to prepare me for this job and the next one, I thought. This branch opened the way to an exciting — and secure — future. I could go all the way.

During theses first few weeks of the job, I spent what little free time I had away from the office house hunting with Pat. We then contracted for a new two-story home located in suburban Grand Rapids and construction came along perfectly. We would move in the middle of April. Counting the number of bathrooms, I chuckled as I placed a call to my more conservative brother.

"Five toilets, Bro' ... the whole family can have diarrhea at the same time."

"Yeah, I'm impressed," he replied. "I've still only got the one crapper."

I laughed. Having Denny just fifty miles up the road meant a good deal, too. Dad's death, three years prior, had brought us even closer, although we had always had a good relationship. Not a week went by that we didn't talk on the phone about something. Now, we'd be able to see each other frequently as well. Plus, if my family wanted to go to the country, we could just jump in the car and drive there in less than an hour.

I gave my brother an order for a new Olds'. "Wall-to-wall leather in there and all the toys."

Running Grand Rapids meant a lot of things and all of them good. Money, for one thing. From early indications the job had the potential of doubling what I'd made in my last position. Plus with all the money we had made from our last home in Detroit, we were already in good shape. Money in the bank, plenty of IBM stock owned, the struggle of making ends meet in our early years was clearly over. We had arrived, our financial and social life in perfect order, my ego bursting with satisfaction and pride.

And then came the message: "Max, a Mr. Fitzpatrick in Detroit called. You're to call him back. He said it's urgent."

Funny, I thought. *Never heard of him.*

I returned the call. A bland voice responded. "Yes, Mr.Beardslee. I'm an auditor from Atlanta headquarters heading up a team visiting your region. Let me refer to my notes..."

◆◆◆

With effort I roused myself from the grass, brushed the loose dirt off my pants and turned toward the Olds' feeling a building frustration manifesting itself in a desire to smash something or someone, to release the emotion in my body before it consumed me. Noticing a rock the size of a suitcase jutting out from the edge of the bank, I walked over, bent down, wrapped my arms around the stone and pulled as if my future depended upon getting that boulder out of the ground. Struggling, I balanced myself and drew it up to chest height. Then it started to slip. I took a step to the edge of the bank, leaned precariously forward and let go, my aching arms falling like a lifeless puppet's to my sides.

I watched the gray mass disappear into the creek's dark waters, noting the resemblance to my situation. The rock had probably lain beside that bank for years. In just one moment of time, I'd made it disappear — not so different from someone picking me up and heaving me over the side of IBM. And now I was sinking just as deeply as that boulder in the dark murky waters of my uncertain and confused situation.

Three

WHEN I GOT HOME, PAT KISSED ME ON THE CHEEK, AND ASKED HOW my visit with Denny had gone. "Fine," I replied. "Talking with him helped. Anybody call?"

"Yes, you missed a phone call from Gene Brandon. He's coming to Grand Rapids in a week to handle your termination paperwork," she said.

Seven days after the firing, Brandon landed in Grand Rapids. We met at the same airport where Fillmore had verbally fired me; however, this time around I knew it would be done in writing. With little attempt at conversation, he snapped open his briefcase, reached in and pulled out a pay voucher. The personnel man placed it on the table between us. Forty-one thousand dollars

"Your last check will come in the mail in a few days," he said as he pulled out some other papers and shoved them and a pen toward me, indicating that they needed my signature.

I signed the necessary forms, fighting my misty eyes, not wanting this guy to know I'd been devastated by having the job I'd prized so much taken away from me, and got out of there.

After the lonely drive back home, I puttered around in the yard for the rest of the day, but nothing I did felt right. All my motions seemed clumsy and awkward, like a newborn trying to take his first steps.

That night from a thousand miles away Chance called. "I'm all set to see Larue at the chairman's office. Can I tell him what happened to you? Have you thought about it?"

A voice in my head screamed of being labeled a Judas. As I listened to Chance's battle cries I felt the energy drain from my body. I had no fight left. I sat down on a chair near the phone.

"Sorry, Arnie. You're trying to help and I appreciate it, but I can't get on board." A disappointed Chance hung up.

Maybe Larue would draw the connection and independently look into it. Maybe — but I doubted it. Why should IBM go out of its way for me if I wouldn't try to correct the injustice for myself?

The next week produced nothing to impede the increasingly rapid flow of negative aftereffects of my job loss. My appetite and my energy continued to dissipate; I slept fitfully, if at all. School was out, a blessing so that Pat could occupy herself with the kids as opposed to her zombie-like husband. I performed minimally, speaking only when spoken to, not initiating any dialogue with either Pat or the boys. I retreated farther and farther into the fragile shell of my inner self.

I tried playing golf with a friend a couple of times to get myself out of my malaise, but clubs were left strewn all over the course. They'd fall, totally forgotten, from my hands onto the course after a shot, and not only would I not notice but I wouldn't realize I'd left them behind until the next time I needed them. "You're taking this too hard, Max. Relax. It'll all work out," my golf partner reassured me.

"I don't know. I just stay so damned worked up all the time. I feel mostly stupid and guilty, but I also wonder why I feel stupid and guilty, because what they got me for was a miniscule thing. I know that, but right now I feel useless to anyone or anything."

"Yeah, I can understand how you must feel," my friend said, "but it'll only be the end of the world if you make it that way. Don't forget the talent that got you ahead. You can use it somewhere else."

After a quiet dinner — they were all quiet now — Pat reached down and pulled at a loop of my sagging pants. "How much weight have you lost?"

I said nothing, just stared at her with unfocused eyes unable even to find the energy or desire to focus them.

"Hey, are you okay? You don't talk any more. Do you realize that? You're going through whole days without saying anything to me or the kids," her voice sounded panicky.

I nodded my head, jostling my eyes back into a normal sight pattern, and replied, "I guess so." I stuck my hand down the front of my pants and felt the empty space that Pat had noticed, surprised at the size of it.

I didn't tell her that the cigars stayed at the forefront of my mind, incessantly bashing around in my head and blurring my thinking by enveloping my thoughts in their pungent smoke. In fact, I'd taken the event that caused my dismissal from IBM and poured it, like Miracle Grow, on my psyche with such force that I felt guilty not only about the cigar deal but about much of my past life as well.

This was something new to me, a man who had always been good at moving past mistakes and faults with forgiveness for self and others. Now, I was rehashing events: some I'd not thought of for years — dropping out of engineering at college, all the times I'd ever gotten drunk, not being at my dad's side when he passed away, and others more recent, including a one-time act of unfaithfulness (just one more "perk" of a corporate lifestyle, at the expense of my family and personal values).

"I'm struggling, Pat, big time. So if I appear to be ignoring you, it isn't that I want to, I just can't focus on a damn thing other than my own misery."

God help me. I got up from the table, leaving my wife sitting there with an abandoned, hurt look on her face. Just when she had thought I was acting a bit more normally, I fell back into my silent withdrawal.

I wandered into John's bedroom. "Hey, John. How's it goin'?" I asked, hoping to dig out whatever had caused him to be in a perpetually bad mood.

"Hi, Dad. Okay," he said, no enthusiasm in his voice.

"Well, how's summer treating you — glad school is out?"

Again, a listless, "Okay," but this one was followed by, "I'm worried about you, Dad. I can tell you don't feel good, because you never talk to us anymore. Some guys I see, that I met at school ... their dads used to work for you, and..."

"Go ahead, Son," I said knowing what would come next.

"Well, they know you got fired and Dad, they weren't mean to me or anything, but..."

I motioned for him to continue while feeling closer to my son than perhaps I ever had.

"Well ... they wonder if I'll have to move 'cause you won't be able to get a job here, 'cause everybody'll know you got fired."

Not having an answer to that, I told him I loved him and closed the door.

The next morning, again sans breakfast, I told Pat I was going into town for the day. "Gonna look up Larry Brannon, and hit him up for some office space," I said. She looked pleased that at least I was doing something rather than sitting around the house staring into space.

Like others I'd known, Brannon, who'd joined IBM a year ahead of me, had decided that IBM operated with too many rules, so he got into managing a wholesale appliance distributorship for his father-in-law. Brannon endorsed the office space idea with enthusiasm.

After a tour of his operation, Brannon showed me to my new office, an unused storage room on the second floor of the warehouse. I looked around the shadow-filled room in which a skylight offered the only relief for the windowless enclosure. Brannon returned to work, while I examined the thin veneer desk covered with dust, silently opening its empty drawers.

I sat down in the faded chair, opened my briefcase and busied myself working on a resume. After two hours I had only five lines on the sheet of paper. I wadded it up and flipped it in the general direction of a trashcan sitting in the corner just as Brannon walked in.

"Hey, Beards', let's get some lunch."

In the restaurant, we turned the conversation to mutual friends from my previous tour in Grand Rapids. "Hey, have you heard from Jack Orlop?" Brannon asked. Orlop was one of the best new-account salesman either of us had ever known and the premiere peddler in IBM's Grand Rapids location when I went through training. I related to him how Orlop barged in on me my second day as branch manager.

Jack had swashbuckled his way into my office, a well-worn buckskin coat covering his broad shoulders. "Beardslee, with you in charge, if I had any IBM stock, which I don't, I'd sell it." Friendly banter from this former biology teacher who had made such an impression on us all.

He sat down and immediately lifted his scuffed, snakeskin cowboy boots up on my desk. "I'm in the horse racing business. Breed 'em and race 'em. Quarter horses is where it's at," he informed me. Knowing of Jack's penchant for action of any kind, I figured not a bad match.

During my previous time in Grand Rapids, Orlop had most of the dozen or so support people readily adapting to his fun-loving style. He easily charmed the entire branch support team into working with his accounts to the chagrin of management, who couldn't control him. After four big sales years, Orlop left IBM to go into his own business. Too much structure for his freewheeling, blustery style.

Brannon and I shared a needed laugh as he imagined how Orlop would have sauntered into IBM, cowboy boots and all. While Orlop just plain ignored the rules while working for IBM, I struggled to live within them. At first the freedom of a remote sales territory made it easy. Each promotion, however, brought me added visibility into IBM's fishbowl. Toward the end, I had pretty much conformed to dress code and paid more attention to rules of conduct while selling. I guessed in time, I'd probably have conformed all the way, wearing a game face every waking moment. *Ugh*, I thought. *At least I won't have to do that.*

Brannon and I drove back to the warehouse, where I once again busied myself in my resumé. This time I made more progress. With a full page of data ready to type, I left feeling a bit of my former self-confidence returning. *Hell,* I thought, *the stuff looked good enough on paper. I should be able to get a job pretty easily. Now, if I could just clear my head.*

That Sunday I visited Orlop, watching him give my middle son, Steve, a pony ride. After failing at convincing me to buy a pony for Steve, Orlop turned the conversation to my firing. "Hey, no big deal; I never figured you'd last this long at IBM," he said.

After Brandon's similar remark, I reacted strongly to Orlop's words. *Damn it, I sure as hell felt qualified to run the place, and the people at the branch seemed to enjoy my leadership. Had I acted as a perpetrator to the job or what?*

"Why do you say that, Jack?" I asked, glaring at him.

"Hey! Take it easy, Max. I didn't mean nothin' bad about it. It's just that you're no IBM kinda guy. Never were. They're a bunch of stuffed shirts." Jack rolled his eyes upward in disgust. "You broke a rule and got caught. So what? They got more goddamn rules than this barn has horse shit."

"Big business is not for you. Every big company is gonna have a shitload of rules, like the one that got you. If it wasn't that one, it've been another. And I know you ... you probably broke a helluva lot of 'em." He snorted and smiled wryly. "This time you just got caught." He walked away to bridle a colt, leaving me to ponder his remarks.

Back at the house Pat told me Ed Schwartz had called. I'd worked for Schwartz at IBM, but he'd left the company before I did, not fired but offered a demotion. He'd told them to "shove it." I called the Detroit number Pat had written down.

After the customary "I heard what happened," Schwartz asked, "Will you consider working for me in Detroit?" Not wanting to move back but feeling that some kind of job option made sense, I agreed to see him the following day.

Later that night Pat and I talked about the possibility of going back to the Motor City. "It's okay, if we have to, honey," she offered.

"Grand Rapids has been harsh on both of us. But having only lived here two months, I kinda hoped we could stay."

In the morning, I drove to Detroit anticipating my meeting with the one guy who had the best chance of understanding what I was going through. That was another reason I agreed to talk to him.

Schwartz, who now held a regional sales manager's job with a computer services company, had been my branch manager in Indianapolis in 1975. He'd resigned from IBM through circumstances similar to my own: a voucher submitted as food turned out to be for liquor. Auditors picked it up. Schwartz said it was a mistake, but IBM hung in there pressing the point. Some said that Fillmore wanted Schwartz out of the business and this was a convenient way to get rid of him. Schwartz eventually was offered a demotion; he no longer could run the branch but could stay with the company by taking a job of lesser rank on the divisional staff in Atlanta. Insulted, Schwartz said nuts to IBM.

Schwartz will understand, I thought. *He's been through his own audit. Plus, the former Notre Damer has an added incentive for helping me get back on my feet.*

It was common knowledge at IBM that Fillmore and Schwartz disliked each other. Schwartz believed Fillmore could have looked the other way over his liquor incident, but purposefully let matters take another course to suit his personal desires. *Fillmore wouldn't stop my getting canned, so Schwartz picks up the pieces and settles an old score – that's how Schwartz will view it,* I thought.

Schwartz got right to the point in a most flattering way. "I'd like to hire you, Max. You could move back to Detroit with Pat and the kids."

Schwartz told me the hiring procedure required passing a battery of tests. I normally tested well, but with a cooked mind I couldn't be sure. Nice to know I had a job in hand if I got through the tests though. It would give me a security net and increase my confidence. We parted with a handshake and a promise from Schwartz to schedule his company's tests on another date.

As I walked in the door ready to tell my wife about the Detroit opportunity, Pat shouted from the kitchen, "Roger Martin is on the phone."

Martin, the man who hired me into IBM. Well, I'd better talk to him, I thought.

"Beardslee, this is Roger. What in the hell happened? You were supposed to be my legacy to IBM."

Martin now served as a vice president of Steelcase, Inc., the commercial furniture manufacturer headquartered in Grand Rapids. A popular man, Martin had sat in my chair as the head guy in Grand Rapids until six years ago. He resigned because the next promotion, when it came, required leaving the area. Like many execs, Roger wanted to put down roots and raise his family. IBM in those days meant, "I've Been Moved"; Steelcase accommodated his desires.

I took him through a few details of my last days. Martin sounded sympathetic, but I could only believe he was feeling let down, disappointed in me. He must, since I was feeling so guilty for letting him down. His legacy no longer existed.

Martin lowered his voice before he said, "Look, if you'd like, I'll arrange an interview for you with the director of personnel at Steelcase, but frankly, we're not hiring right now.

I leaped at Martin's suggestion. Getting into Steelcase could be my salvation. We could stay right here, same house, same school, hold the ol' head up high, and get on with it. I'd recently read that most people leaving a job of long duration normally didn't find their niche until the third or fourth try. Steelcase meant big business again; Orlop, well intentioned, had warned me away from going into corporate America again, but, at the very least, it would be a place to get my head clear, then move on if it didn't suit me. *Boy,* I thought, *this sounds damned good.*

The following morning, I drove to an east-side mall and wandered into a bookstore, where I headed toward the business section thinking I might buy a book on resumès. I never made it that far. A hard-back selection with a bright red-and-yellow jacket caught my attention. The word, *SACKED*, was printed on its cover in big capital letters.

Damn, I thought, *that about covers it.* Without even having to open the book, it delivered the right emotional impact — shock — to the recently unemployed buyer. I bought the book and walked out of the store with Pat.

After an expected warm up about the importance of staying busy, the author of *Sacked* discussed how to handle the dismissal during a job interview. He recommended the direct route; I focused on that part, as I would soon face that exact situation during my Steelcase interview.

"Don't dodge it," he wrote. "Assure the interviewer you are over being fired, and that you learned a lesson from it. Don't show bitterness, even though you feel it."

I read another chapter with great interest, one in which the author discussed the emotional problems that can result from being fired. He assured me that they were as inevitable as the shock waves of a bomb blast. I relaxed deeper into the chair. *See. You'll be fine,* I assured myself.

Several medical terms he used that I'd heard before took on new meaning for me as I conducted a self-diagnosis process while I read. I noted that every day I felt more and more of the symptoms he described. Words like shock, paranoia, loss of confidence, and guilt came to life in my undefended mind. However, the last sentence of this particular chapter sent a chill down my spine:

> In extreme instances, the person fired can become severely depressed and ultimately suicidal.

I stared at the words for a minute before carefully closing the book. *Naah. Could never happen to me,* I thought. I shook my head and put the book down on the table.

No matter what I tried to occupy myself with during the rest of the day, I couldn't get those words out of my head. *Could I become suicidal,* I asked myself? I had a lot of the other symptoms ... guilt, depression, lack of appetite, and insomnia, but I didn't feel like I wanted to die. On the other hand, I didn't feel I had much reason to live. *No,* I concluded. *I may be depressed, but I'm not suicidal. Hell, I've loved life, and I'll love it again.*

I suffered an even more restless night than usual, getting out of bed about six times unable to sleep and tired of staring at the dark ceiling and replaying the words in the book over and over again in my head. I began rehearsing what I would say at the interview tomorrow when I was asked why no longer worked for IBM. Finally I fell asleep but awoke early, worn out.

Steelcase interview day. Give them the opportunity to hire Mr. Wonderful. Go the Martin route. I hooked the belt of my pants on the last notch and peered in the mirror. Baggy.

I managed to get lost driving to Steelcase despite the fact that I knew the way to the company's offices, which were only a few miles from our house. My mind wasn't on the road or the interview; as usual it was occupied with more bashing around in cigar land.

Arriving at Steelcase I collected my thoughts and straightened my tie before being summoned to see a pleasant-looking well-dressed man sitting in a spacious office befitting a billion-dollar corporation. When my interview with this friendly personnel czar turned to my reasons for leaving IBM, I tried my many-times-rehearsed spiel as advised in *Sacked.*

"IBM fired me over a box of cigars, because I tried getting the company to pay for them by calling the cigars photocopies. I learned from being fired, and I'm a better man for it," I recited. The words sounded flat as I plowed through more of the awkward material. "I didn't want the cigars for myself … see, they were for a meeting, and I had no way to collect for them. Later on, I did pay for them, because somebody found out about it and told me to, but, nevertheless, I was let go."

The director stayed silent, his eyes on my resumè as I spoke, slowly lighting a cigarette as I finished my recitation. "Now, let's go through that again. IBM moved you here, looked you over for something done months ago and you paid them back before the auditors found out about it. Then they *fired* you?" His tone of voice had gone from friendly to condescending.

"Yes sir." I fidgeted in my chair.

"That kind of action for seventy-seven dollars?"

This was no fun. "Yup."

"And they obviously spent several hundred dollars flying you to Atlanta — twice — to question you, right?" The Steelcase man sounded like a trial lawyer.

I turned back to look him in the eyes. "Yes, sir, at least that much," I answered.

The man stared up at his ceiling before turning to responding and me. "I'm in the personnel business, and in the personnel business we've heard IBM is tough. But, pal, this is playing real tough."

Damn, I thought, *he doesn't believe me!*

"What I'll do is talk to Roger Martin about you, see if anything opens up we want to consider you for, and let you know," the personnel man said with no encouragement in his voice. Abruptly he stood up and left the room ending our interview.

I just sat there for a moment staring at the place where he'd sat. Then I heaved myself out of the chair and followed.

One the way home I stopped at Brandon's warehouse. Being snubbed and disbelieved seemed to justify the guilt I felt about losing my job, thus increasing it all the more. It also reminded me how far I'd fallen from the ranks of the admired, at least in the personnel man's eyes. "Larry, I gotta lie about why IBM fired me. People aren't going to buy the cigar bullshit. Hell, I'm not sure if my own wife does."

Brannon helped me practice a new tale: I'd incurred a marketing practice violation. I got a little too aggressive in describing the competition's shortcomings; I'd even exaggerated them. IBM didn't allow its sales force to badmouth the NCRs, DECs and Honeywells of the world, even though we all did it. I got caught and was offered a demotion. I decided to turn it down, and here I am.

"What do you think, Larry?"

"Sounds better to me than the cigar story," he agreed.

That evening I attempted to hold up Pat's sagging spirits by reassuring her that at least I had one job option even though it meant going back to Detroit. "Plus," I lied, "I feel better."

Immediate guilt overtook me as the words left my mouth. *Maybe I really did deserve to be fired,* I thought. *I'm a liar just like the false invoice proved. I've worked up a lie for my next interview and I lied to Schwartz about wanting the job he offered me. I even lie to the people I love most, let alone to the company I worked for.*

Another week flitted by and my IBM severance check came. *Forty-one thousand dollars.* I idly flipped it to Pat with no feeling at all even though it's amount equaled almost what I'd made cumulatively my first three years in the business.

"Stick it in the bank, honey," I mumbled in a voice sounding listless and flat. As I heard my own monotone words tumble out, their resonance didn't at all resemble the music my voice normally played.

An insurance agent called. IBM's medical policy would expire in a few weeks. Pat talked to him. I couldn't have cared less.

That night Pat, the kids and I played Scrabble. I forced myself to pay attention while fumbling over five-letter words. As I placed the letters on the board, Steve asked, "Dad, why's your hand shaking?"

I held it up and stared at my trembling fingers; I didn't have an answer. Pat looked away.

Three weeks after the firing, I interviewed with another company in Grand Rapids, knowing a few people from IBM had joined it. I flew out to corporate headquarters in Denver the next day and examined the computerized graphics equipment they manufactured while they looked me over. In the afternoon, the president, a mid-thirties, broad-shouldered former IBM regional manager — and a friend of Fillmore's — sat me down "You took a screwing. I checked on it. Are you over it?"

Comforting words, they made me feel a bit better, a bit less guilty since he seemed to be blaming someone other than me. *Plus his high-level IBM friends probably had told him I got screwed. That meant some people at IBM weren't saying what I feared most, that I'd gotten what I deserved.* I didn't answer his question, knowing another lie would just bring the guilt on again.

He looked directly at me. "Look, Max, we could use you. Forget IBM. It's a half-assed outfit. Too political. They wanted Fillmore, couldn't get him, and you left yourself open. The expense account stuff is just one example of their pettiness."

The words sounded like Mozart; my heart floated pleasantly on the notes. My "thank you" was saturated with honest gratitude; it felt wonderful to have someone understand what had actually happened to me. I expressed an interest in the job and spent the rest of the day learning about the company's products. Because, unlike Steelcase's personnel man, these people understood me and didn't blame me, I felt I could work for them.

After spending a sleepless night in a mile-high city motel, I wearily took a cab to the airport and flew to Grand Rapids. Walking into the furniture city's airport parking lot at about ten that evening I estimated that more than four-hundred cars sat parked in the airport lot, and I hadn't the foggiest idea where or which one belonged to me. At midnight, with a face tear-stained from my futile search, I finally stumbled onto the Olds'.

Fumbling with the keys, I collapsed inside the car asking out loud over and over again, "Why? Why? Why? Why?" I just didn't understand... *Why had everything become so difficult? So wrong?*

I forced myself to consider all the calamities worse than mine: cancer, loss of a child, divorce, bankruptcy, combat, crime victim. A long list. *Geez,* I thought. *Getting fired is nothing. There are worse fates than the one you got handed. Get over it.* But I couldn't. I was mired in it like quicksand. And the more I thrashed around in it the deeper I sank.

The words from *Sacked* crept back into my mind. *"In extreme instances, the person fired can become severely depressed and ultimately suicidal."* Carefully, I drove home.

Weeks crawled by. Now two months into the firing, I could fool people on the phone about my mental state but not in person. My appearance had become pretty shocking to those who hadn't seen me in a while, but even Pat who saw me every day noticed my worsening condition: the haggard face, sunken chest, hollow eyes, and listless movements.

"Why don't you go see a shrink?" she offered as she ran her hand through my disheveled hair.

I considered her suggestion. That visit could be something to get me going, but, taking the macho approach, I had talked myself into thinking that psychiatrists saw only those unable to handle life's realities. "I've been in tough straights before, and I'll get through this one, too," I said with force, mostly to convince myself and blot out the inner voice that said I was caught in a tailspin. *"You're emotionally out of control,"* it insisted. *"Go see the shrink."*

That evening while driving home from a restaurant, I heard Steve suddenly shout, "Dad! Stay on the road!" Feeling that the car lurch across gravel and rough terrain I snapped back into reality, jerking the wheel to the left, thus pulling the car off the shoulder where I had let it drift and back onto the pavement. At the same time I shouted at my son, "Mind your own business."

My passengers fell silent except for the periodic sniffles floating forward from the back seat. Pat looked at me with anger and surprise, then stared ahead, her face like a carved piece of marble. My white-knuckled, sweaty hands gripped the steering wheel.

At this point my hands always felt moist, leaving damp streaks on glass table tops and needing to be wiped several times a day on my pant legs. Itching red welts covered my legs. I had bags under my eyes, bags in my pants. *The bag man. A hell of a way to go on a diet,* I thought.

Schwartz called and invited me back to Detroit for another meeting. While driving there, my car ran out of gas; I hadn't even noticed that the gas warning light had come on. I coasted to an exit and bummed a ride from there to get gas.

Arriving late, I apologizing for the delay. Schwartz told me not to worry about it. "You've lost a lot of weight," he commented.

"Yeah, Ed, everybody says that. I'm on a diet," I lied.

After fielding a phone call, Schwartz turned to me and gave me good news. I had scored high on the tests. Ninety-eight percent on the math score. The only negative analysis came from the psychologist. His opinion was that something gnawed at me.

No shit, I thought. *How perceptive.*

"His opinion doesn't matter to me. How does seventy-thousand-dollars per year plus a car sound? I figure that's about twenty thousand less than at IBM for an average branch manager, but you can move up from there." Before I could react, however, he changed the subject.

"Max, understand, I don't really care, but I just came back from a business trip to Atlanta, and, well...," he hesitated, then stated a question. "I thought your firing came from the box of cigars."

Something smelled. *The cigars again.*

"Yeah, it did. Why?"

"Well, I had a drink with a regional manager, I won't say who." Schwartz cleared his throat and then dropped the bomb. "Anyway, the regional manager would only say they let you go over booze, broads and cigars."

Holy shit! I couldn't believe it. Schwartz's words rang in my ears. "Nothing there, Ed!" I blurted. "Who's the lying bastard that said that?"

Schwartz dodged a reply, his eyes looking for a way out of the subject. They found one with the clock. Twelve o'clock, it said. Time for lunch.

On the way back to Grand Rapids "booze, broads and cigars" served as my constant driving companions, heightening a growing paranoia that IBMers everywhere would heap more crap on me. I could hear the conversations.

"Hey, did you hear the latest about Beardslee?"

"No, what?"

"Well, I got it from reliable sources that he was screwing around with some babe in his office and that he drank too much. IBM wanted to dump him, and when someone found out he'd covered some cigars, they did."

I'd known of a couple of guys being fired for a relationship they had with one of the female sales employees. Putting this story out about me would make it sound better for IBM than the truth of the matter.

I had become so deeply enmeshed in the constant replay of the whole scenario that when a thunderstorm blew up a few miles outside Grand Rapids I became completely unnerved. The sudden blast of rain on the windshield and the thunder that made me jump in my seat and my heart palpitate — it also sent the car swerving across the road. I quickly returned to reality and straightened out the car. No damage done.

The wind and lightning frightened me, despite the fact that I normally loved watching nature's work. My fear so consumed me that I made two wrong turns in the subdivision I knew by heart before finally walking into the house.

As I walked into the kitchen from the garage, Pat took one look at me and in an alarmed tone asked; "Max ... what's wrong? You look terrible."

I sat down in a heap on the couch and shared Schwartz's story with Pat, her surprised and angry eyes showing a reaction similar to my earlier one. "Honey, where do they come up with this garbage?"

"I don't know," I replied in a weak voice as I stared blankly at the floor. "I'm going to bed."

On the way to Brandon's warehouse the next day, my car again ran out of gas. Leaving the Olds' where it sat, I took a cab back home. Seeing the cab pull up, Pat walked out into the yard. "What happened?"

"I ran out of gas."

Wearing a frown, Pat called a neighbor to help pick up the car.

"Maybe you'd better see a doctor," she said as she opened the door to leave. The suggestion sounded more like a plea.

"No." I'll be all right," I shouted at Pat and began pacing furiously. "Getting a job is all I need, goddamn it! Right now I feel worthless." I picked up a book from the table and slammed it back down. "And I'm gonna get one right — goddamn — now."

Pat said nothing as she walked out of the door.

With Pat gone, I picked up the telephone and called the ex-IBMer I'd interviewed with in Denver. Yes, they would bring me on board. Then I called Schwartz in Detroit. "When do you want to start, Max?"

Before hanging up, I told each of them the same thing: "I'll start work on Monday," knowing full well I didn't want to make a decision until I had to, amateurishly stalling for time — time that wouldn't solve anything.

Just one more item to deal with: a short letter to Frank Cary, IBM's chairman of the board. I drove down to Brandon's warehouse and banged out the letter in my little office. Short and to the point. I didn't want to ramble.

Dear Mr. Cary:

After twelve years of employment at IBM, I was fired for "premeditated intent to obligate funds." While in charge of setting up a company-sponsored meeting, I altered an invoice for cigars to say photocopies. An audit caught what I did and, even though prior to the audit somebody else called it to my attention and had me pay for them; I was still let go. I did not smoke the cigars personally and could only charge twenty dollars per attendee. Expenses ran higher than the twenty dollars, and I believe I can prove that. Please consider investigating my circumstances as I would like re-admission into IBM.

Sincerely,
Max Beardslee

I shoved it in an envelope and mailed it on my way home.

I decided against telling Pat about the letter. Nothing would probably come of it anyway. Back at home, I apologized to her for my outburst and offered to help make dinner.

"No, thanks. Why don't you play with the boys? They miss you, you know."

"That noticeable, huh?" I replied.

"Yes … that noticeable." I headed off to find my sons.

After dinner she guided the conversation around to my job opportunities. "Two different jobs. Well, we've lived in Detroit before; we could do it again. Of course, the Denver company's job offer would be right here."

How to tell her what I'd done, I wondered. "Pat, I, uh … well, look … while you were out, I told both companies I'd be … you know … starting with them on Monday"

"You what?" Pat shouted. "Max, you can't do that. They'll…"

I cut her off, determined to plow ahead and get her off the subject. "Honey, I don't know why I did that." I tried to sound positive. "But we have the weekend to figure out which of these jobs I'll actually take."

Pat's Irish temper flared. "Damn it, I know this is tough, but those are nice people out there, and one of them is gonna feel you put them on."

I mumbled something about needing more time to figure things out and feeling that saying "yes" to both bought me that time.

Pat showed no signs of getting off the subject any time soon. "But, Max, that's not anywhere how you normally think things through. I still don't understand why you—" I cut her off and headed out on the balcony.

Saturday I fared no better. Unable to focus on which job to take, I just sat languidly around, not talking, not eating, and not thinking. Evening came and was no better. By now I dreaded the night, when normal people slept and I, unable to sleep, would get out of bed and pace around the house.

As Sunday night came Pat busied herself with the laundry, the kids watched TV in the den. We hadn't shared the job situation with them, wanting more clarity so we could tell the kids about our decision in a positive way. Pat now handled their every day needs almost exclusively, shielding them from my fumbled motions.

"Honey, I'm going for a drive," I announced. "When I come back, I'll have the job figured out." I drove around the neighborhood for about an hour, maybe more, and in that time I didn't think about a job at all, no room for that with cigars and other junk filling my head. I left the subdivision and pulled out onto the highway, pressing the gas pedal as the speedometer moved quickly higher. I passed a cluster of trees on the right side of the road as the thought of ramming my car into a tree took hold. At seventy miles per hour, I knew that from the time the front bumper caved in until the steering wheel crushed my chest the whole process took less than a second. A coward's way, but a final way to extinguish the emotional pain I continuously felt. *No,* I told myself. *That's not what you want,* and I turned off at the next exit and headed for home.

When I came back in to the house Pat asked me, in a gentle way, if I'd made up my mind. "Still looks like Grand Rapids, honey. Yeah. Grand Rapids..." I hesitated, unsure whether to continue, but I did.

It didn't seem that I could get any lower, and it was time to come clean with the person who had stood by me throughout my career. I told Pat about the recent one-time act of unfaithfulness I'd had. I asked her forgiveness and watched her leave the room with tears in her eyes.

◆◆◆

After about an hour of staring into space, I hoisted myself out of the chair and went upstairs, entering the living room as a lightning flash threw bright white light into the room, spilling out over the sheen of my damp skin and revealing bright red blotches on my arms. The following rolling turbulence compressed against the windows making them rattle and matching the volcano-like violence I now felt. My brain seemed ready to explode, the pressure against my temples like a vice, pushing tighter and tighter, the discomfort more than I could bear. I didn't know how I'd gotten to this state of misery, but I felt no confidence that time would bring me back to normal. Time seemed to make things worse, each day a little lousier than the one before.

I did know this much, that soon I'd have to do something to cut out the pain and only one option appeared to be open. It was one I hadn't wanted to dwell on. It had become apparent to me, but I had just let it tumble around in my head without allowing it to take root.

Living had become an unbearable chore. Hell, I wasn't living; I was existing and doing so in a worse fashion than those people so physically damaged that they were dubbed "vegetables." I had become worse than a vegetable, however, since I seemed physically inactive but possessed a mind that raced out of control into the black hole of misery. It wouldn't let up; I could not escape. Ever. I felt trapped and doomed to a life of agony, a burden and shame to those around me. *Everybody, including me would be better off if I wasn't around anymore,* I thought. *God, I must be insane to be thinking this way, but how much more pounding could I take?*

Think about the jobs, I commanded myself. *Which job? Why don't I care? Why can't I think? Why am I so miserable?*

I fumbled for a smoke. *Screw IBM. Screw it all. I don't want to go through any more. Put myself out of my own misery. I'm gonna blow.*

Pacing around the house I thought about just two things. Living, and what that entailed, and not living. Feeling cold sweat ooze out of my palms, I cursed. "Goddamned worthless hands, quit sweating. Stop it." I wiped them off on my pants. In a few seconds they were soggy and spongy again. I looked in the mirror; a garish reflection looked back, the look of a madman. Sick about what I saw, I quickly turned away.

At 6:30, I crawled back in bed, curling up in a fetal-like ball. Pat stirred as I pulled the covers up over my damp body.

"Max, are you all right?" she asked in a sleep-laden voice. I rolled over and faced her. Before I could stop them, the words stumbled out.

"Pat ... I'm suicidal!"

Four

O H, GOD! NO!" PAT SAID, HER EYES WIDENING TO AN ABNORMAL SIZE as she quickly sat upright, then scrambled out of bed. She bolted down the hall, shutting the doors to our kids' bedrooms as she went, then ducked into the guest bedroom where I soon heard her on the phone.

Dumb-assed stunt, I thought shaking my head at myself. *Now you've really done it. Why'd you say that?* Regretfully, I couldn't recall those words. I'd said what I'd said.

Moment's later I heard a car pull up in the driveway. Curious, I went to the window. My sister, Marcia, and her husband, Tom, who lived just a few miles away, had rushed over. *Must have been who Pat called,* I concluded. Hell, I'd just uttered the condemning words minutes before. I heard them come in and muted conversation in another part of the house, but I remained in the bedroom, pacing back and forth, faster and faster.

A few more minutes passed, and Pat walked back into the bedroom. Startled, I stopped pacing but remained silent, afraid for the stupid words sure to follow.

"Let me give you a reason to live, Max. We'll get you through this" Pat said gently while slowly undressing before me. Her light robe fell to the floor, then her nightgown. Walking up to me, she pressed her naked body up to mine. She held me for a moment, then took a step backward, looked at me for a reaction, found none, and began unbuttoning my pajama bottoms. They fell to the floor in a heap around my ankles.

"Come on," she said, taking my hand. "Get in the shower with me."

Pat tenderly hand washed me with soap, watching for any sign of interest. I just stood there, stone-faced, hardly feeling her touch, watching the spray fly off both our wet bodies.

"Now wash me, Max," she said, picking up my hand and placing the soap on my palm. I looked at the soap and began like an automaton to wash her. As slowly as my hand moved over her, my emotions started to awaken, but they were not those of passion or sexual desire.

Quickly, an almost overwhelming sadness overtook me. The family's breadwinner and main man was broken. I had let them down and hurt them terribly. I admitted to myself that, after I had left the sales rep job in Traverse City, I'd been like a fighter being groomed for the champion's role; only after completing six years of carefully-staged matches, I'd been knocked out in the first round of the championship fight held right in my hometown. And that had left me with no fight at all. The soap slipped out of my hand and landed with a thud at my feet. I looked at Pat.

"Kiddo, I've gotta get help. I gotta go somewhere for help."

Her naked wet body pressed hard to mine. "I know, honey. I know."

Getting out of the shower, I quietly toweled down, watching Pat do the same. While dressing, Pat kept glancing at me, a worried frown stamped on her face. Slowly putting on a long-sleeved shirt and some slacks, I walked over to her and helped her fasten a necklace. "You look good, clothed or naked, kid ... always did. Remember our first shower together in Maine? The one at the naval air station where we checked in as husband and wife?"

She managed a smile. "I sure do."

Now, dry and clothed, my always-tidy and organized wife packed some clothing and toiletry items for me while my brother-in-law made the necessary calls. Marcia and Tom knew quite a bit about the firing; I'd used Marcia's typewriter for some resumè preparation and told her about it then. Now, I needed to walk out the bedroom door and face them, ashamed over my cowardly display but nevertheless needing them as never before for help. I took a deep breath and stepped through the doorway.

As I entered the living room where they both sat, an embarrassed silence engulfed us. Marcia broke the ice by giving me a hug. "Come on, brother, let's get you some help."

In a few minutes, we were on our way. Tom did the driving while I sat silently in the right front seat, Pat and Marcia in the rear, trying to put together why I felt suicidal. *Damn, suicide? Why suicide? How could I have let myself get this depressed? How could I even be thinking of dropping out on Pat and the kids as well as friends and family?*

We drove into an office park complex dotted with look-alike one-story brick structures. The one we parked in front of held no outward signs of busted minds, inside no signs of any kind whatsoever. Walking into the lobby, I saw nothing different about this place than a nursing home I'd visited when my grandmother moved into it. As I waited to be admitted, one difference became apparent — a buzzing noise that I soon figured out meant doors locking and unlocking. *That made sense,* I thought. *Patients in here are restricted from leaving of their own volition.*

The admission form called for a "reason of visit." In large handwriting, I wrote "Suicidal." *Call it for what it is,* I figured.

The admissions clerk looked right at me after reading my response and hesitated before acting. She then reached over and pressed a buzzer mounted on her side of the counter, and I heard a door click open. Turning around, I watched a young, dark-haired attendant wearing starched white dungarees and shirt walk though the door and approach me. Taking my elbow in his hand, as if I was an aging invalid needing assistance, he said, "Follow me."

I picked up my belongings and turned to face Pat. She waved, her small hand trembling. *This is it,* I thought. *I'm about to pass through a locked door and into a New World with no return. All of this over a lousy fir-*

ing. Why me, God? Why didn't I handle this better? Am I a coward, God?

I turned away from Pat and toward the metal interior door. The orderly led me through and it closed behind us with a loud, ominous click as the lock slipped automatically into place. We walked down a vacant hallway, passing windowless doors, the sounds of our footsteps all that could be heard. My nose twitched at the smell of antiseptic strong in the air. The attendant led me into a small room with two beds, two chairs, a desk, and an attached bathroom. Neat and clean, the setting resembled that of my freshman year in a Michigan State dormitory.

The little rational thinking I could do limited itself to an internal lambasting for whining at my own wife about feeling suicidal. Then she responded by giving me the most tender of scenes in the shower, and I stood there like a goddamn eunuch. Not even enough energy or desire to make love for old times' sake.

But, here, alone in this small room, an eerie calmness crept into my mind and body locking out all else. *Like before a storm,* I thought, *when the sky turns green and the air stagnant. Before all hell breaks loose...*

Sure enough, the tranquility faded away rapidly. As I sat motionless on the bed looking at my stark surroundings my pulse quickened and my breathing began coming in gasps. Remembering the lecture I'd heard when I was in the air force about symptoms of fear, I knew I'd started hyperventilating.

Supposed to breathe into a sack, I recalled. I looked round urgently. *No sack.* I lit a smoke and paced the floor, wondering where my roommate had gone. His belt lay on the extra bed and his toiletry kit sat neatly on the nightstand.

Unable to stand the silence any longer, I walked toward the lobby without speaking to any of six or so patients and staff members I walked by. Looking around, I expected someone to lead me back to my room before I made a run for freedom. Nobody seemed to notice. When I reached the metal door out of the ward, I placed my hand on the cool knob and tried to turn it. It didn't budge. Locked.

Walking back to the room I lit another cigarette. My brain felt as if it was glowing as hot as the tip of my Winston. Yet, a new sensor kicked in — smell. Yeah, I could smell it all right. Fear.

I sat down on the bed and held my head with my hands. *God, I thought, I'm blowing up. Please, Lord, make the pain go away. I can't handle this.*

My eyes settled on my missing roommate's belt. I stared at it blankly at first, then an idea hit me. Jumping from my seat, I grabbed it, moved quickly to the shower stall in the corner of the room and attached it to the metal rod holding the shower curtain. Then I made a loop of it around my neck. *Must be a skinny guy,* I thought. *No surplus to work with.* I hesitated for a moment.

This is it. The end. By God, I must be crazy! I don't care. I don't care! I'd rather die than feel the pain.

Do it, said a voice in my head. *DO IT!*

I jumped up in the air, hands behind my back, knees bent and feet tucked up to my buttocks. With luck, my neck would snap.

Crack! Still conscious I landed on the floor, hard, and wondered about the cracking noise. Not my neck at all but the sound of the shower rod being jerked out of the wall. The burning sensation in my brain continued, now even hotter.

Find another way, Beardslee. My eyes darted around the small room. Not many choices. They settled on the porcelain toilet in the corner. *I've got it! Stick my head in the toilet, and hold it there until I drown.* I crawled to the toilet and kneeled on the floor beside the bowl, then, after taking a deep breath and holding it, dunked my head into the chilly water and pulled the flusher. Water rushed around my head, but I pulled my head out of the bowl. Two attempts later, I raised my drenched face out of the bowl, gasping for air. I stood up and mopped my face with my sleeve.

Now holding my pounding, flame-filled head, like a caged animal I paced the room. Back and forth, back and forth. Then I noticed the walls. Concrete blocks. *I could ... maybe ... run into them hard enough to break my neck or crush my skull. The now unmerciful and unbearable pain would be gone.*

International Business Marionettes

I moved to one side of the room, got down into a football crouch, and hesitated before running with my hands behind my back, tentatively, at the solid wall. At the last minute, with a burst of determination, I dove straight at it.

Wham! The noise of my skull hitting the wall filled my ears as I fell to the floor. Still conscious. Slowly I got up, gasping and coughing, and resolutely backed up to the end of the room determined to go again before my nerve failed me. I got down into another football stance, ran, this time faster, and leaped off the floor and dove for the wall.

Thud! I lay for a moment on the cool floor to take stock of my condition. Nothing broken. The headache had worsened. *Not surprising.* Picking myself up, I could taste blood in my mouth. Three more times I charged at the block wall before I gave up, cautiously feeling the top of my head afraid of what I might touch. Lumps. Huge lumps, but no blood. My head felt broken even if it wasn't.

You can't even kill yourself successfully, I thought. *You don't deserve to be alive.*

I sat down on the bed once more and placed my head in my hands. *Am I insane, I asked myself? What is sanity?* I pondered the subject for a few minutes before concluding I must be crazy. How else could I explain my behavior?

Okay, now that my mental state has been established, I thought logically, *there must be a way to accomplish my goal. But how?* I looked around the room once more, this time noticing the window. A new idea managed to cram its way into my pain-filled brain. *I'll break the goddamn window and get to a highway where I can throw myself in front of a passing truck!*

I walked to the small desk on the other side of the room and picked up a wooden chair. It wasn't too heavy but, by placing it in front of me, it would serve as a shield when breaking the glass. Much like before, I stood opposite the window and prepared to throw myself against it. One, two, three ... Go! I flung the chair and my body straight into the glass. A shattering sound filled my ears as I landed half out of the window, the chair falling on the grass outside.

It worked! I thought with elation. I could feel the sting of cuts on my skin as I balanced on my hands, which were spread out on the ground below and covered with warm blood. I pulled my legs over the remaining shards of glass and the ledge.

Falling to the ground outside the decimated window, I staggered to my feet and began to run. All my parts were working; the cuts wouldn't prevent me from making it to the highway. Out of the corner of my eye I saw a tall, bearded man dressed in white. He was standing about thirty yards away from the window, but when he heard the crash and located the cause, he started running toward me.

Must be an attendant, I thought. *Well, I'll out-hoof him.*

I moved with purpose, hoping to find a busy road and become a pedestrian accident statistic. Some thick foliage along a sidewalk afforded cover, so I darted into its middle, stumbling through the brush. Like the madman I was, I rushed forward frantically. Winded, I struggled with each breath and each step but kept going, the hot sun forcing sweat onto my bloodstained shirt. I wiped my dripping face with my hand, smearing blood across my face.

Over my own heaving breaths and the pounding of my heart and head, I became aware of another sound — the whooshing of cars travelling at speed. Pushing branches aside, I exited on the other side of the bushes. Immediately I spotted the familiar four-lane highway to Lansing.

Good, I thought, *it won't take long now. The seething and aching will stop, because my brains will be splattered all over the highway.*

Approaching the side of the road I thought, *how simple. I supply my tortured, miserable soul and the driver supplies the force. No weak shower rod or toilet tank, and no more ramming my head against a concrete wall.* I strategized how to end it. *Pick a truck, one with a flat nose so I can't be flipped over the top, and just step out in front of it... Easy.*

I stepped closer to the highway and then hesitated. *What about the truck driver? I'll burden some poor bastard with my death. He'd never forget it.* I shrugged my shoulders. *Sorry, buddy,* I apologized in advance. *There's no other way.*

In a few minutes, an eighteen-wheeler came barreling down the highway. My side of the road. Flat nosed. *The driver won't be suspicious if I just jog beside the road,* I thought. The truck rumbled closer, sending vibrations up from the pavement through the balls of my feet. *Can I do it?* I queried myself as I jogged lamely now along the shoulder.

Yes. I picked up some speed and my stride lengthened as my insanity peaked. Now, said the familiar voice in my head. *Go!*

I stepped off the shoulder and into the driving lane. The startled driver swerved, his air horn signaling his displeasure, but my motions had been timid. I had not jumped out far enough to ensure my early end. I moved back onto the shoulder. *No balls. No nerve. You really are a sad, sorry case, Beardslee. You truly don't deserve to live.*

I made two more half-hearted attempts.

The hell with this. Maybe, just maybe, I don't want to die, anyway. I don't seem to be able to pull a suicide off, so I must not really want to.

I sat down on the hot tarmac, pulled my knees up to my chin and wrapped my arms around them. I rested my chin on my knees. Anger, guilt, defeat but mostly confusion swirled around in my pain-filled head. One minute I wanted to die and now, the next minute, I wanted help. "Please, someone help me," I pleaded. "God, can't you hear me? Oh, God."

A police van drove by, the driver wearing a blue shirt with a badge reflecting the bright sunlight of mid-afternoon. His eyes met mine with recognition. The van stopped and slowly backed up until the front window became even with me. With a gentle voice the driver said, "Come with us, Max."

He knew my name! Relief flooded my tired, battered body. I climbed inside the van, falling limply against the seat.

"Do you want to go home?" he asked.

The thought made me want to laugh. He had no earthly idea just how insane I felt or what I'd tried to do in the last hour. Nobody did. I took a deep breath, letting the air rush out my mouth noisily. "No, officer. I don't want my wife to see me this way. Take me back."

This time around, a white-coated attendant led me to what the hospital called the "quiet room," a cement-block cube about eight-feet up, down, and across. Clean and sterile, flooded with white light. A bed in the middle of the floor, nothing else. Sticking a needle in my arm, a familiar-looking bearded attendant smiled, then walked over and stood in a corner of the room. He looked vaguely like the same guy who saw me flying through the window, but I couldn't be sure.

"A doctor will be in to see you in a few hours," he explained as he settled against the wall. "I'll be with you until he gets here."

Well, I thought, *bring him on. We wouldn't lack for things to discuss.*

Fiddling with the syringe, the orderly said, "I've been here six years and that's the first time I remember a window ever being broken. How'd you do it?"

"With a chair," I told him matter-of-factly.

"Oh yeah? Well that window ain't supposed to break, no matter what."

What the hell, I thought, *who cares about the window?* "Do I win a prize?" I asked.

The orderly grinned. "Only prize I know of is another charge on your patient care records. Did you know I tried to catch you?"

So it was him, I thought. "I saw you," I mumbled. Nobody had to know how desperate I'd been. Nobody had to know about running into the wall or playing traffic tag. "Now can I be left alone?"

"Sure," the attendant replied with a grin. "You'll sure as hell be safe in here."

After what seemed like ages of just sitting there on the bed, the seething in my brain subsided. The burning, hurting sensation was replaced with one that felt almost pleasant. Had the shot eased the pain or had I returned to my senses? I didn't know the answer, but I did know I felt happy to be alive, lumpy head and all.

International Business Marionettes

Into my isolated cubicle entered a kind looking man with a balding head, a generous nose and an aged stoop. He nodded an acknowledgment then he introduced himself to me. "My name is Dr. Victor Rosenberg. I've been assigned to your case."

I bypassed the outstretched hand, jumped off the bed and hugged him. "Damn, Doc, am I glad to see you!" The little guy looked embarrassed as I let him go. "You see, I've been in this cloud ... couldn't think ... got all whacked out of shape ... damn near killed myself today, but you know what?" I exclaimed.

Doctor Rosenberg stayed still, his face expressionless.

"I didn't do it. No siree, and boy am I glad I didn't," I grabbed the doctor again. This time he looked annoyed.

"I'm glad you're feeling better," Doctor Rosenberg said as he pulled away from my embrace and brushed at his coat. "I know why you were admitted. Tell me, what were you thinking when you broke the window? By the way, that's a first around here ... supposed to be unbreakable."

Attentive, watery eyes stared at me as I described the seething sensation in my head, becoming so unbearable I'd devised ways to make the pain go away. "I dove head first in the concrete block wall of my room. Tryin' to break my neck, I guess." He ran a gentle, liver-spotted hand over my bumps. "I almost jumped in front of a truck, a flat-nosed one so I wouldn't flip up in the air."

Doctor Rosenberg got up as if to leave. "You may have been temporarily insane for part of today. The window, for example, I don't think you could break it right now. I work with some criminally insane patients at another place. They can do things that require almost super-human strength.

"Try to think about some good things in your past," he recommended before departing, adding that he'd see me sometime the next day, shutting the door firmly behind him. I stayed alone for the next few hours, feeling foolish but thankful to be and feel alive, not at all depressed. I felt rather happy, in fact.

Pat came to visit me in this cell-like room that evening. Looking around, she appeared amazed at my Fort Knox like accommodations. "How're you doing, Max?" she asked in a dejected voice.

I wanted my wife to feel half as good as I did. "Honey, I'm doing great," I almost shouted. "Damned if I don't think that whatever went on today broke something loose and freed me up. Honey, I'm telling you, I couldn't feel better."

Pat's face appeared to brighten at my enthusiasm. She said, "Well, I hope so, cause something else broke loose as well. The broken window cost us four hundred and eighty dollars, and I just got done paying for it. If I hadn't, you'd have been booted out."

I smiled sheepishly. "Guess I felt my Wheaties, huh?" Thinking about my dive through the window, I shuddered. *I must have been really desperate using strength reserved for the insane as Rosenberg had said. Insanity could be the only explanation.*

Pat ran her hand gently over the lumps on my head. She'd been told of my head-ramming escapade. After she left, another attendant gave me a tranquilizer, which I gladly accepted. I curled up on the hard bed and before I knew it had lapsed into the best sleep I'd enjoyed in weeks. I didn't move once until the door opened and an attendant brought me breakfast the next morning.

Not long after I had eaten I got moved to a ward for the moderately impaired, only getting glimpses of the more severe patients through the heavy wood and glass barrier of their separate wing. I could tell which ones were deeply disturbed by their eyes. Some had vacant lenses flooded with darkness, others wild and staring, a drug or drugs compressing their pupils to pinpoint dimensions. Still others possessed a permanent look of pain, but always their eyes signaled wounded minds. I wondered if I'd looked like them just twenty-four hours ago. *Did I look like them now? Now that I felt almost normal again?*

I was impressed with the facility itself. This intimate first look at a psychiatric center revealed clean rooms, a cafeteria serving tasty food, and a patient, pleasant and cheerful staff — not at all what I'd imagined a mental hospital to be. I'd figured on a dark and dreary place filled with bent over bodies clad in dirty and foul-smelling clothing, mumbling to themselves, eating food out of bowls with their hands. *I've watched too many old movies,* I decided.

That afternoon, Dr. Rosenberg started therapy sessions with me. A novice at this, I expected a couch upon which to lie or a key ring at which to stare. None of that. His cramped office shared two chairs, a cluttered desk and several framed diplomas brandishing his medical credentials.

The old doctor started by explaining yesterday's events to me, "Max, you were temporarily insane. I diagnosed you as such judging by the abnormal strength you found to break the window." He paused.

"So, why don't you tell me what's been going on?"

Briefly I recapped the whole mess. Cigars ... audits ... being fired ... and the weeks that sent me into the darkness of despair. "The main thing, Doc, was the guilt. Couldn't flush wanting to revisit my meeting with the waiter thousands of times, trying to change the outcome or something, I guess. And then I started feeling guilty about everything I'd ever done. Hell, I even felt guilty about feeling guilty."

The doctor showed interest in what he called my "guilt manifestation." Rosenberg explained, "People can sometimes lose their normal way of filtering their emotions; love, hate, success, failure, depression, guilt, loss of confidence. In your case, probably from the intense shock you endured, something misfired causing your filters to clog. That threw all your sensual perceptions into one area ... in this case, guilt." The doctor made some notes on a pad before he continued.

"Now I want to know why that happened. It could have been from the shock; it could have been from something you've subconsciously harbored for a long time. I'd like to know a little more about your childhood.

"Take me back a bit, say high school." I got comfortable in an overstuffed chair and thought about high school. A happy time ...

Max Beardslee

◆◆◆

With butch-cut hair wax, a clamp on tie, and liberal amounts of acne cream to blot out the teenage curse, I decked out for the athletic awards banquet. This annual event highlighted social happenings in our small town of Sheridan, population six hundred. Two gas stations, a grocery store, Wally's Barber Shop, and a Rexall drugstore. The Carnation condensery was the largest business in town employing sixty-odd people to process canned milk.

Most of the town turned out for the banquet. My younger brother, Dennis, sat next to me fidgeting uncomfortably in his unaccustomed dress clothes. Marcia, my older sister, was away attending Michigan State and was, therefore, not present. I'd had a good senior year and was pumped up about my chance at getting some individual recognition.

The master of ceremonies' voice boomed over the loud speaker "The most valuable football player as voted by the members of the team is split between two players ... Gene Byers and Max Beardslee." A skinny, gangly kid of one hundred fifty pounds with size-eleven shoes, I broke out into a toothy grin as I jumped from my seat, passed the paper-covered tables with fold-up seats and trotted to the podium to receive my award. The coach handed me a trophy with a small inscription: Max Beardslee, MVP 1956, Sheridan High School. I beamed with pride.

Mother taught English at the high school, which had proved awkward for my sensitive disposition. A few fights ensued when classmates called my mother various unmentionable names when she declared them ineligible to graduate or move on to the next grade. I knew, however, as did the others, that she taught well. Tough, but fair. Mother participated in any and all the social activities in our town as well as helping supply the home-cooked food.

My dad measured as the third largest employer in town with a force of six at his Olds' dealership. Dad's Main Street business made him a prominent man in the community.

International Business Marionettes

Despite my award I was blessed with little natural athletic ability. I was just one of those gung-ho kids who cramped up in the fourth quarter from burning up all my adrenaline during the first three. I'd practiced hundreds of hours learning how to come off the ball. In a forty-yard dash I moved no better than average, but off the ball I could knock a bigger guy on his ass.

We competed for the county championship and, although we lost that game, enjoyed a strong season. The fine print in the *Detroit Free Press* listed me as all-state honorable mention. In the spring of 1957, seeing my name in print, a tiny inked bit of recognition, convinced me all the effort had been worth it.

♦ ♦ ♦

As I related my childhood to the doctor, I reflected on how my character, developed early around my attempts at sports success, ideally suited the masterful recognition schemes IBM would induce later in my life. "I'm a pretty gung-ho guy, Doc. When IBM laid out all those quotas, I took them real serious. Until I made the almighty numbers, I played the game hard. Probably too hard, like I did in athletics... Learn anything, Doc?"

He muttered something indistinguishable and slowly shook his head. *So much for therapy.* "I'll see you in two days," he said.

Feeling more alert and attentive every day, I rose early in the mornings, ate hearty meals and slept well at night. During the day I attended group therapy sessions that included receiving information on stress management and symptoms of manic depression. I also took a workshop where one could putter around making belts, clay pots or even painting on real canvas, something I tried but the results looked dismal. The mental institution bore minor unpleasantness, but at least I was insulated from the realities with which Pat had to deal.

The day after I'd been committed, an IBM exec named Jim Barton called the house intending to make an appointment to discuss the letter I'd written to Frank Cary, IBM's chairman. Pat concealed her surprise, as I had never told her about it, and bluffed by saying I would be at the airport the next day to meet him, knowing she'd have to go in my place and fight this one alone. The possibility of her husband enduring a long-term illness, losing her home to the bank and having no way to support the children had her more than worried. She was panicked. She wanted this opportunity to work IBM over for the pain she felt the company was causing her and her family and to try and ensure some assistance.

When the appointment time arrived, Pat called Barton's room from the hotel lobby. Unable to suppress her frustrations, she gave Barton most of the lowlights right over the phone. "Max has lost it, I'm losing it and I need your help."

After hearing Pat's impassioned plea for help, a surprised Barton said, "I'll be right there," and rushed to the lobby.

Barton, unprepared to deal with an emotional woman rather than an ex-employee, seemed uncomfortable when he stepped off the elevator. After a few moments, he put his hand reassuringly on Pat's shoulder and said, "I'm sure IBM will help, but I need to make a few calls about this." With that he turned and disappeared into the elevator again leaving Pat standing in the lobby.

An hour later Barton returned. He had called the chairman's office and the vice president of personnel. "IBM has agreed to giving assistance on the house and medical bills, Mrs. Beardslee. We'll help."

As Pat shared the details of the conversation with me that night at the psychiatric clinic, I felt encouraged that Pat got her licks in, but I also felt relief that she'd found an outlet for her frustrations, although I doubted anything good would come of it. However, a commitment by IBM to buy our home was something.

On August 18, fourteen days into my stay at the psychiatric center, Dr. Rosenberg discharged me. By getting up at the proper hour, enthusiastically participating in the day's activities, and repeating to the staff and psychiatrist that I couldn't feel better, I had fooled myself as well as him into believing that I was operating normally once again.

International Business Marionettes

Once at home, however, I slowly regressed. This time paranoia reigned as the dominant factor in my thinking. I constantly convinced myself that everyone was whispering about me and saying negative things behind my back. I interrogated Pat about some anonymous phone calls we'd received. Just breathing on the other end. I thought for sure it was Martha with the M-M-M-M-M license plate. *Damn her. Why couldn't she leave me alone? She was probably spreading wild rumors about me throughout IBM, while crowing to her personal friends that she'd brought me down.*

The next week, I met with Barton at the airport. He had with him a letter offering to dispose of our house, but I refused it. "Nope. No thanks. For one thing this says we'll have to pay broker fees and all of that. For another, we don't want to move."

I then moved the conversation toward the meetings in the Fillmore regime, but I did so with no feeling of conviction, no fight, Barton impressed me as a man going through the motions, bored that he had to be there at all. "I'll write down the names of people you can contact who will prove I could only collect twenty dollars tops to fund outside expenses. They'll also tell you no way would twenty dollars cover all that stuff."

I didn't mention the Sugar Loaf cover-up, not wanting to get Blaylock into real trouble. *I'd been booted. Let it go at that,* I told myself, though I had real problems understanding why Blaylock had done nothing to save my job. In my almost-daily fantasy, Blaylock, the wonder kid, would call IBM, confess the plot, and save me. *Where in hell was my white knight?*

Barton listened but the way his eyes wandered around told me he didn't view my story as any big deal. And, frankly, neither did I, and that was why I still couldn't understand why I had been fired.

The medium-height executive stood up and said he had to go meet his "next case." *Sounds a bit like a psychiatrist in the psycho ward,* I thought. Indeed, I wasn't far off in my analogy as he offered a bit of information about it. "This guy had a total mental breakdown on the job," he said, his tone of voice subtly implying that my "case" didn't stack up to some others. "The pressures of quota got him. He was behind, moved out on his wife and kids and started drinking a great deal. Then, one day, he just broke down at his desk."

Screw you, Barton, I thought, *and IBM as well. The poor guy who blew up over a blown quota needed help, sure he did, but so did I.*

Back at home, Pat kicked the hassock as I watched her face flush when I told her about my conversation with Barton. "Let's check on Barton," she said, and picked up the phone with determination on her face.

She called Chad Russell, my key witness toward the twenty-dollar limit. He'd been in Blaylock's office when I complained about expenses, asking Blaylock to raise the limit. "No — nobody has contacted me about anything. I sure hope they do, though. I was in the room with Max when he asked Blaylock to raise the limit."

Pat thanked Russell before slamming down the phone.

The phone rang. Schwartz. Pat told me she had called him and the company in Denver to explain why I hadn't arrived at work. Still, he invited me to Detroit. From the eleventh floor of the American Motors Building, he gave me reassuring news.

"Forget the past month, Max. If you're okay, we'll still hire you and move you back to Detroit." The next day, I drove to Detroit and met Schwartz at his office.

"Want to read something Fillmore said about you to an employment agency, Max?"

"Sure," I replied, curious about it, "why not?" He showed me a handwritten reply from Fillmore to the employment agency Schwartz used. "Beardslee left IBM under questionable circumstances. I tried to save him, but couldn't. He got the highest morale index as a branch manager in the twelve-branch region and doesn't even know it. The results came in after he left."

As I read a few more comments Fillmore made about my career at IBM, I reflected over him having at least mustered some kind of fight to keep me in the company. *Well, Christ,* I thought. *I'm glad he did. I thought he took my dismissal personally, and this adds credence to it.* I felt proud of the rating, too. Grand Rapids had been moving in the right direction. "Thanks for showing me Fillmore's comments, Ed. It helps to know he's saying good things about me."

Before returning to Grand Rapids, with false enthusiasm I accepted Schwartz's job offer while secretly doubting my ability to work at all. I agreed to begin on the following Monday.

Arriving back in Grand Rapids, Pat noticed my continuing despondence. Hell. I couldn't hide it. As I attempted to pacify her by saying that once I went back to work full time I'd be too busy to dwell on the past, a mental fog moved in and settled on my brain. It wasn't painful like the burning sensation I still remembered so well, but it did cause concentration problems much like the cigar smoke that had enveloped my thoughts not so long ago. *Maybe work would burn off the haze.* I hoped so.

After a three-and-a-half-month layoff and two weeks in a mental institution, I tried to psyche myself up about starting this new job. *Come on, Beardslee. You can pull it off,* I said to my reflection in the bathroom mirror the day I was to begin. But little remained of my former self, and there was no inner response to my pep talk. I could not even pat myself on the back for fitting into my old suits again.

For two weeks I managed to arrive at the office, but I never did a semblance of work. Early in the day, I'd sneak out of my office, go to the ground floor of the American Motors Building, pace back and forth, and then ride the escalator up and down for hours. During this period I began experiencing mental voids, lapses where I only marginally knew my surroundings. I'd be standing in the lobby wondering where I was and, once I figured that out, I'd wonder which floor my office was on. I had to walk over to the directory in the lobby to figure it out. I kept these aberrations to myself, assuming that one more trip to the psycho ward and any chance of retaining this job — or any other — would be gone.

When one of the company's sales reps made an appointment to make a presentation to me, his new boss, I spent half an hour staring but not seeing as he flip-charted me with the standard features and benefits of his program. At the end, he earnestly asked, "What do you think, sir?"

I hadn't heard a word of his presentation. I looked at him and bluntly replied, "A fine program. I've gotta go."

His face fell. He'd expected a hard charger; that's the word Schwartz had spread about me. No evidence of that today. The salesman walked out shoulders sagging.

A week into the job I flew to Chicago for a software convention, marginally managing to get on the plane, into Chicago, and find my way to the convention center. There, I did nothing but pace and walk for several hours, returning to Grand Rapids for the weekend.

Home life was no better. I had little to say to Pat — or anyone else for that matter, spurned all offers of food, slept three to four hours each night, and didn't even acknowledge the children's existence. That weekend dragged into an awful scene of silence and memory loss on my part. I shuffled around the house not bothering to shave or even bathe. Pat could see it. She sent the kids to my sister's house so they wouldn't have to. "Max, I'm trying to reach you, but nobody's home. If you want to talk, I'm here. Okay?"

I nodded my head and limped through the weekend, hardly ever uttering a word.

On Monday morning, I drove back to Detroit. As I parked my car in the lot, I realized that I had no recollection of how I'd gotten there. Later that morning, I tried to interview a job candidate, but when I asked him questions I made no sense at all. My mind said, *"Talk, Beardslee, talk,"* but after a while no words would come out. I excused myself and left the room. The applicant just stared at me in total confusion.

Schwartz was out of town on business most of this time, so my behavior largely went unnoticed. When he returned for a few days, he requested a meeting with me. As he entered my office, his eyes revealed his shock. I stood before him, ten pounds lighter than when he'd left, with dark-purple half moons under my eyes and only half the whiskers on my face shaved off. My suit was wrinkled and baggy, my shirt unpressed.

Quietly, Schwartz advised, "Get out of the office, go see your psychiatrist and try to work things out." He ushered me to the door.

I drove back to Grand Rapids, thoughts confined in a bubble-like sphere. My thinking couldn't escape the hazy ball that had never left, just gotten thicker with each passing day at my new job. My thoughts lazily bounced off its undefined sides as I tried to understand the messages of my frazzled brain. My efforts reaped nothing but a deepening feeling of impending doom. I didn't know the specifics of the calamity, only that its coming felt imminent.

Five

I SHOULD HAVE BEEN ABLE TO DRIVE HOME BLINDFOLDED. INSTEAD, although only one road traversed between the two cities, I hadn't a clue about where I was driving until a landmark jostled my memory. I recognized the turnoff, made it and proceeded home accompanied by my feeling that something bad would happen. What? When?

As I walked into the house early, Pat showed her alarm by quickly asking, "What went wrong? Why are you home?"

"The job, honey, I wasn't hacking it. Schwartz figured it out and advised me to get back here and see a doctor. By the way, are you okay? Are the kids okay?"

"Yes," she replied with a quizzical look. "Why? You look really worried about something?"

"Yeah, I am. How about the news? How's Russia?"

"Not a thing new about them that I heard. Why?"

"You sure?" I replied, still sure something lay amiss.

"Yeah, I'm sure," she said and shook her head at me in disbelief. "You sure are acting strangely. Come on, help me fix dinner and tell me about what happened at work."

I told her some, but not all, of what had been going on. After dinner I suggested that we take a long walk in the subdivision, hoping it would work off the gloom. I eased into bed still depressed and anxious and fell into a fitful sleep. Twice I woke up to nightmares;

I couldn't remember the details but knew the subconscious screen of my mind had been playing hideous movies.

I woke up early, slowly easing out of bed so as not to wake Pat. I walked over to the window. A soft orange glow threw early shadows on the lawn, while fall-colored leaves rustled, their edges sparkling with morning dew. Pleasant and serene. The house lay quiet but for a clock ticking in the hall.

Yesterday's fear of impending doom had turned to a dread of certain calamity that now consumed me. My hands shook as I formulated in my head a picture of the upcoming event. Waves of fear washed over my senses flooding out all other thoughts as I locked onto my vivid delusion.

As the truth dawned on me, I thought in horror, *Oh, my God. I know what has happened. The earth has fallen out of orbit and is now being drawn toward the sun. The world will end today.*

I looked at Pat's sleeping figure. She looked so peaceful. *Why didn't she know about this imminent catastrophe? Everybody knew about it, didn't they?* I gently shook her.

"Pat. Pat! Wake up."

My wife opened her eyes, bewildered by the hasty awakening, then saw the terror reflected in my eyes. I started babbling.

"Pat, you and John, Steve, and Chris are going to heaven this very day. I love you all very much. I'm going to hell."

Pat looked into my glazed eyes and knew I was over the edge again. "Oh my god," she said as she pulled away from me. The terror in her eyes belied her thoughts.

I watched as she slowly moved out of the bed and inched toward the walk-in closet. I could understand being afraid of death, but why was she acting like I was threatening to take her life away? Before I could elaborate, my mind rationalized her behavior as a mother's desire to save her children from the world's end.

Keeping her eyes on me, Pat quickly found clothes, dressed and moved toward the door. Once out of the bedroom, she went to the kids' rooms and dressed them as well and invented a reason, to which I was not privy, to leave the house with them.

I watched all this from where I stood in the bedroom, not moving except to go to the window and watch my family leave. As the car disappeared down the road, I decided that Pat's actions were appropriate. She must know the end is coming soon, I thought, and is taking the children somewhere safer than our house.

I don't know how long I stood at the window before the phone rang, but it startled me out of my mental ramblings about what I was waiting to see happen outside those panes of glass. Still in my pajamas, I walked over to the bed, sat down and answered the phone. I heard the sound of my mother's voice.

"Hello, Son. How are you feeling? Seek and I want to come over and see you." *Pat must have called them,* I thought. But I didn't want my mother and Seek, short for Seekell, to venture outside.

"Don't come over," I commanded and hung up. *They'd be safer not traveling now.* Plus, I was convinced my private secret had been told — it was my fault that the world had begun its destruction — and I didn't want anyone, not even my mother, to come and confront me about this deed or, worse, try to punish me for bringing disaster upon them.

Yes, the truth was clear to me: I'd be found guilty of bringing about the coming calamity and others might want to kill me for bringing impending death upon them. *I can't blame them,* I told myself, *but I better take some precautions.* I moved to the interior of the house, to avoid being shot by an irate neighbor.

When I heard a car draw up to the house, I got down on my hands and knees and crawled to the front door, peering out the side glass. Before I could even see the car and identify it, Mother opened the front door, looked at me crouched on the floor and with upturned brows and wide eyes exclaimed, "Son, what are you doing? Are you all right?"

Standing up I exclaimed, "No, I'm not all right. Haven't you heard?"

Seek, the distinguished, tall and lean, white-haired businessman who now served as my step-dad, stepped in front of Mother as if to protect her. When he saw me, he put a strong, firm hand on my shoulder. "Heard what, Max? We only heard from Pat that you're mixed up."

Mixed up? Why the hell would Pat say that? I thought she understood what I had said this morning and had taken appropriate action. I wrinkled my forehead, eyebrows almost touching, in confusion.

Before I could reply, I heard another car in the drive and leaned over to peak out the curtain again. A paddy wagon drew up alongside Seek's Cadillac. *Ah, now I understand. Pat thinks I'm crazy again and has gotten a court order to have me re-committed to the mental institution. And here they've come to get me.*

As the police handcuffed me, I didn't fight. *We'd all be dead in a few hours anyway. What did this turn of events matter? Soon nothing would be left to matter.* They led me toward the van and I looked over my shoulder for my mother and Seek. She was nowhere to be seen. With illusion as my only reality, their absence just confirmed my fears; they had died and were on their way to heaven.

My God, I thought. *The end of the world has begun already.* I looked around for more telltale signs. Gusting winds blew suddenly scattering the decaying leaves of fall that had sparkled just hours earlier but now performed a dark, macabre dance over our lawn. There was not another person in sight.

Ah, ha. All of civilization has begun shutting down right here and now. And it's my entire fault, I thought sadly. I hung my head and stepped into the van. Riding through the subdivision I peered through the small glass window of the van hoping to see survivors but saw not one.

At the asylum, familiar staff members whisked me into the quiet room and lifted me onto the bed. I lay there wondering how they and the policemen had survived. Very strange, I had no explanation for their endurance. They left me in the room, a scowling nurse shutting the thick metal-and-wood door of my room behind her. Double bolts snapped in place. I got up and peered out of the small, four-inch square piece of reinforced Plexiglas on the door.

Suddenly my heart began to pound on my chest and my breath

to come in gasps. *Trapped! The world is coming to an end, and I'm caught in here,* I thought. *Oh, good God! What am I going to do?* I went back to my bed, and lay there, cold sweat oozing from every pore.

Some time later, the double locks snapped open. Pat walked in, startling me with her presence. *What's this? She's alive? How can it be?* I remained lying on the bed, afraid to get up.

My deluded mind scrambled for an answer, and, of course, found a crazy one. *She must be an angel,* I concluded. *That's it! Pat, thank God, is an angel.* I sat up and reached out to touch her arm, unsure if she would be solid. I found her skin firm and warm. "Pat, your spirit has left your body and made its way toward heaven. God, you're an angel."

I talked rapidly, as if playing a piece of music in a staccato manner, but enough of it registered for Pat to understand what I believed. The more she understood, however, the more her normal expression disappeared and a look of shock replaced it. Wide-eyed she stepped away from the bed as if I carried a communicable disease. Looking at the door frantically, she stood aghast as I continued to talk.

To Pat's relief, Dr. Rosenberg soon entered and asked her to leave the confining cubicle. She looked at me once more, this time with almost pathetic sadness, and left. I focused on Rosenberg. I had figured him for dead, too, and was surprised and pleased to see him standing before me.

"Doc, you're an angel. Good! I knew you were a good guy!" I said with enthusiasm. Rosy', as Pat referred to him, took on a mournful look as I continued. "I know your spirit is presenting itself to me. This isn't you ... I mean; this isn't the solid, human, alive you. I need you to get a message to Pat, John, Steve, and Chris. They're somewhere in heaven or on their way there ... and Mother and Seek, my sister and brother, too."

I grabbed the lapels of Rosy's lab coat and pulled him toward the bed, saying desperately, "You're my last chance to get a message through. I want my family to know I take solace in the fact that they've gone to heaven," I said imploringly as I pulled his face closer to mine.

Rosy', tired beyond his seventy-plus years, had already worked most of the night with a suicidal patient at the prison hospital. My junked-up head could wait until tomorrow. He leaned backward, grabbed my wrists and with surprising strength yanked them off his coat. Then he turned and walked out without a word. The door slammed shut behind him, the locks clicking into place seemingly more quiet in comparison.

I lay back on the bed for what seemed like eons. I didn't know how long I had been in the room when the bolts snapped again and in walked the familiar night nurse. She looked different though. Large darkened rings circled her eyes; hideous eyes sunken with burned out, blackened coals for pupils. *Either dead or dying,* I thought, pulling away from her. She looked ghoulish. I heard someone screaming for her to get out, looked around for the source and realized the sound came from me. It was my own voice I heard.

More immeasurable time elapsed and then the door opened again, and my brother, Dennis, came into the room. I pressed his arm and deduced that it was filled with embalming fluid. It had to be, since the skin didn't just pop back the way it should; it filled in gradually. Another angel.

As I stood beside him, I could smell beer on his breath. *Strange. Did angels drink booze?* This angel looked annoyed as it said, "What in the hell is going on in your mind, Bro'? You gotta snap out of this!"

Afraid to grab an angel, although I desperately wanted to, instead I shouted, "The world's ending! Don't you know anything?"

Denny shrugged his shoulders and left the room followed by familiar sounds of bolts snapping into place.

Darkness now enveloped the room totally. *This is it,* I thought, drawing myself up into a ball. *Whoever's left, we're all gonna die now. The end has come.*

Staring into the dark, I envisioned how the world's end would progress. The earth had spun out of orbit and had drawn closer to the sun, causing the polar ice caps to melt. Millions of people had already drowned from tidal waves and the ensuing flood.

Oh, my God! I jumped off the bed in a panic, ripped the sheets off my bed and stuffed them against the crack in the door to postpone the inevitable seepage of water and — a new threat — the blood of my fellow "inmates." I tried to see my handiwork in the pitch-dark space then lay back down on the bare bed. My eyes staring into the darkness, I spent the night in the small room in terror.

The humming of what I figured to be an exhaust fan kept me company until a faint and intermittent squeaking sent me into a new fearful frenzy. *Oh, God. It's the nurse with the burned out eyes mopping up blood! It's the sound of her squeezing out her mop from the wringer mounted on the pail. She must be the last person on earth still alive, and she's determined to outlast me because she knows I caused the end of the world.*

The squeaks grew fainter and I imagined the nurse's movements becoming weaker and weaker. The squeaking ceased. I waited to hear the thud of her falling to the floor, but I heard only silence. *She's too far away. She must have died. I'm the only one alive. Oh, God.*,

Hours of terror passed as I wondered what would happen to me and relived my part in this disaster: Frank Cary, IBM's chairman, had been the first to die. His wife screamed to her neighbors, "It was Beardslee, he did it!" before she too dropped dead. I still lay curled up in a ball on the bed. The smell of fear filled the small cubicle in which I lay. It became difficult to breathe. *Too little oxygen...*

I got up, stumbling around in the total blackness, my hands feeling for the walls. I thought about Eichmann and Hitler, visualizing what hideous experiences their souls must have been forced to endure after their death. I formulated in my mind the millions of agonies these murderers had caused. Screams from inside gas chambers as deadly vapor snuffed out lives. Exploding shells hitting unsuspecting bodies with their accompanying flames. Terrified mothers clutching screaming babies. Soldiers dying, crushed by the treads of oncoming tanks or blown apart, their lifeless limbs littering the ground. All of their evil, conspired atrocities, the collective agony of the millions of people they slaughtered, had been compressed and recorded into Hitler's and Eichmann's miserable souls for eternity.

They must have been sent to Satan's hell, not hot and fiery but a hideous opposite — black, slimy and cold. The Nazi criminals' souls, joined by others equally as evil, lay imbedded in freezing thick slime. Since I had caused the end of the world — the "sin of sins" — my treatment surely would be worse than theirs.

I made a blind journey around the room, feeling the block wall, looking for a way out. I found none.

Oh, why am I the worst of all sinners? If only I hadn't been so guilty I could have become an angel like Pat and gone to heaven. I fashioned a vivid image of Heaven in which each spirit earned a custom placement with God. His hand guided their spirits anywhere from pure heaven to Satan's hell, with millions of levels in between these two awesome extremes. Each spirit was delivered precisely to a level commensurate with its worth in God's eyes.

I tried to guess to what level my wife and three children's spirits had risen. *By now they all must be enjoying spectacular views of the universe.* I drew my sole source of comfort from that vision.

Time dragged, and periodically I pinched myself, astounded to find that I still lived. Suddenly the door opened and with a flick of a switch an attendant sent the cell from blackness into blinding light.

A trick, I thought, as I squinted and blinked at him. *Must be another angel.*

The tall, lanky, bearded aide who saw me escape entered the little room. "You've been in here a long time. Would you like to go out for a walk?"

I nodded my head.

As solidly as the other corpses who had visited, he led me into the locked anteroom just outside my caged room. I expected to see bodies lying in heaps on the floor or slumped in chairs where they had died. There were none. *Odd.* I looked out the large Plexiglas window, and in the area just past this one I could see patients walking around. My confusion made my head hurt. I knew the world had ended.

The Lord must be playing tricks on me. The bearded man led me out of the anteroom and through the control room. Here attendants operated the hospital's nerve center, and kept themselves apprised of all that was going on throughout the hospital. I stopped facing the rear of the combination control desk and admission desk and looked around for cadavers again. The people at the desk were still alive.

To my right was a glass door opening to a doctor's examination room. As my bearded attendant busied himself with his friends at the desk, I inched toward it and peered through the glass, then jumped backward in fright. Here lay the evidence for which I had been searching. A body with bright orange hair lay on a cot within the room. I stepped forward and looked again, clearly seeing matching orange stitches connecting the hair to the cadaver's head. *Strange, was it just a mannequin?* I couldn't be sure.

I turned back toward the control desk. *Were the flowers perched prettily there real or plastic? Could flowers even grow in the atmosphere created by the earth's destruction?* I moved closer. *Plastic, just as I suspected.* I desperately wanted to look outside and see if grass, clouds, trees, and people still existed there. *I can't be sure what is real or a trick in here, because the attendants or angels control all of it, but outside ... now that they can't control.*

On the other side of the control desk was a door marked "Exit." I had to get outside and see for myself what lay there. Without warning, I ran forward and scrambled to climb on top of the control desk, then dove with arms reaching outward toward the door, all the while keeping the handle within my sight. I landed on my head a few feet from the desk, with plants and phones tumbling around me.

Amidst the following commotion, I was lead back into solitary confinement. Gradually, hours or days later, I came to the conclusion that while the world at large had ended, something strange had occurred here at this private asylum. Life still went on here.

International Business Marionettes

Why? Did God have something special in mind for those of us here?

I was moved to the closed ward. The common denominator among patients here appeared in their demented eyes. I attributed their wild and rapid eye movements as a sign of approaching death.

A new sensation accompanied me to this ward — a feeling of motion created by a vibration in my feet. Maybe this new delusion was just the misfiring of my mind or maybe it was caused by the steady flow of green, liquid-Thorozine highballs that I was now being given. The most powerful drug psychiatrists had at their disposal, Thorozine was reserved for only advanced psychotics. Even the most active of patients was reduced to whimpering shells with enough of this depressant. Delusions, however, had proved to be one of its side affects, thus fueling my pre-existing, non-drug-induced ones.

With the help of this anti-psychotic drug, I decided that the vibration meant I actually was moving. In fact, since the world no longer existed, the Lord was flying the whole mental institution to Heaven at the speed of light with his power. The building had been converted to a spaceship with reinforced windows, walls and ceilings to withstand the vacuum of space. The vibration in my feet was caused by the powerful motor generating the force to propel us.

The Lord must feel special compassion for mental patients, I reasoned. *All, except me, of course – an as-yet-undiscovered stowaway on this heavenly-bound vessel – could expect to earn a special place in heaven.*

Based on my previous vision of heaven, I was sure that we would be making numerous stops along the way; individual patients would have to be dropped off at their designated levels with God making the decision based on one's mortal actions and experiences.

After examining my new surroundings and the ship's passengers, I found a seat next to the exterior windows of the building. The world outside was masked in darkness and mist. I wasn't surprised, for I had always imagined outer space to resemble what I now saw outside.

An elderly woman patient sat down beside me and began telling me about a beautiful star she had seen. Pointing out the window, she asked me to look at it with her.

Ah, yes, she knows where she is going, I thought. *The star is where she will get off.*

Sure enough, some time later she hobbled up to me, placed her hand on my shoulder, and said, "Goodbye. It's time to go now." Then she walked out a door and disappeared. I knew she had left the spaceship, instantly exploding in the vacuum of space, thus releasing her spirit and allowing it to be positioned at her earned Heavenly level.

In her absence, I became terrified that my presence aboard the spaceship would be noticed, although such a discovery appeared inevitable. I would be thrown off, my body exploding into pieces and my spirit bouncing downward from level to level until ultimately plunging with horror into the sludge with Eichmann and Hitler. This was God's way of proving to all sinners that heaven existed; let them be subjected to a glimpse of it to serve as a final tortured remembrance of what afterlife could have been while enduring the infinite and awesome horrors of hell.

After being given my nightcap, another Thorozine highball, I went to my room and drifted yet deeper into my delusions of the fate awaiting me.

During the course of that frightful night, I was transferred from one room to another. I wasn't conscious enough to remember but awoke in a new room with an old priest sleeping in a second bed against the opposite wall from mine. His breath came in uneven gasps. Groggily I sat up and hung my legs over the side of the bed. After pushing myself to a standing position, I walked over to him, curious as to his intended place in heaven. I leaned over to touch him, to see if he was real, but my eyes latched onto his thick satin cossack folded on a bedside chair. I ran my hand across its smooth, cool surface.

An attendant entering the room suddenly startled me. I stood up and took a step backward. The attendant purposefully strode toward me and pushed me out of the way so he could examine the priest. He spoke to him with kindness, while glaring at me. Other attendants frequently visited him as well.

A famous religious person, I decided, *racked with pain caused by the end of the world ... caused by me. Probably the only priest left on earth to perform last rights on other dying people. The priest will be placed at the highest level of heaven, thus completing the spaceship's mission.*

Why was I his roommate, I wondered? *Was I supposed to confess? No. My sharing his room was contrived by God as a special punishment for me as soon as the spaceship stopped for the priest – the last stop – I'll be allowed a glimpse of this highest level of bliss then thrown out to begin my hideous journey to hell. It wouldn't be long, now.*

Frantic at what appeared to be my inevitable fate, I walked to the door separating our closed ward from the control desk. *What could I do to save myself?* I peered through the little window. *Not many angels left, now,* I noticed. *Looks kind of deserted out there. The spaceship must be approaching the end of its God-directed journey. Nothing I can do now but wait.*

I got back in bed, my arms wrapped around my knees, awaiting the expected summons to the spaceship door. How would it come? A booming voice? A power lifting me off the bed? A flash of light preceding the devil, who would make a personal appearance for the soul who'd authored his increased membership?

I must have dozed off, the drug finally knocking me out completely, for when I next opened my eyes the sun was shining through the window. I sat bolt upright in bed. *Wait a minute,* my maligned mind thought, *what is this? Sunlight? I'll be damned,* I thought. *Heaven has a physical as well as a spiritual side.* Not only does the spirit enjoy all the beauty of the universe, but also this priest is going to be allowed to live in a physical sense as on Earth.

A verse from the Lord's Prayer drifted into my head – "On earth, as it is in heaven." I repeated it over and over under my breath.

I can't take this waiting any longer, I thought. *I've got to get this over with. I've got to get my journey to hell started. But how?*

Maybe if I walk over and touch the priest, it will offend the Lord or his angels, and I'll be kicked out, I thought. Taking several minutes to work up the courage to perform the action that would set into motion my demise, I walked up to the bed, bent over and placed my hand on his chest. With my face near his sleeping form, I whispered, "Father, if I touch you, I believe everything will get started."

The old priest rolled over on his side, looked up at me with sleep in his eyes and pulled the covers over his balding head I heard his muffled voice say, "Son, you need to see your doctor."

His statement caused some loose circuit inside me to become connected again. The delusion ended as quickly as it had started. I re-examined the priest's religious garment hanging on a closet hook. Luxurious satin from just a few hours earlier had converted to common polyester. I put my nose up to the cloth. *Pew! B.O.*

The door to the room opened, and I turned, my delusion returning for just a moment. *Maybe the touch had worked!*

No. It was only the bearded attendant. "Come on, Max, time for your Thorozine."

The waking nightmare had ended. The earth had not. I hadn't died, and suddenly there seemed no reason for guilt, no reason for my life — or anyone else's — to end.

You fabricated the spaceship and the angels, I reassured myself, *thank God. Oh, thank God!* Relief flooded my overworked brain. *I wouldn't be going to hell after all.*

"Come on, Max," said the attendant, this time tugging on my arm.

I smiled at him, then shuffled out into the hall where my bare feet moved from the cold floor into a warm puddle. I looked down at the yellow liquid then up again. A large man, who met my gaze with an innocent stare, stood opposite the door to my room zipping the fly of his pants. As he turned and walked away without a word, the last vestiges of illusion drained from my mind and reality took their place.

I carefully lifted my feet out of the puddle and followed the attendant down the hall to take my place in line, obediently awaiting more of the green liquid in the paper cup. The worst was over, of that I could be sure.

Six

THAT MORNING DR. ROSENBERG HELD AN HOUR-LONG SESSION WITH me in which he discussed my delusion. "You know, you were in solitary for six days before we moved you in with the priest. I didn't know you were still delusional, or we wouldn't have done that. But a week in there, that's a long time, fella."

I nodded, comprehending what he said but too groggy from the drugs to say anything and too tired from my tortured brain running on overdrive. I understood his words, however.

"Do you clearly know there's a life out there, a life we want you to join someday?"

"Yeah, I know it, Doc. And I'm damned thankful for that. This horror I went through — What caused it?"

"Well," the old doctor replied, " I think it was that guilt manifestation I've discussed with you before. You took the firing and manifested it, or enlarged it, into an event thousands of times more serious than it was. What's more serious than causing the end of the world? Nothing. In other words you took it as far as it could go." The doctor took off his bifocals and wiped them off before summarizing. "But in a way, as horrible as you imagined it, I believe it was good. Now I believe we can get you back up and keep you there."

"Yeah, I see what you mean, Doc," I said through dry lips and a mouth feeling as if it were stuffed with cotton. "And from where I've been, I mean relatively speaking, I feel like I've come a long way, even since yesterday. Although I'm real tired and weak today. But, uh, how far back up, as you say, can I come?" I asked searching for a forecast.

He hesitated before he replied, "I don't know, son. I don't know. I'm thinking, however, that shock therapy might help."

"Jesus," I stammered, fear rising in me. "You mean wire me up in the head and all?"

The doctor attempted to allay my obvious fear. "What the shock does is force a controlled convulsion and perhaps break up any calcium deposits you may have in your brain. The priest had shock therapy. He believes it helped him. Why don't you think about it, talk to him about it? I have to have your written consent."

I shook my head. "No, Doc. No. I don't want it," I said in a raspy voice as thoughts of *Frankenstein* movies filled my head.

"Okay, you're the boss," he replied, his sad, watery eyes looking down at his notepad as he scribbled a few lines.

After a lecture to me about the importance of thinking about past events of pleasure and joy, Rosy' told me he would cut down my drug dosage. "We've had you on a maximum dosage of Thorozine for a week; that's most of the reason why you are groggy and slur some of your words. In a couple of days you'll have more stamina." The old man then doddered out of the room.

An hour or so later an attendant entered my room, looked me over and frowned. "Your clothes are all wrinkled and dirty. We need to clean you up. You're gonna have a court hearing this afternoon." I gave the attendant the small pile of clothes that I had, sans the ones I wore, and he returned them in a couple of hours, folded and clean. Still quite foggy, I slowly dressed and waited for the hearing.

A Judge Stoppels, with my wife present, took one look at my shabby condition and committed me to the psychiatric hospital on an indefinite basis. "Next hearing in ninety days."

◆ ◆ ◆

International Business Marionettes

The ensuing dozen or so days brought about further healing of my exhausted brain. Probably the doctor had been right. I had no place to go but up. The reduced amount of drugs also helped me right myself since they didn't contribute to delusions beginning again. Still confused and disoriented, I nevertheless felt I was making progress, and so did the staff.

"Atta boy, Max," a nurse congratulated me one morning as I came out of my room freshly showered, shaven and neatly dressed. "Keep it up, handsome, and we'll be moving you on out of here."

Pat visited me two or three times a week, and while I didn't always remember what we talked about, it felt good to see her. Mother and Seek and Marcia and Tom also came by at least once a week. As the fog slowly dissipated from my wounded mind, I looked forward to their visits.

One day, Pat spent two hours with Rosy', discussing my situation. "I'm afraid your husband's condition may be irreversible," he told her, a message not relayed to me by her until several months later. Dr. Rosenberg painted a picture of a future limited to the most menial of abilities, like working for my brother as a janitor. A tough report for Pat to handle.

Pat's closest friends shared concerns that she would soon collapse under the pressure. She assured them and me that she was fine. She had to keep going. The children needed her. The affects of her ordeal showed not in her attitude but they were etched on her exterior; she looked tired and thin.

In the meantime, I continued the long climb out of my fog slowly, each day just a hair better than the last. But the progress seemed sustained. I could now watch a television show for a few minutes and comprehend it. Shaving and showering every day, I started washing my own laundry and returned to the workshop where I fumbled with making belts and pots. I also began to take note of other patients, striking up basic conversations with them, reaching out for any type of human contact. I even got into a routine of having a cup of coffee with the morning nurses before breakfast.

On a night in early December, Pat brought all three boys over for a visit. We met together in a small doctor's office. Seeing them all there together, I completely broke down, crying uncontrollably. Through sobs and nose blowing, I managed to hug them all and tell them the tears were over how happy I was to see them. John and Steve cried too, while little Chris shied away, not at all sure about what he was witnessing.

That night I lay awake for a long time thinking of family. *My* family. Still disoriented, I tried to figure out what my family meant to me. *Everything,* I concluded. *IBM means very little now.* I dozed off into sleep.

On December 8, our six-month policy with Prudential ran out. After my first hospitalization, Prudential wisely opted to cancel my piece of the rock. Rosy' and Pat made plans to send me to the Veteran's Administration hospital in Battle Creek, sixty miles south of Grand Rapids, where my air force service allowed me to stay on the house.

Two months after the hideous delusions and six weeks since my walk in traffic, some of my circuits — which felt to me as if they had burned out from too much voltage — began to splice themselves back together. This affected little things at first, like watching an entire program on TV and, later on, carrying on conversations with patients for more than a few minutes.

I told Dr. Rosenberg I wanted to go home. "I feel fine and going home would solve the whole insurance problem." This time he didn't buy in to my self-analysis.

On December 9, court orders arrived transferring me to the VA hospital. That night, a black, comely young lady in for schizophrenia hosted a farewell party for me. As she proudly held her self-baked chocolate cake high for others to admire, I cried the tears of joy that I had been able to develop close relationships with a dozen or so of these unfortunate people; and tears of sorrow that I would now have to leave them and my safe cocoon. After downing a hunk of the rich tasting cake, I shot several games of eight ball, satisfied at my returning hand-eye coordination and ability to focus on the game.

International Business Marionettes

Pat and my brother-in-law, Tom, drove me the hour or so to Battle Creek. I was upset by Rosy's decision, which I only marginally understood. And Judge Warwick had backed it up with his signature.

Saying goodbye to Tom and Pat, I checked into Ward 29B of the six-hundred-bed hospital. 29B held the three-dozen or so sickest patients in this massive facility. I found out that standard operating procedure brought new patients into this ward for evaluation; all but the worst got reassigned later.

The ward looked strange and different from the private facility I'd left two hours earlier. Just two rooms housed all thirty-six or so of us in this all-male ward: a large day room for walking around or watching TV and an equally-large room where we all slept with a small metal locker at the front of each cot. No privacy, no way to be alone with one's thoughts.

Once in the ward, a cold meat sandwich on a paper plate materialized; the last place had real china. *What the hell*, I thought. The sandwich came free. *What do you expect, Beardslee? The Hilton?* I ate it, since by now my appetite had returned to normal, and it tasted good.

After finishing the sandwich and putting my suitcase under my assigned bed, I mingled in the day room with the really severe cases. These men walked around talking to themselves or exclaiming about the voices they heard. Occasionally they would stop, their arms stuck straight out in front of them as if for balance, and shift their feet back and forth in a rocking motion, an affect of their prescribed drugs. Some had tongues hanging out of uncontrolled, distorted faces. I watched one middle-aged patient smoke a cigarette right down to the stub, letting its glow burn his unfeeling fingers. And their eyes — always the anguished eyes — gave away their advanced state of mental illness.

Still suffering from a lingering disorientation, I did figure out that almost everybody in there was in much worse shape than I. As unaccommodating as these new surroundings appeared, that one thought provided me solace.

Fortunately, I occupied this tragic ward just one night but a bad one it turned out to be. A huge bear of a black man threatened me for no discernible reason other than that he didn't know me. Pretty well gone mentally, he stuck his head in my face so close I could feel his hot breath on my cheeks and said, "If you don't stay out of my way, I'll bop you one on the head."

That sleepless night, in the one huge bedroom housing all the ward's patients, I kept a watchful eye on the bear.

Assigned to a "normal" ward the following day, I joined others in the routine of daily therapy followed by physical education. Fired in May, now in December on this morning I finally felt good about myself again, the last of my disorientation slipping away during the night. I could only believe I'd been wrapped in thick layers of shock for most of the time since I'd been fired, a few layers of it peeling off in the Grand Rapids hospital and then a massive husking of the remaining layers taking place last night. *Well,* I thought, *maybe passing time and the experience of 29B shocked me back into reality. Well, why not? I was shocked out of it. It's about time. It's taken eight months.*

A joke told by one of the patients caused me to laugh, the first laugh in about 240 days, I figured. By noon I noticed I could go through a series of thought processes in an almost normal way, or at least what I'd known as normal last spring. I felt tremendous relief at having dumped the bag of guilt I'd carried for so long. That heavy emotion had slimmed down gradually in the last few weeks until I felt as if it had now disappeared. Jumbled thoughts no longer bounced around in my head, intertwined one minute and separated the next. I could focus on one subject and hold it through a normal thought process, disposing of it when it no longer held my attention.

The second day on this ward, a sad-faced, scruffy, bearded psychologist called me in to join the daily group therapy sessions he conducted complete with incense to set the mood. He suggested that for this session we discuss how our lives had evolved in the most recent past.

International Business Marionettes

We went around the circle, each person telling his own story. The best one came from an airplane kleptomaniac who forced real laughter from my humor-starved soul as he related stories of his ten-year compulsion for stealing airplanes. He believed that a witch's spell held him in bondage, so there was no real hope of him breaking the airplane habit.

Another man forced me from my preoccupation with my own problems by offering me his to consider. This outwardly normal fellow with curly hair and friendly eyes had been assigned as the ward leader, and his tragedy sounded the worst. It had started with a picnic lunch with his wife at a public park. He'd even brought fresh flowers for her. Later, a spirited argument started and grew out of hand, and they both fell into a pond. He climbed out, but she did not. He still loved her, but now her drowned form was his only remembrance. Tears formed in his eyes as he said, "And now I face manslaughter charges."

When my turn came, I picked a subject appropriate to my returning sense of sanity — why I was so hooked on IBM and what I'd learned from my twelve years in the company. With eight mental patients listening, I spoke in what seemed to be a logical manner with complete sentences for the first time in eight months. And, boy, did it feel good!

"Okay, guys. Let me explain to you how I got as hooked on IBM as Fred, here, got hooked on heroin." Fred, a recovering addict sitting next to me, grinned, showing the gap in his front teeth.

I started at the beginning with how I had gone into the job interview knowing IBM wanted engineers but I only had a degree in business. I described how difficult the training had been and that only my pride saw it through. "I was overwhelmed with the difficulty of the material I had to learn and the pace at which instructors covered the new and uncomfortable ground. Four years into the job, making my yearly sales quotas but not standing out, I almost resigned from the company for another opportunity," I told my captive audience. "Certainly I hadn't been so committed to IBM at that juncture.

"The change came when I gained my first big promotion to an advisory marketing representative, which was accompanied by a move to Detroit. In Detroit, while still pretty low on the ladder, I stumbled onto an idea that blew up into a marketing plan IBM adopted worldwide. I called it 'Operation 30/30.' As it gained momentum IBM called it 'BOLDER,' " I continued.

"Flushed with the success of that experience, I earned six more promotions in the next six years until the last big one that brought me all the way back to Grand Rapids. Each step of the way, I made friendships, received solid coaching, developed business acumen far beyond an MBA program, and deepened my conviction that IBM was a special company, the only one worth working for.

"Each new success I enjoyed had me naively believing I could just keep earning promotions until I retired.

"Ultimately, from the high appraisals and measured accomplishments of sales statistics, my defenses came down. I played offense, sometimes recklessly. The hell with defense; that was for the guys who needed the structure to hold them up.

"Failure no longer entered the picture, guys," I confided in them.

I shared with them how IBM gradually became my life. "During the day I worked for IBM. A Company man. Nights and weekends I socialized with IBMers. My vacations were planned around its One Hundred Percent Clubs, the three-day events always held in sunbelt cities for those who had made their sales quotas from the previous year. And IBM's benefits provided my family all they needed in the way of medical, dental and retirement coverage. Just as the IBM sales mentality dictated, my whole life evolved around three little letters. Failure became the worry of other people. The IBM way had me Teflon-coated by intense training and exposure to all facets of the job I'd risen to. Stock purchase plans, retirement plans, relocation plans, medical plans, life insurance, the whole enchilada. My future was insured."

Pleased I had recovered to the stage I could discuss my having been sacked in objective, rational terms, I shared it with the group.

"The worst had to do with the precise way I was fired. First, they categorized me like a guy who cheated on his medical bills to make money — you know, worked a deal with his doctor to be billed for services he didn't receive.

"Then I'm fired from the job I focused on getting for years. And all this happens after being dumped in the same town I started from, giving me unwanted visibility for the whole goddamn affair."

I turned to the airplane thief. "Maybe my career had a voodoo curse on it."

The group gave me a good laugh over that one. I was enjoying this. "Quite a few people in Grand Rapids knew I had struggled through training, almost washing out," I continued. "Others thought my style of openness, lack of conformity and disdain for IBM's structure would lead to my demise. And after I thought I'd converted the last of the doubters by becoming the head guy in the Western Michigan region, what I really did was prove them right by being fired for going against the rules."

Concluding, I filled my new friends in on Schwartz's demotion over a liquor invoice, his resignation and his interest in my circumstances. "But when Schwartz told me about 'booze, broads and cigars,' my already waning confidence shattered into a million pieces."

I paused for a moment to contemplate the cigar deal. This time I felt no guilt and lauded my improvement, concluding my talk by telling the group I'd been a recruiting error. "IBM should never have hired me. I really never fit what they wanted from the very beginning, but they molded me into someone that could succeed in their environment. And I had a hand in it, too. I allowed it, and for the most part, wanted it. A willing participant. At the end, with their help, my mug could have been put on their recruitment posters. Plus, I had become a guy who couldn't relate to failure. Failure belonged to other people in other companies. So, when they told me I'd failed, my well-programmed brain blew a circuit."

I put my arm around Fred's shoulder. "Now, Fred, here, is taking Methadone to get rid of his heroin addiction while I endured a world-class guilt trip to flush IBM out of my blood." My airplane klepto' buddy led the applause as our psychologist snuffed out his incense, signaling that our therapy session had ended.

My psychiatrist, a busy guy from being assigned over one hundred patients, spent a few minutes with me in the ward the following day. "I watched you play water volleyball in the pool today. You hit some good shots and played hard, that's good. Your therapy counselor also tells me you are active and vocal in his group. By the way, in my notes, here, he believes you had a psychotic break. Know what that is?"

I shook my head.

"Well, it's pretty much like, 'here today and gone tomorrow.' And the reverse holds true. When a person comes back, he or she comes back fast, like you appear to be doing."

"I don't think it was a clean break, Doctor. I think it was the guilt manifestation Dr. Rosenberg talked about that took about four months to consume me. But I do think an incident I had in 29B might have helped bring me back faster." I told him about my run in with the bear.

"I know who you are referring to," my tall, wide-shouldered psychiatrist replied. "A guy in bad shape. He'll never get out of here. You will. And, you might be right: his threats, and forcing you to focus on them might have brought you back faster." Thumbing through his clipboard, the doctor concluded, "I've got to go. You seem to be in pretty good shape, but because of the description in here of your extreme delusion and a prognosis of long-term, even permanent damage, which, by the way, I don't think you have, I need to observe your progress for a while longer."

I thought about my guilt-induced delusion. *Yeah, I'd gone on a nasty guilt trip. Goddamn Guinness material, it was. But I sure don't feel guilty, not any more.* I was eager to return to a normal life, but this time I didn't press the doctor for my release.

Pat visited me after about the fifth day, saying she thought I looked and sounded better. Good input, on the mend at last.

Ten days later, the psychiatrist told me he had signed the necessary papers for my release. After handing me a prescription for Elavil, a mood elevator, I said goodbye to him, as well as my new-found friends and checked out.

Seven

FIVE DAYS BEFORE CHRISTMAS I WALKED OUT OF THE HOSPITAL AND got into the plain Olds' in which Pat sat waiting for me. She'd sold the Toronado.

"Welcome back to the living, Max. Nice to have you back. You done playing psycho man?"

I laughed, glad that she could make light of the past few months and able myself to see the humor in her comment. I felt good deep inside about the healing that had taken place and the progress I had made since my mental failure had held me in the clutches of insanity.

Pat drove me to our new home, which I'd never before seen. As she ushered me through the cramped condominium located a couple of miles from our former spacious home, which now lay in IBM's hands, I thought how luxurious the condo looked compared to my accommodations over the past months.

Unpacking my few possessions — two shirts, some dirty underwear, three pairs of pants, and shaving items, I watched the Elavil drop from my shaving kit onto the bed and spill out of its container. Picking up the capsules, I dropped them into the toilet and flushed it.

"I won't be needing them," I said aloud as I watched them swirl around the bowl and disappear.

The kids came home from school and gave me a first-class greeting. All of them talked at once and each wanted me to give them my undivided attention. While I could hardly hear what they were saying and I was tugged and pulled by their little hands in several directions at once, I enjoyed every second of this reunion. Their presence made it feel like old times, like nothing had ever happened. As they jibber jabbered, they made enough sense for their ol' man to catch up on their news. After a little rasslin' match, I helped them with some homework and joined them for television then tucked them into bed.

While I spent time with my sons, Pat fussed around the condo. Now we had some time to spend together, and we did so without tension or discomfort. Indeed, we acted naturally around each other talking about the kids, money, bills —normal stuff discussed in a normal manner.

"You can pay the bills any time you want, Max. I'm sick of 'em."

"Yeah, hopefully I can still deal with numbers." I picked up the checkbook and noticed something wrong.

"Hey, how come this thing only has your name on it?"

"Oh," she flustered, "I forgot to tell you about that. Judge Warwick. You remember him, right? Well, anyway, he has you under a court conservatorship. What that means is that you receive an allowance from the court: two-hundred dollars a week. The rest of the money is in my name."

Well, I thought, *can't let the small stuff get me down.* "Okay" I said. *No big deal. I'll go see the judge one of these days and get the conservatorship dissolved.* I then paid a few bills and let Pat look at the checkbook register. "Looks okay to me. Want a drink?"

"Why not," I replied as Pat headed for the tiny kitchen. I hadn't had one since September. We agreed to give the IBM thing a rest for the night and made love instead.

Lying in bed with Pat cradled next to me, her head on my chest, my hand on her breast, I thought, *maybe, just maybe, life will get back to normal.*

The next morning after a sizable breakfast — my weight back to a normal one hundred eighty pounds again since the return of my appetite — I went for a walk. I wanted to get out of the condo and think about the future, a future that now seemed manageable in every way. Walking briskly, my steps belied my renewed confidence. I felt ready to move forward with my life as quickly as my legs carried me forward on the sidewalk.

Noting a pay phone booth, I called up a lawyer in Detroit who had been referred to Pat by friends. Pat had talked to Fred Amrose while I was hospitalized but hadn't ever followed through. After explaining to Amrose who I was, he acknowledged knowing most of the facts, so I got to the point. "Mr. Amrose, I'm looking for a lawyer. Interested?"

Amrose acted hesitant in taking my case. Getting aggressive. I said, "Either your law firm commits to litigate my case right now, or I'm going to walk across the street to the largest law firm in Grand Rapids: Warner, Norcross and Judd."

Amrose still hedged. "I don't want wishy-washy bullshit, Fred, I want a yes or a no."

"Come down to Bloomfield Hills tomorrow," Amrose replied.

"Yes, sir!" I responded, liking his no-nonsense decision.

Excited by this turn of events, I slammed the pay phone back in place and retraced my steps home, anxious to share the news with Pat. "Do you remember Fred Amrose?"

"Yes, I do. I liked him when I spoke to him that one time."

"I'll be heading into Detroit to see him in the morning, thanks to you. Be spending a couple of days there, or whatever it takes to go through the firing." My enthusiasm seemed infectious and Pat encouraged me to do what was necessary while voicing her disappointment that I would be away again. I called our friends, the Wagners, who had recommended Amrose and arranged to stay with them while in Detroit.

The next morning, I snatched a couple of suits, ties and shirts and drove the three hours to Bloomfield Hills, a suburb of Detroit, thinking logically and clearly about the facts I could prove. *This time, no holds barred,* I thought resolutely. *I'll even tell the lawyer about the cover-up my friend Blaylock had ordered.* Loyalties needed to be put aside. I knew I'd have to use a heavy hammer to dent IBM's armor, but I felt confident that it could be done.

Several times I had to force myself to slow down, anticipating with excitement what lay ahead. When I arrived at Amrose's office, the average built, average dressed, nondescript lawyer with a face holding promise of great intelligence greeted me with enthusiasm.

Working six to eight hours a day at the law firm, I saw little of anyone but Amrose. Over frequent lunches, usually spent discussing my case, we formed a solid friendship. I saw little of my friends during the week and returned for home duty on weekends.

As my case began to take shape, Amrose dug through his firm's archives and surfaced with a Michigan law that made illegal the act of forcing employees to patronage employers by buying them things. That law would be the crux of our case.

Next, a strategy session. I argued that we should go the Open Door route, writing a long letter or report to the chairman once again. I figured a satisfactory response to such a letter could save me from months of legalese thereby replacing a dwindling pile of cash with a bigger bundle years faster.

Tom Criswell, the firm's counsel, wanted to file suit. Criswell's way would have forced me to use the state-sponsored contingency plan where lawyers cashed in on up to half of any settlement. My way allowed a pay-as-you-go plan with the firm for at least a few months until I ran out of money. The bulk of the settlement, if we could get one early, would flow to my family and me. And if it dragged on, or didn't work, then we would file suit under the rules of contingency.

My logic prevailed. We would try the Open Door first. As I signed the legal representation agreement, including my insertion of bonuses for performance, I thought this is just like IBM would have done it. Through IBM, I had learned the power cash has as a way of motivating people. Always in IBM the incentive plan worked to drive sales people beyond "normal" performance. Going over one hundred percent, the payment plan picked up by paying more per sale.

At lunch the next day Amrose shifted our conversation to points of law. "As I hear you describing the recognition meetings, I always come back to the same thought," he said in his low-key, even-keeled voice. Amrose wiped his glasses before continuing, giving me the feeling something important loomed in his gifted mind.

"Now, as you know, you were technically dismissed for premeditated intent to obligate IBM's funds."

I nodded my head and replied, "Yup, that's right; like I planned on calling the cigars photocopies ahead of the meeting."

Amrose continued. "Well it appears to me that, in fact, IBM premeditated with intent to obligate *your* funds. It's just the opposite of what they've claimed."

Amrose's point hit home like a jolt of electricity. I dropped my fork on the plate and slammed my fist against the palm of my hand. "That's it, Fred! That's it! We'll one-eighty the bastards! Perfect! Yeah!"

The thousands of self-incriminations I'd endured over and over vaporized in that instant. Damn, I was proud of Amrose. "They premeditated with intent to obligate my funds! Wait till that asshole, Hampstead, hears about this," I exclaimed jubilantly. Jumping up, I ran around the table and hugged the embarrassed but smiling lawyer.

After lunch, I called Pat and, trying hard to contain my excitement, told her about Amrose's strategy. "I'm going to deliver the hardest hitting Open Door those pricks in Armonk have ever caught, and you're going with me. We'll fly out there and stuff it down their throats. Okay?"

Her enthusiastic response, the first in months, indicated that the news had revved her up, too. "Yes, I want to go. Okay!"

I felt good about her attitude. I wanted her on board to share in any reversal we could get done. She deserved that satisfaction as much as I did.

By January twenty-fifth we had the Open Door's final version almost ready. Victory seemingly within grasp, I drove to a station-ers' store with Amrose and acquired one-hundred and fifty dollars worth of binders made of the best leather they had in stock.

Amrose's face took on a perplexed look. "Just curious, Max, but why are you buying the real good binders?"

I had a ready reply. "Because, Fearless Freddie, I want to use better stuff than they do. Sets the stage for what's inside." While at IBM I'd always fussed about using the cheap company binders for holding proposals that asked prospective customers for hundreds of thousands of dollars.

By this time, Amrose was staying after hours with me each evening, and he had brought in extra help to type the documents. I drove home for the weekend, excited over our clear strategy and ready to relax in advance of my sure-fire success. With my focus back to normal, I romped and played with the kids and Pat. Later, I played Chess with John on a K-Mart chess set Pat had bought. I noticed not only how well he played but that when I moved the pieces my hand stayed steady as a rail.

I returned to Fred's law firm on Monday, and late that night we completed the *pièce de résistance*: A twenty-nine-page letter followed by sixteen tabbed attachments. Everything indexed. One original and five copies, each bound in cowhide. I grabbed one of Amrose's fountain pens and in a spirited mood asked him to witness my sig-nature, a bold John Hancock-sized one. After saying good night to my well-appreciated lawyer, I drove to my friends' home and shared a nightcap with them, excitedly voicing my optimism.

The next morning, I called up Jack Trice, IBM's corporate resi-dent manager for the Midwest Region. Trice, a former sales exec', wound down his last years with the company by taking a person-nel-related job. Only six other people covered the entire U.S. in that capacity. Knowing he reported directly to the chairman's office as the eyes and ears of IBM's Midwest population, he'd be perfect for launching my quick-hit strategy.

His secretary told me he'd been called out of town. Undeterred,

I dialed Trice's residence and talked to his wife. "Please tell Jack I'm going to Open Door the corporation and want his assistance in setting it up."

Mrs. Trice sounded excited. "I sure will," she replied. She'd come across as delighted about what I planned to do. A good sign. *Maybe the Detroit outcry after my sacking had reached her ears.* An hour later, Trice's voice had me on the phone.

"How are you, Jack?"

"The hell with how I am, Max, how are you?" Trice gave me a warm greeting, much different than the treatment from Paulos. After the preliminaries, he told me he'd heard I was back home.

"Yes, I'm fully recovered ... feel great."

"Well, what can I do for you?" Trice asked.

"I want to fly to Armonk and deliver an Open Door in person," I said. The words shot out as quickly as pellets out of a shotgun. *I'm talking too fast,* I thought. *Slow down.*

"Why don't you tell me about it?" Trice openly asked.

"Yeah ... okay. Sure. Jack, IBM fired me for premeditated intent to obligate funds. My Open Door will reverse that." I paused, letting the remarks sink in. "My contention is exactly the opposite. IBM premeditated with intent to obligate my funds. Got it? Understand?"

"Yes," he said in an even keel voice, disguising which way he might feel about my plan. "I'll have someone from the corporation contact you."

"Okay, Jack, and do me a favor, will you? Keep Paulos and Hampstead in the dark about what's coming."

Trice replied, "I can't handle it that way. Policy requires notifying affected divisions about an Open Door."

Another goddamn IBM rule, I thought. IBM had rules for everything. Nothing was left to chance. Once, as a sales rep in Traverse City, I'd even been ordered to attend a retired person's funeral and — as per policy and procedure — to sign the guest register in a manner that indicated my employment at IBM. Everything one did at IBM had to be checked against some thick manual or another, some-times stifling the fast action necessary for success.

After getting my phone number in Grand Rapids, where I would be returning that day, we hung up.

The next day, my home phone rang. Bernard Striker, one of IBM's seven administrative assistants to then IBM President John Opel, made the expected phone call. After a businesslike warm up about my grievance he said, "I know you want to come and see me, but I want you to mail your Open Door."

"No way, Mr. Striker. Absolutely, no way. It's being hand delivered."

Striker, sensing my determination, backed off and committed to a next-day, two o'clock meeting at IBM's corporate headquarters in Armonk, New York, home of their ruling *junta* and a place foreign to me. Not once during my twelve years with IBM had I been called to or had reason to visit the Company headquarters. *That's probably normal,* I thought. Not much reason for sales types to visit the place that put out all those policy manuals. Early the next morning, Pat and I flew to Detroit, where Amrose met us at the airport. We could rehearse and still make our 9:00 A.M. connection to New York. God, I loved saying that IBM premeditated the obligation of my funds as opposed to me premeditating to obligate theirs! The phrase that had caused me so much grief before now gave me great pleasure.

In turn, I almost convinced Fred and Pat that we would get something other than lip service in New York. "IBM has a heart. As soon as these guys who surround Opel, no slouches, I'll tell you, understand the real truth here, they'll jump all over it. They're paid to right wrongs."

Flying higher than the plane we rode on, I shifted away from the window seat and faced Pat. "Honey, IBM has a heart and we're going to find it. When Striker hears what we've documented, we'll be having dinner with Mr. and Mrs. Opel at their private residence tonight. It'll happen!"

I could see skepticism in Pat's raised eyebrows. This was no small task to pull off, I knew, but I honestly believed I could do it.

I didn't see how we could miss. I tried to get her to at least believe that our argument stood a good chance of getting us the desired outcome — an admission of guilt on their part and a fair and equitable monetary settlement to be determined later.

"IBM premeditated to obligate my funds, Pat, and that's against the law. Opel has a heart. He'll see us."

At the Hertz counter in LaGuardia, I boldly asked for a Lincoln or Cadillac. Like the binders, I wanted the best. No luck. Pat and I jumped in a Buick with a map of the area, and I sped up the highway, anxious to reach the combat zone. Pat kept warning me to slow down, watching the speedometer hover at eighty-five miles per hour, but I couldn't. Lustily singing college fight songs, I prepared to meet John Opel.

Arriving in Armonk, we followed the signs directing us to IBM's Grand Poobah. Pulling into the visitors' lot, I glanced at my watch. Twenty-five to two. Good! A little time to spare. Pat inspected my carefully-selected striped tie and dark blue suit. Even my wing tips were shined a glistening black. *Out-image the image-makers,* I thought.

I hauled the cardboard box out of the rear seat; six thick binders filled it to the top. Opel would get the original. Frank Cary, chairman of the board, would read one as would Tom Watson, Jr., a member of the board of directors and former chairman of the board. The fourth went to Nicholas Katzenbach, former attorney general of the United States and IBM's head lawyer. Striker's name appeared on number five. I retained the last one.

Pat and I walked into the lobby ten minutes early for our appointment. I looked around the lobby as my stomach registered my disappointment at the surroundings. *What the hell is this,* I wondered? *No waterfalls? No museum showing off IBM's ancient iron? Nothing but sterile walls and chairs. Not even any plants.* I'd expected something elaborate to mark at least the entryway of this famous corporation so well known throughout the world as the largest producer of high tech products. *What a let down,* I thought.

In the middle of all this low-key decor appeared a glassed-in cubicle in which sat a skinny kid in an ill-fitting sport coat. I walked up to the Little-Lord-Fauntleroy type and in a too-loud voice declared, "I WANT TO SEE BERNARD—" Suddenly I couldn't remember his last name. To mask my embarrassment, I shouted to Pat, "WHAT'S BERNARD'S LAST NAME?" as if I was not put off in the least.

"Striker, honey. Striker."

"RIGHT ... STRIKER. BERNARD STRIKER."

The kid grabbed a phone and dialed.

A couple of people furtively glanced my way, probably figuring an irate computer user had arrived.

Three or four minutes passed while I paced up and down and Pat sat quietly on a couch before a receptionist arrived and asked politely, "Are you the Beardslees?"

"Yeah, that's us," I said less loudly than before.

"Mr. Striker regrets to inform you he is running a little late. He would like you to come back at three P.M."

Just like that he planned to make me wait. As far as I was concerned, she might as well have said, "Look, buddy, Striker will get to you when he can."

I exploded. "THAT'S TOTALLY UNACCEPTABLE! I FULLY EXPECT TO MEET WITH MR.STRIKER AT THE AGREED-UPON TIME. THAT TIME IS NOW!"

Words seemed to stream out of my mouth before I could even think them. *You're out of control, Beardslee,* I cautioned myself. *Take it easy, bud.*

By now, several people had turned to see from whom the loud and obnoxious voice emanated, echoing in a lobby that had heard few. Fauntleroy looked like he wanted to duck down in his cage.

I couldn't shut up. "YOU GO BACK AND TELL MR. STRIKER THAT I'VE WAITED ON IBM FOR THE LAST TIME. I WANT TO SEE HIM RIGHT NOW!"

The receptionist tossed her hair over her shoulder, sniffed at me and then high stepped away, tall heels on long legs thudding on the carpet.

Pat came up to me, put her hand on my elbow and said in a hushed voice, "Calm down, honey," but I think she liked the commotion I was making.

I liked it. It felt good. No more subservience. No more intimidation. No more sweaty palms. No more "Yes, sirs" and "No, sirs" to stupid-assed questions about cigars. In just a few minutes, down the hall at a brisk pace walked a tall, black, dignified-looking IBMer wearing a navy blue three-piece suit.

Bernard Striker. Striker's even-voiced greeting with direct, penetrating eyes, started to make me comfortable, a good first impression. The man guided us down a hallway and into a drab room not much different in decor from the lobby. *Geez,* I thought, *they've even got these dinky cubicles in Armonk that I've seen in other less prestigious IBM facilities.* I hauled out the top book and dropped its leathered cover on the desk. Bang!

"This is for John Opel."

Bernard showed no emotion. A cool customer.

I then started showing Striker what he would find beneath the covers, flipping tabs as I did so. "Here's a list of all the crap I had to buy and what it cost." Another tab. "Here's the Operation 30/30 strategy I authored a few years back that will help pay for your retirement." I flipped to another tab. "And some information new to IBM: Look at this section, Bernard. I got ordered by an IBM executive and a friend named Blaylock to cover expenses at a resort called Sugar Loaf." No holds barred.

I continued my tirade almost ceaselessly. "Look at this — Look at that." Striker sat to my right at the small conference table looking a bit perplexed and as if he didn't understand why he had to be the one to handle this when there were seven administrative assistants serving John Opel.

Whenever Striker would come up for air, I would hammer on him. And when I was taking a breath, Pat picked up the ball. "We can prove that Max could only collect twenty dollars apiece," she said. "We can prove that he always had to spend more than that.

We've got witnesses."

Bernard had it coming from both sides. Like Custer's last stand, I thought and almost laughed out loud.

I continued flipping through the tabs, "Here's documented evidence showing I was a fruit cake. The psychiatrist's report said 'And then Mr.Beardslee told us he thought the mental institution served as a spaceship.' " I smiled remembering...

I flipped to another one. "This is the Michigan law we say you guys broke. Another tab. "Here's a copy of my personal check for the cigars." Another. And another. Striker glanced at his watch.

"What's the rush, Bernard?" I asked, feeling rather powerful, despite the fact that Striker didn't seem fazed. "We've come a long way," I added, then felt embarrassed as a dab of my spit fell on the open sheet. I quickly flipped to the front of his binder hoping he hadn't seen it and had him read the cover letter:

To: Mr. John Opel
         President and Chief Executive Officer, IBM
         Old Orchard Road
         Armonk, New York 10504

Subject: IBM's Open Door Policy.

I would have written to you sooner, but, for reasons that will soon become clear to you, I couldn't. Let me put it straight to you, Mr. Opel. I believe I can establish that IBM premeditated with intent the obligation of my funds before I premeditated with intent the obligation of yours. In other words, you got to me before I got to you.

Bernard disdainfully thumbed to the next page, figuring I would make him read all twenty-nine pages, but I flipped his copy to the last page, watching his masked eyes dip down to the print.

"Read this, Mr. Striker. It summarizes my position rather poetically." I wanted some deep-dish dramatics in the letter, and had thought long and hard about the close.

As an outpatient of a mental institution, over the recent Christmas holidays, I taught my son John how to play chess. He is ten years old and has a high logical aptitude. We play on a two-dollar K-Mart plastic chess set. My wife, frugal by nature, is being extremely so until we get back on our feet.

One of the things John learned about chess, Mr. Opel, concerns the pawn. It is difficult for the pawn to reach the end of the board but, if it can, it picks up strength. In my career with IBM I played every piece on the board except the king. At the end I played the pawn. It has taken me eight months to reach the end of the board and pick up strength, but I've done it. As I consider my letter to you, and what I know to be true, the following phrase is now appropriate:

CHECKMATE!

Max Beardslee

As I read the letter to myself for what seemed the thousandth time while Striker read it for his first, I felt elated. Telling IBM's business leader, one of the most powerful in the world, that he had no moves relative to my case did wonders for my general attitude.

Time for a trial close.

"Well, Bernard, Pat and I expect to meet John Opel yet this afternoon. As you can see, there has been a huge mistake made here."

Striker's brown eyes looked at me with surprise, then flitted around the room uncomfortably. "I'm sorry, but seeing Mr. Opel ... today ... is out of the question."

I couldn't give up. Pat needed a sign that this whole idea was a sane one on my part, or I risked her feeling that the security blanket she wanted back remained out of reach, my whole strategy a waste of time. The only way to do so meant gaining the CEO's attention — especially since we had a hard time even gaining Striker's interest.

"Bernard, when John Opel finds out that everything I say in here is true — that I've been packaged as a person who took money from employees and put it in my pocket while Operation 30/30 contributed more to IBM than any other strategy IBM has had privy to in a long while — you may get your ass chewed for not exercising good judgment."

Striker stayed firm. "I'll run that risk."

I kept it up. "Well, maybe he'll see us tomorrow."

"Not likely."

I hunched my shoulders in resignation. Enough. I didn't need to beat my head against a wall. I had literally already tried that.

After giving Striker the number where we could be reached, Pat and I drove to downtown Armonk, a small well-preserved village built in New England tradition, to celebrate. I felt proud of my wife and told her so, feeling we had made a strong call on Striker.

We found ourselves giggling over glasses of wine, reviewing our crossfire tactics on Opel's tall administrative assistant. Justice would swiftly arrive, I thought; however, Pat still wasn't so sure.

We were staying with Dean Hamilton, one of my closest friends in IBM who recently had been reassigned to a marketing group near Armonk. That evening we relaxed with him and his wife, enjoying a long and boisterous Italian dinner.

Hamilton seemed to enjoy my regained enthusiasm. From his deep, raspy voice came what I perceived as praise and recognition. "Max, as regards Operation 30/30, my group has taken the strategy you developed overseas. It is now used worldwide."

Jeesuhs, I thought. *Timely information.* The sales strategy I'd thought up in the mid-'70s had been adopted all over the United States already. I'd been told a couple of months back by Jack Horner, a guy in a position to know, that the idea had put tens of millions of dollars into IBM's coffers. At the time my plan was initiated, I'd been handed some "attaboys" but those looked like nothing compared to its result.

When Striker confirmed the next morning that we wouldn't be seeing Opel, Pat and I flew back to Grand Rapids, quiet and pensive, our mood octaves lower than just two days earlier.

On the last day of January, Striker called me at home. Instead of the expected apologies I'd planned on hearing from him, including an admission of error, he told me Atlanta's General System Division, home to Hampstead and Paulos, had complained about my personnel records being subpoenaed because of a Workman's Compensation action Pat had started.

"Look, Bernard, some judge ordered the action; of course I'll be willing to drop it provided that you get to cracking on my case."

"Sorry," Striker bureaucratically replied. "The comp will have to be dropped more formally. It'll have to be done by a signed document."

Yeah, yeah, I thought, *another blasted rule.* "I'll send you a document which I want you to read and reflect on for a few days before you make up your mind."

◆◆◆

At home I did nothing but mope, watch TV, make calls, and — argue. Almost every day now Pat and I argued, mostly blowing up over incidentals. I knew the cause; I had gotten her all pumped up when we flew out to Armonk, and now, like a sail on a windless day, Pat felt flat. Arguing, at least, blew up some wind.

The resentment she directed at me by criticizing my decision to use the Open Door rather than Amrose's partner's outright lawsuit built anger in me, thus aggravating the situation. The embarrassment I also felt about believing that IBM would make an honest attempt to establish the truth of my case and acknowledge it, when obviously they had no intention of doing so, served as pure oxygen to fuel my anger.

A bad situation, I thought. Rather than confronting the problem, however, I avoided it by staying out of the house for long periods of time.

Five days after my conversation with Striker, the paper he had promised arrived by Federal Express. I noted that it cost IBM fifty-six dollars to have it hand delivered to me. I'd been fired for seventy-seven dollars. The logic of it all didn't add up.

Plus, it had taken four whole days for them to even get the letter written. *No urgency, no sensitivity, just stonewalled bureaucracy,* I thought. *This crap had to cease.* While the IBM field offices moved pretty fast, when documents got to IBM's sales division headquarters in White Plains, New York, and Atlanta, they bogged down in the machinery of "in" baskets and multiple levels of management sign offs. Now I could add IBM's corporate headquarters to the latter category.

I spent a minute or so reading the document. *Jesus, what a lethargic response to my missile. David and Goliath. I needed a bigger slingshot to get them to move, let alone to fall.*

I called Striker. "Bernard, this says if I am willing to suspend the Workman's Compensation action you will investigate the Open Door. Like I said, I suspend the action and am so notifying my lawyer."

Bernard's cool response: "I have to have it in writing."

Getting madder by the minute, I shouted, "I'll send you a goddamn telegram, okay?"

"No, I need your signature on the letter."

I slammed down the phone, banged out a two-sentence letter suspending the Workman's Comp action, and mailed it first class. I then called Bernard for four straight days to see if he had received it; "No," "no," "no," and "no," replied the man.

On the fifth day Striker conceded. "Okay, we'll take your word that the Workman's Comp litigation will be dropped."

The following morning a man named Art Kaufman called me, introducing himself as an IBM corporate director assigned to my Open Door. Two weeks had gone by since Fauntleroy summoned Striker's secretary. I'd been wrong about IBM leaping all over this thing. It was more like foot dragging, it seemed.

In no mood for lip service or sugarcoated intentions on Kaufman's part, I bore down on him. "Look, part of this says you gotta handle Hampstead, president of the General Systems

Division. You got enough clout to do that?"

He replied in an authoritative manner, "I'm a corporate officer, directly assigned to the CEO's office in this matter. That gives me the authority to manage anything that needs to be."

I believed him.

"I want to meet with you next week to review the Open Door," he said.

"What for?" I asked without waiting for an answer. "The god-damn letter says all there is to say. I don't understand why you want to see me in Armonk, but I'll be there."

In midmorning a ringing phone brought Pat and me out of an argument over IBM's real intent in asking me back to Armonk; I was advocating that they would get to the heart of my Open Door while Pat took the position that they would broad brush it away. We both tried to grab the phone at the same time, but Pat beat me to it. I pulled the receiver away from her, gave her a shove and ordered, "Get the hell out of the room."

With a piercing glare at me, she stomped out.

"Hello," I answered angrily.

"I'm with Prime Pest Control, and—"

I cut the salesman off before he could go further with his pitch. "Hey, I like bugs. Goodbye."

Embarrassed by my physical expression of anger toward Pat, I needed to find out how upset she was. I didn't have to look for her to find out.

As soon as I'd hung up, Pat entered the room. Anger filled her face as she said succinctly, "I want you to move out. There's too much stress between us and all we're gonna do here together is continue arguing."

I couldn't get myself to say what I wanted to say: to offer an apology, to ask her to let me stay. The best I could do was, "Hey, you don't want to live with me, you know where the goddamn door is. I'm not leaving."

"Fine. You want it that way? *I* will." She turned and went to the bedroom where she pulled the suitcase down from the closet. Pat packed some clothes, waited for John and Steve to get home from school and then packed the kids into the car, curtly telling them, "Get in, we're moving to your Aunt Marcia's."

With my family loaded up, the kids stared balefully at me out of the car's windows. I stood there, feeling like chump of the year. Putting the car into gear, Pat rolled down the window and motioned for me to walk closer to the car as it inched away. Looking up at me, distress in her clear voice, she said, "You weren't an IBMer. You were an International Business Marionette."

Eight

P AT'S PARTING SHOT RANG IN MY EARS. "AN INTERNATIONAL BUSINESS Marionette." *Yeah. A puppet. She's right. And this whole mess with IBM has my strings so knotted that I can't move. I wonder if my strings are more tangled now than they were when I worked for IBM.* I wasn't sure, but I did know I had gotten so twisted that I misspoke my lines and lost my greatest fan.

Just a few weeks before I had Pat in my theater, positive that our appearance in Armonk had gone well and rooting for a pro-Max curtain call. Now, my last scene, angrily shoving her around, had changed her review from love to anger and fright. And if I had scared her off, a person who loved me and who knew me well, I could naturally assume that my way of presenting myself to the world scared others as well. *Well, that could work for or against me with IBM,* I concluded, as I turned and walked through the front door. With my family, though, it was definitely counterproductive.

I shut the door behind me and looked around the condo. Empty. The furniture and knickknacks still stayed all in place, but without Pat and the kids it felt empty.

This added more fuel to the angry fire burning inside of me. *If it wasn't for IBM's unwillingness to take on their problem relating to me and find a solution in a timely manner, I wouldn't have all these issues at home,* I thought, blaming IBM for my own inability to separate personal and professional situations from each other. I decided to vent my current anger at IBM, where I believed it belonged. Kaufman presented a good target.

I walked into the kitchen, looked up Kaufman's phone number and called him at home. Without even offering a salutation, my angry words spilled over the line. "Screw it, Art. I'm not coming to New York."

"Why not?" asked a surprised Kaufman who immediately recognized my voice.

Unable to control my anger, I shouted, or maybe even screamed into the phone, "Because there's nothing my visit can accomplish. Everything — I mean everything — that's relevant has been stated in my letter to you. Seeing you is just wasting time and counterproductive."

Kaufman, to his credit, tried to calm me down, but I would have no part of his attempted conciliation. The anger I had lain so close to the surface for the last few weeks had now bubbled over. I could no longer control it, not that I had much luck before. "I've been caught up in a bureaucracy that treats me like a little kid," I argued.

Kaufman could have told me I acted like one, but he politely did not.

I rambled on. "You guys fart around taking a week with your rules on Workmen's Compensation. Hell, in a week, you should have had this thing figured out. You bastards owe me that. What do I get? Lip service, stalling, rules, and regulations.

"I've got the king in a checkmate position, but because none of you guys have shown him his position on the damned board, he doesn't know it yet."

Kaufman, in a soft voice, said, "Okay, Max, I understand. Can I speak to your wife?"

"You could if she was here" I snapped. "She's moved out."

Kaufman remained silent for a long time. "Max ... ah ... do you think you may still be mentally ill?"

He touched on a point I hadn't even known was sore, but boy did it hurt. I exploded with rage. "HELL, NO, I'M NOT MENTALLY ILL. I'M MAD. YOU GUYS GIVE ME LIP SERVICE.

"I'VE LOST ALL CREDIBILITY WITH MY WIFE. THIS AIN'T RIGHT.

"YOU GUYS AT THE TOP ARE SUPPOSED TO BE SMART AND TO HAVE A HEART. YOU AIN'T GOT SQUAT!"

I took a deep breath. "Look, Art, just please do this. Get going with the guys who will tell you about the twenty-dollar limitation. Then get going with the guys who will tell you I complained about the expenses exceeding twenty dollars apiece. Then get your lawyer, Katzenbach, to read the goddamned law we sent him. Then ask yourself this question: Who spent whose money? It's all there, goddamn it! Goodbye."

I slammed the phone down and stomped into the living room, still steaming with anger. *It won't matter if they bungle this. The facts won't change over time. I can always get people on the stand if I have to go to court, but damn it, that's not the way to settle this. The way to settle this is with fair play, with IBM's Open Door Policy. Screw it. If I have to I'll kick the door open. Go to Armonk and picket the place until Opel agrees to see me.*

And when I get this IBM thing turned around, I should be able to win my wife and my kids back. That's right. First things first.

A private war. Just Big Blue and me.

The phone jangled me out of my fantasy. I slowly walked back to the kitchen, picked up the phone and sat weakly down on a kitchen stool.

"Max? It's Marcia."

I'm not surprised, I thought. "Yeah."

"Pat and the kids just landed on my doorstep. She says—"

Not wanting to listen, not wanting to talk, I interrupted. "I can't talk, Marcia."

Marcia's husband, Tom, got on the phone. "Max, why don't you come over so we can all talk this out?"

"I don't want to talk, Tom!" I yelled. "Just send her back here where she belongs." I slammed the phone into the receiver with such force that it bounced out and landed clattering on the floor. I just stared at it then walked away; the beeping sound of a phone left off the hook too long fading behind me.

Back in the living room again, I paced back and forth across the rug. My body pulsated with too much energy to let me sit down, but as the anger abated I found my mind sorting out my current position. Pat and my kids had moved out, a court conservator doled out allowances to me like a parent to his child, and the Open Door stayed closed. Zero for three.

Besides that, I felt angry much of the time. And that feeling wasn't all that much more pleasant than the guilt I'd felt months before.

I knew blowing up at Kaufman did no good for anybody, least of all me. My anger lessened for a moment, allowing me to think more clearly and logically.

Feeling suddenly worn out from my anger, I slumped into an over-stuffed chair. *Kaufman had some nerve asking me if I was sick. Who wouldn't be mad if they were in my shoes? Or wouldn't they?* I couldn't be sure that I knew how normal people reacted to things anymore. I hadn't led a normal existence for quite some time.

I wondered if I deserved to feel so indignant or if my anger served as a displaced and irrational emotion enveloping me in self-righteousness? *I have every right to be upset at IBM,* I finally concluded. *Even if they decide that the facts warranted my firing, highly unlikely as that might be, they owe me an honest investigation – and a vigorous one, too.*

On the other hand, while my anger at IBM may be justified, extending it into matters beyond IBM, like taking it out on my family certainly was not.

I reviewed my struggle to get IBM to give me a fair shake this time around. Like a climber on the Eiger's north face, the most famous of nature's Swiss wonders, I kept pounding in pylons but they wouldn't stick.

What in hell am I really doing here? Dodging reality by banging on a steel door called IBM or living in the reality of truly having checkmated Big Blue?

I got up and began to pace once again as my anger began to swell once more. *No one will ever understand either side of my flip from the norm. They won't be able to relate to my mental illness, and they can't know the anger and frustration I feel over being tossed out of IBM. This is not the time to get cold feet over pushing IBM around.*

"They deserve to get screwed worse than they screwed me," I

said aloud. My words sounded hollow with no one to receive them, but they renewed my conviction.

I'm having a hell of a time getting off the base of the mountain, I thought, *but, dammit, when I get to the top ... and I will ... the view is gonna be spectacular.*

I returned to the kitchen and placed the now-silent phone back in its cradle. Then I picked it up again and punched in the number to IBM's Armonk office. After the usual secretarial screening, Kaufman picked up.

"Art, it's me, Max Beardslee. Look, I won't shout or anything, okay? It's just that what I asked you to do in the last phone call could have been done by now. Anyway, can you tell me anything new?"

"Yeah, the interview process with Fillmore, Hampstead, Paulos, and Blaylock has been initiated," he replied.

Hallelujah! Some progress at last.

Then he said something else, something quite humane, especially after my earlier outburst. "A few people around here know about your Open Door, and they are all laughing about your reference to Striker as 'Bungling Bernard'."

Good. The humor over Striker was a good sign. The door seemed to be slightly ajar. After all this shouting maybe I could yet win Kaufman over. "I appreciate the update," I told Kaufman "and ... uh, I apologize about our last phone call."

"Well, look," he said, "I know this thing's gotta be real tough on you. Real tough. Have you talked to your wife lately? Are she and the kids okay?"

Thinking about being apart from my wife reminded me of the blame I put on IBM for my personal problems, and I started to feel angry again. I needed to hang up before I said something I would regret. "Yeah, Art. They're okay. Thanks for asking. I gotta go. Bye."

I sat in the kitchen thinking of the miserable times my family and I had endured over the last nine months that had culminated in this separation, my anger at IBM kept rising all the while. With Pat's words still fresh in my mind, I thought, *Why not cut some of the strings? No need to be a marionette anymore.*

I'll take the offensive. Why not? Nothing to lose. It oughta be fun. A little reverse intimidation can't hurt, can it? Call up the bad guys and tell them it's their turn in the barrel.

I jumped up and walked to the kitchen window thinking, finally, my chance to act out Patton. I watched a chipmunk foraging on the lawn and remembered the eagle painting, in Fillmore's office, holding the rodent in its talons. *Be the hunter instead of the hunted.* I smiled.

"Go for it, Beardslee," I said aloud. This time I didn't hear the emptiness of my unreceived words.

I needed a strategy. My first priority had to be Paulos, I concluded. I crossed the kitchen, picked up the phone again, rang IBM's Atlanta headquarters, and asked for his extension. Paulos' secretary said he'd gone to Armonk, New York.

"Oh yeah?" I replied, with real enthusiasm in my voice. The warmth of satisfaction began to creep into my body. He had to be responding to a command from Kaufman. Attaboy, Kaufman. "Well, look. Please tell Mr. Paulos that Max Beardslee called. He knows me. Let Paulos know he's in line for a big promotion and have him give me a call. I'll tell him all about it."

"Does he have your number, Mr. Beardslee?" she asked.

"Yes, he has my number." Paulos' secretary wanted to be sure Paulos knew how to reach me. She had bought it.

The thought of Paulos' predictable reaction to my message — shock — brought laughter to the empty room, several minutes of mirth in fact. I then moved back to the sink, brewed a cup of coffee and anticipated the pain I'd cause with the next call, I picked up the phone and dialed the same Atlanta number.

"Bruce P. Hampton, please." My words were followed by the barren silence of the hold button until a secretary's voice rang through.

"Mr. Hampton's office."

Forcing some executive timber into my voice, I casually introduced myself. "This is Max Beardslee. I want to talk to Bruce Hampton."

Figuring news of my Open Door had reached the ears of this divisional commander, I believed he would feel obliged to pick up the phone. He'd be aware that I'd used a point of law as a reference and probably that I accused IBM of the same thing for which they had blamed me. He'd be confused, not wanting to take the call but concerned that if he dodged me I'd use it against him in some way.

"Bruce Hampstead." A firm but neutral voice.

I figured right. "Is this *the* Bruce Hampstead?" I let my sarcasm slowly drip on the line. Expectedly, his voice turned cold.

"What do you want?"

No problem responding to that question. No problem at all. "I'll tell you what I want, Hampstead," I delivered the rehearsed message with staccato words. "You packaged me up as a bad guy. You said I took IBM money for personal gain.

"Nothing could be further from the truth. You fired me, because, as the new divisional president, you wanted to set an example. You blew me away without bothering to verify the facts; the real story reads a one-eighty. You assholes premeditated to obligate my funds, not the other way around."

Had he hung up? Nope. I could hear his unsteady breathing, like he was taking in big gulps of air. Damn, had I ever felt better? Nope. I showed this big shot no respect, and he listened anyway — at least so far.

"Hampstead, I think I have IBM by the balls. I'm trying to settle with you guys without suing. It's quicker, but, by God, if Armonk doesn't slap your hand for the stupidity of what you did, then I'm going to sue Big Blue's big butt. You got upset about Fillmore bending the rules and creating a Taj Mahal operation in Detroit, so you went after him. But when none of your thousands of regulations would bring him down, you found one that could take out one of his palace guards. And your snake, Paulos, grabbed it. Hell, he *premeditated* how to use the rule to get me. With his syrupy voice and way he got me to explain things and to set myself up, the only thing he was interested in. Well, as a man once said to me, IBM can't afford to be emotional. It's gonna be expensive on you guys."

Knowing my words had to be stinging this loftily-positioned, fourteenth-floor exec', who probably heard his first rebuke in a helluva long time, I pressed on.

"And, one more thing, Hampstead ... your vocabulary." The "mitigating" thing had always bothered me. Time to get it out.

"The day you fired me, you told me there were 'mitigating circumstances.' You later denied ever saying that, but you and I both know you said it, and you didn't even know what the word meant. Shame on an IBM divisional president for having a limited vocabulary like that."

Silence on the phone.

"Are you still there?"

In a voice passed through crushed ice, he responded, "Is that all?"

"No, it isn't. One last point. The day I got fired, the last thing you told me was, "I wish you well." I'm returning the favor, Hampstead. It's the last thing you'll hear from me. I wish you well."

Click. The kitchen was silent.

"Damn, this feels great!" No one to see or hear me gloating. I chortled at myself and did a little dance on the linoleum.

After aiming at John Opel, Hampstead meant nothing more than loose change to me. *Everything has its relevance and perspective in time,* I thought. *In my days as a marionette, this guy, the president of my twenty-thousand person strong division, could send shivers up my spine. Now, he means nothing. Nothing.*

Walking into the bedroom, I tried not to notice the places where Pat's things were missing. I put on a warm-up jacket, hat and gloves, and walked out of the condo. I stretched my arms high above my head, noticing how alive the cold air made me feel. I reached down and touched my toes, then began jogging over the gray, snow-covered urban terrain. Retracing my phone calls in my head, particularly the one to Hampstead, I felt elated that I'd been able to get my licks in personally. With my confidence high, I jogged with purpose and energy through the blustery afternoon.

When I returned I pressed the hot button on the stove, filled the teakettle and leaned against the counter waiting for the cozy whistle to blow. Two miles of running had cleared my mind. Now I needed a little hot liquid to thaw me out. Then, maybe, I could figure out a way to get my family back together.

As I sipped the steaming brew, lost in thought, the piercing ring of the phone sent hot tea like a geyser splashing onto my hand. "Shit," I said as I jumped away from the cup, then placed it hurriedly on the counter. I looked at the phone. It had to be Kaufman or Striker giving me hell for stirring up the pot.

Striker. "Max, we can't have this," he opened.

"Have what, Bernard?"

"You know what ... calling up Paulos and Hampstead and harassing them."

Feeling too pumped up and too mindful of my past tendency toward being intimidated to let his words sidetrack me, I silently vowed again, no more intimidation. Never — from anybody. I laughed and replied, "Is great big IBM scared of little old me, Bernard?" and hung up without waiting for a reply.

Bullshit, I thought. *This thing will never get straightened out until I talk to Opel.* I picked up the phone and called Armonk knowing it would be close to impossible to get the man on the phone. After being routed by the Armonk switchboard toward the general direction of his office, a pleasant-voiced lady named Alma said, "Hello."

Matching her pleasantry, I asked her if she worked for John Opel.

"Yes."

"Are you a secretary?"

"Yes."

"How many does Mr. Opel have?" I queried, interested in that little tidbit myself. How many to serve a man responsible for the direction of the company and its four hundred thousand people?

"Four."

I figured four sounded about right. She acted friendly and, judging from her job serving one of America's most powerful corporate chiefs, I assumed she had to be competent as hell. "Well, John Opel knows of me, but we've never met. Would you let him know I'm on the phone?"

"Sir, he's in a meeting, but I'll let him know you called."

I stayed polite. "Okay."

An idea struck me "Please talk to Bernard Striker. Do you know him?"

"Yes."

"What I really want to accomplish is to get a letter I wrote to Mr. Opel into his read file. Would you discuss my suggestion with Mr. Striker?" She assured me she would.

The next day, Kaufman called. He had interviewed Chad Russell, Ken Albright and Paul Beckman in Detroit.

"Did you verify from Russell that I could only collect twenty bucks per meeting no matter the cost?" I asked.

"Yep."

"Did you talk to Albright about the Sugar Loaf cover-up?"

"Uh ... yes, I did."

Well, that oughta do it, I thought. *Kaufman now knew I'd been ordered to bury expenses, that I couldn't collect more than twenty dollars per branch manager and that I spent more than twenty dollars for most meetings. Time to go for the close.*

"Are we ready to settle?"

Silence on the other end. Just as I planned to ask Kaufman if he still was on the line, I heard, "I need to talk to some more people."

"Who?"

"Fillmore, Blaylock and Hampstead."

Reluctantly, I gave him that but wanted to cover some new ground.

"Okay. Are you willing to look into the contribution Operation 30/30 made to IBM?"

I had previously noted a hesitance on both Striker's and Kaufman's part to do anything about 30/30, and I didn't understand why. Kaufman, again, hesitated. I couldn't let them bypass 30/30. Having them see my contribution to IBM and examine the resultant sales increases seemed a necessary needed step in softening them up to see my side. Then, let them draw a comparison between that and a box of cigars. Let them.

"Art, it'll make you feel a hell of a lot better when you write the check. Look into it, please?"

"Okay, Max. I'll look into it."

This call has gone well so far, I thought happily. *Kaufman sounds friendly. Maybe I should quit while I'm ahead. Nah.*

"Art, in reading my Open Door have you found anything to indicate I wasn't telling you the absolute truth?"

"No. "

"Can I talk to Mr. Opel?"

"Not yet."

"Okay, Art ... and thanks," I said honestly, the first time he'd heard that from me.

Two more days went by spent in the lonely confines of the condo, which was ensconced in the cold and snow of a typical Michigan winter. With nothing to do but think about my situation and ponder my life over the last eight months, I began to play around with the idea of writing a book about what had happened to me.

The idea entered tentatively at first with judgements of unworthiness pushing it out but persisted in returning. I reviewed the possibility. In the worst case, I thought, maybe I'll learn something from writing it, like whether I was predisposed to go whacko, or maybe I can dig something deeper out, like how IBM's culture affected my psyche. Yeah, I thought. I oughta go to the library and check out a couple of books on organizational psychology.

There must have been some link between working for IBM for so long and then getting fired and going crazy, I thought. *I certainly couldn't envision myself having endured a mental failure over being fired from a tire distributor, even if I was its head guy. But maybe it's not just what a company does or sells; maybe it is more a company's culture and organizational structure that make the difference. Maybe it's how people are treated that creates such a strong hook that being forced to leave causes unbearable pain in employees. Maybe if I just wrote about IBM, readers could get interested in the book.*

I wasn't sure, so I decided to let the idea stir for a while and made myself some lunch. Later in the day I decided to give the book idea a chance. *It can't hurt to just put something down on paper and see how it goes,* I thought. So, I made some notes about what I would include in the book. *Well,* I thought, *I oughta make it fair. IBM had its good points.* They made pretty good products most of the time and their history of growth appeared excellent. I outlined the founding principles of the company, like respect for the individual and how that didn't apply at all levels. *Yeah, that would get it started,* I thought.

Pleased with this new development, one I viewed as a constructive way to use my time, I decided to give myself a break from my solitary confinement. I'd had enough of that at the asylum.

I drove over to my sister's house. Marcia and Tom were off at work, and Pat acknowledged a curt hello before leaving me with the kids. I played pool with Steve and John, finding some relief from my anger and preoccupation with IBM by laughing with Steve, who had to strain to see over the table let alone make a shot. The boys acted like living away from home and from me was okay, but I knew they had to feel like gypsies. This was the third house they had moved to in less than a year.

After a while, I sought out Pat, hoping to make amends. We talked privately and without success about our fragmented family. "Max, I want you to move into an apartment so the boys and I can have the condo back."

Not what I wanted to hear. I wanted her to weary herself of living with my sister and move back in with me or, better yet, for me to get enough momentum going with IBM so she would regain confidence in my ability to give her and the kids some stability in their future.

"Pat, I can't do that. Look, I think I can stop acting like an ass if you move back in."

"NO," she shouted with real conviction in her voice.

"WELL, I'M NOT GONNA TAKE AN APARTMENT," I shouted back. Hearing our outburst, the boys came upstairs to see what was going on. Embarrassed, I muttered a goodbye to them and stormed out of my sister's house. As I backed out of the driveway Pat walked out and motioned for me to stop.

"Yeah," I snapped.

"I think you ought to see Dr. Rosenberg. You aren't right yet. You're still off … not like before but…"

I cut her off mid-sentence by slamming the gas pedal down and sending the car out onto the road.

Back at the condo, I decided to occupy myself and vent my renewed anger by keeping the pressure on IBM. I called Kaufman. Not in. I left a message.

After about ten minutes, he called back. "I talked with Paulos and Hampstead," he informed me, no confidence in his voice.

"Oh yeah" I said with interest. "How'd it go? What did they say?".

"I can't tell you anything, only that I talked to them," he replied. These guys, the first he'd talked to at his level, seemed to have taken the wind out of his sails. He sounded less confident and less sympathetic.

"Art, did you tell Hampstead I can't see settling through the Open Door route unless he is demoted?"

An unenthusiastic "yes" came down the line.

"Well, did you get into the twenty-bucks stuff, that I could prove IBM forced me to spend more than I could collect?"

Kaufman deferred from answering. As he continued his evasiveness, I built up a head of steam, wanting to move the ball. "Art, you don't seem to be making anything happen. So, I've gotta see Opel," I stated angrily.

Kaufman lamely replied, "The right time hasn't presented itself."

"Damn it, Art. I've had it. I'm going to talk to Opel with or without your help." Collecting my thoughts, I continued. "I'm gonna hire a detective to get Opel's home phone number. Now, you know me. Somehow, I'm going to get it."

Hanging up, I then picked up the phone again, this time dialing John Opel's secretary, Alma. I forced my voice to sound calm.

"Alma, please get my letter into Mr. Opel's weekend read file. I don't want him embarrassed when I call him at home this weekend, and he hasn't read it."

Alma sounded shocked. "You're going to call him at home?"

"You bet. Gotta run, Alma. Don't forget."

With just two days to cover that bit of braggadocio, I grabbed the phone book lying next to the phone and looked up "Detectives" in the Yellow Pages. After a couple of guys declined my request by admitting they could not obtain the phone number I needed, I noticed the ad on the next page. Who could miss it? "FatMan Detection Agency."

The ad filled the dimensions the name implied using a half page to proclaim: "The FatMan, International Private Detective — City and State, Nation and worldwide." According to the ad, this guy handled everything: "Marital problems, child custody, kidnapping, embezzlement, runaway teenagers." And he had a whole slew of devices at his pudgy pointers: "Shadowing, Invisible Powders, Magnetized BumperBeepers, Closed Circuit Video Television, Manual or Radio Controlled Photography, Moving and Still Infrared Telescopy." Plus, the ad claimed, "No Assignments Too Large or Too Small. First consultation: FREE — NO OBLIGATION," and then closed with a personal message from the FatMan himself:

"The anxiety of not knowing can be more cruel than the truth." His scrawled signature followed this.

My kind of guy, this FatMan. His ad begged for the unusual, the tougher job.

I dialed the number at the bottom of the ad. An aggressive male voice answered. After a few minutes of discussion about what I needed, FatMan said he could handle the assignment.

"One thousand in advance and more later," he notified me brusquely.

"How much more?"

"Varies...," he offered, then paused before adding, "might need up to nine thousand more."

Shit, I thought. *That's a hell of a lot of money for a phone number and address. But, I need that phone number and address more than anything else I can think of right now. Hell, I can cover the advance and deal with the remaining balance later.*

"Okay." We agreed to meet later that day.

After completing that call, I rang up my brother's secretary and asked her for the checking account balance of a small car leasing company I owned. I had opened it when dad died, four years prior. She kept the books for me at Denny's dealership, making my overhead next to nothing. The judge and court appointed conservator didn't know about that account. I liked her reply. My normal allowance just got enhanced by twenty-one hundred dollars.

"Good. I'll be up this afternoon to get it," I told her.

Late in the day, I met with the FatMan — an experience in itself, in a parking lot near downtown. He lived up to his moniker. Huge. Bigger than Fillmore. Rumpled clothing. Black on gray over black. An oversized head holding hazel, intelligent-looking eyes. "Did you bring the money?"

"Yeah, FatMan," I replied, surprised at my calmness.

After I forked over the one grand in hundred dollar bills, FatMan made his prediction: "I'll have this fellow all figured out by Sunday. His phone number *and* address."

This guy looked and sounded better than the characters in an old Charlie Chan movie. With exaggerated actions he moved faster than his bulk implied and spoke with a voice clear and confident.

FatMan called me the following evening and in a hushed voice informed me, "A penetration will take place most imminently."

At two in the morning, awakened by the ringing phone, his whispered words hung in the darkness of the bedroom: "Penetration has started."

Six hours later, on Saturday morning, the phone rang again, this time his mystery-tainted words were, "Penetration has been completed."

Later that afternoon we met in a vacant parking lot. The FatMan wanted more money for his efforts. Nine grand more. I looked at his king-sized face. *I may have been crazy,* I thought. *I may even still be crazy ... but not that crazy.*

"You're ripping me off, FatMan."

The FatMan pursed his lips, looking annoyed. "There aren't five guys in the U.S. who could have gotten the job done this fast. You get what you pay for. I'm the best."

"Hey, I figure all you did is bribe some telephone operator. I'm glad you did, but—"

"No, I didn't," the FatMan cut me off. "He's too important a person to do it that way. I really flew to New York, got a rental car, drove to your man Opel's house, penetrated security, and read his kitchen phone — a wall-mounted yellow one — with a pencil flashlight." I promised to pay the FatMan something more as soon as I could get more money from my leasing company.

In turn, the FatMan said he'd revisit his expenses, maybe he'd come down a bit. "Not a commitment, mind you, but I'll look at it," and then handed me John Opel's home phone and address.

Glancing down at the greasy-looking piece of paper in my hand, I sniffed then smirked in satisfaction.

Not an hour later, after practicing what I would say over and over in my mind, I dialed the expensively gained ten-digit number. I took a deep breath and let it out slowly as the numbers registered. *This is it. I'm going to talk to the man.* Then I heard an all-too-familiar signal.

Busy. The damn line was busy! Working up my nerve again, I re-dialed the number a minute later. It rang through. All right! The voice of a teenager answered the home phone of one of America's most powerful businessmen. Heart pounding, I attempted a calm voice.

"Hi. This is Max Beardslee calling John Opel." I thought I said it just right, as if we were buddies or something. The young man said his father had gone out of town. A setback.

"Oh, do you expect him back this evening?"

"No. Dad and Mom drove to Vermont for a weekend of skiing."

Wanting to keep the son friendly, I casually opened up the conversation. "I'm an acquaintance of your dad's, and I need his help on a matter involving me and my family. Would you let him know I called?"

The son sounded anxious to please. "Sure, let's get the spelling of your name and your phone number." After giving him what he needed, I hung up.

The next day, I tried again. The same young man answered. I got as far as, "Hello, this is Max Bear—" before hearing the clicking sound of a phone being hung up. I hadn't planned on scaring John Opel off, but I'd done it. He probably thought a deranged former employee was preparing to gun him down. Calling definitely no longer served as an option.

A thousand bucks for nothing? No. There was still the address. No problem. I'd send a telegram to his home and foster an even more frightening mental picture than the phone call could ever accomplish. Now, as the saying goes, he'd know I not only knew his number but where he lived as well.

The telegram, dated February fourteenth, 9:46 P.M., served as an apology.

> I REGRET MY CALL ALARMED YOUR FAMILY – STOP – MY INTENTION WAS TO HAVE YOU INVOLVED IN MY OPEN DOOR – STOP – YOUR SECRETARY, ALMA, HAS IT IN HER POSSESSION – STOP – I WENT TO CONSIDERABLE TROUBLE TO OBTAIN YOUR HOME PHONE NUMBER IN THE HOPES OF GAINING YOUR ATTENTION – STOP – I WILL NOT CALL YOUR HOME AGAIN – STOP – SINCERELY, MAX BEARDSLEE.

I added it up. I had mastered Opel's home phone, which, hopefully, would show my determination to get him involved. I had his home address, so I could at least communicate with him on a one-way basis.

The next morning, Kaufman called as I expected he would. "Back off calling Opel's home," he grimly demanded.

No surprise to me that he had heard about the phone calls. I wanted the Babe Ruth effect of being able to slam a homer on the pitch I called.

"Maybe, Art. It depends on whether you get off your dead ass or not."

"Hey, your case takes up all of my time," he assured me and then added, "Today Mrs. Opel brought your telegram into the office personally. Mr. Opel is out of town. She thought it must be important."

Hot damn! That's what I needed, an executive's wife's perspective. I toned down my shots at Kaufman, deciding his patience was wearing thin, and I needed to keep him in my camp.

"Look, Art, I apologize, I know you're trying."

After hanging up, I went to see Roger Martin. He was one of only three outsiders who had read my Open Door. *Talking the situation through with him should help*, I thought. *It'll give me some perspective.* When I arrived he greeted me with, "Hey, Max. You don't look so good."

I shrugged his comment off and filled the Steelcase exec in on the FatMan and the call to Opel. I summarized my feelings: "I feel like a soldier who has been blazing away right down to his last round, Roger. I just don't know if I've hit the target or not."

Martin thought my strategy would work but suggested stepping away from the fight for a few days. "Go visit a friend, Max," he suggested. "Give it a rest and let Kaufman and the others work in peace."

"I've got a buddy in Florida. I guess I'll fly down there and spend a few days with him."

Martin nodded his approval. "Get out of town for a few days. It'll do you good."

The guy I had in mind was Tony Lucido, a close friend of mine from the old days as bachelor Lieutenants in mid-sixties Germany. Working now in Tampa as a lawyer, I could put his logical mind to good use helping me sketch out the possibility of a book on my IBM experiences and relax a bit on the beach as well. I assumed I'd receive a favorable response to my planned visit and was right. When I called and asked him if he was prepared for a visitor, in his usual amiable fashion, Lucido said, "Come on down."

I called Pat. "Honey, you can have the condo."

"Oh? Why the change of heart?" she said skeptically.

"I'm tired. Exhausted, really. I'm on my way to Florida. Be staying with Tony."

Pat viewed this latest move with mixed emotions. "I wonder whether you are going down there because you are still unbalanced or because you really need the rest."

"You don't understand, do you?" I replied, not liking the reference to my mental state. "Can I see the kids before taking off?"

"Sure," she said.

"I'll come by tomorrow," I said, and we hung up.

The next day, I drove over to Marcia's, picked up Pat and the kids and drove them to a Chuck E. Cheese's pizza parlor. Getting settled into a booth, I attempted to explain why I was going to Florida, how I felt and what I was going to do next.

"Guys, this is like a war, only they aren't real bullets. Got that?" Three nods. Their interest perked up at the reference to war.

"Anyway, your dad is trying to get his reputation back. It's a big company, lots of big cheeses in it, like Chuck E. here, that I need to argue with." More nods. "I pretty much have fired all the bullets I have, only the bullets are words and letters, see. And IBM trained me to fight hard. Like all those computer sales I've told you guys about."

I hoped they understood. "So, uh, I'm pooped, and need to get away for a few days and think about everything." Pat listened to what I had to say. Maybe I reached her through my explanation to my sons.

After paying the bill, we all drove back to Marcia's house. As the boys got out of the car I gathered them all in my arms and said,

"You'll be moving back into the condo. Mind your mother and brush your teeth." I then kissed the boys goodbye and called, "I love you guys," as they turned toward the house. As they slowly walked away, I got back into the car and looked at Pat, her blonde hair done up in her usual ponytail. She looked relieved that the housing issue had been solved at least temporarily.

I asked her, "Do you know I really need to get away?"

"Yes," she replied, "you do need to get away from the IBM stuff for awhile, but be careful. You're still not fully recovered from whatever you went through."

"What are you worried about, Pat?"

"I'm worried that you ... that you're still mentally ill ... not like before where you suffered from guilt and depression but almost the opposite, like you think you can do anything."

I thought about what she said for a minute. "I'll consider what you said; I always have," I said placing my hand lightly on her cheek.

My wife stepped out of the car and then turned to face me. "Goodbye, Max. I hope the trip works out. Let me know if you hear from IBM."

Judging by her demeanor, I concluded that our marriage fell definitely on the far side of the growth curve. Only a heavy dose of IBM settlement — or me getting another job — could hold it together and head it back upward toward renewal again.

That afternoon, carrying only a small duffel bag full of warm weather gear, I caught a flight to Florida.

Nine

*D*amned good to be in Florida, I THOUGHT, WHILE SEATED IN AN AIR-conditioned tenth-floor bar, above an office building, sipping a cold drink. The window offered an elevated view of Tampa, matching my mood. The trip had been the right thing to do. For the last three days I'd been enjoying the beach and Florida's hot sunny weather, a big switch from February's blustery slush that I'd left behind in Grand Rapids.

On my fourth day in Florida, I waited for Lucido to join me. I'd also been enjoying Lucido's friendship and the chance to catch up with what he'd been doing. Leaving all the catch-22 stuff of being a young, single lieutenant in Germany behind, he had put himself through a tough three years of law school. After two years as an assistant district attorney, he had become an accomplished criminal lawyer in the city. In a feigned British accent, last night Lucido had summarized his cops and robbers role reversal.

"First ya learn how to put 'em in, then ya learn how to keep 'em out. Keepin' 'em out pays better, matey." An English major in his undergraduate days, Lucido delighted in speaking in the half-dozen idioms he'd mastered.

I glanced at my watch. *Lucido should have been here by now. Well, the rest of the world operated with less structure than IBM, and good for them. He'd be here.* As the J & B settled in, I reflected on the long conversation I'd had with Tony and Vera the night before. Some pretty heady stuff had been discussed. I hoped Tony didn't view me or my plans as grandiose.

I remembered how Lucido had shuffled his feet and glanced with raised eyebrows at Vera when I told him that after the IBM settlement I could lease a Boeing 747 and take all my friends, certainly him included, on a trip around the world. The idea had caught on as the wine we had drunk began taking me on a flight of its own.

What the hell. I soon would be able to afford it, I thought. *It wasn't such a far out idea, and it would be a hell of a lot of fun.*

Lucido showed open disbelief when I told him about the banquet. "When the investigation is over, I'll be vindicated. And what I'll ask IBM to do is to host a banquet announcing their error. I'll ask for senior IBM executives to attend and, because IBM will want to cooperate, they'll go along. One person I'll ask for is Tom Watson, Jr., son of IBM's first leader.

"Now, get this, Tony; Watson is a former ambassador to Russia and a pal of Alexander Kosygin, his counterpart. I'll ask Watson to invite Kosygin along. Kosygin can witness first hand fair play in America."

Tony said "That's bullshit, Max, you won't be able to get that done." But, I thought I could.

Looking up to signal the waitress for yet another drink, I noticed two beefy policemen enter the bar. *Those guys must be off duty,* I thought. *I don't see any kind of disturbance going on here.*

As I watched, the policemen surveyed the room. One of them looked in my direction, and when his eyes lighted on me, he paused, then elbowed his partner and leaned over and said something to him. The partner followed suit.

What the hell? Why are they heading right for my table, I wondered. *What did I do? Nah. They must be looking at the guy behind me.* I turned and looked over my shoulder. The table behind mine sat vacant. *Damn, damn, damn! They want to talk to me!*

"Are you Max Beardslee?" the cop who had recognized me first asked.

Stay calm, I ordered myself. "Yes, I am. What can I do for you, gentlemen?"

"I'm Officer Chappel and this is Officer Higgam. We need you to step outside."

"What for?" I said, my voice surprisingly controlled.

"We'll explain outside," he said and took my arm in his large hand. The pressure of his strong fingers made his point clear. These cops were serious.

Was this another Lucido prank, I wondered? The pretty waitress intentionally looked away as I got up from the table. *Where in hell was Tony,* I wondered. With the best military bearing I could muster, I walked outside into the bright sun and sticky air. *No sense letting these cops think I'm a patsy,* I thought.

"Put your hands behind your back. We're going to put handcuffs on you," ordered the bigger of the two officers as we approached a county police car.

"Officer, what the hell is going on?" I asked in an irritated voice, while doing as he asked. The cold metal fell heavily against my wrists. I feel like a goddamned criminal for Chrissake. I remembered all the implications of the words "premeditated intent" that I had felt after getting fired from IBM. The handcuffs would have seemed appropriate and justly deserved then, but not now.

"All we can tell you is that we have a signed court order to deliver you to a psychiatric care facility."

I felt my face flush and sweat begin seeping out of the pores on my forehead and on my upper lip causing an unpleasant tickling sensation. I wanted to mop my face with my sleeve, but the cuffs restricted such motion.

Another mental institution? Shit. This can't be real.

We drove north out of the city, a ride void of conversation other than the car's two-way radio chatter. Fifteen minutes later, we arrived at a sprawled-out multi-storied white building with no visible name. I noticed a round sign with a yellow happy face painted on it hanging on a faded post out front. "Yes. You've come to the right place," the happy face seemed to say. "This is the loony bin."

I was led into the hospital lobby and my handcuffs removed as the cops identified me to the nurse at the reception desk. Determined not to lose my recently returned sense of humor, I cockily asked, "Can I get a room with a view?"

A male attendant, attired in the familiar white shirt and pants, arrived and said he was taking me to the Intensive Care Unit of the hospital. ICU? "Follow me," he ordered.

My humor disappeared and like a chameleon anger became the color of my voice and actions. I stood up, began walking toward the door and exclaimed, "Fuck you, I'm not going." The nurse picked up a telephone, dialed a number and announced in a brisk unfeeling voice, "RED ALERT ... RED ALERT." I could hear her words crackle over the hospital intercom. Within seconds, the lobby turned into wall-to-wall white uniforms as five guys ran in and then out the door after me. Two grabbed me by the arms as I began sprinting down the walk. They dragged me backward into the hospital as I looked forward at my last glimpse of freedom. This scene felt too familiar for my liking.

After stripping me of watch, wedding band, shoelaces, and belt, they literally carried me up the stairs to the second floor and past a steel door manned by a uniformed guard.

I had thought that this kind of treatment, without explanation, could only occur in China, Eastern Europe or other non-democratic societies. *Wrong, Beardslee. It's happening to you,* I thought. They continued carrying me like an invalid criminal down the hall and through a door into an office, where they not so gently put me down on an armless wooden chair. I sat facing an overweight female shift supervisor.

After a little paperwork and a lecture about my uncooperative entry, the unfriendly lady assigned me to a two-bed room. "Two phone calls per shift, Mr. Beardslee. Four a day," was her parting comment as one of the attendants ushered me to my room.

Looking around, I noted the rotted mattresses, threadbare

sheets, worn flooring, and stained fixtures in the bathroom. As I paced in line to use the one and only pay phone, I studied the other patients on the ward, dismayed to see that most of them appeared to be severely mentally ill. Unshaven, unkempt, two with uncontrolled drooling, many rocking from side to side in the now-familiar manner caused by too many drugs pumped into their bodies. And their eyes — always their glazed, deadened eyes — gave them away. A Ward 29B replay. I had seen it all before and I had no desire to be seeing it again now.

Finally working my way to first in line, I called Lucido's office. Not there. I knew he had a switching device at the office.

"Goddamn it, splice me through to his home!" Lucido's fiancée came on the line.

"Vera, you're not going to believe this, but I've just been picked up by some cops and dumped in some funny farm north of the city. Please put Tony on the phone!"

"Max, neither Tony nor I can talk to you. I'm sorry." Click.

I felt like a leper just hit with a bucket of ice water by the only people who would come near me.

Obviously Tony had something to do with putting me in the psychiatric center or he and Vera would gladly and willingly have talked to me. Someone had told them not to.

I made my second call collect to Pat. I hoped she would know something. Impatiently I drummed my fingers on the metal shelf in the booth as I waited for the connection. Finally someone picked up. I took a breath as I anticipated speaking, then held it as I heard a computerized operator say, "The number you have dialed has been changed. The new number is unlisted." *Damn it,* I thought, *divorce was one thing, that might be justified, but cutting me off from communicating in this time of need seemed a nasty deed.*

Damn! Slamming the phone down, I looked frantically around the booth for a phone book. *I had to find the number of a lawyer. Where was the goddamned phone book?*

"Mr. Beardslee, your two phone calls have been used up. Please let another patient use the phone," said the supervisor, who'd been glaring my way the whole time.

I turned to face her, and with an effort to control my frustration and anger, I politely said, "Ma'am, I need to make another call. This is important."

"So are the other calls. Making more than two is inappropriate."

I looked at her for a moment, realized she wasn't going to budge an inch, turned and stormed to my room. I kicked the door shut and leaned against it, trying to calm down.

A kid of eighteen or so said, "Hello," as I turned around. I muttered a hello back at my new roommate before lying down on the mattress. I turned my back to him, unwilling to get acquainted.

After what seemed to be several hours, the night supervisor ordered me to down some tranquilizers, telling me they would help me sleep. I took them but spent instead a sleepless night waiting for morning and my chance to see a psychiatrist and convince him or her that I should be discharged.

As dawn and a tasteless breakfast arrived, I was already up. I could feel the effects of the previous night's drugs, which put me into slow motion and dragged me down, wearing off, but I stood ready for an expected appointment. Some doctor would show up the first full day; they always did. Not until I had picked at a limp bacon and lettuce sandwich at lunch, however, did a medical professional seek me out.

Dr. Myron Heileman arrived, looking like he could stand a haircut and some shoe polish. This slight-of-build glassy-eyed slouched man with dandruff on the shoulders of his multi-colored sport coat introduced himself as my new shrink.

After talking for a few minutes about what seemed to me to be unimportant matters, such as the weather outside and whether I drank a lot, I challenged him. "I'm not mentally ill, and I expect to be immediately discharged. Now!"

Heileman wrote some notes on his clipboard, gave me a look that said, "You're kidding aren't you?" before responding. "I don't know about that. I have additional rounds to make," he mumbled and then shuffled toward other areas of the ward.

During the course of the day, I struck up a conversation with two members of the hospital staff. From them, I learned that according to policy here, like at the VA hospital, patients start out in the section reserved for the most mentally disabled and from there could only hope to earn their way out.

Despite this similarity, the condition of my room was just one indication of the differences between this facility and the other hospitals I'd been in. The staff acted casual and unconcerned about patient conditions, as did the psychiatrists. In the Grand Rapids and VA hospitals, the facilities were clean and well kept, the attendants acting professional and considerate. Attendants here looked like high school dropouts earning minimum wage.

I just about confirmed this fact when I struck up a conversation with one young, friendly attendant by asking him how long he'd been working at the hospital. He told me this was his first day.

"Oh, where were you working before this?" I asked.

"I worked at McDonald's," came his reply.

The attendants also possessed no idea of what patient care meant. Their interaction with patients appeared to be janitorial, confined to cleaning things up, as opposed to therapeutic, offering hope or encouragement. In fact, the attendants seemed almost repulsed by the patients, acting as if they were afraid to touch one for fear they might get a communicable disease.

I quickly noticed that most of the attendants and staff overworked one word, so much so that it took only about four hours of being in the facility before I wished it were banned from the vocabulary of the human race. In much the same manner, IBMers would pick up a word and overwork it. In the sixties, everything was "super." In the seventies, "Good luck and good selling," concluded every memo. Just before I got fired, "ubiquitous" made the rounds.

The asylum's staff deemed almost everything as "inappropriate." Smoking in your room was inappropriate; abusive language was inappropriate; talking to children in the adjacent ward was inappropriate; visiting another patient in his or her room was inappropriate; talking more than three minutes on the phone was inappropriate; and, as I'd found out within a half hour of being at the hospital, making more than two phone calls at one time was inappropriate.

The rules reminded me of those at IBM.

After trying to take part in "outdoor therapy" without realizing I hadn't been cleared for it, I was forced to take pills containing stronger stuff than I had received the night before. My lids were so heavy there was no way to keep them open. I remembered the old cartoons where the characters used toothpicks to keep their lids up when they were tired. *Those sure wouldn't be enough for me,* I thought as I lay down on the filthy mattress.

Fate hands us strange turns sometimes, and this has to be one of its strangest, I thought. *I came to Florida for a stress-free rest and now find myself locked up in a small cell. To boot, it appears that nobody gives a damn about my situation, and those closest to me figure I belong in a place designed to hold the crazy.*

I curled up into a fetal-like ball as self-pity swept over me. *Why in hell had Martin ever hired me? Why did I ever accept his offer? Why? Goddamn it, why? If none of that had ever happened, I wouldn't be here in this filthy hole now.*

As I thought about how and when IBM entered my life, and such a promising life it had seemed to be, I dropped off to sleep.

◆◆◆

September 1967

After five years in the air force, the last two as a captain managing the Officer's Club at a Strategic Air Command base in northern Maine, I'd become bored and unproductive. The military grapevine spilled out glittering stories about the national economy and large "civvy" salaries. Promotions in growth companies could be earned rapidly, offering a better deal that the military's slow, mandatory time-in-grade methods.

At the age of twenty-seven I viewed myself as behind my college peers, most of whom were already well entrenched in civilian life, having avoided the military and heading directly into business. *I at least know what I want to do,* I thought. *That will help me get a jump-start.* I had done a lot of thinking about my car-dealer father before leaving the air force; he had been a successful salesman, and I figured I could be, too. *I'll get a job in sales.*

After clearing the base, leaving behind Pat, by then the perky, quick-tempered Scottish/Irish young lady had been my steady girl friend, I arrived at my parents house in Michigan with just five-hundred dollars, a Blaupunkt stereo and a used Volkswagen. From there, I visited my alma mater in East Lansing, only an hour from my parents' home. Walking by hundreds of students younger than I felt strange as I located Michigan State University's job placement bureau.

A bulletin board mounted on a plain gray wall advertised hundreds of jobs all over the United States. One ad stood out: Three letters with eight horizontal lines through each letter printed in bold blue — IBM. The ad conveyed a message of fast growth. And with growth would come promotional opportunities, I figured. Hmm. IBM, I thought and searched my memory for recognition of the company. I've heard of 'em but that's about it. Still, I can apply.

I read the rest of the notice showing IBM recruited on campus that very day and a footnote mentioning that IBM applicants must possess a degree in engineering. *Damn,* I thought. *No business graduates. But, what the hell, the job description looks interesting, so I'll apply anyway. The worst they can do is turn me away.*

Sporting a pair of unshined shoes, and a friend's shiny-blue, ill-fitting suit, I decided to have a go with this vaguely familiar company. Heading for a plain interview room with two chairs and a table, I found one of the chairs occupied by a well-dressed gentleman.

"Hi, I'm Roger Martin," said the friendly man on the other side of the table. Martin, who informed me that he held the job of IBM branch manager in Grand Rapids, was a good four inches taller than I was and wore a three-piece tweed suit of obvious quality. He had his large feet encased in heavy-looking wing-tipped shoes. As he plopped his big boats on the interview table, his casualness pleasantly surprising me, I noticed that on Martin it was the shoes that looked shiny, not the suit. His demeanor impressed me as being comfortable with his station in life, unlike many talented senior officers in the air force, disgruntled with their work and promotional opportunities.

After the normal discourse of job descriptions and a background review, he discussed the subject of hiring engineers. "I usually hire engineers" he said, adding, "a personal preference of mine...," he paused to chuckle, "even though I have an economics degree from the University of Wisconsin." This gave me hope.

"We can teach people business," he continued, "but we can't put brains in their heads. The engineer generally has the brains or he couldn't have graduated."

I could not refute his logic and mentioned that the first year of college I'd been an engineering student, but not why I'd traded that major in for another. (My two-year engineering stint at Michigan State had been a real ball buster.) Martin left an opening by concluding that he did, on occasion, hire business majors such as myself.

"What can you do that you consider unique?" he queried.

I gave it some thought, then smiled. I didn't know if this was what he wanted, but it was unique all right. "I can spell words in descending sequence from the letter closest to 'z' in the alphabet to the letter closest to 'a'. Martin comes out T-R-N-M-I-A."

Since he seemed impressed and encouraged me to continue, I enthusiastically spent a few minutes demonstrating this ability.

Since that trick seemed to be what he wanted, I offered to demonstrate a similar ability. "I can count in my head the total number of letters in ten- to twenty-word sentences." I paused for a moment then proved my point. "The sentence, 'International Business Machines manufactures computers,' has fifty letters in it."

Captivated, Martin tested me with a few words and phrases of his own choosing, thus building an easy rapport as I enthusiastically fielded the rest of his business-related questions. Managing the Officer's Club involved putting out profit and loss statements and understanding the numbers. Martin asked several questions about cost of goods sold and bar control and seemed to appreciate my admittedly-limited knowledge of business.

"You'll hear from me in a few days," he concluded before sending me to a room filled with two dozen other apprehensive people, mostly college-graduating seniors, all there to take IBM's one-hour aptitude test. The test was a requirement for all IBM computer sales job candidates.

"This test is designed to find out how fast you can solve basic problems. Most of you will not finish in the given time," the proctor informed us. When we gained the okay signal, I opened the test booklet and read the instructions.

Well, I'll be damned, I thought. The first part of the test showed various mixed up letters of the alphabet and asked what the next letter logically should be. One had to figure out what pattern emerged and then fill in the missing letter through multiple choice responses. With my alphabet hobby so recently demonstrated, I figured this had to be my lucky day. I loosened my tie, relaxed and dug in, thoroughly enjoying the pained expressions of the others taking the test. I completed every answer on the first section with time to spare.

Two weeks later the offer came from Martin. Ten thousand and five hundred dollars per year as a sales trainee. *Corporate life, whatever that means, here I come!*

In garb that imitated Martin's own, plus a bit too much hair spray on my curly head, I drove lost in thought to my first day of work. I wondered how fast I could make it to the top and visualized what the world might look like from that position.

IBM trainees, my new peer group, impressed me as a collection of fairly intelligent looking people all of whom were packed into a large 'bullpen' with manuals stacked high into tall uneven white columns on plain desks lined up in even rows. Most employees seemed to walk fast and spend a lot of time on the phone. Every male — and men appeared the clear majority — wore a white shirt and shoes like Martin's. Forty-pounders, they were referred as. All their suits were fashioned of dark cloth of various colors, the primary one being blue. Of the twenty or so people in the bullpen, only four were women, also in blue, with white blouses. *I will need to go shopping and buy some "uniforms,"* I figured.

At the front of the bullpen, a select few commanded Spartan offices about the size of ten-foot-by-ten-foot cubicles. Only Martin's office appeared spacious and well furnished. I picked up a pile of manuals from my marketing manager, who gave me sketchy instructions on how to prepare for my first class, a Kansas City-based eleven-week assignment.

After two weeks of reading technical manuals — with little or no comprehension on my part, mind you and becoming acquainted with the other five trainees — all engineers true to Martin's preference, I decided that becoming an IBM computer salesman had been a good choice. The other trainees and I talked about the sales rep's big cars out in the parking lot and the pre-occupation Martin held with his sales force. Clearly the sales jobs held the prestige. Two of the trainees, earmarked to become systems engineers supporting sales reps, had misgivings about their career selections.

I flew to Kansas City and checked into a class-B hotel, later discovering this to be standard fare for new employees.

The next morning, thirty apprehensive trainees huddled in a classroom. Twenty-nine wore white shirts and forty pounders — including me, the thirtieth a female mathematics honors graduate from the University of Tulsa.

The transformation from club operator to computer whiz proved to be a painful one. Eleven weeks of highly technical subject matter fire-hosed with lectures eight hours a day plus a study load of several hours every night and most of each weekend rapidly squelched my enthusiasm for this new career. I wondered why the hell I had joined up but decided to stick it out and force fit myself into this group of brainy people out of pride — certainly not out of job satisfaction.

Day after day and night after late night, I forced myself to focus on the totally foreign material. Bits, bytes, IOCS, DOS, hundreds of words and acronyms with new meaning to memorize. Days ran into weeks and weeks into months while IBM's training never got any easier.

My first air force assignment involved tactical weapons and later I'd served a tour with Strategic Air Command, so I'd been exposed to heavy structure. I'd managed to observe it while not having to endure it, however, because in both cases I managed to get reassigned as manager of the officers' clubs. And now, this IBM environment looked as bad as anything I'd seen in the military. I was concerned about how I would fare with so much structure — especially since my previous tendencies had been to avoid it or go against it.

The instructor made clear how things were to be done within IBM's elite sales force. "Always present your business case with flip charts. Always open the presentation with features, followed by benefits, followed by conclusions."

Kind of like an assembly line, I thought. *No room for creativity in this place. Do it the IBM way.* And most of the trainees learned that way well, never straying from the norm. I imagined that all the IBM sales reps probably did the same.

A puppet factory: To earn a passing grade, trainees had to allow themselves to be tied to IBM's strings of conformity. We were forced to give presentations almost daily, and the criticism of our style came fast and furious. If any student deviated from the instructor's recipe, he was called for it. The way to get through a presentation was to give it IBM's way.

Only in the last week did the pace lighten up. One morning, instead of another dull lecture the class manager announced that we would witness a sales presentation by one of the Kansas City sales hot shots, billed as having made big money the previous year. I thought, *Great, what do these mysterious people, IBM's elite big-money-making high rollers, look like?*

Our hero arrived at the appointed hour dressed in an expensive blue three-piece suit, a white buttoned-down-collared oxford-cloth shirt, a striped tie bulging out of his vest, and wing-tipped shoes mirroring bright reflections from the fluorescent lights. He had lots of hair perfectly combed and lacquered.

The successful peddler's announced objective included speaking with intentional flaws. He would then entertain theories from us peons about the errors he had made. After a half hour of pointing out basic advantages to buying IBM's products, in an aloof and flat manner, I felt encouraged that I could breathe more life into a subject than he had done.

The man then opened his pitch for criticism. "Who heard the intentional flaws in my presentation?" he cockily asked.

One hesitant trainee responded that he sounded glib. Another, more aggressive person, said he had not justified his proposal, another said he didn't apply the benefits to the company.

I had noticed early in his presentation that he used the word "okay" a lot. In my short tenure with IBM, I had realized the company owned hundreds of buzz words and acronyms that most IBMers overused, and which actually limited their vocabulary. "Okay" and "Super" led the list. As this guy grabbed okays like a kid in a candy store, I decided to keep count, believing it not to be an intentional flaw at all, but the man's unconscious adaptation to the boring IBM vocabulary.

I raised my hand next and he called on me. Considering the risk on my part of butting up against the system before speaking, I decided I wasn't willing to just accept things the way they were. I clearly said, "I think your intentional flaw was saying 'okay' sixty-eight times."

His face flushed, and he cleared his throat while throwing an embarrassed glance toward our regular instructor. That flaw hadn't been built in. It had sneaked in on its own.

My comment terminated the critique as well as the question and answer period. Other trainees congratulated me later for winning one back over the hundreds of criticisms we had received while becoming immersed and sometimes lost in the IBM production line.

That night, at the bar, several of us zeroed in on the hellacious odor of the men's room, agreeing that tension and poor diet, accompanied by booze and caffeine, made it so.

Finally, we endured our last day of training. After a final flip chart presentation, we were dismissed with a closing statement: "Final scores are posted in the back of the room. Everybody passed."

I was relieved. Most of my test scores had been down toward the bottom. I got up and walked to the back of the room. Scores were ranked by trainee, high to low, an IBM custom; information was never given without a sorting sequence of some type. The name Beardslee appeared, second from the bottom.

Ten

I WOKE UP TO PAINS IN MY NECK AND SHOULDERS. WHERE AM I? I thought. Slowly the memory of being placed in solitary and taking the drug returned. I'd been in the cell for the night I guessed.

I banged on the door. In a few minutes an attendant snapped a dead bolt, opened my door and told me I could go back to my room. Standing up, my body aching from the hard and lumpy mattress, I gladly obliged.

Back in the ICU, I ignored the other patients, too caught up in my own problems of captivity to bother with them. After three days of impatient existence, fed largely with feelings of injustice, I pinned Heileman down when he showed up for rounds. "What in hell are you going to do about me, Doc?"

The doctor stood there hunched over for a few seconds grinding his jaw muscles like he had chewed on something he didn't like. "I have diagnosed you as a manic depressive."

Unintentionally playing into Heileman's diagnosis, I leapt off the bed like a tiger whose cage had suddenly been opened and glared at him, pent up emotion ready to be unleashed. He moved backward a step with fright in his eyes, then regained his composure, smiled knowingly and shook his head like a parent at an unruly child. My action had only served to convince him all the more that I demonstrated manic tendencies and not the frustrations of involuntary captivity. "I'm not manic and I'm not depressed — even while in this dump — but I am pissed off, and you would be too."

I moved closer, within inches of his white jacket, to confront him. I could see little beads of perspiration forming on his forehead. He stepped backward again. "How can a doctor diagnose anybody in the little time you've spent with me? Come on!"

Heileman made no comment as he looked down at his chart, made a hasty notation, shoved his pen into his jacket's breast pocket, and shuffled out of the room.

Almost every night, now, I was administered a heavy drug. And every night I had vivid dreams, mostly about IBM and how I operated within its tight confines. My memories of kowtowing to IBM's top brass continued to anger and aggravate me to such an extent that I had to find some way to feel powerful and self-confident again. Intimidation served as my remedy for preventing a fall back into a subservient role, thus I incorporated an eye-for-an-eye policy with the hospital staff.

The four-till-midnight ward supervisor's chair usually got filled by the ample derriere of a licensed practical nurse named Peggy; she was not only fair game but an easy target. I worked her over pretty hard about her vocabulary — she'd fallen into the "inappropriate" rut. I'd been less than a big hit with her then, as well as when I found out Florida's minimum regulations called for an RN as opposed to an LPN to be in charge of a shift.

"Therefore, you appear to be inappropriate," I informed her proudly.

She had grumbled something under her breath and glared at me.

The next night I renamed Peggy. The day room patients and Peggy heard from me that her new name was "Brunhilda." Built much along the lines of a fireplug, I figured Peggy would have blended in better with the old Nazi regime as she snapped orders in a loud authoritarian voice. Her recessed, ball-bearing-like eyes squinted with fury as I worked her over. *She'll bear watching,* I warned myself. *She might come after you.*

I also began to take notice of and talk with my fellow patients on the ward. The children in the adjoining ward gained most of my interest, however. Kids hadn't been admitted to the other two asylums; seeing them now on a frequent basis reminded me of my own children safely housed a thousand miles to the North.

After talking to a youngster one evening — despite the fact that I knew it wasn't allowed — and returning with him past the door separating my ward from the one housing children, I yelled out a good natured salutation.

Peggy heard me and couldn't let my salutation pass, "Talking to the children is inappropriate." In a voice that fit better in the German High Command, she ordered me to my room.

I stalked off, slamming my room's flimsy door with enough force to knock a nearby glass exit sign out of its mounting. It shattered on the bare floor.

"RED ALERT ... RED ALERT," the words spewed from the fireplug and into the PA system.

As four attendants raced up to me, I picked the lead guy and dove at him. A perfect tackle. Down he went like a sack of wheat. In moments, however, they had me pinned down and then bodily picked me up and carried me out the back of the ward into the entrance of the solitary confinement wing. This time, I noticed that the hallway housed five small cells with barred doors. Glancing through each of their small windows as I got carried down the hall, I saw that a young teenager with big dilated eyes sat huddled in the corner of one of them.

"What's he in for?" I asked as we continued past his door.

"Drugs," came the curt response as the attendants stopped. They abruptly put me down, and one attendant opened the door to another cell. "Get in." He shoved me into the bleak cubicle.

A few minutes later a nurse came in carrying the expected medications. *They put that kid in a cell like this for doing drugs by choice and then they force them down my throat,* I thought wryly. *Typical.*

The nurse's nameplate said, "Borchek." An unusual name, I

thought, just like the person most responsible for me being in this hell hole — Lucido. "Watcha got, this time, Nurse Borchek?"

She glared at me. "Mr. Beardslee, inappropriate behavior such as you just demonstrated will not be tolerated."

"Right you are, Nurse Borchek, but my question is, what kind of drugs are those?"

"Dalmane," she curtly replied. "It's an anti-anxiety drug."

"I didn't know I was anxious," I replied, "but you would know best, wouldn't you?"

Ignoring my sarcastic comment, Borchek handed me a cup of water with one hand and the pills with the other. I took them from her obediently. *So much for not being subservient,* I concluded. She waited until I doused the pills down with water before leaving.

Feeling their numbing effects in just minutes, I curled up on the board-like mattress thinking about the man with the unusual name who'd so enthusiastically endorsed my trip to Florida.

"Yeah, Max, come on down. Stay in my condo. You're all set," Lucido had said when I called him. I'd carried with me a propensity for seeking out friendships with unusual people, and Anthony J. Lucido proved no exception. *Some friend,* I thought.

Of the four hundred officers on the American Fighter Base located in West Germany over a third remained youthfully single. One hundred wore multi-zippered flight suits flagging their vocation as fighter pilots. In three years, Lucido earned the reputation as the liveliest of the single officers. My name appeared not far down the unpublished list.

Neither Lucido nor I flew the fighters. In my case and his, not being able to pass the eye-chart portion of the physical kept us grounded. As "ground-pounder" bachelors, we turned our attention to one of the few places where recognition could be gained in this fighter-pilot-dominated setting — piling up significant records for getting into mischief, which we mostly accomplished using our pal alcohol as a catalyst.

Lucido delighted in putting people on. He would comfortably

assume several dialogues and impersonations on the free stage offered by Germany's G.I. bars. Of only average build when he arrived on base, he had worked himself up to immense strength. He got me involved in weights as well while trying to convince me that a mixture of vinegar and honey remained the undiscovered health drink to enjoy while lifting steel plates for several hours duration.

Remembering the foul-smelling drink made me aware of the stench in my cell, much like the odor of decaying rodents. Groggy from the pills, I managed to sit up on the threadbare mattress while squinting at the low-wattage bulb hanging from the high ceiling. I remembered my club officer stint in Germany. "Skater" had been my nickname, so earned from confessing to initiating a late-at-night false alarm in the single women teachers' quarters, causing them to flee the building in various states of dress.

The colonel I had confessed to spread the word that I was a helluva guy for taking the rap for some unsavory other lieutenant. He believed I was covering for somebody else! Instead of being in big trouble, I'd skated.

Shifting on my hard mattress, a smile crossed my lips as I thought of the considerable skating I'd done at IBM, particularly in the early years. My thoughts drifted to my second IBM training class where the props got knocked out from under a supposed spit-and-polish presentation. No one had ever found the instigator...

I had studied the prerequisites for my second class much more earnestly than I had for the first, this time determined not to get behind the educational power curve. A manager who worked for Martin took me aside and gave me advice:

"Keep your nose clean, Beardslee. Martin thinks you can sell, but there are limits to his patience."

Flying into Cincinnati I checked into the New Baltimore Hotel. By comparison, the seedy hotel made the Kansas City hotel resemble a palace, IBM's glamour clearly reserved for the more advanced in rank.

All IBM sales training classes began with the election of student officers and, once the votes were tallied, telegrams wired to the branches announced the winners. Gaining a leadership position in training looked good to branch management; they knew trainees who led here would usually lead later on in their careers. Knowing that, and looking to keep on the good side of Martin, I opted to run for president of the class.

Kip Stawski, a former quarterback from Iowa State, acted as my campaign manager. The broad-shouldered naturally athletic Stawski had a face with close-set eyes. The combination earned him the nickname, "Joe Bananas," and he proved an effective campaign manager.

My main competition came from Bruce Ruede, an outgoing *summa cum laude* from the University of Detroit. I got elected president by one vote and Ruede defaulted to the vice president, or "veep" as they were called in IBMese. A good start; the telegram would go to Martin.

About two weeks into the class, we took our first major test. IBM training was intensely competitive, a prelude to the competition higher up the sales ladder — with the illusion being that the better your grade, the better your chances of a good sales territory assignment. Actually, class grades had very little to do with first assignments, but we didn't know that.

The class roster, mounted on a prominent place in our training room, showed every test score, ranked high to low by the cumulative scores. Later, in real sales situations, published branch rosters would show our sales against our quotas, ranked in the same high-to-low sequence. Hiding poor performance in IBM sales, be it during training or in the real world, proved impossible. Some sales people thrived on the recognition scheme and it caused them to work harder, to strive for the success that would keep them on the top of IBM's charts. The majority silently resented the constant competition and openly disclosed ratings, knowing that the bulk of the IBM population escaped the charts and that only a small percentage of the sales force could ever manage constantly to be at or near the top.

When the results came back, Bananas found he had finished dead in the middle of the pack, which was not to his liking. He believed, as most of us did, that living in IBM's middle ground meant an average territory assignment since real opportunities lay reserved for those with the most potential.

That evening while relieving the stress and disappointment in a bar, the well-oiled Bananas sang the blues about being average. We talked it over.

The next day, Stawski arrived in class with a sign hanging from his neck like a restaurant "sandwich" advertisement covering the entire upper half of his body. Neat letters spelled out, "MY NAME IS JOE BANANAS. I AM AVERAGE."

While most of my classmates sought to learn to live in the average category of IBM's ranking scheme, I spent a lot of time trying to figure out the paths to standing out. Did every top IBM exec excel in training? I chose to doubt it, thus precluding myself from failure. Later I discovered the truth, and it wasn't far off from what I had chosen to believe: Within IBM, illusion held more importance than fact. Training scores provided just one rung on the ladder, and a rung easily skipped over if one proved nimble enough.

However, enough illusion existed about grades to keep us all hauling ass. We weren't taking any chances.

Just as the trainees wouldn't have tried so hard to earn good grades if they'd known it wouldn't make much of a difference in their sales assignment, people or businesses rarely would have bought anything from IBM if they knew all the facts about the products. Customers really bought based on a mental picture of what IBM could do for their business. The mental picture acted as the illusion.

As an example, we were all taught to paint a picture of total confidence when discussing the subject of computer installation, showing impressive arrays of computer packages and conversion tools we would provide for the prospect. We did this because we felt if the prospect or customer knew the real workload and disruption we were about to cause, he wouldn't buy from us.

The class seemed split down the middle. About half of us fawned the instructors, while the other half wisecracked and looked for ways to break the tedium. One overbearing ass kisser from the fawning group aggravated us all to no end by acting aloof and continuously extolling the virtues of the West Coast. Ruede, Stawski, and I agreed that our acquaintance from L.A. needed to be whittled down a bit. Strategies rose and fell like nervous pigeons before we settled on one that seemed sure to throw our West Coast colleague. We selected Stawski to make the hit and got on with it.

Every member of the class was required to give a half-hour presentation that counted for about ten percent of the total grade. L.A.'s pitch came due the next day. In the back of the room, an alcove with translucent smoked glass panels presented us with our opportunity. As L.A. began his presentation, Ruede and I sat up front with Stawski intentionally positioned in the back. About five minutes into the presentation, Stawski got up, went into the alcove, dropped his trousers and pressed the cheeks of his ass against the glass. A classic pressed ham.

The three of us anxiously awaited L.A.'s reaction. Our West Coast yuppie, the only one in the room who could see Stawski's hairy fanny, lost his composure. With his eyes straining and mouth unnaturally held open, he completely lost his train of thought. By the time the rest of the class began craning their necks to the rear, Stawski had stepped away. Success.

◆◆◆

An unoiled hinge signaling the opening of my cell door brought me out of my drug-induced mental wandering. Nurse Borchek had arrived with dinner. Plastic silverware, paper plate, meat loaf, and Jell-O. *Not exactly the Hilton.*

I put the untouched tray in the corner, returned to the mattress, lay down facing the wall, and dozed off.

Eleven

I HADN'T BEEN ASLEEP FOR MORE THAN A FEW MINUTES WHEN THE DOOR'S squeaking woke me again. Peggy walked in accompanied by two guys in white. Expecting to be left alone for the night, she surprised me with her visit. Further, I didn't like what she held in her hand — a needle.

"What the hell is in the needle, Brunie?"

"More Dalmane, your favorite tranquilizer," she said with sickening sweetness.

"Are you proud of the fact that you can order people around and blast their fannies full of drugs?" Not to be deterred, Peggy quickly replied, "Pull down your pants and roll over, or we'll do it for you!" I complied once again, despite my desire not to be continually drugged. I seemed to have no choice but to be subservient. It didn't feel good, nor did the shot. The fireplug jammed the needle in with eye-watering force and left without another word. There would have been no use in fighting though, and it felt all the more demeaning to be held down while someone yanked off my pants and stuck a needle in my butt.

Lying on the mattress all night, I slept fitfully. Even the added tranquilizer could not subdue my anger. *How could I be in such a place? Screw these people! I'm not just going to sit idly by, full of drugs, and take this shit! Dogs are treated better,* I thought.

The night passed slowly, and my only indication that morning had arrived came from the arrival of an attendant, who unlocked my door and motioned to me that it was all right to leave. Walking down the hall to my room, I noted the clock hanging in the open day room. Ten-o'clock. I'd been in solitary for sixteen hours, far beyond my normal ten or so.

Drinking coffee in the ward's dingy day room, a cluttered area with a battered TV set always blaring, I watched a schizophrenic try to convince others he was the son of Howard Hughes. Trying to shake the hangover from the last night's shot, I sat slouched on a couch until an attendant told me my wife was on the phone. I walked to the hall phone where incoming calls came in.

"Hi, Pat!"

"Hi, Max. I just called to tell you I'll be coming down on February twenty-seventh for your court hearing."

The hearing, required by Florida law to determine my mental health, was just two days away. I felt encouraged by the news of her visit.

"Good! Bring me a few clothes and say hello to the kids for me," I said excitedly.

The night before the hearing, Pat visited me at the hospital. Looking good, nevertheless she acted restrained, unwilling to open up to me. I could feel the invisible wall between us, especially when I hugged her and she responded dutifully but without real warmth or feeling.

She updated me on the three boys. "They are all doing well in school. They don't seem to be too upset about where you are. I told them you are getting some rest in a hospital."

Wanting Pat's support, I attempted to show her mental normalcy by talking to her in even tones about being locked up in the place.

"Do you know that Tony never once hinted at the action he ultimately took?"

"He talked to me, Max, and said he thought you were still mentally ill." There it was again.

"Well, I'm *not*. Sitting here, talking to me, do *you* think I am?"

Pat looked away, not answering. I put my hands on either side of her head and turned it to face mine directly. "Pat, will you support me in court tomorrow?" She didn't reply immediately, and I just looked at her fixedly waiting. I dared not hope.

She wouldn't return my stare. "I don't know, Max, you look and sound okay tonight, but you have done some weird things lately."

"Okay," I replied, letting my hands drop away from her face. "I guess I have, at least to some people. But think about it, will you? I'm telling you I have never felt better."

Pat nodded her head again, but this time in a less convincing manner.

I decided to change the subject. "How much money do we have left?"

"We're down to our last forty thousand." That meant we had gone through about seventy thousand dollars since I left IBM; the sale of our last home at a big loss had a lot to do with the erosion.

"What's going on with my Open Door?" I queried her.

"IBM has little to offer, other than that they are aware of your status. I've asked for assistance on your medical bills — you know Prudential has dumped you — and the guy, Kaufman, he says they'll give me an answer."

As Pat got up to leave, I said, "I need you to talk about this conversation. To tell the court I sounded okay."

"I'll think about it," she said as she walked out the door.

I listened to her heels getting fainter in the distance and thought about our relationship. Getting tossed into another asylum added fuel to her desire for a divorce, as did Dr. Rosenberg's prognosis that I would possess menial capabilities only upon my release. I appreciated her coming down to Florida and checking in with me despite all that. How many spouses talking divorce would do that?

Despite Pat's promise to think about giving me some support in my plea for freedom, I knew little chance existed of getting released unless I got off my dead ass and cooked up something special. I'd be fighting long odds. I needed to go into court looking and sounding like a businessman with some kind of plan. And I needed to be clear headed, almost impossible from the drugs I ingested.

Luckily, I'd been able to fake taking my drug dosage that night, usually two sleeping pills, and I was able to stay awake into the wee hours of the morning working on my strategy in the day room. A graduate assistant in the math department of a local college assisted me. She was also in for manic-depression and we'd gotten to know each other fairly well. I chose plain-old straightforward logic as the thrust of my planned message. I reached all the way back to the tenth grade for basic mathematics, putting together theorems, hypotheses, arguments, conclusions, and recommendations as my friend insured that my definitions fit. Each recommendation had the same ending: immediate dismissal from the happy-faced funny farm.

Pleased with my night's work, I neatly trimmed my two-week-old beard and put on a blue suit Pat had brought down for the occasion. As I left the ward, leather briefcase in hand, an attendant told me I could pass for a shrink. In the hearing room sat my wife, the obligatory court-appointed attorney, Doctor Heileman, and Judge Studley, an elderly gentleman with a hearing aid who would be presiding. To Judge Studley's left sat a court reporter.

The room appeared stark, absent of tables. The judge commanded a large oak-finished desk, while the rest of us sat on plain folding chairs.

Judge Studley warmed things up with a pointed direction to my wife. "Do you believe your husband can represent himself today?"

Looking at me, then away, she replied, "No, your honor … I don't think so." Then she dropped her head and didn't look up again for several minutes.

Studley then asked me the same question "What about you, Mr. Beardslee. Do you believe you can speak for yourself?"

"Yes sir," I quickly responded. "I'm ready."

"Well, then, I'll allow it. Now here's the procedure."

Heileman would testify first and then the judge would hear from me; from there he would render a decision. Heileman, eyes looking at the floor or out the window, brushed dandruff off his plaid sport jacket as he gave a fifteen-minute monotone diagnosing me as manic-depressive.

Finally, came my turn. "Your honor, how much time do I have for rebuttal?"

"Six minutes."

Six minutes for a sanity hearing was all I could have! With the court reporter pounding away, I played defense attorney. Reading from a notepad, I began, "Your Honor, members of the hearing," I glared at Pat and my lawyer, "I am Max Beardslee and will represent myself today.

"I call your attention to the scraggles on my face. I am trying to grow a beard, as opposed to any lackadaisical personal hygiene contributed to a mental illness."

Warm the judge up. Let him know that I was aware of how I looked, I thought, *and let him see I know how to conduct myself "appropriately."*

"This hearing is to determine if I am mentally ill. There are, as you know, various degrees of mental illness. I will spend no time on these degrees. My arguments will substantiate and prove that I have full mental faculties. I will further substantiate the use of these faculties since December of 1980."

This judge is going to buy the blue suit and preparation. Go for it! I cleared my throat and continued.

"I would like to now introduce the definition of the word, marionette."

Quickly, Judge Studley responded, "Young man, I am well aware of what the word means."

"Uh ... yes, your honor, but just for the record." Holding aloft a Webster's borrowed from the asylum I entered into the minutes that "marionette" meant the object of control of others. "And, your honor, that's all that's wrong with me. Others control me."

From there, I hurried through all the arguments I had, namely the preparation I'd jointly accomplished with Amrose in laying out my case against IBM, and the rationale behind my trip to Florida.

"I'd fought a battle, your honor. All I wanted was a little R 'n' R, not confinement."

At the end of each of them I gave the same summary. "Conclusion: I possess full mental faculties. Recommendation: Immediate release from the hospital."

As I read my last argument, I began formulating an idea on how to close. Done with the written material I folded up my notes.

The judge had seemed to pay attention; *Maybe I had a shot. A creative closing and I may have it. Time to try the idea I'd been formulating the past few minutes.*

"I have one final point to make, your honor."

The old judge glanced at his watch and said, "You have one minute."

"Your honor, I notice you wear a hearing aid … Can you hear me all right?"

Studley tightened up his jaw muscles, shifted in his chair, and in a baritone voice responded with, "Mr. Beardslee. I can hear you just fine."

"Exactly my point, your honor. You may be able to hear a fly crawl around on your desk with the technology of your hearing aid, but society will always suspect you cannot 'hear well' because you wear one." The judge moved forward in his chair and, peering at me through his granny glasses, looked less than happy.

"A couple of months back, I was mentally ill, about as sick as a person could be. No question about that. But, now that I'm recovered, society views my previous mental illness like your hearing aid. They don't think I 'hear well,' so to speak."

The judge gripped his high-backed chair hard, looking like he wanted to reach across the desk and belt me. The fly analysis had upset him. "Young man, you're out of time," he said dismissing the hearing with a firm pronouncement: "Mr. Beardslee will be confined in the mental institution for an indefinite period of time. Next hearing in ninety days." The gavel fell.

I slammed my briefcase shut and walked out of the room with

the policemen at either side. I was disappointed about the decision, but I felt good about what I'd tried to get accomplished.

Out in the hall, Dr. Heileman gave me an offhand compliment. "The judge gave you more time to testify than I have ever seen before. And, I found your remarks lucid and logical."

Fat lot of good that does me.

The cops drove me back past the familiar smiling face sign. Pat was waiting for me there, and we moved into the visitors' room for a leisurely and long conversation about the kids, money and our future. Our marriage had unraveled for all the obvious reasons. I had been out of work for several months, we were almost out of money, Pat had to cope alone with three boys suffering the stress of having a dad lingering in a mental health facility.

When I'd pursued the Open Door with IBM, Pat had supported it, but the brush-off treatment I'd received subsequent to the Armonk ultimatum had damaged her confidence in having anything come of it — and her confidence in me.

My opinion still differed from hers. I knew I had them dead nuts. To me, it was a question of when, not if. To Pat, it was all over.

"Pat, I'll need a lawyer to get me out of here, somebody better than that kid I had today. What about it, will you help me get one?"

Her response, slow to come, didn't take long to hear. "You think you are so damn smart, get one yourself." Then she smiled at me like she used to when we would joke with each other, and said, "You did a reasonably credible job in court, but I'm not going to get you a lawyer. If these doctors think you are well, they'll let you out."

She showed me the invoice the hospital staff had given her amounting to several thousand dollars.

"Jesus, this dump is expensive," I exclaimed. I glanced at some of the details. One of those was a charge from the head psychiatrist of the hospital, a man I'd never met. "That prick billed me one-hundred dollars for a visitation he never made!"

The perfect medical scam. In a hospital full of mental patients, many of them pretty well cooked, a psychiatrist could charge away at will. What proof could a relative provide if challenging the bill? Patient testimony wouldn't mean squat. I could just imagine the scene, the lawyer asking, "Did Dr. Trotsky see you fifteen different times in February?" and the patient's response, "Yunnh, garrunh, expez."

With my wife watching, I crossed out the charge.

"Max, IBM will probably pay the bill."

"Maybe, honey, but I want them getting their money's worth."

Pat once again brought up the subject of divorce. "Speaking of lawyers Max, I've talked to a lady ... who, uh, specializes in divorce."

I said nothing. I knew that divorce could only be headed off if IBM came around. Besides, I wasn't so sure anymore that it ought to be headed off. I loved Pat, but our differences had become apparent through the IBM ordeal.

The crisis had pointed out some incompatibilities in how we viewed life; crises often magnify the heretofore unnoticed. She wanted a stable husband, one who worked for a large company and enjoyed security. I would never again want to be part of a big corporation.

"I may file, but I want us to stay friendly, and I'll certainly hang in there until the boys and I know you're okay."

By now I had resigned myself to the idea of a divorce and I knew I could handle it. I didn't challenge her, especially since I was not sure I wanted to. "Do what you gotta do, honey. I'm probably not gonna be to your liking anymore. I'm different, now ... hope I stay this way. But IBM owes us both, and when I'm out of this dump, I'll get the job done."

I got up from the table, walked over to Pat, who rose to meet me, and gave her a hug. "Have a safe flight back," I said. This time she hugged me back and as we pulled away two sets of sad eyes met. Even though divorce appeared probable and she'd irritated me with her non-support when I got incarcerated and in court, Pat had performed an admirable job, all in all — especially with the kids.

Twelve

THE NEXT DAY, BORED WITH MY OWN SHENANIGANS AND WITH NOTHING much to help me while away the hours, I focused on why I took the IBM firing so hard. The whole episode haunted me. I needed to understand what had happened to me and why. Had I been predisposed to have a mental breakdown or was there some mysterious grip IBM had on me that I didn't fully understand?

I knew I'd have a chance to take a closer look during a counseling session I had scheduled with a lady therapist named Ms. Habel. I'd met the short mid-forties brunette briefly, and the other patients raved about her. My first impression of her had revealed a person who seemed to show interest in her work — an exception at the fort.

"How do you want to proceed?" I asked.

She offered a ready reply. "Just talk about how it was when you worked at IBM. Probably somewhere close to the beginning. From there we'll see how it goes."

"Okay. We'll start in Traverse City. As soon as my first-year training was over, that's where IBM sent me."

"Fine," she replied, "I've vacationed there, before, a charming little city."

◆◆◆

Max Beardslee

When I returned from training, Martin informed me that he had an opportunity for me. A sales rep' had transferred from a small town up North; I could replace him. Traverse City, a town of about twenty five thousand people, sat nestled in the northwest corner of Michigan's lower peninsula on Lake Michigan. Several nearby towns held populations from a few hundred upward to ten thousand. Surrounding hilly terrain made for a beautiful winter recreation area, and in the summer sandy soil produced an abundance of cherries, adding a diversion to sailing and golf, the area's prime draw in warm weather. A flourishing business district rounded out the town with light and diversified industry.

Replacing a salesman headed for so-called greener pastures in a bigger territory, I arrived in Traverse City. Green as a spring apple but with some solid leads my predecessor had given me and an aggressive, "I-can-do-it" attitude, I immersed myself into the job. Having started after mid-year, the sales plan rules said I needed to accomplish half a year's quota in the four remaining months to qualify for IBM's One Hundred Percent Club, an annual recognition event for sales people who had made all of their year's objectives.

My first-year quota included getting four businesses to install IBM computer equipment that previously had none. By selling two new accounts, a dairy and a small hospital, I made the half-year objectives in those four months, thus allowing me to attend our Club event the upcoming spring.

Living in a lakeside cottage rented from a customer, I enjoyed this vintage year by calling on existing customers, attempting to make new ones, and most of all, trying to figure out this complex job. One comforting thought carried me: as little as I knew about computers and their advantages, I knew more than most customers.

In February of 1969, facing my first full year of quota, I attended a two-week manufacturing and distribution class in Chicago. Manufacturing and distribution industries contributed almost seventy percent of IBM's revenue. IBM systems engineers, who knew how to program and set up computer installations, worked side by side with the sales reps', who needed to fully understand what manufacturers and distributors should do with their IBM equipment. Ergo, this education would help me make a living, and I looked forward to it.

The class enjoyed a set-up around a fictitious operation, called "The International Milk Bucket Company." To humorously dramatize the management problems and challenges of a daily manufacturing operation, instructors role-played various management positions as well as personalities ranging from gay to alcoholic to General Patton-like styles. This creative way of presenting material allowed us all to begin understanding the complexities of a manufacturing operation and how to sell to different types of people. By far, I graded this training the best I'd ever gotten from IBM; the only one that, in my opinion, avoided the structured assembly-line method.

At the end of this class, all students formed pairs and made sales moves on the International Milk Bucket Company. After six months at IBM, I no longer tried anything out of the ordinary with my classroom presentations. Creativity seemed something the company's executives didn't want or even appreciate; I had gotten no rewards for any of my attempts to do things my own way, whether that way be better than IBM's or not. I had already decided to save my "creative genius" for the territory where nobody watched my techniques. On the other hand, my partner had not as yet figured that out and my attempts to warn him went unheeded.

The day before our final presentation we heard a lecture on creative closing techniques. Taking it to heart, my partner deftly produced a large tube of Colgate toothpaste from his pocket while talking about the profit squeeze occurring in American manufacturing. Continuing to drone on about IBM's remedy to the problem, he started squeezing the stuff into the instructor's ashtray. The IBMer's eyes studied the gooey mess while a look of disdain slowly spread over his face. I managed to contain myself for about five seconds before I burst out into laughter. The instructor in turn squeezed our grade down a few notches.

Off and running in 1969, I attended my first One Hundred Percent Club in April — the reward for making the numbers in 1968. About sixty percent of the marketing force made this all-important objective in a given year. The forty percent that did not received intangible punishment in the form of increased tension created by the knowledge that missing quota two years in a row could mean dismissal. With base salaries averaging only eight thousand dollars, they also suffered from lack of income. New sales reps like me could expect to make twenty thousand dollars per year or more in the late sixties by accomplishing annual sales objectives.

My first One Hundred Percent Club, IBM always held these in a sun-belt city, took me to Los Angeles. Thousands of IBMers of all shapes and sizes from all over the United States gathered together there to celebrate a united accomplishment; they had all met or exceeded their previous year's annual sales quotas.

The three-day event, filled with plenty of leisure time, had a major impact on the IBM peddler, particularly the first-time visitor. IBM executives presented special awards to the top sales reps' in the nation. Like the old television experiments subliminally flashing soft drink logos thousands of times over normal footage, an underlying motive of IBM's One Hundred Percent Club was to show average achievers the recognition and money given to the top marketeers, thus motivating them to run for the top. Positive brainwashing.

IBM's top executives, all former peddlers themselves, attended these functions. After observing the brass and formulating opinions about what it took relative to style, appearance and career accomplishments to make that elite group, no question existed in my mind; I wanted to strive for that goal.

The top guys looked, acted and sounded the way I had imagined. They spoke in confident voices while sporting expensive, well-pressed suits, crisp starched white shirts and heavy black wing tips. Outwardly, they appeared to like and enjoy their jobs, animatedly mingling with the mass of us, always appearing positive, and alert. Even during social activities, however, they always wore their game faces. An IBM exec stayed on duty twenty-four hours a day.

On the way back from the West Coast, I joined my free-spirited buddy, Jack Orlop, for an introduction to the bright lights and action of Las Vegas. Without much effort on my part, I managed to lose all of my money within twenty-four hours. Orlop won a few thousand.

The top salesman in Grand Rapids for the year, Orlop smacked of charm that attracted customers like teenagers to a phone. While much of the sales force clung to a rigid set of standards, Orlop proved an exception, wearing light-colored suits instead of dark and quite often taking a customer to lunch, having a highball or two and then returning to work. The IBM standard said if you did have a drink, even with a customer, you were to go home for the rest of the day. Not Orlop. I envied him as I succumbed, albeit slowly, to IBM's way of life while he never did.

At eleven in the morning, dead broke after my gambling spree, he invited me for breakfast to the Sands Hotel, where he was staying.

"Jack, your wife is here with you, isn't she?" I queried, suddenly remembering that he hadn't mentioned her, let alone called her to tell her he was still out gambling.

"That's right. So what?"

"Well, you've been out all night. I'm not sure I want to share the heat with you."

"Naah. Don't you worry about it," he said and waved me off. "She's used to my IBM late-night shenanigans. Anyway, I'll make sure she doesn't stay mad long, if she gets mad at all." He grinned and grabbed me by the arm.

As we entered the room, Orlop's wife glared at him predictably. He had left the room some twenty-six hours before saying he was going down the hall for a bucket of ice. She wasn't pleased that he showed up a day later, never having let her know where he was, and without even one cube.

Before she could say a word, Jack wisely threw all of his cash in the air and, with a wide grin, informed her, "Honey, the money is all yours."

Thinking of getting married myself, I wondered at that time how much most IBM wives endured. *Probably less than Orlop's,* I conclud-ed. *And, he made a lot of money.* Jack told me had made thirty-two thousand that year at IBM, while making only eight thousand as a teacher three years before. Maybe Mrs. Orlop enjoyed the money.

Orlop's wife managed a grin and seemed ready to forgive him as I discreetly headed for the door.

Upon returning to Traverse City, at the ripe old age of twenty-nine I decided to take the big plunge and proposed marriage to Patricia Dorsey. Pat and I had been dating since my arrival in Loring Air Force Base, Maine four years prior and had since main-tained a long-distance relationship. She had visited me once for a week during training, and we called each other once a week on average during the year that I had been with IBM.

After our honeymoon we rented a one-story, lime-green, cement-block house near downtown Traverse City. Charming, no. Humble, yes. Next came IBM's world-renowned two-week sales school where the last strings would be attached to this IBM sales rep' and the full assembly completed.

Anticipating little trouble at sales school, I eagerly packed myself off to Baltimore, Maryland. I figured that if I could make quota the previous year, I must know my stuff. Plus, I was off to a good start for the year. I had a surprise coming.

On our first day, each student gave a privately video-taped sales call to an instructor. My simulated call attempted to initiate some interest in a small-town banker; I completed it thinking I had done reasonably well. The instructor then asked me how long I had been with IBM. I told him over a year and said with no lit-tle pride in my voice, "I made one-hundred-fifty percent of my objectives last year."

The instructor couldn't believe it. "You did," he responded

incredulously. When he played back the videotape, I couldn't believe I had either.

My eyes wandered to the floor rather than being focused on my perspective customer; I picked my nose and fidgeted; and I asked too few questions about the customer's needs as I amateurishly tried to small-town charm the instructor this way and that. With absolutely no substance to my sales call, I appeared to be the main character in a B-rated movie.

That instructor did me more good than anybody in my early career by brutally tearing into me for thirty minutes, including "You didn't qualify the prospect. You didn't understand what his needs were. You didn't take the call to any conclusion, such as what the next step oughta be. This call was, frankly, horrible."

My skin burned. Working my butt off every day for the next two weeks, toward the end of the training I got better at it.

Sales school's daily assignment called for the class to be broken up into groups of five, giving individual presentations within the group; the class and the instructor would then critique the individual results. Group feedback allowed one of the few times a grunt trainee could do his or her own criticizing, thus this fleeting moment of power caused occasional abuses. One lady, in particular, caught the brunt of it in this case. As her peers picked her into small pieces, I could see her face redden over the gushing stream of criticism. Feeling sorry for her, I kept my mouth shut. Looking embarrassed, she hastily got up and walked out of the room in tears, leaving a puddle on her chair. One had to be thick skinned to handle sales training.

Three of our class of thirty could not handle the pressure and criticism, departing for their regular IBM homes to await a fate that could go one of three ways: re-assignment into the systems engineering ranks, a second try at sales school at another time or dismissal.

The day of graduation, the president of IBM's Data Processing Division, Jack "Buck" Rodgers, addressed our group. Buck, a tall,

Canadian Royal Mountie look-alike usually clad in charcoal gray pin-striped suits, that year wore the cloak of flat revenue from the recession of 1969. Like the rest of us, he also had a quota that required taking in more revenue than the year before, and he wasn't making it. Rodgers gave the class a brief "State of the Union" message before entertaining questions.

"What new products are we going to announce in the short term?" came first.

Rodgers quickly admonished the questioner. "IBM never pre-announces its products. In fact, it is a violation of company policy to do so."

Another new rep' tried the same question another way. "Mr. Rodgers, I'm well aware that you cannot disclose unannounced products, but I wonder if you would comment from your perspective about IBM product-line shortcomings?"

Buck liked the question. After asking the questioner's name and branch office location, an illusion that he might honor the attendee with a call to his branch manager, he described the need for a new lower-cost punched-card system with disk file growth capabilities.

A hard glare followed one fellow's question, another's, creatively asked, obtained the answer. The product got announced within the next fifteen days as the IBM System 3. With graduation behind me and this experience firmly rooted in my memory, I renewed my goal of making it into the ranks of IBM's top brass. Back to the patch.

In the spring of 1969, with an army of federal lawyers getting ready to launch an antitrust action against the company, IBM "unbundled," or started pricing its services separately. Since its inception, IBM had offered all of its services under one price: hardware, software, education, programming support, and systems engineering services. This was referred to by the Fed's lawyers as "bundled" pricing. By pricing hardware, software and services separately, IBM created a picture of offering the competition a better chance, thereby slowing down the Fed's for a while.

Mass trauma swept through many of IBM's largest customers as they realized they had to pay forty dollars per hour for a systems engineer who most knew only earned from fifteen to twenty-five thousand dollars per year. IBM's major accounts stayed awake nights trying to figure out how many millions of extra dollars they might have to spend.

The sales and marketing areas felt this change dramatically, since most major customers wanted to digest this fundamental change in IBM's pricing before moving ahead with any new purchase commitments. Computer installation decisions were delayed at every level, wreaking havoc on the commission-dependent sales force and throwing plant shipment schedules into an unpredictable mess. In the midst of this, frantic phone calling on the part of IBMers occurred at every level.

One call that IBMers talked about on the tie line circuit — IBM's internal telephone network — went to an IBM veep, Jack Guth, in Chicago. After his umpteenth phone call about unbundling, Guth, known for his salty, direct manner, casually responded: "EGBAR."

"EGBAR?!" exclaimed the exasperated caller, "What the hell is EGBAR?"

Guth calmly replied, "Everything's Gonna Be All Right."

Unbundling made little impact on me, a guy who made his living from smaller accounts. The System 3, not unbundling, held the big news for me. Two models were announced, a punched-card shuffler and a more expensive disk-storage model to be available in 1970. The System 3s initially rented for one to five thousand dollars or could be purchased for about forty times their monthly rent. In that era, only those companies believing the computer would serve for a long time or have a decent market value at the end would buy one. In general, less than ten percent of IBM's customers purchased their computers during the '60s. The System 3 matched the needs of the first-time user as well as being a natural for upgrading IBM's slow and antiquated card-read/punch accounting systems.

Within two weeks of announcement, I had sold eight System 3s, making my 1969 One Hundred Percent Club objectives a sure bet. The year held up, and I made a good living: twenty-five thousand dollars, which was reflected in my home and lifestyle.

Pat also greeted me with wonderful news; her face glowing with pride, she said, "Honey, I'm pregnant." The Beardslee clan would expand. I gave Pat a big hug and popped a bottle of wine.

During the 1970 recession, IBM endured a sluggish first quarter performance. Panic permeated much of the sales force as the market eroded and competitors sold disk and tape drives to IBM's larger accounts. During this period, many of IBM's customers returned equipment that had been replaced by the competition's. Ergo, the commission plan showed the sales rep's at less than zero: more leased equipment had been removed than sold. The reps' owed IBM money. Future sales would only get them back to even. Salespeople started leaving Big Blue in alarming numbers while personnel grunts stayed busy trying to stem the tide.

In answer to the company's poor start and with the intention of giving the sales force special training for rough times, IBM hurriedly constructed a forum, called "Marketing in the '70s." Every peddler with any large account (defined by having eight hundred thousand dollars or more in equipment installed or on order) received divisional orders to attend. Because I managed one large account, Martin sent me.

IBM conducted these classes concurrently in its three executive educational facilities. I went to the one in Endicott, New York, the first home of IBM. Each location had a normal plant facility, a golf course, clubhouse, and tennis courts for plant personnel and retired employees. They also had hotel-like accommodations for customers coming from all over the world to attend executive educational offerings. However, the Endicott facility offered only small Spartan rooms, and a lobby with ample quantities of *Fortune*, *Forbes* and the *Wall Street Journal* lent a clearly conservative image.

About thirty peddlers made up my class, for the most part all of whom could be dubbed seasoned sales reps exhibiting foul moods developed from enduring competitive erosions back in the field. We endured the training non-stop, twelve to fourteen hours a day, before returning to our featureless hotel.

I'd never taken kindly to intensive mass education and this venture proved no exception.

During the last couple of days, we broke up into teams of four and were given business usage and financial justification assignments for IBM's slow selling System 7. The System 7 had been a unique design for IBM. In addition to digital, or number-deciphering, capabilities offered by standard computers, it offered a series of ports allowing it to be connected to many kinds of instruments. The System 7 had been designed, in analog terms, to accept input-measuring highs and lows of instruments or chemical contents of liquids and solids.

The Digital Equipment Corporation (DEC) had grossed hundreds of millions of dollars from their computers both standard and analog input; IBM wanted a share of that market. None of us knew at the time that the System 7 would eventually parallel Ford's Edsel.

There wasn't enough time for each team to present its System 7 assignment, so to ensure completion of lab work by everyone, our education tutor, a Harvard graduate who bored us every day with stories about "Hahvahd," announced a lottery. Each team drew a number; the team with the losing number would then make a presentation.

When our spent team met at the hotel that night grumbling over the assignment, I pointed out the low odds — one in eight — our team faced of actually being picked and advocated running the risk by ignoring the lab work and going out on the town. "Come on guys, the risk is worth the reward."

"Okay, Beardslee, but if we get selected, you're making the presentation."

"Agreed."

The next morning, my blood-shot eyes watched "Hahvahd" spin

the dial. Round it spun and stopped on four. *Oh, no ... our team,* I thought. *Shit.* My teammates sweated it out, wondering what, if anything, I would do. I wondered the same thing.

It took ten seconds to walk from my seat to the blackboard in the front of the room — the exact amount of time which I had to put a presentation together. My booze-sodden mind fought for something, anything.

"Ladies and gentlemen, the IBM System 7 will revolutionize the measurement of whiskey consumption as we know it in the free world."

That woke 'em up. Me too. *What next?* I wondered.

I blathered on. "As you may know, several thousand retail bar prospects exist in the United States alone, but rather than the standard method of interfacing the computer with inverted bottles of liquor and measuring consumption, I've got a better idea." Picking up a piece of chalk, I attacked the blackboard with a complex series of boxes, arrows, and logic symbols; the class continued to pay attention.

Toward the bottom, I drew a crude room with a door, and on the door I scribbled the word, "MEN."

In this room, I scribbled a square and labeled it "URINAL."

Amidst growing laughter from the audience, the chalk continued to scratch a series of zig zag lines — commonly called "thunderbolts" in the computer world — connecting the urinal to a System 7. Only partially successful in maintaining a straight face, I proceeded to show how with the analog "port" the System 7 could measure the alcoholic content of liquid hitting the urinal and with the digital portion of the computer could measure the number of shots consumed. When I had finished my design, the blackboard resembled that of my Japanese economics professor back at Michigan State.

"Lads, with this invaluable system, which we call IBOWACS, meaning 'IBM Body Waste Bar Control System,' we can draw precise conclusions as to how much money should be in the till."

Everybody but Hahvahd roared, delighted at this diversion from IBM's fire-hose method of education.

"Are there any questions?" I asked innocently.

My classmates, who saw my query as a way to avoid another boring day with Hahvahd, asked several. "Will it factor for the portion of pee splashed over the side?"

"Yeah, it does that."

"Can it distinguish brand names?"

"Well, uh, it's pretty accurate on that except for the wines. It mixes up Boone's Farm with *Château Neuf du Pape.*"

After answering more bizarre questions, I concluded the discussion and sat down to applause and laughter.

The instructor had, for the first time since I knew him, nothing to say. That afternoon, I made a trip to see the education center manager. He made up for Hahvahd's silence with a crisp message about the seriousness of the class. "You're all here because IBM is not doing well. We're trying to help you turn it around. And while I certainly admire a little humor once in a while, you're overdoing it. Do I make myself clear?"

"Yes, you do. But can I offer one piece of advice?" I asked riskily.

"What's that?" he snapped back.

"That you put a little creativity into your education, like they did with the International Milk Bucket class in Chicago. Then we wouldn't get so damned bored. Stick your head in class. Half of us are having a helluva time staying awake." I got up and left.

◆◆◆

The calm Ms. Habel couldn't help but chuckle over that story. "Let's take a coffee break, Mr. Beardslee, and then continue."

◆◆◆

As part of IBM's internal education classes, normally managers from IBM would be invited in to discuss topics outside the prime content of the class. I found these informal sessions provided a way to find out what went on in the other divisions outside IBM's myopic world of sales and marketing. On the last day, a scholarly looking man approaching retirement and introduced as one of the best historians in the company, entertained our group of thirty frazzled IBM students.

Wearing two hearing aids and bent over with age, this old gent used a powerful voice and twinkling eyes to hold us totally enraptured with stories of IBM in the forties and fifties when all the company's peddlers wore hats and sang songs at sales meetings.

He also talked about the classic computer punched card, which always comes with explicit instructions not to fold, spindle or mutilate. These cards sport tiny numbers printed in rows — a row of twelves at the top, then elevens, followed by zero through nine, with the nines on the bottom. Instructions for placing the cards into a card reader always are given as twelve edge or nine edge first, face down. This great old gent concluded his presentation with the wish that when he passed, he be buried in Endicott, "nine edge first ... face down."

We loved his unhurried, salty dialogue; he proved to be one of the few speakers I ever heard at IBM who spoke from the heart. And he closed with a bang. When asked whether Tom Watson Jr., son of the founder and current chairman of the board ever visited Endicott, the home of IBM, the old gent slowly replied "No ... his yacht won't fit on the Susquehanna."

With class dismissed, we left quickly and loudly, glad to be rid of Endicott and its bare-bone facilities but happy to know how to focus on contending with sales in the '70s.

By that spring, I had been selling long enough to be convinced several advantages existed for those fortunate enough to be marketing an expensive technical product in America. For example, only a few sales people had the training and sales skills to perform, making for a reasonably secure career; demand exceeded supply. Also, the commissions could be large. I felt, however, that one of the most beneficial aspects of being a salesman came from involvement with customer executives, which proved to be a requirement, when selling a system to any first-time user.

Most of my customers owned their own companies. Conversing with them and analyzing their strengths and weaknesses through a reasonably in-depth survey of their company occupied much of my time and gave me insight to small business owners and several kinds of companies.

Mike Horstman, who owned Traverse Bay Marine (TBM), a thriving snowmobile wholesaler, typified the high-income business owners I came to know. In the summer of '70, almost three years into my IBM career, I had TBM earmarked as a sales target. Having already sold them two computer installations justified by their spectacular growth, I had made plans to sell them a third.

TBM's first computer system, the IBM 1130, offered me a major challenge. This early entry-level disk system originally had been designed to do problem-solving work. Later, it was expanded for commercial use, such as billing, payroll and inventory control. To make this first sale, I had to convince Horstman at length that computers did not make errors. "However, if information went in incorrectly, it would come out the same way. GIGO: Garbage In, Garbage Out."

Horstman occupied the plushest office I had yet seen in Traverse City, decorated with stone walls and custom leather furniture. Allegedly, a double-barreled twelve-gauge shotgun pointed at the entrance to his office hung underneath his massive mahogany desk. Having already learned that illusion was more important than fact, I always passed through that doorway a little more quickly.

During several hours with the doubting owner, I explained parity checking circuitry and other functions, summarizing that in no way would mistakes like a wrong part number or a wrong price be entered on a file or printed on an invoice if it had been input correctly.

Several months after installation of the first computer, which had been working to satisfaction, Horstman called me at home. "Max, this goddamn computer is going crazy. Can you get down here right away?"

When I arrived at Horstman's office — walking quickly through his office doorway — he picked up off his shiny desk several invoices and immediately began using them as evidence of the computer's lack of capabilities.

"Look at this crap," he ordered, banging his fist on his enormous desk. "This customer, right goddamned here, ordered part number 8910, which we have loaded into the computer as an Arctic Cat Snowmobile Model C for thirty-two hundred bucks. See that?" he asked while looking at me and jabbing his finger at the invoice. His voice resounded against the stone walls of his plus office as he continued to speak and gesture angrily.

"Now, look here, goddammit."

I did. On the invoice with 8910 was the price and description of a pair of nine-dollar snowmobile goggles. To further complicate matters, the computer had reduced the on-hand inventory of snowmobiles by one, but not the goggles.

Horstman proved conclusively to me in a matter of a few minutes that, while the computer printed the part number the dealer ordered, thus proving it had been input correctly, the description and price that it printed back out made no sense at all.

"What about all this GIGO shit, Max? Huh?"

I couldn't figure it out, but I knew I needed to before Horstman exploded. The proverbial light went off in my head, and I asked, "Didn't you have a routine maintenance check done on the system recently?"

"Yeah, a couple of days ago. Why?"

Ah, ha, I thought. *The problem can probably be traced to the questionable technical aptitude of our customer engineer.*

I should have immediately suspected his involvement, because this particular customer engineer held a rare attribute: He could walk into an account enjoying perfect stability and destroy it in a few hours.

"Can I use your phone?" I asked.

Horstman handed it to me without a word. Hurriedly, I called the best IBM repairman I knew, Bob Cronover, and asked him if the other customer engineer could possibly have done anything to cause the foul-up. "Yeah, he could have," he replied. "I'll be there in an hour."

Cronover, a large and quiet man exuding so much confidence that one felt it when he entered a room, cracked the problem in a couple of hours. The inept customer engineer had misaligned the 1130's read-write heads so that information read into its processor got written back on its disk exactly ten cylinders away from where it should have been. The net effect had us billing out wrong items at wrong prices, destroying inventory control and erroneously updating accounts receivable information.

Horstman called me into his office upon notification the problems had been cleared up. "I like the way you got on top of my problem, staying late until it was complete. And you relate well to my people. Ever consider leaving IBM? I could use a sales guy."

After discussing the opportunity with my wife, I called Horstman and declined. I had worked so hard to master my trade I wanted to see how good I could get. Leaving then, I would never have the chance to know. That was the last time I would ever consider leaving; in later years as rapid promotions took over and my income picked up, I began to believe I would be with IBM until I retired.

While I could say that my continued work with IBM became the snowmobile company's loss, it also became another company's misfortune. Not long after I turned down Horstman's offer, I took on a challenge with Chef Pierre, a young dynamic fast-growing maker of fresh frozen pies and desserts. In the fall of '70, IBM's sales of the System 7 — of the liquor-measurement fame — fell far below forecast. Sales reps' like me did not buy the company's marketing spiel as word filtered down that the System 7 represented a nightmare to install. Even the most basic installation aids remained unavailable. Just to interpret programming instructions, one had to read them in hexadecimal, a computer numbering language clumsy and time consuming to interpret.

From missing revenue forecasts and incurring cost overruns, IBM's development people had prematurely released these turkeys hoping field personnel and customers would somehow get them installed — somewhat akin to a general ordering his troops to battle with brand new rifles but their bullet clips only half full.

IBM headquarters' marketing staff personnel, who were on salary as opposed to field sales people who were on commission, noted the dismal performance of the product and drew on the old IBM motivational standby — money. They put one hell of a bonus plan together making the System 7 commission dollars two to three times greater than any other IBM product of comparable price. Their solution reflected their attitude that "If money will fix it, then, by God, we'll fix it!" Even from my still lowly position on the totem pole, I noted that the company was funny about its usage of money in other ways. While other companies picked up the kinds of expenses incurred to run first-class events — like I would later see Fillmore put on, IBM approached such things with a stingy attitude.

Chef Pierre, recognized as the fastest growing company in northern Michigan, was owned by two large Greeks. Obviously the company represented no namesake. Chef Pierre made thousands upon thousands of frozen fruit pies every day. During twenty-four hours and three shifts a day, hundreds of white-gowned employees rolled, sifted, mixed, boxed, and stored these delicious desserts. As pies came off the assembly lines, they were boxed, labeled and put onto pallets. From there, forklift operators drove the pallets to a staging area. The storage process concluded when a different set of drivers operating small cranes, hoisted the pallets into one of several hundred locations within a warehouse bigger than a four-story-high football field and kept at a constant twelve degrees below zero.

I surveyed this mammoth freezer and noted that, although the storage methods got the job done, inefficiencies existed that might be handled with automation. *Damn,* I thought, *if I could find a use for one of these System 7s in the freezer, I could make a few thousand dollars. But I'll need some help.*

I called David Crandall, the branch System 7 specialist, and asked him to join me in this venture. "Look, Crandall, I think we can sell one fast here."

A few meetings with the Greeks convinced them that a System 7 could act as a Super Clerk figuring out where to put all the pies randomly by first-available slot closest to the front and efficiently getting them out again for shipment all over the United States. The big deal came from the random storage. Not having to reserve space for each label type promised big savings by increasing the total storage capacity of the freezer.

"Okay, we'll buy one," said the president, Pete Dimitri, frustrated from his futile attempts to increase warehouse efficiency by other means. "But put a rush on it. Our new freezer opens in a few weeks."

We didn't tell Dimitri that the IBM systems engineer who wrote all the software, which we proudly called "Dynamic Warehouse Allocation," had cast some doubt on the reliability of his programs by quitting IBM before they could be tested. In addition, we didn't tell him that to install the System 7 in record time we would have to borrow components from IBM education centers and stick them in the Chef Pierre warehouse without a system performance test. The unavailability of new components was an augury of doom, but in our haste and greed we set the system up in this manner anyway.

With the Greeks home in bed, during the first night of operation Chef Pierre's vice president of production, Bud Gerow, and I watched the System 7 pick pies like an octopus on a shrimp run. Super Clerk helped us load up seven semi's in the course of eight hours, a Chef Pierre record. However, it also failed to update all of its records properly — a nasty little trick none of us yet realized had been played upon us.

Returning home the next morning, I had breakfast with my wife, too excited about this unique design to sleep. "Honey, those Greeks are going to love me ... Super Clerk really knows how to pump out the pies."

Pat, comfortable in our newly-built ranch-style home, asked, "Oh yeah? What's so special about 'pumping out pies'?"

I proudly taught her the pie business. "Chef Pierre can now randomly store cherry right next to apple, which is right next to blueberry. Before, they had to reserve separate space for each product. Now they can mash them together, freeing up additional space. And it can always find the oldest pies first, rotating the inventory as it goes." I sketched on a napkin the way Super Clerk worked.

"Plus, it always picks a slot near the front of the warehouse, if available, saving the poor-assed crane operators who work at twelve degrees below zero a helluva lot of time."

After breakfast I drove back to Chef Pierre figuring I might be invited into the personable Greeks' executive offices for lunch. Donning a fleece-lined parka, I walked toward the freezer and approached the large double doors. I pressed the switch giving me access. As the twenty-foot-high doors broke the seal, instant heat loss pulling frigid, frosty air out into the main warehouse, my eyes met with a totally unexpected scene.

Instead of the efficient and organized flow of pies, a dozen weary warehousemen stared glassy-eyed at a mountain of pies stacked all over the floor and aisles of the freezer entranceway, thus snuffing out the usual orderly flow. Forklift drivers with full pallets from production sat queued up about a dozen deep waiting to add to the mountain. Hard-hatted foremen barked signals into their walkie-talkies sending all available personnel to the warehouse. As I surveyed this scene, I thought, *Even the Three Stooges could not have improved on this chaos.*

Spotting Bud Gerow leaning against a wall and stubbing out a cigarette into a nearly-empty cup of coffee, I walked toward him tentatively, my apprehension increasing with each step. Black stubble protruded from his face, his shoulders slouched forward.

Gerow, who was our key Super Clerk benefactor, possessed experience spanning a dozen years in production. A hardened veteran of assembly-line foul ups, I had heard that he rarely cursed or got overly upset. So when he said, "Beardslee, the goddamn System 7 is a piece of shit! Fix it, or I'll set it out on the curb," I knew I had trouble on my hands.

Gerow, through bloodshot eyes and tightly rippling jaw muscles, continued the saga. "Hey, we've sent semi-drivers over to the Holiday Inn. It'll be days if not weeks before we dig through this mountain of crap and load them up."

Donning a parka, an executive luncheon with the Greeks a distant memory, I joined the warehouse ranks; Super Clerk knew all the tricks. I watched a warehouseman place a card asking for raspberry pies in the reader . The computer promptly responded by clicking out a brief message on the console typewriter: "Not Available in Warehouse."

Gerow, peering over Super Clerk, looked even more frustrated. "Goddamnit, we just put some in there two days ago. Where in hell are they?"

A production man asked Super Clerk for a storage location to put away a pallet of pineapple turnovers in the half-full warehouse. With electronic speed, our System 7 once again responded through its typewriter: "No Warehouse Space Available."

A crane operator then asked for a pallet of cherry. Immediately, Super Clerk typed out the aisle, row and bin location of the cherry pie. Glad to get away from Gerow's glare, I rode with a loader to the designated area.

"For Chrissakes, there's no cherry here, just apple," said the crane operator through the ski mask covering his face "What the hell are you guys at IBM trying to do to us? I burrowed myself deeper into my mackinaw, ignoring the man but wondering the same thing.

Because the pies were, by design, stored randomly to maximize available space, finding a flavor and size of pie now meant wandering around the frozen warehouse and looking for it, which is exactly what Crandall and I did for the next twelve days and nights. I went home once in a while just to catch a few hours of sleep. The freezer gobbled up all waking moments except for the dreaded occasions when we were summoned to the Greek's offices — not for lunch, nor, for that matter, for much talking, but for listening ... listening very intently.

Dimitri rarely found occasion for ill temper, but when he did, he would squeeze a handball to its original factory compression causing the cords of his massive forearms to pop out. He did so frequently during our forced appearances while voicing displeasure. "Hey, I've managed growth compounded at seventy percent a year. My people have torn down entire assembly lines and replaced them with new ones. And over all that time, where fast growth can cause foul ups, this IBM computer you sold me takes the cake, no goddamned pun intended."

Traverse City's tiny airport stayed busy with incoming flights of lab technicians, programmers and field managers all sent from IBM to help solve the problem. Because the normal debugging software that would find problems in a few hours for other IBM computers had never been developed by IBM's lab for the System 7, our technical types ran "core dumps." These showed the contents of the computer memory in several pages of funny looking numbers written in the awkward hexadecimal numbering system, while trying to figure out which files had not been updated and why. On the twelfth day, the programs became operable, and on the thirteenth day Super Clerk got the job done. On the fourteenth day, I slept for twenty-four hours.

In the aftermath, we discovered additional foul-ups. For example, a semi-truck arriving in New Orleans had left Traverse City in reasonably good shape. However, the pies it carried arrived in what the frozen food industry terms a 'hot' condition. They had not been sufficiently frozen before leaving, because Super Clerk failed to figure out how long they had been in the freezer and we had no manual back-up procedures to prevent such an event from occurring. So, strawberry shortcake soup was served as the product of the System 7 ineptitude.

My experience highlighted the System 7 installation efforts going on all over the United States. Who took the burden of the toll? The good old loyal IBM customer who didn't know about over-advertised, under-developed IBM projects. They bore the financial burden of making System 7 work or, as was often the case, threw them out after huge expenditures of dollars and manpower trying unsuccessfully to make them do what they were purported to do.

The head marionette — in this case the System 7 product manager who lobbied for extra commission money — pulled the money string, thus making thousands of us sales people dance.

During a phone call a few days later, I bitched to Crandall about the lousy headquarters support for the System 7. I was looking for agreement for my view, but he gave me his very different version of the big picture instead. "Hey, what would you do if you were in headquarters? IBM has bet big bucks on the development of the system, but the support isn't there. The company can't just throw in the towel. The field people have got to make it happen, have got to make the system sell and work. If you ran the company, you wouldn't have it any other way."

I adamantly disagreed. "David, now, really ... whose money fixed it? Chef Pierre's money and other IBM customers money in similar situations did the developmental work on the software."

"Well ... that is true," he conceded.

In fact, Chef Pierre's program eventually got used by fifty odd frozen-food distributors on the East Coast. A brochure called "Dynamic Warehouse Allocation" was produced by IBM's marketing team to tell prospective customers all about Super Clerk and the amazing feats it performed in the warehouse.

◆◆◆

Ms. Habel finished scribbling and stood up. Five feet tall, tops. "Okay Mr. Beardslee, this was good, but let's call it a day."

"Is this helping you understand why I blew a fuse, Ms. Habel?" I responded.

"Oh yeah, we'll figure this out," she concluded.

Thirteen

August 1971

I HAD MADE IBM'S HUNDRED PERCENT CLUB FOR THE THIRD YEAR IN A row. During a sales meeting Martin announced that I was the first of twenty plus sales reps to make their annual quota. The tall leader in his conservative tweed suit called me to the front of the room and handed me a plaque plus a lapel pin recognizing the occasion. A proud moment.

Sales management looked for those who could make things happen, and they were starting to place me on the plus side of the ledger. Conversely, from Martin's sales force of about twenty, twelve new faces had joined in the past three years, replacing those, like Orlop, who had left. With half the sales force having less tenure than I, I became the veteran.

The next month I had an even prouder moment when Pat gave birth to our first son. John Maxwell Beardslee made his debut to the world weighing in at seven pounds and eight ounces.

I was a very proud papa.

I managed to finish the IBM sales year at about one hundred and fifty percent of quota with money in the bank and a savings account started for John. In February of 1972, my branch manager, Martin, resigned from IBM, taking a job with Steelcase, Inc. as director of Data Processing. Most of the sales reps expressed surprise about Martin's move. Becoming a branch manager — one of the most prominent posts within IBM's sales division – posted odds of at least one hundred to one, and here was a guy who had beaten these odds giving up what he had worked so hard to win.

Does the grass always look greener on the other side no matter what the view? I wondered That question needed an answer, especially since I definitely had my sights pinned on beating the odds as well.

The new leader came from Chicago. In his late thirties, Joe Schmidt sprung out of a group of budding executives fondly nicknamed the "German High Command" because of the high percentage of Deutsche last names on their staff, headed by Jack Guth of EGBAR fame. While watching Schmidt accept the baton at the branch announcement meeting, I formulated a plan to get promoted. Having made up my mind to stay in the company, and with my commitment all the greater since the snowmobile wholesaler job offer, I needed a bigger challenge. Making it to the Schmidt/Martin level looked like a long shot, but marking time in Traverse City would be like having no odds at all.

Schmidt made a big hit with me during his inaugural speech. He hauled out a picture of a mule and said, "Some people behave this way standing in the middle of the road and refusing to move." He then held up a racehorse and said, "Some people can really run. I'm anxious to find out who can run in this operation."

I definitely wanted to show him my speed and my track record. I figured from the racehorse analogy that Schmidt would offer free reign to his people, but in the months to come most of us found him over-controlling in nature and openly grumbled about his "tougher-than-Martin" style.

I, however, was not put off. Giving the racehorse stuff continued consideration, in July of 1972, I paid a sales call on Schmidt. "I want to earn a promotion and try to become a marketing manager, Joe."

The call went well; Schmidt, an athletic looking man of average height, always a hanky in his suit coat and expensive monogrammed white shirts on his back, understood that I was determined to be moved up and offered me a way to do so. A troublesome but high-potential corporation named Kysor Industries formed the basis of his offer. One of their divisions, Dexter Lock, appeared ready to throw IBM out and go with the competition. "Think you can straighten out the mess in Grand Rapids for me?"

I nodded my head, not really knowing if I could but not about to turn down an assignment Schmidt viewed as critical.

Kysor was comprised of six manufacturing divisions scattered throughout the Midwest and Southeast. I would continue to cover the corporation headquarters near Traverse City, in Cadillac, Michigan, as well as picking up responsibility for Dexter Lock, located in Grand Rapids and the challenge for my ticket out.

Schmidt knew that the people at Dexter Lock, the nation's third largest door knob and lock set manufacturer, didn't like their current IBM sales rep, and Control Data Corporation (CDC) had started sales activity that could lead to IBM being booted out and CDC being invited in. Dexter Lock had come further along in computer usage than any other Kysor division, but that only represented marginal success. If the most advanced of Kysor's divisions went to the competition, the rest could well follow suit.

"Beardslee, you take the Lock Company over and get it and the other divisions in bed with IBM. Do that, and you're gone," said Schmidt.

"I can do it, Joe. Talk to you soon," I said as I headed out the door. I didn't feel the confidence I exuded. I didn't know Dexter at all, and Schmidt implied IBM was way behind in the race with CDC.

An amicable, easy-going Canadian named Duncan Stilson occupied the corporate controller's chair at Kysor's corporate headquarters and also had responsibility for corporate approval of divisional data processing recommendations. Kysor's divisions, such as Dexter Lock, had to go through him before they could order any computer-related items.

I viewed Stilson as having the swing vote. If the divisional presidents remained passive about choice of computer vendors, he would rule the day. As managers of profit centers, however, if these presidents could be persuaded to get aggressive and take a stand on the issue, they would make the decision. Since Stilson had become entrenched in the CDC camp, I needed to make sure these other execs cared about what happened.

Stilson would normally have been an IBM marketing rep's dream — aggressive, motivated and naive about data processing. With those characteristics, a Stilson type would sign up with IBM purely out of fear of failure with the less-known "Brand X." But not Stilson. Over the years he had built up a distrust of IBM's ability to deliver what it said it could and a belief that the company's products were overpriced. He also felt that IBM salesmen had taken advantage of him. Different IBM reps in different towns, myself included, had given him and his divisions a lot of hot air about IBM's software offerings to the manufacturing industry and subjected him, personally, to several boring slide presentations.

Quite a few of Kysor's divisions used some combination of IBM equipment. When Stilson measured the real benefits of computer usage in these divisions, he found that three of them had paid IBM hefty sums of money and gotten little return on their money other than achieving payroll and invoicing automation.

On more than one occasion when I had made a sales call to his office, he had raised his clipped English-accented voice and laid on me his favorite question: "Max, how could these divisions be into computer use for several years and barely have automated payroll?"

A tough question followed by a lame answer. "With your help, Duncan, we need to lay out goals and timetables to move them ahead. It can be done."

My strategy for beating IBM's competition usually meant outhustling them. Simply load many hours in the account interviewing employees, understanding the kinds of computer applications they needed and talking with the decision makers — making me and IBM extremely visible in the process. I started arriving at the doorknob and lock set manufacturer around eight in the morning, which was no mean trick as it required maneuvering one hundred and forty miles of bad roads from Traverse City to Grand Rapids.

In its infancy but an obvious 'comer, IBM's disk version of the System 3 offered my best bet to beat CDC. The System 3's display station capability could bring the manufacturing people and the computer closer together.

I had an idea that the best way to head off CDC would be by doing a demonstration for Dexter Lock in Rochester, Minnesota, where the IBM facility that made System 3s was located. I decided to use a "show-don't-tell" strategy, actually allowing the Dexter execs to see their company's own data displayed on terminals with keyboards connected to the computer. This setup, called workstations by most people, had been dubbed in monosyllabic grunts as "tubes" by people in the industry. Seeing actual Dexter Lock work accomplished easily on the tubes using IBM-provided software might force Dexter Lock out of the bore-assed dullness the IBM slides had elicited and into a feeling of excitement and anticipation about what IBM might be able to do for the company.

My Traverse City-based systems engineer and I worked in Rochester for a couple of weeks getting Dexter Lock's data to run through an early version of the rebellious IBM software. I then convinced Schmidt that IBM should charter a flight to Rochester for the demonstration and split the bill with Dexter Lock. Thoroughly first-class, I thought. From Schmidt's personal interest in the account, he signed off without question.

I then approached Dexter Lock's president, Don Kolkman, with my invitation. He agreed and made the decision not to invite Stilson but to bring four other top Dexter Lock execs along. My marketing manager joined us on the IBM side. Out to Rochester we flew.

The demonstration with Dexter Lock's records went well. Kolkman asked the right questions about using the system to make knobs and locks and let out a long, "aahh," as he peered into the tube and saw parts and engineering data from his company light up on the display.

"I believe you're starting to understand the needs of Dexter Lock. A first-rate demo. Very interesting," he commented.

I thought to myself, *Beardslee, you done good.*

Seven people occupied the return charter that cold winter night — the top five Dexter Lock execs, my boss and myself. In high spirits from our accomplishment, the account actually seemed to be winnable, we broke out the booze. Dexter Lock's vice president of administration, second only to Kolkman in Dexter's decision process, enjoyed a dozen highballs thousands of feet over the frigid waters of Lake Michigan. We landed in Grand Rapids three hours after the normal dinner hour. All but one of the Dexter Lock execs turned up the collars on their heavy coats and headed for the parking lot. The vice president of administration wanted to eat.

"Howshabout a nishe lobschter before we call it a night?"

My marketing manager and I drove our inebriated decision maker to Sayfee's, the only restaurant in Grand Rapids serving live lobsters at the time. Entering the lobby we hung up our snow-covered coats and waited for the Maître de. Tired of waiting, Dexter's veep weaved his way over to the lobster tank and peered down at his potential dinner. Without warning, he stuck his suitcoated arm into the tank up to his elbow, grabbed a huge three pounder and hauled it out, taking plenty of saltwater and sea weed with it.

Thrusting the snapping crustacean in front of a dumbfounded Maître de, he declared, "I want thish one."

After a few more unneeded drinks, the veep's feast arrived. Our waitress carefully pulled a bib over his sleeping face. He tasted little of his handpicked dinner.

Wining and dining customer execs served as an important part of the business. Getting an executive away from his place of business afforded opportunities to align oneself with that person more closely and often to gain a perspective later used to help close a sale. Such meetings usually went much better than that with my lobster-eating friend, who slept through most of it. Kolkman fast became an easy executive to see. He seemed to enjoy having me around and discussing matters with me, not all of it business. During one of these meetings the fortyish executive told me he liked gambling. "Card games, dice, horse races, you name it." A few days after our Rochester trip, I gave my final presentation and proposal to Kolkman. Schmidt came along and, as was his habit, arrived late. When he walked into Kolkman's palatial office, Schmidt found the two of us on our hands and knees, whooping it up while shooting craps against the Dutchman's credenza.

"The point is four. Come on, Little Joe," shouted Kolkman, not even looking up when Schmidt entered the room.

Schmidt, an avid crapshooter himself, stopped short of joining us. Later, back at his office he told me, "I don't think much of your written proposal, but you sure as hell have account control."

My tall, craps-shooting president sent a letter up the line to Kysor's corporate headquarters recommending IBM over CDC. A tight-jawed Stilson, recovering from this unexpected turn of events, called me into his office and gave me an off-hand compliment. "Beardslee, you're a tough sonovabitch to whip. Personally, I think CDC offers a far superior solution than IBM, but you have convinced Dexter Lock otherwise. I'm frustrated but will not block their decision." We shook hands, two adversaries at odds but with mutual respect.

The next day, I paid a call on Schmidt with Kysor's order in my hand. "Great job, Beardslee," he said. "You'll be gone in thirty days." And I was.

◆◆◆

July 1973

Stephen Dennis Beardslee came screaming into the world — a family of four — quota met.

And a family functioning fairly well. Although Pat did not enjoy the long hours and trips away from home my job called for, by and large we enjoyed life in Traverse City, having a large circle of friends from the professional community of the city. When the promotion opportunity materialized, Pat supported it.

After spending the last five years as the only IBM computer salesman in a small northern Michigan town, that fall I started a new job in Detroit. Like every other sales rep at IBM, being promoted meant a huge change in responsibility and lifestyle as we joined IBM's unglamorous world of staff. Now out of the direct firing line represented by commissioned sales reps, we moved to a regional or headquarters location, in my case regional, to serve as salaried specialists in a given area.

When moving into IBM's staff area, some people got assigned to one kind of computer, others to a specific customer, augmenting the field team. Still others got assigned to support a certain set of software programs for a particular industry. No matter what the assignment, staff personnel could no longer earn membership into the One Hundred Percent Club, since they were out of the sales game, rather we were in these jobs hoping to earn assignments back to the field as managers. To get from point A to point C, one had to go through the misery of point B.

My assignment was to the Great Lakes Region regional headquarters in Detroit. The big three automotive accounts of General Motors, Ford and Chrysler justified much of its existence; the regional manager held an important job, responsible for fourteen branches and approximately one billion dollars in annual revenue.

About fifty of us, occupying two full floors of a suburban office building, reported through others to the regional manager, handling specific assignments to assist him in running his billion-dollar empire. All of us had been successful sales representatives or systems engineers, a prerequisite for getting promoted to a staff job.

In this job, we no longer had to fight the daily quota battle of making IBM's revenue numbers. While this relieved us of some daily stress, it also meant that we were no longer paid sales commissions.

Pat and I found a nice two-story house in a suburb north of Detroit. I observed that IBM hadn't cornered the market as masters of illusion; street namers were pretty good at it, too. Sturbridge Road, Wood Brook subdivision, Farmington Hills. As I surveyed our new domain, I noted no bridge, no woods, no brooks, no farms, and not one semblance of a hill. But living in the big city proved to be exciting, the neighborhood was friendly and every weekend somebody hosted a backyard party.

In 1973, software revenue accounted for only two percent of IBM's multi-billion-dollar computer-related revenue. Software's bottom line profits, however, totaled eight percent, or four times the sales number. IBM's high profits in software came from the simple fact that the packages could be duplicated for pennies and distributed for a few dollars, much like the booming Microsoft Windows market today. With my newly created staff job, IBM wanted to interest the branches in the software side of the business. IBM could sell more of this profitable commodity if the branches could get their salespeople to generate customer interest. And, if the customers became interested in the software, they would buy hardware with which to use it, commonly called "drag".

My job encompassed three areas: First, discover interesting software programs written by customers, called installed-user programs (IUPs); and then negotiate a contract with the customer for its sale to others. Second, encourage already-overworked IBM systems engineers in branch field offices to develop software they felt had potential for several customers, referred to as "Field Developed Programs (FDPs). Lastly, promote these two types of software, plus "Program Products" — IBM headquarters-developed programs — to branch sales people. The latter category enjoyed recognition through their abbreviated name, "Pee Pees."

The Pee Pees caused my first visit to White Plains, New York, "Grand Poobah" country and headquarters for the Data Processing

Division, one of only two selling divisions IBM then had in the United States. The other, much smaller one called the Office Products Division, located in New Jersey, sold non-computer products, such as typewriters and copiers.

One of the largest staffs ever assembled outside the military worked in White Plains; several thousand IBMers occupied acres of buildings. As I followed yellow arrows painted on the floor toward my four-digit cubicle destination, I could feel my normally high energy drop and depression creep into my usually "up" mindset. I thought of the thousands of people working inside these dinky little work areas constructed like boxes with no windows, just four plain white walls to occupy their view. The cube dwellers' unhurried pace differed from the fast-moving branch and staff people back in Detroit. With such a drab, energy-draining atmosphere I could understand why. I appeared fashionably dressed, not one of my more noted characteristics, compared to the dated suits and ties of the "cubies."

Arriving at my assigned cube, I talked to its dweller about the planned timing of a software announcement I'd be responsible for managing in the region before we broke for lunch. Thousands of IBMers all looking alike in their dark suits, white shirts and striped ties jammed the elevators and escalators for a trip to a football field-sized cafeteria. Spiffed up forty pounders, many adorned with metal heel savers, caused our lunchtime jaunt to resemble an old fashioned clogger hoe down.

Mystified, I turned to my host. "What's with all the heel savers? Don't they pay enough to cover new shoes out here?"

My host, a former sales rep from Des Moines, replied, "Just a fad. Some veep wears them."

Amazing, I thought, *how most IBMers emulated their superiors in dress and mannerisms; even something as trivial as heel savers caught on. Here in particular, emulating the leadership appears to be the main concern.*

"Christ," I said to my cohort, "how can you handle this after Des Moines, Iowa?"

"Not well, pal, not well. The job is boring. I stay busy because I want to get out of here and back to the field. But for thousands of these guys and gals this is their life. This is all they want to do. And, most of 'em, hey, I've been here eight months, they ain't killing themselves." I noted the unhurried pace, myself, peering into crammed break rooms. My host then shared a story with me about a highly paid woman on staff who had been waiting for six months to make a presentation to IBM's CEO on banking trends. That had been her only assignment. With nothing to do but wait for the appointment, already cancelled a few times, she told my host she was looking for a job outside IBM.

There seemed to be two worlds out there, I thought, *the field and regional staff where the workload remained large and matters were handled at a fairly brisk pace, and this other world at divisional headquarters where the workload stayed small and things moved slowly. Well, that I could do without.*

Finishing my business, I left White Plains knowing I could never handle that kind of environment. A sterile place running at an unhurried pace, with most people so specialized in what they did for a living I couldn't believe they would have much value to any company other than IBM.

Back at the Detroit region, I wrote and mailed several letters to branch managers and their subordinates, marketing managers. I watched my letters go unerringly unanswered until one of my new peers, Fred Falbo, took me aside and explained the facts. "Nobody gives a damn about software, Beardslee, it's too small of a deal. My advice is do what you can to exist, and then ask for a transfer to some other area."

Falbo also hinted at the need for visibility when wanting to earn promotions and advancement in the company. "Some branch manager has to notice you and believe you are the best guy out of the fifty or so of us up here. And he has to have a job opening as well. Tough odds. This software stuff ain't gonna get you noticed, because the branch manager has bigger problems to contend with, like selling computers."

I listened to what he said, knowing that the highly-coveted next

I listened to what he said, knowing that the highly-coveted next rung up the ladder, the job of a marketing manager, could be achieved only by being noticed in a positive way. *My current job might keep me skulking in the shadows if I'm not careful,* I thought.

Falbo, assigned to staff a few months ahead of me, had drawn the Chrysler account, IBM's third-largest customer in the Detroit district. Only GM and Ford paid bigger bills to IBM. Because of Chrysler's importance, Falbo's job held more interest from sales leaders than mine, therefore, more visibility.

Following my letter with a dozen phone calls to the branches brought Falbo's point home. "Max Beardslee, here... Yeah, the new kid doing software. I'm anxious to appear at your next branch meeting to explain how IBM software can help your sales reps make quota."

Their answers were always similar, saying, in effect, "I'm more interested in how IBM is going to make its tape drives competitive with the other guys. I'll let you know if I can work you in."

A clear message filtered through: "Fuck off."

As I plodded through the first three months of this job, I had to agree with Falbo — software lacked pizzazz. I decided to heed his advice, biding my time while looking for some new job opportunity within IBM.

◆◆◆

January 1974

That winter, IBM created the marketing arm of the General Systems Division (GSD). GSD spun away from the Data Processing Division (DPD) with an announced objective of providing better service to existing and potential customers with smaller system needs. The new line-up featured DPD selling the big- and medium-sized mainframe computers and GSD pushing the small- and medium-sized mini computers, while the Office Products Division (OPD), functioning for twenty years with no significant change in mode of operation, continued to sell typewriters and word processors.

IBM's newest marketing organization promised more action; I wanted in. However, when GSD's first roster appeared, transferring several thousand field and staff people from DPD to GSD, I was disappointed to find my name missing.

Amidst all of the people shuffling, Ted Sanders, a former marketing manager from Chicago, became my new boss. Sanders, well groomed and openly friendly, headed up all industry-oriented marketing programs as well as software in my DPD region. His new environment, however, quickly grew tense. The System 370, so widely acclaimed as IBM's system of the future, was only selling well in their larger versions. The big players, like General Motors, had traded in their large 360s, but the thousands of customers using smaller 360s were holding back. This presented DPD's — therefore Sanders' — biggest headache and prevented us from reaching revenue objectives for the intermediate systems. After attending his umpteenth briefing about why the small and intermediate Series 370 computers fell flat, Sanders called me into his office. "Beardslee, you're pretty creative. Think about a way to sell the small System 370 and report back to me in two weeks."

Sanders personified "Theory Y" management, the type of boss who believes you should "give the horse a track and find out if he can run." In other words, give him free reign. Most managers in IBM would have qualified the assignment with a dozen parameters reflecting their own viewpoint — "Theory X" management.

The System 370 had the computer memory and file capacity to accomplish several tasks at once — called multi-programming, but it did not have much Pee Pee software available to guide the hardware. The only companies capable of using multi-programming to capacity enjoyed staffs of twenty programmers or more. Those thousands of System 360 users with small staffs, targeted by IBM to convert to the System 370, could not touch it.

IBM's execs argued the sluggish sales problem based on the interests of the group they represented. Finance wanted to cut production to reduce capital expenditures. Manufacturing, not wanting to miss its production revenue target, opted to add more unwanted features; the sales force couldn't cope with what they had. Staff Marketing, sitting on the hot seat for advocating the 370's design, needed to meet its revenue forecast. Its people busily mailed more half-baked slide sets out to the burdened field to explain the benefits of a System 370. Meanwhile, sales branch managers, missing quotas and suffering lower personal incomes as a result, asked for increased sales force commissions for selling the system to customers — another "money-will-fix-anything" strategy.

My own analysis, derived from conversations with sales reps from all over the nine-state region, quickly showed that IBM's customers ran scared from the perceived sophistication of the small and mid-sized 370. All of the new buzz-words that accompanied it onto the market implied complexity — virtual this, direct access that, data sets, paging, longitudinal redundancy checks — which trade publications, like *Computer World,* overstated. Computer managers cringed at the thought of the conversion nightmare that surely must be embedded in this new system. A lot of companies like Kysor existed out there, and these customers felt that making the new features of the 370 work, mainly the communicating terminals or tubes, would be another busted play. They clearly saw the need for tubes but felt unsure of their ability to install and use them — unlike millions of people today who take for granted their ability to enter and display data through PCs or workstations.

What I also felt in my guts was that a frightened IBM sales force also delayed customer acceptance. *That's a new twist,* I thought; *IBM salesmen and systems engineers actually feared the System 370 as much as prospective customers. If customer staffs fell short in mustering a conversion effort, then both sets of people could kiss their home life goodbye; they'd be the ones hassling with the conversion for as many hours as it took to get the system up and running.*

The field force's fear lay subconscious but caused shallow sales calls, people only going through the motions. Salespeople found it hard to articulate the increased productivity and savings possible with the system since they themselves didn't believe these aspects existed or were readily possible to achieve. Thus, sales reps rarely discussed what customers wanted to hear: that conversion to tubes could be made.

Customer perception posed the last hurdle to the System 370's success. In these medium-sized businesses a cut below the Fortune 500, many of the execs responsible for the managers of the computer department had already been burned from previous failed conversions and had experienced the delays in actual bene- fits that the IBM sales force assured them would be there. A grow- ing number of Duncan Stilson-types doubted IBM's one-time unmatched integrity. Overall perception concluded that few com- puter projects got done on time or met their goals of increased management information and productivity within the organization. "Why should this new IBM system be any different?" they asked.

While I mulled over Sander's assignment, I read about a set of Pee Pees that simply could grab data out of a computer and display it on a tube. The tube operator could also conveniently send the data back to the computer. *Hell,* I figured, *this might do it.* Excited about the possibilities, I huddled up with Ralph Pennington, a tal- ented systems engineer on staff, and explained my ideas to him in detail, starting with the new software products we had to work with.

"Ralph, the picture I'm getting is clear as hell. Now, I gotta try it on you."

"Go ahead," the graying systems engineer, noted for his ability to manage complex projects, said.

"The sales force is overwhelmed by all the technology incorpo- rated in the 370 product line. It's like going to a beach resort. The place is stacked with good looking babes, but there's so many of 'em a guy doesn't know where to start, so he never starts at all."

Pennington grinned at my analogy.

"And the customer is equally confused. He doesn't know how to relate. The only reason he believes there's probably some goodness there is because IBM says so. And that's beginning to get old. He doesn't totally believe what IBM says anymore.

"What if we could come up with a way to show the customer and the IBMer the benefits of the system. A hands-on demo with real live customer data. The customer will see something exciting for a change, like his own records displayed on a tube as opposed to a four-hundred page printout that makes him want to puke. Got it so far?"

Pennington nodded for me to continue.

"Well, just getting him excited is half the battle. Now that the customer sees for the first time a use for the new technology, he has to be convinced his people can make it happen. Install it and make it work. Right now he might believe an IBM data center can make it work, but what about his people?"

I moved closer to Pennington. "Now, that gets addressed by having his people do all the work instead of us. The executive will see his data displayed and all the talking will be done by his people who did all the programming using the new software programs from IBM."

"Now, you know how big customers come into the Data Center for a week at a shot and get damned little done. Right?" Pennington nodded his head, having had his share of those sessions.

"Well, when the customers come in here this time, they are gonna be turned around fast. We'll need to teach the sales force what records the customer needs to bring with him on magnetic tape, how they are to be formatted and blocked, etc. That'll be easy. From there it's one, two, three."

The exhilaration of my idea made my words come out quickly, but Pennington stayed right with me and picked up on the idea. "One, teach them how to retrieve the data and get it displayed on the tubes. That's day one. On day two, have them do it. Have them write their own demo for their executives. That'll put the workload on them, not us, and get them interested. That's day two. On the third day, have the customer executive show up, and have his own people give him the demo. At the end of the demo, the IBM sales rep gets off his dead ass and explains the benefits in dollar terms — the business case for buying the 370. The customer will already be convinced he can install it and the sales rep will fuel that conviction by showing him the payback is there. That's it, Ralphie. And, for each sale we can expect from three-hundred to eight-hundred thousand dollars in revenue."

My idea sounded simple enough, but one last issue needed to be addressed: getting IBM's commitment.

"Now, Ralphie, boy, you know how hard it is to get new ideas off the ground around here, right?"

Ralph nodded his head, and said with conviction, "Yeah, I know." His staid boss had stymied him more than once when he suggested ways to improve usage of the Data Center.

"Well, my boss, Sanders, is a good guy about creativity. He likes it and is not worried about the politics of who takes credit for what. And Sanders' boss, Grabe, is desperate for some sales in the mid-range product line. Timing is everything and our timing is perfect to demand everything we need right goddamned now."

I paused for a moment, and felt a tinge of doubt flow through my body. "Will it work, Ralph?" I asked.

Pennington looked at me with a gleam in his eyes. "You bet your ass it will, Max."

So, I did. The next morning I took Sanders through my "show-don't-tell" strategy a full week ahead of his imposed two-week deadline. Sanders bought our program and, after believing we thought we could get a customer that far in three days, he committed his support.

Not willing to wait to put the plan in motion, Sanders grabbed his phone and made a 4:00 P.M. appointment with Bill Grabe, Detroit's regional manager, for the following day, which was no small accomplishment since the regional manager, responsible for one-billion dollars in annual sales, held a full appointment calendar.

I stayed up until the wee hours sniffing the fumes of magic markers as I sketched out my plan on IBM's inevitably-required flip charts. The next morning, with all the horsepower of our regional management team crammed into Grabe's office, I laid it out.

I wanted to use the premise that IBM's customers were scared of the new system, but I knew I had to tone this point down. IBM hadn't been noted for recognizing employees who said, "Boss, the customers are scared shitless." I chose instead to maintain that if the customers knew they could install the System 370, they would want to.

"IBM has been trying to tell customers how to accomplish the conversion, but now we need to show them how," I told my audience. "We need to give them proof that it is possible."

The intensity of my enthusiasm reached the powerful Grabe. His brows knit together as I spoke, and he focused on my ideas as a way out of the biggest problem confronting him.

Next, I explained the program, in much the same way I had to Pennington and Sanders. "And all of the new features are confusing. We're going to focus on the customer seeing his own data displayed and on having this accomplished by his own people. They do all the work, not us, and in a day, not weeks."

Grabe bought it all. "Gentlemen, this has top priority. Whatever Beardslee wants in computer Data Center time and regional manpower, give it to him."

I watched Grabe's staff managers cast their eyes furtively to the floor, pissed that I, who was several levels below them, had gained this commitment. I raised my chin and looked directly at them, inwardly gloating at the transfer of power taking place. A couple of them defiantly tested the water advising Grabe they would have to de-commit other projects, but he responded with a silent stare. With no other comments dared, Grabe stood up, thus ending the meeting.

Pennington and I hit the deck running. As he tested the software I had identified, I got pilot customers lined up for "Operation 30/30." Remembering my sales school days, the name implied a rifle shot rather than shot gun approach to generate thirty sales in thirty days, an unbelievable sales record if we could pull it off. Revenue would come out to fifteen million dollars plus.

The first customer, a manufacturer from Lansing, enrolled in the pilot program, and the first day went off without a hitch

Back at home I couldn't sleep and kept Pat awake half the night along with me. "This deal is gonna be better than Chef Pierre, Kysor and all the rest," I told her. "Because it's not a one-shot program. The efficiency of it will allow hundreds, maybe thousands, of customers to use it. And, honey, best of all, it gets me out of the mundane, no-visibility job I'm in and into one that's fun and rewarding. I could know everybody in the region because of this program and helping them sell computers fast."

As Pat curled up beside me with one arm over my chest, I thought about the ramifications of my 30/30 program. The news of the first order would smoke IBM's tie-lines. *Finally ... recognition,* I thought, and dozed off.

Seven of the first ten companies in the program placed orders averaging half a million dollars apiece — a quick three and a half million to IBM. Word rapidly spread about the high, fast and easy sales rate. Stories surfaced about proud computer managers taking the offense with their executives instead of being pummeled about late payrolls. Bookings ran sixty days in advance for Operation 30/30.

The guys with the heelsavers in White Plains found out about our rifle shot program, as did the industry staff people of the other sixteen regions. Pennington and I spent long hours explaining the strategy as IBMers flew in and out of Detroit on a frequent basis. After two months, Pennington and I told Sanders and Grabe that customers who had completed the program had ordered forty systems totaling eighteen million dollars; thirty-one of the systems were ordered in the second month, hitting our target of thirty. We were on a roll.

The DPD division adopted the program as their total marketing strategy for what they classified as small and intermediate systems, calling their version of it "BOLDER," or "Branch On-Line Data Entry and Response." In a matter of twelve months, BOLDER training reached an astounding four thousand sales reps and systems engineers. At its peak, twelve system 370s circulated around the nation solely to conduct Operation 30/30.

An IBM reporter came to Detroit and interviewed me for insertion in the company newspaper. A two-page article about the program in IBM's *Data Processing News* appeared glorifying the idea.

Fred Falbo and I had lunch. "Beardslee, you personify the adage of 'falling in a bucket of shit and coming out smelling like a rose.' The rest of us are pissed that we have to hear all about 'Beardslee' every time we go in to see Sanders."

"Cheer up, Freddie. I'll sign your copy of the divisional rag, no charge," I said and grinned. Falbo responded with a couple of french fries hurled in the general direction of my head.

Finishing our lunch, I walked back to my office my head buzzing with my success. I thanked my lucky stars for that old thing called creativity. *IBM didn't teach me that,* I acknowledged. *I had it when I walked through their door. And luck, too, that somebody didn't beat me to the punch.* I looked up Pennington.

"Ralph, how come nobody got ahead of us on this?"

The enthusiastic systems engineer had a ready reply. "I've been thinking the same thing. What I figure, as I've come to know you, is that you can put yourself in other people's shoes."

That confused me. "What? What shoes?"

"Well," Ralph continued, "you thought about the programmer, the IBM sales rep, the programmer's boss, the customer executive, the IBM systems engineer. You knew what was on their minds. You knew who was scared, for example, and what it took to strip their fear away. That's why it worked. And, I think it's because you have gotten to know all kinds of people at different levels. You know how they think. Damned few people at IBM do. Do you think Grabe, as an example, can understand what a customer programmer has on his mind?"

I thanked Ralph for his insight and hoped he was right. I had always assumed that everybody thought about all of the aspects of the business Ralph had mentioned, but maybe they really didn't.

As I watched other decisions being made, reviewed, reworked, and delayed, I hit on the heart of the problem. It wasn't that IBM's top execs were incapable of coming up with a solution to the System 370 problem, rather too much structure prevented them from understanding the problem. The people at the top had no contact with and, therefore, no feeling for what a computer program or a conversion plan meant anymore. They had people design new marketing programs while not keeping updated themselves on how customers thought and what they need or what concerns they had.

And the reason they didn't know much about customers was because the headquarters jobs had become too myopic, too specialized. One person did the features section, another did the benefits section, another did the pricing section, another put the slides out for bid, and yet another did the graphics. And that's all they did, day in, day out. Busy or not, they had become automatons who never saw the whole picture.

IBM needed to understand why automotive companies constantly tried to move away from using one man for one job. Active, creative minds became rusty and dull from so much repetitiveness. In 1974, IBM, I concluded, was too rigid and confined in its thought process. The restraining string of structure. *So what,* I concluded. *I'll stay away from it, stay in regions and branches. Then, when I get high enough up the ladder, maybe I can do something to change it.*

While the 30/30 program continued, requiring less of my time as others became trained in its workings, Sanders started giving me more exposure to Grabe. "Grabe's hosting a breakfast at the Hundred Percent Club in Miami, he informed me one day. "Write his opening message for him and pick out an appropriate personalized gift for the two hundred or so people who are attending."

"No sweat, Ted."

This time Theory Y didn't work. Because of the meeting's location, I suggested to Grabe that we give the attendees a book written by an NFL football coach, which I recommended without reading it first. Watching Grabe from the confines of his spacious office, he appeared non-committal, not saying much or looking directly at me as I spoke.

Next, in Sanders' presence, I laid on a real fire-and-brimstone pitch comparing football with sales and suggested Grabe conclude his speech with a worn cliché, "When the going gets tough, the tough get going." Grabe remained quiet.

From his silence I sensed Grabe felt uncomfortable, but I didn't know why. And when the top guy is uneasy, it spreads. I began to fidget and sweat.

Sanders enlightened me after we left Grabe's office. "Bill read the book. You know he's pretty intellectual. To him, it read like a 'Dick-and-Jane' deal, like an elementary-school primer, so forget the book idea, okay?"

I screwed up my face and stared at the ceiling. Yeah, Grabe hit the nail on the head. Pennington had built me all up by telling me I knew how multiple levels of people thought, and then I blew it by not focusing on Grabe and what he needed out of the speech.

Sanders failed at holding back his laughter. Between seizures he wheezed at me, "And another thing ... your pitch won't work. Bill's speech is for breakfast; everybody will be hung over. Grabe won't want a rah-rah deal for that crowd, he'll want a low-key one to blend in with the Alka Seltzers they'll all be full of."

Favored treatment from Sanders and Grabe continued despite my *faux pas*. Sanders, in particular, usually spent time with me every day discussing business, personal lives and lately, how a marketing manager got off to a good start, the latter being my favorite subject.

More recognition from Sanders: "I'm giving you an appraisal of 'one' for the reporting period," he informed me. "Generating a strategy adopted by the division earns you that." All IBMers received annual written appraisals from one to five, with one being the highest grade. According to personnel, only seven percent of IBM's employees earned a one.

Before I could rise all the way to cloud nine, he continued. "On the other hand, your paperwork is only average, but I believe you could do good written work if you wanted to. My opinion is that you don't give a damn about paperwork." (Criticism of my paperwork had been raised before. I focused on his praise and on his conclusion instead.) "If you can handle the paperwork and detail that comes with the territory, you can go a long way in IBM."

Music to my ears. The first formal appraisal I had ever received that actually stressed my long-term worth to the company and a "one" rating, IBM's highest, to boot.

Before finishing the meeting, Sanders also hinted at my popularity and ease at transitioning into a new job, two strengths I had been told of before. After six years with IBM, I also felt I had created my own illusion.

Coping in IBM's everyday work place had not been easy for me; it had been just the contrary in understanding the complexities of computers, conforming, and learning all the rules. My managers, however, believed otherwise. I wondered if this false impression accepted and believed by others bode well for me or not.

Opportunities arose allowing the second wave of people to join GSD. Using the White Plains heelsavers experience as part of my rationale, I viewed the new division as more to my liking. I informed Sanders of my decision the following Monday. "You're a great boss and who could ask for better treatment ... but this new division ... it looks like rah rah and go, go, go. I want to join it." My hesitant words signaled my difficulty in telling a free-form boss who had given me such a high appraisal, and a big raise to boot, that I wanted out.

Sanders, to my surprise, told me he thought I had probably made the right choice. "I hear they are having fun over there, and they certainly need talent. Good luck."

I interviewed with two guys of staff-manager rank in the new division, also based in Detroit, and asked to put together the 30/30 strategy for their region. Instead, they assigned me to a menial job in distribution marketing, putting together a seminar program to sell computers to small wholesalers. The reasonably unimportant job didn't make sense until months later after I caught a crash course in big company politics.

Three months into Operation 30/30 and at the height of its regional popularity, two go-getters from GSD, Dave Crandall, my partner at Chef Pierre, and Jack Horner, considered as the most talented systems engineer in GSD's Detroit area, asked to meet me at my house to talk about 30/30. Four hours later, they felt convinced the strategy would work equally as well in their division.

GSD's customers had been staying away from conversion to a computer supporting tubes for the same reasons as the low-end System 360 users. Several years of IBM small- and medium-sized customer neglect had occurred when all the talent got aimed at the Big Boys. While GSD had been formulated to fix IBM's neglect, it would take months or even years to gain momentum unless some idea could solve the problem.

I told Crandall and Horner they couldn't miss — and they didn't. Within months, their version of Operation 30/30 became known throughout GSD's entire U.S. territory as "the Detroit story." Crandall and Horner didn't receive much credit either. All of it flowed to Tom Murray, the fellow I'd interviewed with when moving over to GSD.

Routinely, I attended a personnel-sponsored class in Atlanta. At the end of it, a veep named Leo Bracken pumped us up about the opportunities in IBM's newest division by offering as one example the "brilliant thinking" employed by Murray. Taking a half hour to describe the program, Bracken attributed the idea for the-three day Operation 30/30 program to Murray!

While hearing Bracken's dialogue, I struggled with the misplaced authorship. How could a company that preached "accomplish any task in a superior fashion," "respect for the individual" and "recognition for performance" ignore all three? I felt indignant and insulted.

That night I called home to check on my family. "By the way, honey, do you know Tom Murray?" Pat acknowledged she did. "Well, today, I had to hear for a half an hour about what a wonderful guy he was for thinking up Operation 30/30."

Pat, who had a more suspicious mind than I did over politics, fired back. "Hey, you gotta blow your own horn at IBM. Nobody else is gonna put the bugle to your lips. You're too nice a guy. Why don't you look this guy Bracken up and set the record straight?"

That night in an Atlanta hotel room, I did some serious soul searching. I didn't know whether Murray intentionally put me in the background to grab the credit or whether the misplaced honors had occurred innocently. I liked Murray ... I didn't want to think the worst. *Ah, win a few, lose a few,* I concluded. *Let it go by. Going to see Bracken would be a self-serving thing to do.* Despite my decision, I learned that the IBM system could not be counted on to give a fair accounting of ideas and results. Another hidden string — the political one.

Relative to politics, I had never worried about recognition before. In the IBM branch it had all been so direct. And who could ask for more recognition than I'd gotten out of my short stint with DPD's division? All I knew about politics came from people, like Fred Falbo, talking about the need for visibility and a mentor. Bar talk said having a mentor ensured promotion beyond the marketing manager level.

Not only had I left my mentors, Sanders and Grabe, behind, my entrance to GSD had been greeted by an insulting misplacement of recognition. *New division, no mentor, no recognition,* I thought. *Just another IBMer waiting to have his strings pulled.*

◆◆◆

Ms. Habel looked up from her writing pad where she had been taking notes. "An interesting side of IBM, Mr. Beardslee. Very interesting. And it helps me understand you, too. You are a sensitive man with thoughts about many different kinds of people. I do agree with your associate, uh, Mr. Pennington, I believe, that you have a rare gift in that regard. It, however, causes you to take things for granted.

"You took for granted that the president who fired you would understand the position in which you'd been placed. You put yourself in his shoes, as Pennington says, believing he would have all the facts before firing you. He *didn't* put himself in your shoes. And you have to understand that most people don't interact on several levels as you do." She made her final point. "You believe that most people think like you do and they don't. That's it for today."

Something new to think about.

Fourteen

Ms. Habel continued to be a breath of fresh air. Two more sessions with her bore more fruit about my assumptive process being faulty. She helped me see that I was different in other ways as well. But none of this information added up to my having become a manic-depressive.

On the tenth day of confinement, Dr. Heileman grinned as he walked into my room, "I've got good news for you."

Sitting up on the bed where I'd been lying, I asked hopefully, "What's the word, Doc? Sending me home?"

"No, but IBM is going to pay for your stay here. I just talked to your wife." Heileman flicked some dandruff off the lapel of his checkered coat. "They've also agreed to take you back into IBM when you get out."

I stared at Heileman unable to utter a word, and then he shrugged his shoulders and walked out, leaving me sitting there with my mouth open — dumbfounded. *Well, damn, that is interesting. IBM never takes anybody back ... for any reason.* I called my wife.

"Hey, Pat, Doc Heileman says you heard from IBM. What gives?"

"Well, Tom and I met with some IBMers in Detroit," she began. These execs had told her and my brother-in-law that Big Blue remained adamant about not forking over the money I demanded as a settlement, but they would pay my medical bills and reinstate me into the company. An IBM lawyer had given Pat papers to that effect and asked her to sign them. She demurred, saying she would talk this new development over with me.

Pat's words tumbled out rapidly. "They'll take you back, give you your seniority, benefits, everything!" Her excitement about IBM's offer was obvious and confirmed my belief about our differing values. Going back to IBM held great promise for her, and I understood that. However, the thought of meeting more Hampstead and Paulos types turned me cold.

"Sorry, Pat, but tell IBM to stick the paper up their ass. I'll get to them after I am out of here. Worse news is their denial of any compensation. That means my Open Door got closed. Is Amrose aware of this?"

"He knows," Pat replied quietly.

"Well, Fred won't be surprised. He always felt my trying to get something going was a long shot. I feel stupid, Pat. I thought IBM had a heart and would leap all over this thing once they knew the facts. I was dead wrong."

Pat was silent; her enthusiasm turning to disappointment so strong I could feel it through the phone line. Changing the subject, I asked about the kids.

In stilted tones Pat assured me that they were fine, then she drifted back to her meeting with IBM. "Will you reconsider? It could maybe even salvage our marriage," she said.

I thought about that last linkage of subjects before answering. "Sorry, Pat. No way would I ever go back. Probably, in the beginning, when you and I delivered the Open Door to Armonk, I would have gone back if they had acted on it. And, we might have stayed married. Not now; I'm not going back even if it makes a difference in our failing marriage." We hung up with little more said.

Even the medical expense payment couldn't be construed as good news. I had learned about Florida's Baker Act, allowing patients the first ten days of private care on the state. After that, they became either discharged or sent to publicly-funded sanitariums as wards of the taxpayers. IBM's having picked up the private tab just prolonged my stay in the run-for-profit funny farm.

And business appeared to be good at the farm. Children aged nine to nineteen filled the ward adjacent to our "bad-guy" section. They earned their fair share of trips to solitary, passing though my ward on the way. One little guy in particular about ten years of age with strawberry-blond curly hair and face and arms thick with freckles caught my attention; he reminded me of Huck Finn. Once or twice every day, he would be carried down the hall kicking, fighting and swearing. When I heard this defenseless little guy coming, which was easy with all the accompanying racket, I cheered him on.

"Attaboy, kid! Keep fighting."

As I also frequented solitary, inevitably we ended up there at the same time in separate rooms. Attendants let us out together to use the latrine. One day my little buddy looked up, confident blue eyes meeting mine and stuck out his hand. "My name is Mike. What's yours, mister?"

My asylum resistant barriers melted, letting the pleasurable emotion of meeting this little fighter after days of cheering him on take over. I handled the kid like he was a prince.

Days later, Mike and I received permission to have lunch on the first floor where the less severe patients ate. I found out that he was relegated to "Fort Fumble" — my name for the hospital — for fighting too often in his fourth-grade class at school. In addition to his too-aggressive behavior, Mike's young mind had become clouded with the conviction that his deceased father had been poisoned by his step-dad. Most of the children housed in the Fort bore trauma of broken homes, and he was no different. From that lunch forward, I always called my freckled friend, Huck Finn.

On the first floor we could talk to children and talk I did. "Do you have any kids?" Huck asked.

I told him I had three boys, their ages, and where they lived. Watching him pick at his food, I said "And, like you, they hate salad."

We talked about baseball and girls, a couple of subjects in which Huck was very interested. A week later, at another luncheon, Huck told me he wished I could be his father; I fought back the tears. Thank God, my three little guys knew nothing of the Fort.

My first month at Fort Fumble came and went, leaving me ample time to review my past with IBM. I felt this analysis was necessary and revealing, having already learned one major point: I'd assumed IBM would know all the facts about Fillmore's meetings and my contribution from Operation 30/30 before they let me go. I'd assumed IBM would adhere to its own principle of "respect for the individual" before taking a course of action that treated me like a common thief.

Communication with Heileman had broken down; my habit of shouting, "QUACK, QUACK, QUACK," when he approached the ward did not help. The doctor told me, "If you don't cooperate I will have to transfer you to a state-run institution."

My quick response: "IBM won't allow you to do that."

He turned and walked out with a "humph."

Believing a long stay at Fort Fumble probably unless I could devise a plan, I started contemplating ways to get out. As my phone privileges came back, I called friends on the outside mounting a campaign for them to spring me. I fully expected a few dozen of them to fly to Tampa and picket the place chanting, "Let Max go!"

None of them showed interest in making the trip, but Heileman didn't know that and I told him more than once to expect the picket line to form soon. I silently chuckled and knew my illusion had worked after he informed me, "Even if you get friends to picket, I won't be coerced into letting you go."

Most of the practicing doctors at the funny farm held stock in the operation; Dr. Mortimer, the guy who billed me one-hundred dollars for nothing, held the majority. Stories surfaced that patients of wealthy parents could always count on Mortimer to provide them with a diagnosis of mental illness if they were awaiting sentencing on charges of drug possession or distribution, thus keeping them out of jail. "My dad's got plenty of money," claimed one teenager I met, "and he'll keep me in here until charges that I sold cocaine blow over."

I asked, "*Did* you sell cocaine?"

With a quick grin he replied. "Yup. Still do, whenever I can get a pass out of here."

Heileman, who showed signs of having a friendship with Mortimer by making rounds with him almost daily, also owned stock in the operation.

From not obeying a minor command on the first floor, the familiar "RED ALERT ... RED ALERT" filtered over the speakers.

Back to my buddies in the ICU and another shot of Dalmane.

Sitting in isolation fighting the tedious boredom of four walls and nobody to talk to, I thought about my phone call to Pat and her obvious disappointment over my adamant refusal to consider going back to IBM. She had enjoyed many friendships through IBM; so had I. The most enjoyable times for both of us had been when I'd transferred to GSD, joining seven other guys hell-bent, just like me, on becoming marketing managers. I became friends with every one of them, while Pat enjoyed time with their wives. We became a tight-knit group...

♦♦♦

January 8, 1975

Fred Brando bought me lunch. "You're a dumb shit for leaving, Beardslee. Grabe and Sanders love your ass," Brando said through bites of a sandwich.

Yeah, his words rang true, but I had an opportunity to join a division with a little soul. And, that's what I wanted. Soul.

"I think I figured it right, Fred."

After cleaning out my desk and saying goodbye to Sanders, I drove to another area of Detroit several miles away to the building housing IBM's newest operation, the General Systems Division. In those early days of 1975, the division tackled new account productivity. GSD had been formulated to sell small computers for both large and small customers.

The GSD execs realized that the days of cold calls were numbered; the company could no longer afford to send a sales rep in a car for several miles to bang on a door with only the hope of generating interest. There had to be a better way.

I was assigned to Werner Koenig, a regional staff manager working on the productivity problem. Koenig, eyes puffed from work and shielded behind thick horn-rimmed glasses, started his life in Germany, coming to the United States in his early twenties. He slowly worked his way through IBM's ranks as a systems engineer, a systems engineering manager and a marketing manager assigned to the Chrysler account. Now, he enjoyed regional staff-manager rank and tended a flock of eight guys all wanting to become marketing managers A.S.A.P.

Koenig had, therefore, people who would do anything. Gung-ho, we were all right. GSD had just announced a new software package called Installation Application Programs, or IAPs. Focusing on a number of different types of businesses, these became our division's answer to Pee Pees. Each of us was assigned a specialty area, which we then had to develop a knowledge of and a technique for marketing systems to this area. We then marketed that strategy to the branches. From our assigned specialty, we developed our own group of customers and prospects in the region. After direct-mail campaigns got sent to potential buyers in a specific area, one of us would visit the branch and hold a seminar for interested potential customers.

Koenig wanted to upgrade the division's direct-mail effort, confined at the time to clumsy, unprofessional looking form letters sent out by the headquarters wizards in Atlanta. He wanted to personalize these letters and enhance the overall quality, thus eliminating much of the requirement for expensive cold calls.

"Beardslee, I vant you to head zis deal up," Koenig told me from behind the plain desk his junior-exec role authorized. "Feldman will be ze first to use it."

Frank Feldman, a quick-witted, dark-haired peddler out of Youngstown, Ohio, was the disenchanted member of our team. A few months of staff work had already left him unsettled about making management a career. Full of self-confidence, partly due to a future seven-figure inheritance, he painfully grunted through the motions of staff work.

Associations became Feldman's assigned specialty area: membership accounting, dues-paying procedures and aged trial balances. Pretty dull stuff.

As part of Feldman's marketing efforts, he bought a mailing list on magnetic tape that included national and regional groups such as unions, business associations and church headquarters. Late into the night, Feldman's tape spun away, sending data about associations in the Toledo area to the printer at the rate of eleven hundred lines per minute. Thousands of letters tumbled out asking an equal number of addressees to attend a seminar.

The database tape had four field descriptions on it: name of the owner, name of the organization, name of the street, and city, state and ZIP code. The owner for one particular organization had been listed as "J. Christ"; his company, "Church of Christ." Our totally logical computer greeted the intended reader with: "Dear Mr. Christ." The body of Feldman's letter explained IBM software, some of the benefits obtained from associations using it and several merits of attending a seminar in the Toledo area on a particular date. His closing paragraph had a variable insert to further personalize the computer's communiqué. In its closing comments, Feldman's letter advised:

> The seminar in Toledo will afford a constructive use of your time, Mr. Christ. We look forward to seeing you there.
>
> Sincerely,
> Frank Feldman

The letter's journey continued through a burster and stuffer process before finding its way to the mailman's bag. Frank audited the mailings by keeping a copy of each letter sent out. However, it was a few days after his mailing before he discovered what had happened.

When the rest of Werner's warriors heard about the snafu, Feldman's personal note to the Almighty flooded IBM's tie-line network.

Our non-existent screening process of mailings continued. The sales reps and managers in the "Family Jewels Division," a moniker a friend of mine gave DPD since that division had the preponderance of IBM's revenues and body count, took a dim view of Werner's twentieth-century marketing ways. In fact, the people at DPD got incensed about the uproar caused by their poor cousins from GSD when somebody like Henry Ford opened a letter from our division telling him his company appeared to be "large enough to afford its own computer." The letter informed the president of this multi-billion dollar company, which, by the way, already possessed hundreds of IBM computers:

> IBM's seminar for first-time computer users, Mr. Ford, will be well worth your time.

The loftily-positioned Ford's of the world bucked the letter down through several chains of command, ending with some DPD manager getting chewed on. The darlings of IBM, in turn, raised hell with us.

Werner's warriors, however, didn't give a damn about the boring editing process, so the letters continued to go out. We even took a bit of pleasure in ignoring their complaints and continuing to do exactly what they had asked us not to.

An unhealthy amount of friction grated within IBM's sales divisions. DPD, the traditional marketers of large computers to large customers, saw themselves as the saviors of the corporation. In turn, they saw GSD as the rejects of the sales force who were too dumb to understand the complexities of DPD's larger systems. Thus, we were relegated to selling small computers. Conversely, we in GSD viewed ourselves as the wave of the future, and DPD as institutionalized, stuffy and pompous.

Only in looking at the Office Products Division, where thousands of sales people sold copiers and typewriters did the two computer divisions see anything alike; we both called OPD's finest, "Opie Dopies" and thought of them as sales reps with no knowledge of technology.

The Opie Dopies, enjoying a twenty-year run of record sales and high earnings, viewed the DPD people as boring, GSD people as immature and themselves as the true peddlers of the company. (DPD and GSD had the last laugh, though, because shortly after I was fired, IBM's sales divisions reorganized, going from three marketing divisions to two, balancing the revenue and body count. In the process, the Opie Dopie division was wiped out. Thousands of OPD sales people, owning no computer background and little or no technical aptitude, got dragged into the two divisions. For them, the move was a sink or swim proposition. Borrowing a phrase from the Cuban exodus, these OPD folks picked up a new name from their unaffected brethren — "Boat People.")

Most peddlers in Koenig's group formed strong friendships that still existed years later. Three, in particular, became close friends of mine. Dean Hamilton, from the hills of West Virginia, could be counted on to provide the wit and excitement. With a perpetual mischevious grin on his face and an open style, his personality suited itself to my own. And like me, he'd earned promotions without emulating others. He said what he thought and found pleasure in his job.

Enjoying a drink or two with him after work, I also learned he loved pranks just like me. Jokes about his short stature notwithstanding, the wiry generous-nosed mountaineer drew record crowds to his seminars aimed at closing new accounts with building contractors.

Tall and gangly Jeff Rentlow appeared the opposite of Hamilton. He was responsible for selling to the manufacturing business, our region's biggest potential market and, therefore, its most important. Just seeing the better part of a foot's height difference in the two friends forced a chuckle from me on more than one occasion. In addition, Rentlow, broad-shouldered and pug-nosed, was handsome enough to be recruiting-poster material for IBM.

On the other hand, Hal Paplonski — balding, overweight, chain smoking cigarettes down to the filter and letting the ashes fall where they may — was not. I shared a camaraderie with this man who was always out hustling some hospital or clinic, representing IBM as the medical industry rep.

Our Monday-through-Friday life consisted of fast food, too many airports, lost luggage, hard-to-haul-around, bulky flip charts and out-of-sequence slide sets. We often re-fought the IBM wars on weekends over too many drinks and too many golf courses to the chagrin of our wives, who stayed at home.

Koenig put me into the wholesale food business, far down the charts in order of divisional importance, but a newly announced industry program dictated his move.

This relatively calm environment changed abruptly when Len Fillmore arrived as the new Great Lakes regional manager in February of 1975. Many things made Fillmore unusual, including the way he got his job earning his promotion directly from branch manager in Chicago. In IBM, the promotion cycle went from line to staff to line, or direct sales, to sales support and back to direct sales. Fillmore moved up from line to line, an almost unheard of step up the ladder. A former defensive tackle in the pros, Fillmore looked physically intimidating. Taller than Rentlow, the IBM executive filled all of the 52-long suit. Appearing to be about fifty years old, Fillmore's sparse silver hair sat neatly combed on his large head. Silver-rimmed glasses framed eyes that looked straight ahead. A hunter.

We got to see our new regional manager in action at the staff announcement meeting and found out Fillmore had developed his management style around those ample physical dimensions used in earning a living by smashing his body into others. The leader's hands cast large shadows as he used them for emphasis in his short but clear introductory message

"I'm delighted to be here as your new regional manager. That said, I've seen where we are and where we have to go. Sales have to pick up now. You all have a big job to do, and I need you to do it."

Fillmore's new sales organization had suffered a lousy start. Everybody needed to block and tackle until the region tracked back on course.

Koenig's raiders periodically pitched their wares to the twelve branch managers who ran the three-hundred-fifty million-dollar-per-year operation for Fillmore. These prima donnas each headed up a piece of Fillmore's regional geography and held our staff tickets allowing us to go back to the field and the lucrative marketing manager jobs waiting for us there. We could expect the branch managers to view us much like those flesh-market victims of 18th century slave trading, only this time they were looking for potential marketing managers.

Paplonski was the most nervous about his upcoming presentation. Solid and fundamental, he overreacted to his appearance, feeling he lacked the so-called IBM executive look. Paplonski typified my belief that what type of style you had was not important as long as you had one, a message I drummed into those who worked for me.

I had witnessed all forms of style employed within the air force and IBM — short and noisy, tall and quiet, good posture and bad, organized and disorganized, controlling and free-flowing. I'd observed that the above made little difference to success as long as one had consistency. Diverse types — those with many styles — acted unpredictably, which often led to failure. Those still seeking their style commonly copied from someone whom they admired, figuring success breeds success. Or worse, copying from whomever their leader was just to conform, believing that would gain them a promotion. This caused further inconsistency in a person's style since they couldn't adapt fully to something unnatural to them. They often acted erratically, expressing one style in one situation and another in the next.

"A good question for any person to ask his immediate manager should be, 'What am I known for?' If the answer comes back, 'Not a helluva lot,' that person should be concerned," I told my people. "That means they lack style."

Jack Orlop had a gregarious, open style. Usually two hundred percent or more of quota, Orlop frequently took his systems engineers to a saloon or two after normal work hours. As a result, they always performed tasks for his accounts whether their managers wanted them to or not. New sales people contrasted Orlop's style against the structured lessons of sales training; from his record of success, they tried to adapt his. Orlop dressed colorfully and acted out his disdain for the reverence IBM sales people placed on flip charts. Invariably, the adaptation efforts only resulted in bad hangovers and no sales.

An IBM veep named Jack Murphy had the reputation of being a real heavy in gray matter, but as a speaker he mumbled and talked to the floor. And as a listener, the tall Irishman habitually appeared to be dozing off. Often, just as the speaker thought he had safely made it through a point, Murphy would interrupt him and bring up a point the hapless person had made several minutes back and challenge it verbatim. That style added fuel to Murphy's image as a genius. Quite possibly, Murphy possessed no more than average intelligence for his position. He locked onto a piece of the pitch early in the game, dozed off, and played it back to keep everybody else alert. Style.

Paplonski's style flunked all the IBM prerequisites for posture, physical appearance and dress, but he could always be counted on to put something special into a meeting. Determined to gun his way through this first one presided over by Fillmore, he put together some toy medical kits – a small doctor's bag containing a stetho-scope, thermometer and tongue depressors — and literature about his program.

Selling the idea to a conservative Koenig and his boss proved difficult, because they never wanted to take any risks with Fillmore. However, at rehearsal the night before, they begrudging-ly approved his plan.

Following Paplonski at the flesh auction, I walked into the room to find every branch manager had his stethoscope on, some were busily taking the temperatures of others and tongue depressors stuck from the mouths of all twelve. The slave traders voted unan-imously that Paplonski gave the best presentation of the day, prov-ing that much of the emulation that went on in IBM was of a lem-ming mentality. It didn't have to be that way; it just was.

Later in the year, Hamilton, by then a Fillmore favorite, gave a presentation to Fillmore with a nervous Koenig present; the super-straight German had warned the prankster prone Hamilton to deliver a plain-vanilla message. Midway through the topic, howev-er, Paplonski nonchalantly entered the room holding a can of aerosol spray. With Hamilton pitching from an easel-mounted flip chart, Paplonski casually sauntered around Fillmore's spacious office spraying away. Koenig's heart almost visibly palpitated as he watched; Hamilton looked at Paplonski as if he thought he had been in the sun too long, and Fillmore, impossible to read anyway, ignored Hamilton's presentation by totally focusing instead upon Paplonski as IBM's Polish marvel slouched around his office. Paplonski then deposited the can on the corner of Fillmore's mas-sive desk, where all could read the label: "Bullshit Repellant."

Fillmore, surprised but obviously pleased that someone had the courage to take a risk in his presence, formally thanked Paplonski, then asked him if he could take the can with him the next time he had to hear a presentation from Leo Bracken, Fillmore's Atlanta-based boss.

Paplonski, basking in his success — he'd pulled off what every-body else feared to try, flicked a few of the ever-present ashes from his suit and replied, "Len, with your numbers I wouldn't recommend it."

Few dared to challenge the structure of rigid business presentations. In this case, Paplonski put some humor into Fillmore's day, and he would be remembered for it. Once again I thought of Paplonski's style, so different it was refreshing.

One could have a little fun in IBM with senior management, but damned few dared or did. Maybe IBM didn't really want the conformity their system produced. Or, maybe, it was two worlds. Headquarters staff, the world of lemmings, and regions, where life was bearable because it afforded a bit more chance for diversion from the norm.

After only four months in GSD, I arrived on the launching pad. Koenig called me into his office. "Beardslee, you are my leading candidate for zis marketink manager's job in Indy. Ve need a goot Stud down zere."

Koenig also told me that I had not been the branch manager's first choice, but he felt sure Fillmore could make it happen — an example of the old political push-versus-pull power that constantly went on in IBM. In April, push won. My promotion came through.

The interview with Ed Schwartz, Indianapolis' branch manager, took place at Oakland Hills Country Club in Bloomfield Hills, a high-rent suburb of Detroit where Schwartz had a membership. Schwartz had moved fast in his career and enjoyed "wild duck" status as a non-conformist, more evidence that a guy like me could get ahead. No fan of Koenig's group, when seeking Schwartz's buy into their plans for seminars in his branch, staffies either waited an hour to make a call on him — he intentionally made them wait — or forgot about it altogether. In addition, IBM's grapevine had it that he and Fillmore argued about how a branch should be managed. Fillmore wanted Schwartz to utilize Fillmore's staff more. Schwartz, either from being naturally stubborn or viewing it as a way for Fillmore to spy on him, ignored Fillmore's desire.

International Business Marionettes

After accepting Schwartz's offer, I glanced at the mahogany paneling in the men's grill of this country club setting. *Nice. Really nice. I want this kind of environment someday,* I thought I vowed right then and there that I would get it.

In IBM, every promotion got a party. Accepting the standard Cross pen set (IBM literally kept Cross in business), I took stock of the situation: seven years with IBM; recognition from both management and peers; two paychecks a month; medical and dental benefits, the stock plan and a retirement program. In short a hiring hook of long-term security firmly implanted. *What the hell,* I thought, *this can go on forever.*

Fifteen

B UT IT HADN'T GONE ON FOREVER. I LOOKED AROUND MY BLEAK ROOM at the psychiatric hospital to which I'd just returned after being released from solitary. Clearly I definitely was not enjoying the warmth and comfort of my five-bathroom home. Nor did I experience the mahogany-paneled luxury of the country club and the company of important business executives. Here I languished in March 1981, not only unemployed but spending forty-five days living against my will in a dismal and dingy psycho ward.

Under fairly miserable circumstances, I had managed to carve out a tenuous social position in my new environment by challenging the people who privately owned this place of profit and by helping other patients avoid manipulation and intimidation. In doing so, I probably performed for myself the best therapy possible by feeling un-intimidated and needed and getting my mind off my own problems. Each time I questioned the staff over some indignity or another, I felt more sure of my own mental state. I even began to enjoy my new self and, to some extent, my stay at the hospital. I particularly found pleasure in working with the other patients in my ward and helping them find dignity and respect in an environment almost designed to make them feel the opposite. A regular Jack Nicholson, I was.

Every night at about quarter to eight patients from the ICU were herded into a padded elevator and taken down to the first floor.

From there we shuffled about fifty yards down a corridor and through a door to a fenced facility outside the hospital building, where we gained an hour of freedom from the monotonous ward.

During our walk down the long passageway from the elevator to the exterior door we became tempting targets for stares and taunts from the first floor patients. This held especially true given the fact that about half of the thirty-or-so ICU patients clearly exhibited the characteristics of advanced stages of mental illness and could only marginally communicate or walk.

That evening our expedition to the outside felt particularly dehumanizing. One first-floorite even spit on the fellow who sometimes claimed he was Howard Hughes' son. I decided I'd seen enough of that kind of treatment, and the next day before our trip outside I rallied the Fort's sickest. "If they treat us like cattle, we'll act like cattle," I told my sickies, and then carefully explained my plan to those who could understand.

The next night, fifteen people lurched down the first-floor hall doing their best imitations of cows. "Moo ... mooh ... mmoohhh." The attendant in charge, not destined to ever work on rockets, promptly entered into my medical records, "patient observed mooing like a cow," but our first floor audience got the point by backing off. The taunting stopped.

The next night, my ICU pals eagerly anticipated our next event. "Okay, you bunch of loonies," I said. "We made our point last night, now let's show those gawkers on the first floor a little class."

It took several minutes to line up my drugged up, bent-minded friends, short to tall, front to back. Then we rehearsed our next appearance until it was almost perfect. That night we exited from the first floor elevator evenly spaced out one arm length apart.

"Forwahd ... Harch! ... Hup-two-three-four."

Down that corridor we marched, chests out and shoulders back. Watching the cadence from the rear, I whistled music from the movie *Bridge over the River Kwai.*

Watching the ICU gang, arms swinging evenly, eyes straight

ahead ignoring the taunts, I saw some real pride that night. I felt good about myself for putting some dignity into these people's lives where the day-to-day routine tended to de-humanize them. I also acknowledged that my disdain for IBM's headquarters structure lent itself well here as I looked for diversions to Fort Fumble's maize of rules and regulations.

One of the patients in the ICU, a severely retarded teenaged girl named Judy, had, at the age of twelve, fallen into an empty swimming pool, the skull-crushing plunge severely damaging her brain. Judy, who had lived at the Fort for two years, possessed the mentality of a five-year-old. In addition, her retardation caused her to consume prodigious amounts of food; hospital scales showed two-hundred-eighty-pounds and climbing.

At the nightly nine o'clock snack ritual, Judy loved to work over the sandwiches and ice cream. Every night she would steal extras of her favorite food — ice cream — and take them to her room in the huge folds of her tent-like, frayed dress. The ICU staff, under orders to maintain her twenty-two-hundred-calorie-per-day diet, usually caught her and pried the cups out of her strong, chubby fingers.

One night, I smuggled seven additional ice cream cups into Judy's room. Including the one she inhaled from the snack table, that made a total of eight. Judy begged me to keep it up. I figured, *Why the hell not?* Eating and listening to the bent plastic record of *Old MacDonald Had A Farm* on her dented and scratchy-needled record player constituted her only pleasures.

The next night, I continued my thievery. Judy ate one ice cream cup at the snack table, and I sneaked eleven more to her room for an even dozen. In twenty minutes, they disappeared.

"Go for the Guinness!" a witness urged. So, we did. At the next snack outing, Judy quickly consumed the allotted one and waddled to her room, eyes ablaze at the thought of more. With the white coats busy elsewhere, I heaped my wastebasket to the brim with dozens of Dixie cups before skulking to her room. My new friend dumped the contents of the wastebasket on the room's seedy, sagging bed, her deep-set eyes widening at the quantity of her favorite food. She motioned for me to leave.

Forty minutes went by before I heard Judy call my name. Walking in, I saw her pudgy face smeared with toppings and a wooden spoon protruding through her lips. She grinned, causing the spoon to fall to the floor, and handed me the only remaining ice cream cup.

"I'm full," she said.

Nineteen cups consumed. Over seven pounds of ice cream packed away. A new Fort Fumble record.

The following day, several staff members pushed Judy on the scales and watched the needle hover at the two eighty-five mark. Puzzled attendants scribbled Judy's new score into her records, baffled over her five-pound gain.

Not long after that incident, a lady named Rhonda checked into the ICU. The demure, dark-haired woman with long slender legs, thin waist and thick lashes masking clear blue eyes was a far cry in personal appearance from the rest of us. Large bandages covered both wrists, giving away the reason for her visit. When I saw her sitting quietly in a chair looking a bit lost, I approached.

I sat down beside her on the floor and lit her a Marlboro. "My name's Max. Glad to know you."

"I'm Rhonda. Thanks for the cigarette," she replied. "I'm embarrassed I'm in here."

"Don't be," I said. "No one in here will even think about it, so why should you?"

She laughed. A college graduate and practicing schoolteacher, Rhonda proved to be witty and intelligent. *Hard to figure why someone with so much to offer got so torn up inside,* I thought.

"How'd you end up here?" she asked me timidly.

"Well, I got fired from a company called IBM, and I kind of lost my marbles over it."

"What about you?" I asked. "What's an intelligent and attractive looking lady like you doing here?"

"Aw, my marriage is going to hell. He's a wife beater. Means well but loses it. And, my dad, he's dead now, was like that, too. He beat up on me a lot all the way through high school. The problem is my doctor says quite a few victims of child abuse pick mates just like their parents. Kind of like moths to a flame or something, they call it 'toxic baggage'. I'm trying to understand it."

We talked non-stop, exchanging stories of our mutual fall from prime time, me thoroughly enjoying a discussion with an outwardly normal person who held a variety of interests. I felt an attraction to her as well.

The days passed more quickly with Rhonda on board, and I looked forward to spending my waking hours talking with her. All the while she maintained her dignity, not the least bit embarrassed to discuss her suicide attempt. A week after her arrival, however, Rhonda was transferred to a ward on the other side of the building, separating us with a hundred-foot-deep courtyard. I would occasionally see her in her window and wave, my pulse picking up as she returned the silent greeting with a big smile. *Beardslee,* I said to myself, *you're smitten with the lady. Yup,* I answered myself, *and it feels good. As good as the promotion I'd gained from Detroit to Indianapolis.*

◆◆◆

May 1, 1975

"Indianapolis is the thirteenth largest city in America," Fillmore, said, his eyes focused on mine. "As I analyze IBM's potential there, Indy oughta be duck soup. You'll be handling a large new account unit, and if you can do what I think you can, we'll get you back here in a few years."

I listened intently to those words from the big man. Fillmore had relatives living near Indy. That, plus Indianapolis making up one of the region's largest branches, meant we would be seeing a lot of each other.

"Thanks for the promotion, Len." And, boy I meant it. I'd only been on Koenig's staff for four months, so judgment had been quick. Hell, I'd only been out of Traverse City for eighteen months, and I knew IBM rarely moved people from city to city in less than two years. Now, I'd be going to the Promised Land of big commissions, leaving staff and joining the line as IBM's newest marketing manager. I felt wonderful.

IBM allotted fifty-six days to buy a home, sell ours and get moved to Indy. If we exceeded the short time allotted for our move, then any extra living expenses in Indianapolis while Pat and the kids still lived in Detroit would be borne by me. An IBM move required hustling.

I spent a couple days with the tall, aloof fellow I was to replace. As he explained how his people were doing, I saw clearly that he operated with a Theory X management style all the way. Assuming all of his people were mules in the middle of the road, he gave them written daily and weekly goals as to the number of calls to make, proposals to write and industries to call on. Then he met with them at given intervals to see how well they were achieving these goals.

As a result of my predecessor's over-control, all eight people he supervised disliked him. *What a surprise,* I thought with sarcasm.

With my numbers-happy predecessor leaving the next day, I patiently kept quiet as he stumbled through the unit's year-to-date performance at my inaugural marketing managers meeting. The group had suffered as much from customers requesting that their equipment be taken out or cancelled as they had enjoyed installing systems with new customers.

Schwartz, the man who hired me, turned to me at the end of the staff meeting. "Beardslee, you've got a job to do. Making the unit quota in only eight months from zero means you must run at one-hundred-fifty percent for the remaining months."

I tried to fashion a look of confidence, but inside I felt very little.

With my "first-things-first" approach, I analyzed the potential of my diverse flock: four females — unusual in an era of male sales reps — four males, and one male trainee. Two of the peddlers, Eric Gunderson and Ken Albright, appeared to have impressive potential. These guys had distinctively different styles, establishing once again that some type of style, any type, was better than none.

Gunderson, a quiet, smart man of average height and weight with money motivation, had hunters' eyes — keen without a sign of fear. A top earner the year before, he always wore a three-piece suit sporting a second-generation pocket watch and chain.

Albright burst with voltage. Young, fast-talking, fresh off an Indiana campus as a fraternity leader, the highly energized man wanted to be president of IBM. Albright had posted a big track record after two years in the sales game. His organizational habits, the best I'd seen, got him out in the territory early in the day. Go, go, go. His dress of rumpled suits, disheveled hair and scuffed shoes, much like mine, remained of secondary importance. After those two, however, performance fell off dramatically.

My new unit's major objective required selling and installing sixty thousand "points" of business by the end of the year. IBMers at all levels broke business down into points representing equivalent dollars of leased revenue per month. A typical twelve-hundred-point system meant that the computer system rented for twelve hundred dollars per month. Its purchase price would be about forty times that, or forty-eight thousand dollars. In order to meet our objectives we needed to put about fifty computers into installations that had none with the emphasis on leasing them as opposed to buying them. IBM had not yet made a push for purchasing them as they would later in the decade.

May came and went in a blur: we'd attained only about fifty percent of quota. June flew by, becoming our first month to make the numbers. Decisions started to climb in volume and an acceptable amount of those showed "yes." We had a shot at making it.

I relished this new job, which built on things I had been taught by others, by allowing me to teach them to people who needed the education, and the lucrative commission opportunities I'd assure for myself by having successful graduates.

Schwartz's other marketing unit in Indianapolis didn't fare as well as mine. With established customers as their client base, their objective was to get those same customers to buy more. This senior, experienced unit had never really gotten out of the blocks since GSD's marketing inception in 1974. Not only wasn't it making its quota, but its players had bad morale to boot. Bad morale, like the flu, can spread. The best vaccine I knew was to keep my people so busy that they wouldn't have time to hear the other unit's people bitch. My operation, suffering from this disease when I arrived, now appeared healthy with the people meshing and enjoying their jobs.

After a couple of months at the helm, I started to relax a little in my job. Our first month of making quota was out of the way, and Pat and the boys were beginning to enjoy living in suburban Indianapolis. I even had a bit more time to spend at home now that things at the office were going smoothly.

Time for a little fun. Gunderson hosted a "flush the past" party at his antique-filled house in Zionsville, a suburb of colonial-village-inspired architecture in north Indianapolis. A prerequisite for the party required bringing along something that was a negative reminder of our not-so-successful past. A good-sized bonfire built in Gunderson's driveway offered a disposal for the bothersome items.

Gunderson threw in his new-account pen-and-pencil set, a standard award for a large new sale. Usually treasured by a sales rep and displayed on his or her desk for several years following the sale, Gunderson's customer had cancelled the equipment before it ever got installed. Albright walked up to the blaze, throwing in a letter from a customer turning in equipment to IBM. Everybody threw in something.

After his offering to the fire, Albright walked over to me and put his hand on my shoulder in a 'you're-an-okay-guy' kind of a way and said, "Well, Beardslee, what are you tossing in?"

I had prepared for this moment, and giving him a mysterious smile I casually sauntered to my car. I came back with the hated four-inch-thick control book left by my predecessor. I announced its author and tossed the book into the fire.

I gave a short speech, which took longer than intended because of the many pauses for beer toasts, about taking on the region and becoming the top new account generator. We watched long flames lick away at the files of damnation. Customary for any morale booster, we all proceeded to get very drunk. A perfect way to bury the past.

The next day, while nursing a cup of coffee and noting that even my hair hurt, Schwartz buzzed me and asked me to come into his office. "I heard about your bury-the-past party. And while I think the theme sounded good, goddamn it, Max, those letters you burned documented poor performance."

With a swollen tongue I said, "Maybe so, Ed, but the reps resent the fact that they're in the file."

I watched Schwartz purse his lips and screw up his face, an expression he used whenever he felt annoyed. "Well, burning control books was dumb; what if some of your people are not right for the business? That stuff documented a case to get them the hell out."

Schwartz had a short fuse. I picked my words carefully. "Ed, I'm accountable. If they can't hack it, I'll take them out, and they will understand why they need to go. I'll have the credibility to do it."

I felt good about my relationship with Schwartz even though I knew I hadn't been his first choice for a marketing manager. It was more a political issue than a problem he had with me personally.

Schwartz and Fillmore perpetuated a long-term feud. Schwartz had worked in Indy before Fillmore inherited the region and, when promoted to the position, had chosen to continue living in Detroit. He commuted six-hundred miles on weekends rather than reside in this central Indiana city. Fillmore's Patton-type forceful personality had been working overtime in an effort to get Schwartz to move. In addition to Schwartz's commute, his vocal expression of dissatisfaction with Fillmore's regional support programs, for no good reason, caused an all-the-more-strained relationship between the two men.

I tried to address the conflict and my place in it when I was interviewed by Schwartz for my current position. I knew even then that Schwartz did not like Fillmore and that Fillmore had forced Schwartz to accept me into his operation. I assured Schwartz I would be loyal to him despite the politics that had been played.

He had an interesting response: "I don't want your loyalty. I want your commitment to the job. Screw loyalty." An unusual statement from an unusual man. My observation had been that loyalty played big on management's list of priorities.

Now that all the basics had been covered and my people had started to work like a team, I focused on bringing them into the mainstream of general IBM sales life, getting them to focus on what IBM in general expected of them and how to make IBM's vast resources work to their benefit. One thing I wanted to find out was how well they would respond to short-term motivational goals like contests.

IBM behaved like a marketing company with numerous and ongoing themes and contests to increase the reps incentive. This bent might very well have been influenced by its chairmen of the board — to this date there had been eight — all of whom had come from a sales background. In addition to the divisional and regional motivational schemes, each branch made up its own.

Despite the differences in motivational programs, one could always find some form of visible recognition plan in place at every IBM branch in the United States; recognition seemed to be the most common method used for increasing incentive and motivation. These programs, however, usually consisted of a monthly sales performance ranking by individual — more like a competition among sales reps.

Invariably, the customary charts bearing the result were stuck on the walls in a prominent place. As they gathered around the newly-posted charts, most reps already knew their standing, but the black-and-white type served to remind IBM's sales force of the nakedness their position carried. Being on the bottom of the chart made one feel generally miserable, while being on the top brought a feeling of euphoria. In either case, a great amount of stress was involved with earning a respectable place on this list. Couple this with the pressure of making quota, and for some the situation became a nightmare.

A friend of mine who worked in a White Plains, New York, mental health facility (White Plains is where the largest IBM population resides) told me several stories about IBMers admitted to the psychiatric center for help after mental or emotional breakdowns. These patients' malady, she said, came from the stress of internal IBM competition and despair over not making or struggling to make their quotas.

Despite this reality, however, the majority of IBMers reacted positively to these motivational techniques. Indeed, the success of the programs justified their perpetuation.

Every branch also used some gimmick to announce any orders that came in for a particular day. The prevailing viewpoint was that the more visible that gimmick, the better.

Detroit had a complicated horn-buzzer-alarm contraption. The bigger the order, the more complex the action. A small order was recognized with a blast of the horn while a really large order got all three going off at once with an ear-piercing racket. Pittsburgh had a model train that would be set in motion with the details of the sales applied to the caboose.

Akron used a big plaster gorilla some politically-astute marketing manager had acquired at an amusement park in honor of their branch manager, Jim Gonzagowski. Because most people didn't want to sort through his name, we called him "Gonzo." He fit the billing. A custom-made five-feet eleven-inch frame held together a lumpy two hundred and seventy pounds capped by slicked-down dark hair over close-set eyes. Attached to the frame were two inadequate arms. Whenever one shook hands with Gonzo it became physically impossible to be more than a couple of inches away from his belt buckle. Looking a little like a gorilla, he was really a gentle and likeable guy. Gonzo tried a little Patton stuff on the troops, but they responded to him for what he was, an easy touch.

A large order got the gorilla paraded around the office on a platform held shoulder high by six or more sales people.

These recognition reminders could be a lot of fun and satisfied the desire of each branch to break away from the divisional theme and achieve a bit of individuality.

"Pat," I said to my wife over dinner one night, "all we have is a little dinky bell that never gets rung when a sale is made. I need to come up with something better."

Watching five-year-old John disdainfully pick at his salad, Pat thought about it. "How about a big gong like you see in those mystic Oriental movies?" she offered.

"That's it!" I shouted, startling my son so badly that his hand hit his salad bowl and tipped it over. I looked sheepishly at Pat, then said, "A big-assed gong to beat on when we get a sale! Perfect. What's for dessert?"

I put Albright and Gunderson on the project first thing the next morning. "At least four feet in diameter surrounded by a heavy wooden frame, that's what I want."

They didn't disappoint me. Within two weeks, a metal fabricator had designed a gong hanging from a four-by-four cherry wood frame. The gong ringer, a hardwood engraved handle with a head made of chamois wrapped around buckshot, capped it off.

With my team gathered around me grinning, I gave my muscular trainee the first swing. His broad shoulders and thick forearms produced a resounding *"BONG!"*

It delivered the message I wanted: levity and attention when a sale came in. The gong resided right outside my office, many times startling me with its resonant message.

By the end of October, our unit not only consistently met monthly objectives, we had a shot at being the top producing unit of the twelve in the region dedicated to new account sales. We were figured to run neck and neck with the new account unit in Cleveland.

My relationship with Schwartz, other marketing managers, the regional support team, and, most importantly, my sales team felt smooth and clear. I had Detroit's staffies wined and dined when they hit town, knowing they had flexibility about where they spent their time. The more time in Indy the better. I even helped Schwartz's relationship with Fillmore by getting him to appreciate the importance regional-sponsored seminars could mean to making branch revenue and new account numbers.

During a light moment after work, with feet up on his desk, Schwartz shared with pride something he'd accomplished. "Beardslee, I've been working on getting the president of the division, Jack Rogers, into the branch for months. He's finally agreed to come in two weeks. One of the things I want him to do is to make a sales call with you on your best high-potential opportunity. How about Bessire Foods?"

I had to hand it to Schwartz. Getting Clarence B. "Jack" Rogers to Indianapolis had been no small accomplishment. Rogers had nineteen thousand people in his employ, most of them involved in the manufacturing of computers as opposed to selling them. Consequently, with his time constraints he visited no more than eight to ten sales branches in any calendar year. Knowing that at least six levels of management stacked up between me and Rogers, whatever my assignment I intended not to screw it up.

Roger's visit allowed us to tell him first hand how a typical branch in the Midwest operated in 1975. Rogers would give a short "State-of-the-Nation" presentation to all one-hundred-plus members of the branch and make a couple of customer calls on swing accounts representing significant business opportunities for the waning months of 1975.

Bessire Inc., a multiple-location distributor of food stuffs and equipment to the baking industry, had installed a series of terminals in their seven distribution locations, which were, in turn, connected to a large computer managed by a service bureau on the East Coast. When Gunderson uncovered them, he found out they paid heavy fees to a service bureau and suffered from too little flexibility with that service. This company was a natural for us to penetrate.

By the time of Roger's visit, Gunderson had proposed Bessire use seven IBM System 32s, at the time IBM's most popular computer for first-time users. They were worth about fifty-thousand dollars apiece. If Gunderson could pull this deal off, it would represent one of the more significant multiple-system orders in all of IBM. Setting up a meeting with the president and controller of Bessire had been easy: they wanted to talk with our division's top guy before committing their multiple distribution locations to IBM.

I opted to drive Rogers to a restaurant on the northeast side of Indy to have a quiet business lunch with the top two execs from Bessire. Wearing this responsibility uneasily, I drove the road from IBM's branch to the restaurant the day before the meeting. Thus, I ensured that my planned route had no detours or other congestion problems. *Everything looks good,* I thought. *Should be a snap.*

As Rogers would be accompanied by his administrative assistant, I needed to consider what to do with him. Divisional vice presidents and those with positions even higher were authorized to have administrative assistants to help them through their busy schedule. In turn, administrative assistants were viewed as candidates for top exec jobs in the future. Working directly for an exec gave them insight into how the top guys planned their day. Hoping to be in that position one day, I wanted to make a good impression on Rogers' assistant, a rather bland looking fellow named Ed Lautenbach.

Turning to Albright I gave him my idea. "Ken, I want you and Eric to escort Lautenbach to the Indy 500 racetrack. I talked to him on the phone, and he seems to be looking forward to it. You never know about these administrative assistants, though. Maybe he's trying to appease me; but set it up, okay?"

My whiz kids had it worked out that Lautenbach would tour the track in an open convertible with a vice president of the track. The veep would explain the heritage of America's biggest race and highlight some colorful victories. So far, so good. My shoes enjoyed an infrequent shine before Schwartz's management team met Rogers and Lautenbach for a private breakfast at the hotel that morning.

Rogers epitomized the executive image all right. Quiet, with intelligent-looking features, he spoke slowly and in an even voice that seemed to say he was the master of all he surveyed. I couldn't help but compare my style of animated gestures and speech with his. *Did his mannerisms represent those of all the people at the top?* I hoped not, because that would preclude me.

While I remained convinced one only had to have a style to be successful, with IBM's penchant for conformity, especially further up the line in headquarters territory, I might have to do some cutting and pasting to make it up the corporate ladder's last rungs.

Afterward, Lautenbach took me aside. "I've got all kinds of messages waiting for me to deal with. I'm sorry, but I'd better cancel out on the visit to the track."

Shit, I thought. *Albright and Gunderson had worked hard arranging the visit.* Arriving back at the branch with only a few minutes before our lunch with Bessire, I collared Albright. "Lautenbach is crapping out. Says he's got too many messages to contend with. Will it bother the track guys if you cancel?"

Albright, decked out in a new charcoal-gray three-piece suit for the occasion and forty pounders glistening from a professional shine, slammed a manual on top of his desk. "For Chrissakes, Max, they busted their ass setting this deal up. I committed to supplying them typewriters for next year's race and all kinds of crap to pull this off. I don't want to have to break this."

Normally nothing phased Albright; his nervousness at snubbing Indy's most visible kingpins bore consideration. We needed to think this through carefully but had no time to do so.

"Ken, have the track guys ever met you or Gunderson?"

Albright, with an apprehensive look on his face, responded, "Nope, it's all been done by phone."

I smiled, "Well, then, grab Gunderson. One of you play Lautenbach and one of you play you. I don't give a damn which of you is which. You guys know how to do it."

Albright rolled his eyes back in his head, and a broad grin broke out of his wide, intelligent face. "Done!" He strode off to break the news to Gunderson as I walked into Schwartz's office.

There stood the president: lean build, average height in charcoal gray pin stripes and a vest. His tired eyes looked at me expectantly. "Mr. Rogers, uh, Jack, we're all set for lunch. I'll brief you on the way to the restaurant." My sweaty hands gave Rogers the typed brief I had compiled about Bessire.

On the way to the restaurant I seemed to field the questions Rogers asked me about Bessire and my career with IBM to his satisfaction. *If they don't screw up the meal, and if Albright and Gunderson handle the track,* I thought, *it'll be a great day for old Maxie.*

The execs from Bessire met us at the restaurant door. Promptly ushered to a table where menus quickly appeared, I thought, *so far so good.* The day before, I had asked the restaurant manager to give me their most experienced waitress, explaining the importance of the meeting. An attractive young lady, not the senior one I'd expected, did a professional job, and Rogers seemed to be thoroughly enjoying himself as he assured the Bessire execs that multiple-systems hardware and software support would be in place if they gave us their business. As lunch wound down, Bessire's execs made all the right noises about buying seven systems.

Wiping my continually perspiring hands on the napkin, I got up from the table to thank the waitress and pay our bill. As we stood only about three feet away from the table, in a low voice I said, "Great job, young lady, and as pre-agreed, put a twenty dollar tip on the tab." Since she wasn't the waitress I had asked to have wait our table, she also was not the one who knew about this pre-arranged tip.

"A TWENTY DOLLAR TIP!" she exclaimed.

I skulked back to the table, greeted by the smirks of the other three. A few minutes later; the little lady who looked like the daughter every parent would like to have, came over to the table, looked at me and asked with starry-eyed reverence "Are you with IBM?" She enthralled us all with her enthusiasm over working on a business degree at Purdue. "I hope to join IBM some day."

Rogers and I shook hands with the Bessire execs and got into the Toronado. "I believe all you've got to do is go pick up the order," he told me. Thanking the president for his help, I drove him back to the branch without mishap and turned him over to Schwartz, my formal role played out.

"Beardslee, Beardslee, wait till you hear this!" Gunderson and Albright yelled to me as I walked into the office. I thoroughly enjoyed their animated account about how Albright played the IBM exec and Gunderson played Albright. They'd received a tour of the track in an open air convertible, a tour of the museum and a personal dialogue from the track vice president about fuel consumption, concern for safety and crowd control. Gunderson, red faced and talking fast, explained how Albright fielded questions the veep had about Atlanta. Getting bolder as the ruse took hold, Albright had even invited the vice president to Atlanta's IBM divisional headquarters as his guest.

I, in turn, got them going again as I related my blunder with the waitress. Happy times.

Wrapping up the year in a big way, on Christmas Eve Gunderson picked up Bessire's order for seven System 32s. Coming into the office at about six that evening, he wailed away at the gong seven times. His only audience was me. Our unit netted forty-eight new accounts for the year with twenty-two of them gained in December alone. Setting a new Great Lakes Region one-month record, we finished behind Beeman's unit in Cleveland by just two systems — not bad coming from a zero after four months.

Everybody in my unit but one made the One Hundred Percent Club. Albright would be a candidate for his second IBM Golden Circle, reserved for the top three percent of One Hundred Percent Club winners. Golden Circle winners received lavish treatment; they and their spouses were invited to an offshore resort in Hawaii, Mexico or the Caribbean. I made fifty-one thousand dollars that year, thirty thousand of it coming from commissions. And we kept our momentum going into 1976. None of this goose egg crap again for us.

International Business Marionettes

On New Year's Eve, concluding that I had the world by the ass, I gazed out into the empty bullpen. A sea of empty desks, phones and the ever-present piles of manuals. Everybody gone but me. I walked over and rubbed my hand on the gong. Several dents in it reminded me of the incredible emotion I had seen when sales rep after sales rep came up to it and gave it a good whack.

Selling in IBM paralleled an emotional roller coaster. Lose a big deal, get a big deal. Lose another, get yet another. I couldn't resist picking up the four-foot-long gong ringer and giving it my best shot.

◆◆◆

April 1976

In the spring of that year, several thousand IBMers congregated at the Hundred Percent Club. The hazy blue skies and warm temperatures of Los Angeles were a welcome relief for those of us who had endured the cold and windy Indianapolis winter.

In the hotel lobby I ran into Schwartz. "Max, something important has come up that I would like to discuss with you and Mickey." (Mickey Monahan, the manager of the Terra Haute unit, and I enjoyed the closest relationships with Schwartz.) "How about a couple days of golf in Phoenix after the Club?"

An unusual request. I couldn't read this departure from the norm. "What's it about, Ed?"

"Can't say. Will you make it?"

Attendance does not appear optional; besides, what the hell. It should be a good time. "I'll be there."

Later in the day, Fillmore walked up to me. "Will you be back in Indy by next Thursday?"

Again, attendance didn't appear an option. "Yeah, Len, I'll be there." More puzzlement. Schwartz must be getting a promotion and Fillmore would be flying in to make IBM's customary announcement. I enjoyed the rest of the One Hundred Percent Club thinking only briefly about Schwartz's and Fillmore's cryptic messages until I got on the plane bound for Arizona.

I had to wait until our first golf game before Schwartz deciphered the message for me. Disdainfully, I watched my drive hook on the first hole in the hundred degree heat of Pheonix. Swat. Schwartz down the middle. Swat. Monahan down the middle. I wondered as much about the money I would lose as I did about Schwartz's mysterious invitation. I didn't have to wait much longer.

"Mickey, Max, I'm leaving the business!" Schwartz said as I swung. I missed a two footer for bogie. Down two bucks.

"Goddammit, Ed, you'd say anything to win a golf bet," I joked with anger-tinged words.

"I'm serious, guys, I'm leaving," Schwartz insisted. "As a matter of fact, I've already left."

Mickey and I just stood on the green, stunned, staring at the young father of seven children who we knew as a successful IBM exec. He was reputed to be pretty well off from an inheritance, but what the hell had caused this?

Monahan, my one-hundred-ten-percent-Irish buddy, hiked up his plaid pants and said, "Goddamn, Ed, if this is true, let's get off the golf course, go to the room and break out the whiskey."

We drove back to the hotel in silence, but once we had the bottle open and had poured ourselves some drinks, Schwartz took us through his reasons, but not in as much detail as I would have liked. Hoisting a glass of straight scotch, Schwartz pursed his lips, took a long belt then said, "You remember the rehearsal we had at the motel for the kickoff meeting for the new sales year?" I nodded. Monahan, being from Terra Haute, hadn't attended.

"Do you remember all the hors-d'oeuvres I ordered up?" I remembered. About twenty-five of us tore into plenty of chicken wings, meatballs and tortillas. We'd also gone through a hell of a lot of booze. I also remembered Schwartz paying for all of it with his American Express card.

"Well, I routinely turned in the expenses for the food and the booze about a month after the rehearsal, but I called all the booze food." Taking another strong pull from his glass, he continued,

"There was an audit on my expenses." He then muttered some stuff that I couldn't really hear about Fillmore trying to get him for several months, and then continued on with the story. "The bill was for about two-hundred fifty, including the food and booze. Somebody from IBM went to the hotel and found out that half of it was booze. When they questioned me about it, I naturally said submitting liquor was just a mistake ... that I forgot."

"Yeah, Ed," I said, "that's no big deal."

Grabbing the bottle of Cutty Sark, Schwartz capped his drink off. No pretense of mixing it now. "That's what I thought," Schwartz muttered with head down, "but the upshot of it was that Fillmore told me I would have to take a demotion to marketing manager or some staff puke job in Atlanta, so I said to hell with that and resigned."

Monahan and I put our drinks away at a rapid rate. Goddamn, it just didn't make sense. Everybody knew you never, never turned in booze as an expense. At other companies you could do it, but not at IBM. We had a lot of questions, but both Monahan and I could sense that Schwartz didn't want them asked.

Had Schwartz, tired of paying his own expenses in the commute from Detroit, intentionally turned the booze bill in? Had Fillmore tried to nail Schwartz by auditing all of his expenses? Had some asshole from the branch written an Open Door to Fillmore about drinking cocktails at rehearsal? If so, who gave a whit? It was after business hours, and besides, employees had worked late to get ready for an IBM-sponsored event.

The next day, Monahan and I privately discussed the incident. We both guessed that Schwartz probably turned the hootch in intentionally, tired of paying all the expenses and of IBM's dated booze policy. His ego wouldn't handle the resultant demotion.

Too bad, I thought. *I'd hate to have to leave IBM, particularly at the level he'd gained. Well, I'd never mess with liquor expenses, and I wouldn't have to worry about it.* I found myself wondering if my IBM candle blew out, to what other job I could turn. I didn't wonder for long; I had no plans to leave IBM.

With these thoughts in mind, at breakfast the next morning I told Schwartz, "Christ, Ed, there's life beyond IBM out there. Good luck."

Schwartz feigned confidence, "The next job will be easy, better than the one I left, with more pay."

I wondered if he believed it. Fourteen years with IBM down the drain over an improperly submitted invoice. The reason for Fillmore's trip to Indianapolis became clear — to announce Schwartz's departure. After playing a dispirited round of golf, we packed up and went our separate ways.

◆ ◆ ◆

Lying in my room at the asylum I thought about what Schwartz told me after I'd been fired. "From what happened to me, they figure you should have known better, Max."

Well, I thought, *I'd surely put it together wrong: believing expensing booze out as something else would be fatal, but expensing cigars out as something else would not.* IBM had used the rationale of my knowing about Schwartz in their firing process. Thinking my career with IBM was forever couldn't be viewed as a solid assumption either. Hell, in hindsight, I'd bent plenty of IBM rules. With their structure getting thicker and more rigid every year, why wouldn't one of their rules get me the way it had Schwartz and thousands of others? How come I could only come up with two sales guys I knew who had made it to retirement? Because damned few sales types, the riskiest of IBM's professions, retired, that's why. They either made it to the safe-but-boring haven of staff, quit or got fired. But, they rarely finished their days in the field.

As promised, the next week Fillmore flew in to Indianapolis and, with the audience buzzing from speculation over Schwartz's absence, brusquely stated that Schwartz had left the business of his own volition. No mention, of course, of why he'd left. The big man closed the meeting by saying he would return soon "with the best candidate for the job." Fourteen years of Schwartz's fast-rising career covered in a couple of sentences. My flushed face showed my anger over Schwartz's forced resignation.

In a couple of weeks, Fillmore showed up with the new branch manager, Charlie Samuels. Samuels' hooded eyes wore the mileage of hard work. His entire career had been spent in the South, most recently operating out of Atlanta as sales planning manager for the Southern Region.

After a few days, which afforded Samuels time to settle into his corner office, he called me in to his office. "I'd like you all to handle the branch meeting next week," he drawled. "Because it's my first one, it's important that I come across as being a guy who expects first-rate meetings." Samuels leaned forward in his chair, looking right at me. "You're good at making meetings lively. Fillmore told me. Now, what I would like is some entertainment, short skits, in between the business segments to keep it fast paced and lively."

"Okay," I said with indifference.

I performed poorly on this assignment only going through the motions since my resentment of Schwartz's absence was stronger than my desire to make a good impression on my new boss. When Samuels glared at me because the slide projector hadn't been set up right, I damned near gave him the finger wondering why this asshole had gotten Schwartz's job.

I'm not through with the funeral yet, and we're trying to have business as usual. Doesn't IBM management have any respect for the dead?

The next day, Samuels wasted no time in calling me into his office. He talked and I listened. "Beardslee," he said in pure Southernese, "that was a pooor ... pooor ... pooorrr effort yesterday."

Deciding Samuels was owed an explanation I gave him one. "Sorry, Charlie. I really am. Did a piss-poor job yesterday ... yeah, I did. What's worse is I'm not ready for you, yet. I haven't flushed Schwartz out of my system."

Samuels waited before making a reply. "Now, that I know that's the problem, and frankly I guessed that's what it was, why don't we talk about it?" he said sympathetically.

"Okay, look, Charlie ... I'm having a hard time that Schwartz got laid away over his expense deal. Booze was mixed in with hors-d'oeuvres and he gets offered a demotion. Doesn't sound right to me."

Charlie nodded his head. "No, it doesn't. And if there's any more to it than that, I don't know it."

We spent a couple of hours properly burying Schwartz, and I walked out of Samuels' office with a tremendous amount of respect for the man. He had allowed me to pour out the emotion I felt over Schwartz's fourteen years of effort being dismissed in two sentences. While not knowing the true details of Fillmore's relationship with Schwartz, I did resent Fillmore on this day, believing he went after Schwartz because he wouldn't conform, wouldn't move to Indianapolis from Detroit. *And,* I thought, *if your immediate boss didn't like you, he could find a way to get rid of you. Well, I do a good job of picking bosses, I always make sure we get along.*

◆ ◆ ◆

The sound of a bolt unsnapping brought me out of my nostalgic IBM world and back into the reality of musty smelling mattresses and bare walls. An attendant walked into my solitary cell. "Okay, Mr. Beardslee. You can return to your room now. You've been reassigned back to the ICU."

I got up slowly, my muscles cramped from so many hours of lying on the lumpy, hard mattress. I knew what I needed to accomplish. And if I wanted to do it, that would be easy. Get the hospital's staff to like me. I wondered if getting them to like me would conflict with my zeal for avoiding intimidation. *Yeah, it would. Which way would I go,* I wondered, *the way of freedom or the way of principle?*

Sixteen

S ONSA BITCHES. WHEN I GET OUTTA THIS BED, I'M GONNA BUST SOME heads." The slurred voice echoed off the ICU entranceway's dreary walls.

Sticking my head from my room out into the hall of the ICU, I investigated this latest disturbance. A dark-featured fellow with jet-black hair, two days' growth on his face and a gap between his teeth was being wheeled, strapped down tightly on a gurney, into the ward by two policemen. He swore up a blue streak.

"Goddamn fucking flat foots. You gotta have something better to do, you dumb bastards, than to be dragging my tired ass around. Untie me, and I'll bust your balls."

Curious, I walked up to the gurney until the stench of stale booze caused me to back off. Blackened, flinty eyes, one slightly off angle, tried to focus on me as he said "Hey, bub, get me a glass of water, will yuh? I'm about to croak." I obliged without hesitation, holding the paper cup for him as he noisily sucked up the water through split teeth.

He nodded his head when he'd had enough, and I took the cup away. Attendants rolled him still strapped on the gurney down the hallway to one of the four solitary confinement cells; presumably he would stay there until he sobered up.

I had gotten a close enough look at this fellow to regard him as nobody to fool with. Wide shouldered, heavily muscled and a mean looker. That slightly crossed eye topped off a person who obviously stood for trouble.

Besides, I'd overheard the patient care attendants talking while I gave the new patient his water, and they'd made it sound like he spelled bad news. One of the attendants had said to another, "You're new here. Stonehawk ain't. Watch out for him. Last time he was in here he broke another attendant's wrist. The guy quit, scared to come back here because of that crazy Indian. Stonehawk, see, told the guy he'd kill him if he had a chance."

The next morning, noise of a new roommate settling in woke me from a boredom-induced nap. I turned my eyes toward the sounds to see with whom I would now be sharing my quarters. The guy with the flinty eyes stood beside the other bed. Sober now, he silently walked over to my bed and bored into me with his cold, hardened eyes, the right one still slightly askew. *A mean looker,* I thought again. *Shit. Will I ever be able to sleep peacefully again, I wondered? Twelve rooms to pick from and they stick the guy with me.*

I let my eyes meet his, figuring this is one person I need to notify quickly — before he gets any ideas — that I don't intimidate easily. *If I don't do it now, I might be in deep trouble,* I thought. To my surprise, the corners of his eyes crinkled a bit and then he smiled. I took a breath for the first time since I'd opened my eyes.

"My name's Stonehawk, Thurmond Stonehawk. Thanks for the water. That was you wasn't it?" I shook his hand, meeting his full stare as I noted the steel in the man's grip.

"Yeah, that was me. Max Beardslee is my name," I warily replied.

"Nice diamond ring you're wearing," he casually noted. I looked down at the heirloom from my dad. "Yeah, and I plan on keeping it," I said, a warning in my voice.

The man howled with laughter. "Hey, don't you worry none. If I wanted it, though, I could get it," he said with conviction. "Just ask around. Around here, they figger me for a bad man. Actually, I'm just a pussy," followed by more peals of laughter. "Half Indian, I am. Hey, uh, Max, what the fuck you in for?"

International Business Marionettes

I had a propensity for seeking out unusual people, mostly risk takers of one kind or another, and making friends with them. This time, however, without any prompting on my part, I found myself sharing my meager abode in this dumpy den of dysfunctional souls with the most interesting person of them all. Thurmond Eugene Stonehawk. I began calling him, "Chief." This nickname endeared me to him.

As the days passed by, Stonehawk entertained me with endless stories about his life, mostly his career in Vietnam. A fellow who clearly loved to fight, he'd picked up a karate black belt along the way. Stonehawk only remembered losing one fight. Prodded by his fellow Green Berets in a Toronto bar, he'd walked up to a huge Canadian sergeant and laid a roundhouse right square on the Kanuck's jaw. "The sergeant grinned a little bit, picked me up like I was a baby, and threw me through a plate glass window," Stonehawk related, a wry grin showing the gap in his teeth.

While Stonehawk seemingly had no respect for society's rules, he made his own and applied new ones as the occasion arose. Despite his lack of conformity, he had adapted to the structured army life and even managed to get himself into the prestigious Green Beret division, which required all the more discipline.

Like him, I managed to avoid emulating and capitulating for the most part while at IBM, staying largely who I was before I joined. So had he in the army. *Maybe there was some common ground here,* I thought, *despite the fact that at first I thought the man merely a bizarre drunk.*

I asked him about that. "From what you told me, Chief, I can't see you obeying a bunch of officers ordering you around."

"Yeah, a lot of it was a pain in the ass, but I got drafted into the Army. I figured once I got into combat there wouldn't be so many rules. Just kill the Cong. And I did. Got me a bunch of those bastards," he said, a ready grin on his face all the time he was talking. "Once my lieutenant and sarge found out I was good at it, they let me alone. Should've too. Saved that lieutenant's bony ass more than once."

I decided Stonehawk wouldn't understand volunteering to work for a company like IBM with its protocols, structures and politics, nor would he care to learn to live within its strict confines. But, he had figured out a fine line between his own individuality and the army's requirement for conformity. Like a marionette, light of foot. Pull the strings too tight and he would dance up to a higher shelf, where they would slacken enough for him to be himself, at least most of the time. As different as the two of us were in many ways, when it came to individualism versus getting along in the structure, we were a lot alike.

Currently, it seemed, he was hell-bent on tearing up his body with alcohol, a subtle, probably unconscious, way to act out his death urge. I wondered what drove him to drink so dangerously much, and then thought about what had driven me to try to end my life in a much more straightforward and conscious manner. I compared myself, my personality traits and possible predisposition for mental instability, to my roommate. Here was a guy of unbelievable physical makeup who had excelled in the military. Intelligent, too, he could have a lot of opportunities in life.

Outwardly, nothing — not one thing — bothered him. If Stonehawk had been fired from IBM or dishonorably discharged from the army, I believed those actions wouldn't have bothered him beyond the day they occurred.

You could, perhaps, learn from him, I told myself. *What did he have in the way of confidence that I didn't?*

Like Stonehawk, I didn't always follow the rules or like them much. Unlike him, when disciplined for breaking them, whether the discipline was fair or not, I couldn't handle it, at least the last time. He could, or at least I believed he could.

Thinking about our considerable differences, I concluded I cared a damn sight more about my place in society and where I fit than he did or at least I used to. IBM had a dangerous hold on me as I forced my way up their organization. Stonehawk seemed more laid back. He took what came and asked for little, forcing little. Nothing had a special hold on him — except alcohol. Was Stonehawk addicted to alcohol like I had been addicted to IBM, or could he leave it alone?

"Look, Chief, I like you — so understand that I'm asking you this question as a friend. How come every time you get out of here, you go and get shit-faced? Are you an alcoholic? Do you have to have the stuff?"

Stonehawk looked hurt. "Nah, I don't have to drink. But the only way I get out of here is to escape. I know I'm gonna get caught sooner or later so I figure I might as well have a good time while I'm out. To me, getting drunk is a good time."

Uh, oh, I thought, *another similarity. I kidded myself into believing that how I handled business-related expenses was okay. Stonehawk has kidded himself into believing he's not dependent on booze. Well, I hope he's not,* I thought.

Stonehawk had gained a medical discharge from the service a couple of years back. "My liver is a pickled piece of beef," he said grinning, his flinty eyes focused on mine. "I was good for a quart of booze, sometimes two, for several years."

Admitted to the Fort several times before, Stonehawk was well known around the hospital. The psychiatrists didn't believe he would live very long, their predictions based on the heavy damage drinking had caused to his vital organs, particularly his liver and spleen. Diabetes had recently joined his list of ailments. They attended to him in a perfunctory manner; no attempts were made to teach him the evils of booze. *Probably did that in the past,* I figured, *to no avail.*

Stonehawk made a natural ally in forcing the staff to earn their keep since we both shared this pleasure. Indeed, it wasn't long before it became obvious that we operated in a similar manner. Falling short of infuriating the staff, I yanked their strings some, but backed off when they got too tight. Stonehawk operated the same way.

While I had many patients — and even some staff — referring to the hospital as Fort Fumble, within just a few days Stonehawk added a new nickname for all to hear. As he opened a large portable heated container called "Meals on Wheels" one day at lunch, a dozen half-baked roaches came scurrying out. Stonehawk prompt-ly dubbed Meals on Wheels the "Roach Coach." Thereafter, the ICU's faithful could be heard at meal time chanting, "Roach Coach, Roach Coach, Roach Coach!"

About a week after he arrived, the Chief sat down on my bed and informed me, "Buddy, I gotta blow this place. I can't stand it much longer." He'd told me that he had broken out before. Since he had drawn double coverage of staff members who knew his antics, I wondered how he would manage it this time.

"I'd like to get out of here, too. Got a plan?"

"Yes, but I gotta do it solo. Don't worry, if I get out I can get you out."

After discussing various options to escape, we made a pact, which fell short of exchanging blood, but which we took quite seri-ously: The first one out would help release the other.

Another week went by. I decided to continue pursuing more con-ventional and acceptable approaches to getting out of the Fort. However, conversations with my family about needing legal help to fight the court order keeping me at the asylum proved fruitless. My family felt that doctors were more prepared to say when I was ready to come out than lawyers. That logic only worked if the hospital and doctor provided normal patient care. Not so at the Fort.

During my most recent call to Pat, I asked what was new with IBM. "They're not saying anything right now, Max."

Damn, I thought, *not good. Kaufman would have completed his investiga-tion by now. Why not tell me the conclusion?*

Conversations with Heileman remained equally futile. Whacking away at this doctor remained hard and frustrating. He could mum-ble through medical jargon making it damned near impossible to get a regular discharge until he was good and ready.

Ms. Habel proved to be helpful, however. I now saw her once a week. Despite this fact, I now felt convinced that psychiatrists were medical students with unskilled hands who signed up for three years of voodoo to earn a livelihood otherwise denied them. Therapy didn't exist in this place, with the exception of Ms. Habel, unless therapy meant idle banter with Heileman for five to ten minutes most days. He said that if I would take Lithium, a compound that helps balance the highs and lows of those suffering from manic depression, he would permanently transfer me to the first floor and eventually release me.

"Dr. Heileman, you want me to take the stuff so you can write in your charts how much better I am doing and keep me in here, knowing IBM will keep paying the bill. No deal."

After another week passed with no hopes of getting an attorney, therefore, no way of challenging the court order placing me in confinement, I reluctantly started taking Lithium. The balancing drug had no effect, but Heileman started writing in the charts how much better I acted. *What a joke,* I thought.

True to his word, Heileman transferred me to the first floor. Stonehawk had already been there for a few days, having been on best behavior to earn the transfer and facilitate his escape. The double coverage on Stonehawk would slacken, offering him better chances of putting one of his plans into action. My odds of getting out, either through discharge or escape, would go up as well on this ward.

When I arrived, Stonehawk eagerly took me aside and told me he found a partially opened window he thought he could jimmy. Subsequently, he did and off he went, scaling the fence at the edge of the hospital grounds.

After an hour or so, the Chief called me from a pay phone. "Hey I'm out, but I busted my ankle."

I talked in whispered tones with him about releasing me "Screw the ankle. Are you going to stay sober? Get me out of here?" I felt the odds as fifty-fifty at best. If he thought he'd get caught, like he said, he'd merely get drunk.

"Yup," was his only assurance, and that became almost inaudible as the loudspeaker began to blare the familiar "RED ALERT."

"Stonehawk, hear that?"

"Yuh."

"It's a formal sign that you missed bed check." I could hear him howling with laughter.

The second night out, Stonehawk risked going to his own house. But walking up the street, he saw a police car stationed across from his house. As he said it, figuring he would eventually be caught wherever he went, he decided to just postpone the inevitable. Carefully retracing his steps, Stonehawk then sought out the nearest liquor store and bought a jug of Mogen David wine — "Mad Dog" as he called it — and downed it before turning himself in. I happened to be in the outside recreation area when a police car drove up with the warrior. Sadly, I watched the drunken Stonehawk have to be dragged into the building. In the process he tried to take a swing at an attendant half his size but didn't even come close, his fist meeting only air.

"I knew I'd be caught, so I decided to go for it," he later told me. "Why not get a drink while I still could?" I still wondered if he kidded himself about alcohol. Realizing that Stonehawk couldn't be counted on, I vented my anger at him by calling him in the ICU, where he got placed once again. From a first floor ward pay phone, I gave him hell for giving up. "You told me you'd only drink if you'd get caught. Sounds to me like you only drink to drink."

"No, Max, that ain't it. I was gonna get caught."

I wanted to believe him, but I wasn't sure I should. *In any case, I told myself, there must be a better way to approach an escape than his – and a better way than relying on him to get me out.*

I'd been thinking I needed a source outside of the hospital to get me out. My family would not help, and I had no friends in the area other than a former one, Lucido. Reading the paper that morning, the headlines full of mayhem and shootings, I hit on it. Newspapers loved the unusual. And this place, if nothing else, represented that.

Only two newspapers were read in the hospital: the *Gazette,* a morning edition, and the *Times*, an afternoon edition. I made a phone call to the *Gazette*.

After being routed to a reporter, I pressed ahead: "Hi there. I am a patient in a mental institution, and I want to report a number of patient abuses ... Hello ... Hello?"

Having the reporter hang up on me so quickly made me grab hold of my senses a bit more clearly. *Wait a minute, Beardslee,* I counseled myself. *You'd better tone this down. Ease into it. Think about it ... What would you do if you were a reporter fielding a call from a mental patient?*

Forcing a calmness I didn't feel, I called the *Times*, posing as an attorney. "Hello, I'm Bill Shepherd, an attorney for the A.C.L.U. Connect me with the editor, please."

The banter worked. I was transferred to the editor himself, a guy named Banyon. "Mr. Banyon, my name's Bill Shepherd, an attorney for the A.C.L.U. I'd like to take a few minutes of your time to give you what I know about patient care abuses at a local mental institution. If you believe I have a good story, what I'm asking is for you to send one of your reporters over there and interview a client of mine. A guy named Max Beardslee."

"Go ahead, I'm listening," came the ready reply. *Good start,* I figured, *keep building rapport before getting to the meat of my plan.*

"Well, I've been with the A.C.L.U. for ten years and not everything I work on turns out to be news, understand, but this guy Beardslee has convinced me part of the hospital is a holding tank for kids of wealthy parents up for possession or distribution of drugs. The kids duck in the hospital and get a phony diagnosis of some medical disorder to avoid jail. The hospital wins from getting the revenue, and the kid wins from staying out of jail. Got it so far?"

"Yeah" the editor replied, interest in his voice, "Go ahead."

"Also, Beardslee maintains, if the patient shows signs of being able to pay hospital bills for a long duration, that's what he gets — a several-month stay — whether he needs it or not."

The editor replied, "I'm interested, what's the next step?"

Hopefully I had the man hooked; I'd soon know.

"Look, uh, I had to impersonate an attorney to gain your attention," I told him with chagrin. "You've gotta agree I don't sound whacky on the phone, right?"

A hesitant response on his part, "I don't understand."

"Well, I'm the patient ... Beardslee. I'm not an attorney, but I know how you can get a front-page scoop.

"Wait a minute," he said. "You're a patient?"

"That's right and — Hello? Hello?"

A few minutes later, the white coats came. "Come on, you're going back to the ICU."

The editor had given his own unedited impression of my phone call to the hospital administrator. Back to solitary.

To fight the monotony, I asked for a pencil and paper. Maybe I'd be better off concentrating on something a bit more realistic, I thought, and began writing down more ideas for the book I still dreamed of writing. What came out on paper at first were my thoughts on the difficulty I sometimes had keeping my forward momentum going in the hospital. There were surely more reasons to backslide and become angry than there were to be hopeful and constructively work toward the future.

Before I knew it, however, my pencil recorded a much different time when I'd had quite a bit of forward momentum. I was in Indy at the time...

◆◆◆

Christmas 1976 came and went with Pat and me hosting the Beardslee clan, cheered up with the news that Pat was pregnant again. We were excited believing the baby girl we wanted was on the way.

The year-end marketing-manager scoreboard had my name third out of twenty-seven. I managed to finish second in the region for the number of new accounts installed, making my seventh One Hundred Percent Club and fifty-three thousand dollars in earnings — good money in 1976.

A friendly administrative person responsible for entering and tracking orders for my unit transferred in from Chicago and gave me something new to think about. "I need to talk to somebody about some real emotional problems I'm having. Frankly, I trust you and need to lay some things out on the table," Frank McCrary told me early in our association. I led him into my office and shut the door.

McCrary, a black man normally full of humor and enthusiasm, took me through a gut-wrenching story: His wife suffered from terminal cancer, and he did not know how to or even if he should tell his eight-year-old daughter and six-year-old son. Frank also shared with me that his booze consumption had recently approached alcoholic proportions. "I know I'm trying to block out the pain of watching my wife waste away," he admitted.

I decided to handle his situation personally, and a week later Pat and I had McCrary and his wife over for dinner. An attractive lady full of life despite her illness, she talked freely about her terminal cancer and how she felt spiritually prepared. "But I don't think Frank is. Help him at work, will you?" Two weeks after that, she was gone. Pat and I attended the funeral and met McCrary's two handsome children, who were obviously in shock over the loss of their mother.

Not long after his wife's death, McCrary, who was, understandably, devastated by the event, started arriving at work late and inebriated. I saw a personnel guy from Chicago around the office a lot; I knew he was there to figure out what the hell to do with McCrary.

Every day, I made it a point to spend some time with McCrary, one day warning him that I could smell booze on his breath and that the personnel guy skulking around was there to make an assessment of him. It didn't take long for the decision to be made, and McCrary was fired for dereliction of duty. I really struggled with that one, challenging Samuels on IBM's decision and believing somehow I should have helped McCrary more than I did.

"Max, it was out of my hands," Samuels assured me. "The corporation called the shots on this one. Their rationale was that McCrary showed no signs of becoming better, and the thing could not go on ad infinitum."

I wouldn't buy in. "IBM is so goddamn generous in so many ways involving charity, why couldn't they have put the guy in a clinic and tried to dry him out?"

Samuels hung his head, uncomfortable with my line of questioning. "I don't know what all went on there. Maybe they tried to offer him that and he refused. I do know IBM thought long and hard before deciding to let McCrary go. And you did all you could do, too."

On a Friday night a couple of weeks after he was fired, McCrary called me. He seemed to be in a better frame of mind, and we talked for almost two hours. He sounded excited about his plans: "I'm gonna buy a van and take my kids all over the U.S.A."

"Damn, Frank, that's great," I said. We hung up after my assurances that I would help negotiate a good deal for him on a new van. I looked forward to it, genuinely liking McCrary and wanting to be of service.

Thirty-six hours later I sat on the upstairs john reading the Indianapolis paper and for some reason glanced at the obituary page. A prickly sensation grabbed my arms and legs as I saw the name in cold print: FRANK MCCRARY. McCrary had met his maker sometime during the night we had talked. I may have been the last person to ever hear his voice. I had misread the situation totally. While I thought he sounded optimistic, McCrary actually had been lingering just hours away from death: a combination of booze and a broken heart taking his tortured soul.

More personnel types showed up to oversee the situation. Samuels tried to get death benefits for McCrary's two young children, but because he had been fired from the company, it never happened. IBM enjoyed a great reputation for being benevolent because of the money it donated to colleges and universities, the equipment it furnished to schools housing under-privileged children and many other causes, but in this case the company acted callously. Pat and I attended our second McCrary funeral, renewing acquaintances with people we had met just a couple of months before. We met an outgoing couple who planned on taking custody of the McCrary's children and made provisions to give them some clothing and toys.

◆◆◆

January 1977

IBM's General Systems Division announced its first built-from-scratch display station mini-computer, the IBM System 34. Prices started at fifty thousand and went on up to one hundred and thirty thousand. The innovation was a godsend for my unit. We had sold over one hundred System 32s, but the competition had begun to hand us our lunch with their advanced computers; the System 34 could put us back on top.

Sales of the new system poured into the office. With this second fast start to a year in a row, I could smell a promotion nearby.

May 9, 1977

Our long-awaited little girl arrived, except "she" turned out to be a "he." After two normal births, this time Pat endured a painful and drawn out delivery. "You bastard," she said to me through white lips, on her way to a Caesarian after twenty-two hours of labor. "This better be a girl."

"Yeah honey," I nodded, while gripping her hand, "If it's a boy, I'll be in the dog house, all right."

Christopher James Beardslee arrived. Pat radiated with pride as she held our newborn. "If you want to know why I called you a bastard, dear, try twenty-two hours of labor."

The next day Fillmore and his staff arrived in town for the important annual business review. Fillmore not only used formal reviews to determine the status of the branch and its marketing plan but also to eyeball the first line managers. To keep being promoted, one had to pass the intimidating Fillmore's muster.

Spot evaluations judged an individual's capacity to handle himself during a formal, pressure-packed review. The year before, a promotable marketing manager in Columbus had broken down in front of Fillmore's scrutiny of his business plan. The man had run out of words and had to leave the room, feigning illness; he'd be staying in Columbus for a good long while.

I could have been excused from the meeting since I had been up all night, but I felt so pumped up about the arrival of our third child that I drove over from the hospital and gave my presentation anyway. Taking liberties that I believed were there, I flipped over the page of my first chart. It read: "Len Fillmore Beardslee. Six pounds, five ounces." From that start with Fillmore's staff laughing, and even the man himself grinning, the rest of my presentation flowed equally as well. IBM lived off the almighty numbers and my numbers were there.

Not all people with solid sales records got promoted at IBM; the company didn't have the people growth to promote all top candidates. There was, therefore, a subjective side — appearance, unit morale, how well your higher-ups liked you. Without knowing it, but sensing it, I earned Fillmore's vote that day.

By mid-1977, my unit had sold over forty System 34s, all of them entered on the books as uncredited business; in other words, they were ready for delivery but had not yet been counted as sales. Crediting that business would cause commissions to flow and would equal the entire unit's annual sales quota, but there was something I wanted to do before that. Time to go see Samuels.

In his corner office, I shared with the Southern gentleman my short-term plans. "I'd like to move on, Charlie," I explained. My replacement can get off to a solid start by crediting all those System 34s later this year. Whoever got my job would have an excellent start."

Samuels committed to moving me on, but felt that my next position should be in Atlanta headquarters rather than back in the region. Samuels didn't like the fact that I had logged all my time in the Midwest, figuring I needed to see other styles in other parts of the country to help me get a better overall view of the company. "All your time in IBM has been up here in the Detroit area. I figure you need to get more exposure to the rest of IBM."

Remembering my visits to White Plains, I didn't see it that way, and told him so. "My problem is that anyplace bigger than a region, like the Atlanta divisional headquarters, will mean some dinky, specialized assignment. I don't want something so confining." By making a request for a promotion that didnt follow the normal way to proceed — and by gaining such a promotion — I was running against the grain again. But I believed it to be the best course of action for me. I'd take my chances under Fillmore.

"Okay, I'll go along with you," Samuels reluctantly agreed.

In August, Fillmore flew into Indy for a meeting with Samuels. Afterward, the big man talked to me about coming back to Detroit. "I'll have a job available in a couple of weeks. It's yours if you want it."

"I do." It didn't matter to me what opening Fillmore would have. Just getting to the next level and under his tutelage would suffice.

I left the Hoosier State on September first having earned enough business for the eight months of 1977 to put me in my eighth One Hundred Percent Club and to become the Great Lakes Region Recruiting and Training Manager. For the first time since I joined IBM, achieving the coveted branch manager's position became a possibility — although only about one in eight marketing managers promoted upward actually won a branch. I wasn't thinking about the latter fact, however; the only thing I could even believe at this point was that I would be that one who got promoted.

About two weeks after leaving Indianapolis, the branch hosted a promotion party for me. Albright picked me up at the airport and drove me to an apartment clubhouse. At this typical hard-drinking

IBM party, we got into the normal storytelling, roasting and farewell speeches.

At the same time, six IBM wives attended a more subdued good-bye party for Pat. But as the ladies giddied themselves over a few drinks, they decided it would be a great idea to crash my party; their husbands would be delighted to see them, they assumed.

Spouses resented IBM promotion parties as a further encroachment on their already-abnormal home life. IBM exacted a heavy toll from its field sales organizations and the families of people in these divisions felt its brunt. IBMers in these categories worked in a high-stress, make-quota environment of more than forty hours per week with some even working seventy hours or more. Spouses didn't enjoy their husbands or wives spending even more time at IBM-only parties and arriving home late and drunk.

About half of the people I knew, including myself, couldn't shut IBM down at the end of the day. So, before turning toward home we went to a bar and re-fought the battle, later arriving at our houses tired, burned out and disheveled. Spouses put up with lousy hours and extracurricular activities primarily because they felt the company afforded them so much security.

Yet, the spouses saw how their individual IBMers immersed themselves in the corporation nearly every waking moment, thus causing unbalanced lifestyles as well as behavior. The last string on the marionette controlled his or her actions even at workday's end. And, since IBM pulled that string, spouses had no control. Since it was normally taboo, crashing an exclusive IBM party such as the one being held for me was, therefore, not only exciting but a way to regain control for at least one night, anyway.

Midnight's first ill omen occurred as the wives walked up the sidewalk to the Club's entrance and observed one of my sales reps, known for being a gentleman, relieving himself on the shrubbery. As our wives walked by him, he looked back, his dick in hand, saw who they were, and gave them the following warm welcome: "Aw ... Shit ... What in the hell are you doing here?"

International Business Marionettes

Undaunted, our six spouses charged ahead. Inside, the welcome was not much better. Instead of being greeted with, "Hi, honey! Glad to see you," they had to negotiate overturned tables and chairs, cigarette butts on the floor, billowing cigar smoke and empty booze bottles. They took in a scene of about sixty people in various stages of alcoholic disarray, most unable to even focus upon them well enough for recognition. Looking up from the middle of a heated conversation with Gunderson, I saw the ladies faces transition from bright expectations to discerning frowns in the few seconds it took their eyes to sweep the room.

In the corner farthest from the entrance sat George Barton, a mild-mannered, pipe-smoking systems engineer with his right arm around one of Samuels' secretaries and his left arm around another, clearly having the time of his life. As his wife marched into the room and glared at him, Barton coughed up a classic: "My God. Here comes Carrie Nation and her crew!"

The party broke up rather rapidly after that, Barton and his wife being the first to leave. To my knowledge, Barton attended no more IBM promotion parties.

September 1, 1977

I left Indy noting that my promotion out of Traverse City had come on the same day of that month just four years ago. In that period I'd passed through three jobs successfully. This time very little trauma accompanied the change of jobs and towns.

Pat and I enjoyed weekend house-hunting expeditions and, with football season underway, attended a game or two at the same time. We found a new two-story house and signed a sales contract. A good start. The subdivision our Beardslee clan moved into upon this latest move, about thirty miles north of Detroit, appeared perfect. For John now seven, followed by Steve, four, and little Chris, sixteen months, good public schools were within easy driving distance. The money I had made as a marketing manager had taken the pressure off financially. Pat and I enjoyed our new home and new friends, most of whom worked at IBM enjoying a large population of people in the Detroit area, about eight hundred all told. I felt like a gambler on a primal roll. Every turn of the dice would bring another winning number.

Seventeen

PLAYING GIN RUMMY WITH THREE OTHER PATIENTS IN THE DOWNSTAIRS day room, I counted my losses. Down almost two bucks, hard to do at a penny a point. No primal roles today, or for that matter for the ten months I'd been out of IBM; my life of jacks and queens had been reduced to threes and fours.

Hearing a shuffling out in the hall, I asked what was going on.

"Haven't you heard?" said the guy with most of the winnings. "There's an inspection team coming in tomorrow. Today, they'll be putting new mattresses upstairs into the ICU."

Sanctimonious bastards. After spiffing up the place, the Fort's staff will walk around all smiles for the inspection team. Then, as soon as the inspection team departs, the ICU crowd will be back to the stained cardboard they call a mattress. I shook my head, and asked, "Whose deal?"

On three different occasions while I was in the Florida asylum, county or state medical teams arrived to perform inspections. During the first two, I flagged an inspector down and machine gunned away about filthy conditions, unfair incarceration and the Roach Coach but got nowhere. What the hell, I was loony, right? Who would listen to me?

The Fort Fumble administration team and medical staff made television's "M.A.S.H." unit look like a Mayo Clinic surgical team by comparison. Manny Hay, head supervisor of all non-doctors and purported stockholder in the hospital, knew of my efforts to corner these inspectors; I could expect no sympathy from him, especially as I had previously sent a letter to him complaining about the hospital assigning licensed practical nurses as ward chiefs rather than the required rank of registered nurse. With a third such inspection coming up, Hay busily signed orders for wall painting and other clean-up measures while psychiatrists busily schlepped their records into shape.

The Indian occupied himself with devising ways to escape, and I stayed busy plotting ways to influence an inspector. Given my track record during inspections, I was surprised when one of Manny Hay's underlings, a short fellow who, judging from his girth, missed few meals, summoned me into his office. Nervously flicking his cigarette ash into his coffee cup, the perspiring administrator's lips formed the words, "I want you to sign this piece of paper acknowledging patient rights, that you have read and understand the policies of this hospital." The guy could care less about any of that, but he needed to show my signature in his file. It was a State of Florida requirement.

I slammed my fist down on the desk, watching its effect with delight as coffee and ash danced all over his papers. "Goddamn, after forty days and nights in this dump you want me to sign something to make your inspection go okay? Screw you!"

Watching the potbellied man mop up his papers, I abruptly stood up from the table. This, as I suspected it would, threw him off guard. The look of fear on his face made clear his concern that I might attack him. He tugged on his tight pants, tried to squeeze by me and hurriedly left his own office with coffee stained records in tow.

As the inspectors made their rounds this time, I got aggressive with my efforts. Waiting for the group to pass me, I walked up to an important looking guy with a plastic ID tag hanging from a chain around his neck, stated my name, and pronounced, "This place is a dump."

The head inspector stopped dead in his tracks, clipboard in the ready position. I hesitated, surprised by his interest, then took hold of the opportunity I had created and began complaining about the hospital administration's profit-making motives and the general conditions of the facility. But, midstream he interrupted me, made some noncommittal statement and ambled off after the others.

The Fort's head nurse, visibly upset at my latest attempt to call attention to management, stormed up to me and ordered me back to the ICU. Upstairs, Stonehawk and I flopped on brand new mattresses, which were quickly replaced with the usual rotted ones after the inspection team left.

With Stonehawk taking a nap, I opened my now half-full writing tablet. Resigned to ride this place out for the duration, I picked up my pen and thought back to how IBM hired its people. *Certainly with more care than this mental institution had hired theirs,* I thought, remembering my recent experience with the assistant administrator.

I'd held my job as the Great Lakes Region recruiting and training manager for twelve months, spending my time hand picking new IBM trainees. In hindsight, I now saw myself as a recruiting error; Martin shouldn't have hired me to begin with. Unlike most good IBMers, I didn't just accept what I was told or just live by the structure of the corporate culture. I judged rules and regulations as to their legitimacy, occasionally disappointing their authors when I voiced my opinion about them being confining or inadequate. Yet Operation 30/30 and the creativity behind it, my ability to understand points of view of diverse people, those traits paid a lot of company bills. IBM should like creativity and, in that case, did.

But not on expense recovery, no sir. Tom Watson, Jr., son of IBM's founder, had been quoted as saying IBM wanted wild ducks. Yeah, I thought, *as long as those wild ducks fly in formation.*

Yet, I had been quite successful during my career with IBM despite my penchant for flying outside the formation. But I hadn't lasted as long as some like Fillmore. I decided to delve deeper into the question of who made an ideal IBM candidate.

Max Beardslee

December 1977

The Great Lakes Region finished first out of seven at year-end. We rated number one when considering all measurements such as product goals and revenue — a great honor for Fillmore. Amidst the competition of new quota assignments and product announcements, I started 1978's first-quarter hiring program. Hiring for the remainder of '77 was essentially complete, giving me an opportunity to study IBM's hiring plan for the New Year.

The figures called for two hundred new people to be brought into the region's professional categories of sales and systems engineering. Twenty percent of the total was earmarked from minorities and thirty percent for females.

Hiring women required no special effort on my part. In the late 1970s, about thirty percent of Fillmore's professional force of three hundred eighty were women working in sales and performing as well as the men — a far cry from the '60s when the only women hired into IBM were those with a math degree, three cats, no desire to work weekends, and a dislike for flying.

During the '60s a manager's preoccupation with passing IBM's DPAT resulted in the company hiring women with technical degrees like mathematics and to miss out on the growing number of talented well-rounded women who were graduating in other fields, such as business and liberal arts. Although female hiring practices improved in the late '70s, a casual glance in any management meeting proved that IBM management still looked like a men's club.

The forty minority trainees I needed to hire would be a tougher assignment. During the '70s, most of the big companies in America conducted love affairs with top black candidates on college campuses around the nation, needing to do so to meet federally regulated equal employment opportunity legislation. Competition would be tough.

I worked through the existing plan's mechanics figuring that about six thousand interviews would yield two hundred candidates. A thirty-to-one shot of joining IBM. *If the college kids knew those miserable odds, they wouldn't bother signing up,* I thought.

Admittedly, my job didn't entail the kind of harried pace I had while in sales. While some of my brethren, like Monahan, also had been promoted to staff jobs, they had landed positions more related to securing revenue. While they scurried around mopping up the year's close out, I focused on setting up a hiring strategy.

I made the rounds of all twelve IBM branches, leaving behind a "Headcount" plan of men, women, and minorities with branch management to insure they knew the workload required to net their hiring objective. Hiring fifteen people in a branch meant interviewing four hundred fifty — a heavy load.

When it came time for my Cincinnati visit, I paid particular attention. Thomas Blaylock, Cincinnati's branch manager, enjoyed a *"wunderkind"* reputation within IBM. The hard-working former Navy jock had enjoyed a big year, and it was rumored that he was in line to inherit a newly-created regional job, Sales Operations Manager, which had been authorized based on the division's continued revenue growth. Fillmore could turn much of his responsibilities over to the person manning the new chair, and IBM's always-active grapevine reckoned that Blaylock would fill it.

Cincinnati's boss wasted few words on me. Stubbing out an unfiltered Camel into an already-overflowing ashtray, he stated bluntly, "I don't have much time to go through the whole recruiting and training plan with you."

I had wanted to showcase my wares to Blaylock, who very possibly could be my future boss, but it didn't seem I was going to get that opportunity. Putting my disappointment quickly aside, I nodded in understanding.

"There is one thing I would like you to do for me," he continued, looking at me with steady and direct blue eyes. "Find me a stud. Get me an ex-fighter pilot." The former fighter pilot wanted to exercise a common hiring trait, "hire like self."

I could get to like Blaylock, I thought, remembering my air force days of hanging around with fighter pilots, "It'll get done, Tom," I said as I stood up and held out my hand.

Two weeks later I returned to Cincinnati with a former air force F-100 jockey. After a fifteen-minute interview with Blaylock, he was hired. Cincinnati's branch manager clearly was pleased as he called me into his office and said, "Thanks. We hired your man. Just what I wanted. Fast work." I patted my back for at least picking up a few points with this man on the move.

My recruiting and training job afforded me a view of how IBM made its personnel decisions, which, in turn, gave me some insight into the types of people working within the corporation and the corporate culture as a whole. For instance, IBM still used the same hour-long aptitude test to screen candidates for employment. While the Opie Dopies shied away from it, GSD and DPD mandated its usage for every one of their sales new hires. Reviewing the types of questions and the scoring technique, I concluded the test was more for determining IQ than aptitude. A personnel guy I knew in Atlanta confirmed my suspicions. "Yeah, we can draw conclusions about a person's IQ. Yup, we can do that."

The test's first section dealt with associating letters of the alphabet. Its second section showed pictures of objects changing shapes and asked the person being tested to spot the trend and predict the next shape by choosing the correct multiple choice answer. Part three involved basic problem solving. A lot of people had trouble here, especially if they hadn't had to solve math problems for several years.

The whole test consisted of ninety-five multiple-choice questions, each with five possible answers. Scoring allowed a point for each right answer minus a fourth of a point for each wrong one. Unanswered questions counted zero. A slight penalty occurred, therefore, for blindly guessing. The smart applicant would be advised to guess, however, if he or she could nail the correct answer down to two possibilities. The scoring spread out at: 25 to 40 = D; 40 to 50 = C; 50 TO 65 = B; 65 to 75 = A; and 76 on up = A+. Most applicants never knew their scores.

International Business Marionettes

Guidelines from Atlanta called for eighty-percent of the new hires to score A or B. Minority applicants tended to score lower than their white counterparts. The cause for the lower scores came from the selection criteria used for testing. Whites had to have evidence of technical aptitude and above average college grades before they were tested. A black person had only to be black to take the test.

Consequently, hundreds of minorities took the test nationwide with most having no chance of passing. In the process, they falsely dragged down their image amongst the IBM managers. When the annual Equal Employment Opportunity audit occurred, these managers, in turn, would haul out their lists of minorities tested and whine about being unable to find any acceptable candidates. In fact, some managers hadn't really tried to find acceptable minority candidates beyond asking their receptionists to test any minority showing up at the door.

Recruiting had its lighter moments. One of my best occurred at the University of Michigan. As a standard opener, I usually asked about the background of the applicant's father, figuring that if he had a business background it might, sort of through osmosis, have rounded out the candidate's business skills. After one lady enthusiastically impressed me with her academic credentials, I asked her the usual: "What's your father do?"

"Oh, uh ... well, he's in the cookie business," she replied with some hesitation.

Proceeding with interest, and remembering my Chef Pierre days, I queried, "Well, what portion of the cookie business is he in?"

She looked confused so I pressed her. "Distribution?   ... Sales?...Processing?"

With a puzzled look on her face, she hesitated with her reply; "No. None of those."

I blundered on, regretting that I had started this line of questioning. Maybe her old man licked frosting out of the bowl at the end of the assembly line or something. "Well, what does he do?" I finally blurted out in frustration.

"He's the president ...Archway Cookies."

We hired her after she scored the highest DPAT grade I had ever seen — a ninety-two. Months later, I found out that her father grossed a cool forty-million-dollars per year in cookies; I figured my osmosis theory had been well proved.

Concluding preparation to attend a weekend recruiting session, I planned to duck out early one Friday afternoon. Monahan changed those plans when he walked into my office and said in a hurried voice, "Beardslee, brush your hair. Blaylock just got announced in the new sales operations manager position, and there's a meeting in fifteen minutes."

Fillmore announced Blaylock's promotion to his staff and explained the new power structure. Fillmore would keep the branch managers, marketing support guys and personnel under his large wings while Blaylock inherited all sales measurement, budgetary and administrative personnel. Without it being said, we all drew the conclusion that in Fillmore's absence Blaylock would speak for him in any and all matters.

My intrigue with Blaylock intensified. Of the twenty or so branch managers whom I knew on a first name basis, he stood out as the most forceful, fair and comfortable with his expanding assignments. He represented the kind of guy who, having already come a long way in the company, looked like he would go considerably further.

The second day after Blaylock arrived, he left an urgent message for me. Blowing the dust off my unshined loafers and running a hand over my unruly mop of curly hair, I dog-trotted down the hall. Rapping my hand on his door, I briskly walked in, wanting to create the impression of a guy who could hustle.

A lit cigarette in hand, without looking up from his papers, Blaylock said, "I want you to run an important meeting for me. The kind of meeting that can't be fucked up. *Capisce?*"

"*Capisce,*" I said, hoping for conviction in my voice. Blaylock looked up and smiled, pleased that I hadn't shown any hesitation.

With the Camel now dangling from his lips, he explained the need for urgency. "It's like this. We've scheduled a big pow wow, because we're off to a shitty start and have to fix it. The meeting will let us get real precise on what we need done. I want the meeting in a special place. I don't know much about Michigan. You're from the resort area up north, I hear. Get on it, find a place up there."

As Blaylock fell silent, I turned to leave. "Just a minute. Lew Gray (Fillmore's boss) is coming to the meeting. Put him and Fillmore in special rooms. I don't give a shit about what you get for the rest of us."

Other than an order to meet with him the coming Friday to review the arrangements I would have made by then, that was it. No more direction. No more requests. Net guy, all right. And a man on the move. *I do like his style*, I noted once again, Theory Y.

I had previously done some research on these meetings by talking to staff managers who had been the set-up grunts in the past; I had known my turn would come. The raw consensus I had gotten about managing these meetings didn't bode well. Most of the descriptions I was given started with the letter "F" — fearful, fatigued, fun-starved, and fucked up seemed to summarize their feelings.

I did some more research by calling or visiting those who knew Fillmore and his tastes best, as well as those who had been to enough branch manager's meetings to know the ins and outs. "Beardslee, Fillmore wants prima donna treatment on a nickel-and-dime budget," Don Burger, Fillmore's czar of the all-important regional backlog — showing expected revenue from orders not shipped — told me. I respected him and took note of his opinion.

Burger also informed me that I'd be expected to dole out cigars, gum and mints — and not just any kind either — to the branch managers. Gonzo, by then a branch manager in Akron, liked butterscotch mints, and, said Burger, "He'll raise hell if none are available. Also, don't buy Fillmore any big palookas when it comes to cigars. Get the long narrow ones. Hand rolled."

"Okay," I said. "A bitch to deal with, huh?"

"Yeah, it is. They'll tucker you out some. The one I did, I was exhausted when it was over; you can't relax. Something always comes up. Fortunately, they are rotated. You shouldn't get assigned more than one or two while you are here."

Burger added the most humorous advice I received: "No two-liter bottles. Sure, they'll swill the stuff down, but Fillmore likes it in pints and quarts to create the illusion that small quantities are actually being consumed."

Quite the opposite, of course, was true. Since I already considered myself as having earned a Ph.D. in the art of illusion, I bought that part of it. Smaller bottles were a good idea.

Burger hauled out his wallet. "Take some money along, too. All you got is twenty bucks per person for all the extra stuff. That normally won't cut it unless the meeting is real short."

Monahan added the final tip, grinning as he said it. "Fillmore likes to eat, so make damned sure he gets a big slab of something at dinner, preferably from out of a cow."

With all this in mind, I went out to find a location for the meeting, settling on Sugar Loaf Mountain, a ski-and-tennis resort nestled in the sandy hills west of Traverse City. It was also the only place in Northern Michigan with indoor tennis. Fillmore liked tennis, and if unscheduled rain appeared, this would give me a back up.

The Friday review went well; Blaylock liked my plan. After some constructive criticism on how to organize a control book, a report laying out all the different facets of the meeting including travel, agendas, guest speakers, banquets, and golf and tennis he cut me loose.

Albright had just arrived in the region, being promoted out of Indianapolis to one of Monahan's industry rep positions. No more letters to Henry Ford for him, but the principle of seminar selling remained the same. Since I knew his strengths — and I could definitely use them — I grabbed Albright as kind of a grunt's grunt for setting up the meeting.

Two days before the event's start, Albright and I flew into Traverse City and drove a rental car to the mountain. By the time

International Business Marionettes

Blaylock arrived on Wednesday morning, we had taken care of all the logistics. The special rooms for Fillmore and Gray had turned into a furnished condominium complete with fireplace and steam sauna. The rest of the attendees had average hotel rooms.

Huge quantities of the prerequisite gum, mints, cigars, booze, beer, mix, peanuts, poker chips, and playing cards were in the ready. A large fruit bowl, including bananas and fresh cherries grown right down the road, occupied Fillmore's dining room table.

From his vantage point at the table, Blaylock picked at a cherry and fired through my control book in machine-gun-like fashion. "Okay, okay, okay ... What about the chairs? Have to be big ones. Okay, okay...." Each item was mentally checked off.

Fillmore checked in about four o'clock, and I took him over to the condo, showing him where all the booze and condiments resided. He tapped the king-sized bed that Albright and I had rolled into his condo for the occasion with king-sized fingers appearing pleased with the accommodations. After lighting a cigar that I'd specially placed in the bedroom, he asked, "You got Gray's flight schedule?"

"Yes sir!"

"Well, just bring him directly to the condo. Never mind the check-in procedure."

After an uneventful trip, with Gray reading mail on the ride back, as I ushered him into the handpicked condo, I couldn't help but notice the two dwellers' physical contrast. Gray, nine inches shorter than Fillmore, weighed one hundred sixty pounds. Fillmore weighed almost twice that. The difference reminded me of an argument Albright and I had about the need for two king-sized beds for these men. Albright took the position that Gray would resent Fillmore's preferential treatment if he was the only one with the sleeping accommodation.

"No, Ken," I'd argued. "If he notices it, he won't say anything. Besides, putting Lew in a king-size ... well ... we might lose him."

I'd scheduled a tennis match for that afternoon, but as luck would have it, the clouds opened up with a spring downpour. Moving to Plan B, the indoor match came off as scheduled.

Albright worked an adding machine conscientiously adding up all the expenditures made so far that would be paid by the attendees. Gray was taken out of the equation by virtue of his guest status. Expenses to date, including the condiments in Fillmore's condo, prizes for the tennis winners and tennis court fees alone totaled about fifty-three bucks a head — over twice my original estimate.

Wandering over to the courts, I figured I would give Blaylock a general update on that night's dinner and assure him everything was under control. Walking his way, I noted a huge pile of soiled towels wadded up in a corner of the indoor facility. Knowing each used towel added another buck on the bill, I wondered what the forthcoming dunning notices would total. I did some quick arithmetic in my head and the mystery soon evaporated — over sixty dollars per attendee. Blaylock visibly blanched when I told him.

"We can't do that, Beardslee. The per person limit needs to be twenty dollars. I don't give a fuck how you do it, but fix it." And off he jogged to watch the tennis match between Gray, Fillmore and a couple of branch managers.

I took my money problem to Paul Beckman. Beckman, the regional numbers guru, had survived over thirty years with IBM, all of it by playing with the numbers. I didn't tell Beckman the magnitude of my problem, just verified what IBM would pay versus what the branch managers would have to buy. I hoped that at least the gum, cigars and fruit bowl would come out of IBM's hide. No such luck.

Staging my questioning and trying to appear casual about it, I asked, "What kind of expenditures in meetings like these carry low audit risk versus high audit risk?"

Beckman raised his graying eyebrows at the question and stared at me through bifocals for several seconds before replying: "Photocopies, equipment rentals, meals, and meeting-room charges are low risk. Liquor is high risk ... very high risk."

"Thanks, Paul. See you at the banquet," I said and quickly left to ease my discomfort.

Grabbing the calculator, I did a little figuring. After ripping the tape off, I trotted out the door to find Albright and share with him Blaylock's "fix it" order.

"Tell the resort manager to call four hundred thirty-eight dollars of the non-booze stuff either photocopies, equipment rentals or meeting room charges. Absolutely no booze, though. Remember what happened to Schwartz."

Albright, without so much as a blink of the eye, walked off to find Sugar Loaf's general manager. Arriving back a half-hour later, he said, "Done. The shit is all swept under the rug."

My first big test came later that evening with a banquet honoring Gray. Albright had already greased the resort's chef with a twenty-dollar bill saying, "The guy at the head of the table ... make sure his prime rib weighs about two pounds. Got it?" While that detail appeared to be handled, I began to feel the strain that the boys in Detroit had warned me about — the "Four Fs" were definitely in play.

Albright, Beckman and I sat down on the bottom end of the U-shaped table with Fillmore and Gray situated at the top.

After serving started, Albright jabbed me in the ribs as Fillmore's slab of meat arrived. Judging by the numerous raised eyebrows, its size did not go unnoticed

I started to relax, but five minutes into the meal I could see a message being whispered down the table's left side going from person to person. Louisville's branch manager passed it on to me. "Fillmore doesn't like his roast beef."

For a couple of seconds, I felt my heart beating in my throat. Just as I began to panic, I realized the message was a joke — and a hell of a good one. I chuckled and nodded my acknowledgment that I'd been had, then with a sigh of relief began to eat my own dinner. After the waiters cleared away the clutter and brought after dinner drinks, fifteen cigars could be seen glowing around the table. Fillmore wrapped up dinner by presenting Gray with an XXL shirt for his efforts on the tennis court. About the size of a horse blanket, Gray held up the huge swatch of emblazoned cloth for all to see.

I made a mental note to remember that Fillmore and Gray operated comfortably together. *Good,* I thought. *When Fillmore signs off on me for a branch, Gray ought to buy into it solely out of his comfort with Fillmore.* I knew routine endorsement wasn't the case in other regions if Gray felt uncomfortable with the judgement of his regional manager. Some candidates felt they had to have exposure, a much-overused word in IBM, and invented reasons to visit Gray or his staff in Atlanta to be noticed. All I needed to do was hang in there under Fillmore, get my job done and trust him to make the next job happen.

Our banquet spilled over into the condo, where an all-night poker game ensued. Albright and I played waiter until two the next morning when Blaylock gave us the signal to beat it. We felt we had earned an "A" for our efforts and accomplishments and, in a moment of humor, sent a special "fruit bowl" to Blaylock's room: two cupcakes, a cheap cigar, a couple of grapes, and a can of Pabst Blue Ribbon.

Clearly, on one hand we had a manager who wanted the king's treatment — Fillmore, and on the other, one who just didn't give a damn about pomp and circumstance – Blaylock. Frankly, I didn't have an opinion as to whose style was the most effective. It didn't even really matter as long as I knew their criteria. That was the key. *Blaylock's style meant a helluva lot fewer complications though,* I noted.

After placing a request with the front desk for a 6:00 A.M. wake-up call, I thankfully put my head down on the pillow. My last thought, and a rather guilty one at that, was of my cover-up. *I can always undo what is done,* I told myself. *But what the hell, Blaylock knew the ropes, and he'd ordered it done. I'll think about it tomorrow.*

Albright played paperboy early that morning, delivering the W*all Street Journal* to every IBMer's door. Later, a hung-over crowd heard Blaylock and Fillmore take them through two hours of numbers pointing out the region's poor start and ways to fix it. Next, Gray stood up and offered a divisional outlook. Tremendous confidence exuded from this sales leader and his words gave promise of divisional growth and, therefore, promotional opportunities. Brando and others be damned; I had made the right decision by joining this team.

During a break, Albright and I sneaked over to Fillmore's condo for a quick booze count. I had hoped enough liquor would remain to allow for a budget cut by returning unopened bottles for credit, but only one half-full jug of scotch emerged amidst the dozen or so empties. *Damn! Nothing to be turned in for much-needed cash here.*

As our meeting wound down, Blaylock motioned for me to make some administrative announcements. "The airport limo will depart in fifteen minutes. Anybody with a transportation problem, see me or Albright. The refreshments, tennis and so forth, totaled ... twenty bucks apiece."

Too late now. The cover-up had become history.

Albright pre-positioned himself in back of the room by the exit to collect for the incidentals. As people began to leave, I hurried back to join him remembering Burger's advice: "Hold your hand out, or you'll come up short." Two guys walked out without paying, one of whom was Fillmore who could not help but see my outstretched hand.

Another math session with the calculator. Figuring what we had covered and what we had collected versus what we had spent, including the pro shop tab for Gray's shirt, we still fell one hundred thirty dollars short. *What the hell. The cost of doing business,* I figured and wrote a personal check

Blaylock walked up, baggy eyed from the last night's poker game and broke the news. "You guys got an 'A', and, I loved my fruit bowl."

All right! My first test under Blaylock drew high praise from a guy not noted for throwing it around. A solid start under his stewardship.

After Sugar Loaf's last IBMer mounted the bus, Albright and I walked into the lobby bar and got roaring drunk while congratulating ourselves on the meeting's outcome and playing back to each other the averted snafus. We agreed the roast beef prank had been the best. Neither of us talked much about our cover up, figuring that creative billing must be a way of life when you are running these types of events for IBM. The next day, we checked out.

With my first branch manager's meeting out of the way and my plan for reaching the recruiting target of two hundred permanent new hires nicely launched, I focused on getting these raw recruits ready for the trauma of training. In 1978, IBM's first-year price tag for new hires in either systems engineering or sales totaled a staggering sixty thousand dollars, up about twenty thousand from when I'd joined IBM ten years prior. Trainees' salaries averaged eighteen thousand dollars; the rest of the money was pumped into training and related travel, showing that IBM was willing to invest more than the average kid's entire college cost their first year with the company.

Assembling trainees the IBM way resembled studying for an advanced college degree with an emphasis on speaking clearly in a new language: *computerese*. The training program was still pretty much as I remembered it in 1967 and 1968. Three areas were emphasized: the technical side of the business (or what each computer component would do, commonly called "speeds and feeds") as well as computer programming and operation; the financial/usage side (what a manufacturer or distributor is expected to do with his system and how it is justified in economic terms, lease versus purchase, cash flow, etc.); and, last, honing communication skills, both oral and written. Many new terms had to be mastered, including a few hundred acronyms. IBM abbreviated everything, and all of the new terms had to be used carefully. Customers did not speak computerese, nor did they particularly appreciate it when someone else, sales reps in particular, spoke it to them. The terms were primarily for use within the IBM structure.

International Business Marionettes

Fillmore got a training report showing how his trainees ranked against the other regions — one indication of the job I was doing in helping attract quality kids. In turn, I broke his report down to the branch level, ranking them against each other. Occasionally, this data pointed out a lack in training emphasis at the branch level, but more often it showed that hiring the right people produced the right results no matter how much the emphasis on training.

As regional training manager, I hosted a two-day class for all new hires in Fillmore's region prior to their first class in Atlanta. No other region did this, perhaps because none of the other six recruiting and training managers suffered so miserably through training as I had done. Remembering the lousy start I'd endured, I wanted these raw recruits to be prepared.

For most of IBM's new hires, Atlanta training represented the first time their ability to make presentations had ever been graded. The poor souls would soon spend sixty to seventy hours a week in training, as Atlanta mass manufactured its marionettes. I still remembered my ordeal vividly — and my naïveté. I wanted them to know the score up front.

"They're gonna introduce you to the wonderful world of flip charts and crisp, concise thinking. Features, followed by benefits, followed by response," I informed them ominously.

Switching the tone, I acted out several different styles from loud mouth to bashful in going through some basic sales call scenarios, making the point of not letting IBM strip them of their own individuality. "Style is not important as long as you have one. Be yourself and be consistent." I knew, however, a lot of them would lose their style before the end of the year.

As Fillmore's region slowly moved up the new hire training scores, I became convinced that my efforts to take the edge off entry-level training had proved worthwhile.

In 1978, our region hired a number of articulate business-trained women, a far cry from the cat lovers of the '60s, but

Fillmore's geography offered little glamour, as we placed them in such garden spots as Youngstown, Akron, Cleveland, and Detroit.

Soon after training began, Fillmore called my attention to what appeared to be a growing trend: In a number of instances, after the first or second class conducted in Atlanta, single women trainees had returned to their Great Lakes locations and reported to their immediate managers. They said they'd become engaged to a man from "Fill in the blank"

"Fill in the blank" meant Atlanta, Los Angeles, San Francisco, Dallas, San Diego, or Miami. The ladies would push their manager for a transfer to a branch in said Sunbelt location, using future matrimony as the reason. Not so surprisingly, once these new hires arrived in the sunny South, their engagements usually terminated.

Although we put up a lot of fuss about these transfers, no effective way existed to stop them from being approved. After losing one particularly high-potential woman, Fillmore and I mulled it over. He drummed his big hands on his desk, looked up at me with a frustrated expression and said, "You know ... I wonder why none of these ... ladies ... ever fall in love with a fellow from ... *Buffalo!*"

A week into the New Year, Fillmore moved me to the position of Great Lakes Region industry manager. Replacing my pal, Monahan, who'd taken a job in Atlanta, I now managed eight people, all with burning desires to become marketing managers. They covered the region with seminars, scurrying to find new accounts in the region's main industries of manufacturing, distribution and finance. A front-burner job and another step in the right direction, I concluded. Back to the numbers once again, Beardslee.

While sitting in my new office, gloating, Blaylock stuck his head in my office. "Congrat's."

He wouldn't say congratulations, because it would take longer. *Yup*, I thought, *a net guy*.

"Get our purchase revenue going, and maybe you'll be working for me."

Music to my ears. I smiled, swiveled my chair to the side and swung my legs up onto the desk. *Sweet, sweet music*.

Eighteen

TINNY LOUDSPEAKERS MOUNTED ON THE WALLS IN THE ICU PLAYED music not nearly as sweet, however. The crackling and squawking that accompanied the Fort's P.A. announcements of doctor's rounds and pages easily exposed the fact that the vintage piece of equipment operated on its last leg. Just such an announcement snapped me out of my writings about what kind of people IBM ought to hire and awoke Stonehawk at the same time.

Knowing Dr. Heileman would first see a couple of patients nearer the entranceway; I spent the time reading my just-completed notes on recruiting.

> The perfect IBM new hire would be a person knowledgeable about business and the principles behind usage of computers. He or she should have a high aptitude in logical matters. A willingness to conform in dress and mannerisms would be preferable as well as the ability to withstand a consistent sixty-hour workweek.

> The applicant should be engaged or married and be willing to relocate anywhere, any time. Their skin should be thick to withstand the criticism and remolding that accompanies IBM's desire for conformity as well as the pressure of being ranked by sales performance for all to see. They should apply creativity selectively, and if it works, give credit to their boss. Preferably they should abstain from tobacco and alcohol, breed 2.2 kids and drive gray Chevrolet automobiles. They ought to have deep

pockets for shelling out cheerfully at IBM meetings for cigars, gum, booze, and mints and know how to kiss ass.

I laughed at my writing as I closed my tablet.

Doctor Heileman entered my room, gingerly avoiding Stonehawk's mean glance. "How are you doing today?" he asked in his usual nonchalance.

"Oh, about the same as any other day, Doc. Plotting ways to escape from this dump. But don't worry ... no more calls to the newspapers. How are you?"

Heileman heaved a long sigh and shuffled out of the room. Stonehawk, cackling over my mention of the newspaper ploy, couldn't resist a parting shot: "Gonna bill Beardslee a hunnerd bucks for the two minutes, Doc?"

Good question, I thought.

Later that week, Roger Martin, the man who initiated my venture into IBM, called. "My wife and I are in Florida. We want to see you."

Tears came to my eyes as I excitedly greeted Martin and his wife, Joanne, in the visitors' room of the hospital. "Roger, Joanne! I can't tell you how good it is to see you!"

"Maxie, sorry you're in here. We talked to your doctor before we got here. He says you're coming right along."

"Well, nice to hear, Roger, but he's not telling me that. Frankly, we're not real fond of each other."

Martin's daughter had come along and after Martin caught me up on our mutual friends, I asked her how she was doing. She said, "Right now I'm looking for a job ... and having a hard time finding one."

Without hesitation I replied, "Hell, I'll take care of that for you. As soon as I get out of here, you can go to work for the Maxwell Company, a company I plan on opening up."

I had occupied some of my long days with a mental discourse about what I would do when I finally did get out of the loony bin. During the last few weeks, The Maxwell Company had surfaced as an idea. The company would make loans to the disadvantaged, who had worthy business ideas, work with the mentally ill and perhaps even manage mental institutions. I'd need money to get started, but I figured IBM would be forced to provide that through my settlement.

Martin's eyes drifted to the ceiling when he heard my words. *Dammit,* I thought, *I gotta quit coming across as grandiose. Here I sit in this dump with not two nickels to my name, and I'm talking about hiring Martin's daughter; no wonder he rolled his eyes. Am I still messed up, I thought? Well, if I am, I don't know it.* Regretfully, because I really admired the guy, I said goodbye to the Martins.

It seemed that all my visitors showed up at once. Only two days after Martin's visit, Charlie Samuels, my former boss in Indianapolis, and his wife, Dorothy, arrived. My same exuberance showed through. I wanted to talk and talk about all the positive things going on in my life despite the fact that I remained locked up.

When I finished describing my vision for The Maxwell Company and a book about IBM, Samuels sobered me up. "Max, I'd never discount your talents. Never. But, I gotta tell you, from my side of it, you need to be in here right now. You don't look good, and you're hyper as hell. Now, that's no fun to tell a friend, but..."

"Hey, Charlie, call it the way you see it. That's one of the reasons I like you. I just disagree. I think I can do these things. And, if I'm hyper, well, I hope I live my life out this way, because I feel great."

Samuels just shrugged his shoulders. My former boss and I shook hands; I got a big hug out of Dorothy.

In the next few days, Heileman became a bit more friendly and attentive to my needs. Only he knew for sure whether my taking Lithium was by medical design or, as I believed, for medical documentation against my threats of a lawsuit. During my weekly session with Ms. Habel I shared with her my concern about Heileman and asked her what she thought.

"You appear to be fine to me, Max. On the other hand, I'm not a doctor. I also don't believe Dr. Heileman would keep you in here for purposes of gaining revenue or to avoid a lawsuit."

Since I had befriended Ms. Habel and always had been polite to her, she thought I was normal. *Maybe all I need to do is lighten up on the other doctors and staff at the Fort, treat them like I treat her, and I'd get out that way.*

At my request, Stonehawk and other patients attempted to help me avoid more trips to solitary by telling Heileman that the staff looked for reasons to kick my butt into the confining cells. It was hard to tell if he listened to them — or believed them.

Something jelled, however, causing my privileges to be restored and I was re-transferred to the first floor once again. What caused the change of heart — my visitors, my patient friends, Ms. Habel, or Heileman's own conscience — I didn't know, and I never found out.

I, of course, felt good about this change, but something else made me feel even better. By the time Chris Jonesby, on vacation from his job in Germany, arrived on April 29, Heileman informed me that I could soon leave the Fort freely. "You'll be discharged in a few days," he said matter-of-factly.

Since my discharge was now imminent, I was even allowed to leave the hospital and have dinner with Jonesby, the first time I was allowed outside its confines since I had been admitted. The temporary freedom felt wonderful, and I enjoyed every moment of my time with Jonesby.

"Okay, good buddy," I said after dessert. "We've been talking for a couple of hours now. I've taken you through why I should win in a lawsuit against IBM, my failing marriage, my opinion of the mental institution, The Maxwell Company, the book, and Christ knows what else." I looked right at him for emphasis. "Now, here's the sixty-four dollar question — and I want a straight answer: You know me as well as any man alive ... Do you think I'm nuts?"

Jonesby waited a few seconds before his answer. "Naahh ... You're the same asshole I always knew," he said and laughed. " 'Golden Boy' — I used to call you from the stuff you pulled in the air force. The gold's a little tarnished right now, because of the circumstances, but you're okay." I liked what he said; it confirmed my own beliefs.

Jonesby paid the bill. On the drive back to the Fort I told him,

"I know I could just leave with you right now, Chris, but we'll let the normal discharge process take its course. Will you call Heileman in the morning and tell him I'm still the guy you remember from the air force as a favor to help get me out of here, faster?"

"Yuh," Jonesby replied in his slow drawl. "I'll be back in Germany when you get out, but I'll see you when I see you."

I watched him drive away. *A damned good pal,* I thought.

In about ten days a check arrived to cover my travel home with plenty left over for food and hotel rooms. And a day later Heileman breezed in with the expected news. "You'll be all checked out by noon ... and because we like each other so much," he said with a grin, "I'll personally drive you to the airport or car rental agency, whichever way you want it." He paused and then, in a burst of unnatural humor, added, "Wait a minute. Knowing you, it'll probably be a cruise ship."

"Okay, Doc," I replied, good-naturedly. "Glad you can laugh at the end of this deal. Well, so can I. I need to say goodbye to all my friends in ICU and the little kid, Mike, in the children's ward. Okay?"

"Okay."

The only regret I had about leaving was that I would miss my friends left behind to unknown futures. The goodbye process turned out to be long and tearful. Little Mike at first acted cool, severing our close tie with his detached attitude to hide his disappointment and sorrow, but as I shook his hand for the last time, palming him with a five dollar bill for candy and snacks, the tough little bugger's eyes filled with tears. What would little "Huck" be faced with in a fatherless future?

Judy gave me a bone-crushing hug. I laughed, noting the spot of jam rubbed off from her kimono onto my slacks. She, too, got misty eyed. Would she just spend her life in the Fort, stealing and gorging food until she died? Probably.

Brunhilda shed no tears, but even she acted humane. "Gotta hand it to you, Mr. Beardslee. You kept us hopping."

"I won't miss your needles, Brunie."

Lovely Rhonda greeted my sad watery eyes with a pair of her own. A knot worked its way through my stomach as I reflected on the patients I'd be leaving behind. *Not much of a future for any of them that I could tell.*

Except for the Indian. He had a future. Our goodbye, a solid handshake followed by a hand slap, was made for appearances only and a wink over my shoulder as I left the ward had been an assurance I would see him soon. We'd made a deal ...

At noon, I walked out the front door with my duffel bag, glancing up at the misleading sign with the yellow painted happy face, then squinted at the brightly-sunlit world. Out! I was out ... for good! Putting my bag on the pavement, I stretched my arms high above my head and took in as much of the sweet smelling air as my lungs would hold, then slowly let it out. Ah, the smell of freedom.

Heileman drove me to a downtown Hertz rental agency.

Waving goodbye to the doctor, I walked into Hertz full of enthusiasm about my freedom and the future in general. Even the rental agent's reluctance to lease me a car without a credit card proved to be only a minor irritant. "How about a hundred dollar deposit?"

After a phone call to her supervisor, she filled out the forms. "Do you have a preference for type of car?"

"Yes" I quickly replied, reminding myself of my family background, "An Olds' Cutlass."

While wheeling the Olds' out of the lot, the feel of the wheel foreign to me after months of captivity, I felt relief that I finally had my freedom again. However, this feeling was tinged with anger at ever having to be confined at all and for such an extended period. I got angrier as I thought about my thirteen trips to solitary, the worst one being when I was strapped to the cot, the teenaged drug peddlers housed there to avoid jail and the head doctor billing me one hundred dollars for a phantom visit. *Pay 'em back; they deserve it,* I thought. And what better way to do it than the theft of Stonehawk, the man they vowed would never escape again. I'd break him out and then take him with me and get him a job in Michigan.

International Business Marionettes

Before I'd left, the Chief had sworn he would stay off booze if he knew he could remain free. Although I wasn't so sure that he'd hold to his word, I decided that I'd take the gamble, anyway. We made our plans furtively, my role clear. I would spend a few days on the beaches of Florida's West Coast, and when I tired of that, get the Indian. From there to Michigan. If the Chief behaved, fine; if not, he'd be left to his own resources.

Checking into a modest motel near Clearwater, I spent the next few days getting my institutionalized body back in shape by jogging up and down the beach. As I ran by the thousands of vacationers looking as normal as they, I wondered how they would view me if they knew that just a few months back I had lain huddled in a ball, totally delusional in a barred sanitarium.

The day to spring Chief Stonehawk arrived. The sun rose, its rays already melting their way through the slats of the lopsided Venetian blinds in my windows. Rolling slowly out of bed, I couldn't help thinking that so-called foolproof plans were more the stuff of dreams than dreams themselves. While my plan to set him free seemed logical, I could be caught. Getting caught meant a hearing in front of a judge where he or she would be informed that I, a mental patient discharged just a few days before, had attempted to free another patient who had been in and out of mental institutions for several years. *Try talking your way out of that one, Beardslee. A botched attempt could mean long term hospitalization. Well, I won't botch it.*

As I hurried through my morning shower, I began reviewing my shopping list: dark clothing, a small flashlight, bolt cutters. After breakfast, I drove up the coastal road for several hours. Going to another town to buy what I needed was part of my plan. If I did leave a trail of evidence, it would be a difficult one to follow.

Spotting an Ace Hardware store, I pulled the Olds' over and sauntered in, mirrored sunglasses and all. I grinned.

The clerk grinned back. "G'mornin', sir. Bet you need some fishin' tackle. We can sure help you."

"Not tackle ... not today ... need some ... got a bit of fixin' to do,"

I made a point of keeping my back to him as I continued mumbling in a friendly, relaxed tone, trying to downplay my shopping list. Moving down the aisle toward the back of the store, I began to chuckle softly as I imagined how a full-page advertisement promoting the use of Ace bolt cutters made especially for freeing mental patients might look.

The bolt cutters came in five different sizes with handles ranging from about a foot to four feet in length. The longest would cut just about anything, I figured, but would also be hard to conceal. Selecting a middle-sized pair, I went looking for the chain department while keeping careful watch to be sure the clerk was busy up front.

Several reels presented themselves ranging from flimsy links to those strong enough to keep logs from rolling off a truck. Placing the face of the cutters onto a roll that looked more formidable than the one I would need to cut back at Fort Fumble, I squeezed with all my strength. The links broke forcing a length of the chain to clank on the hardwood floor. Looking up in embarrassment, I was relieved to find that no one had taken notice.

Grinning again, I paid for the cutters, a flashlight and extra batteries, two padlocks and some thin wire. I wanted the clerk to think I really did have some fixing to do.

"When I get my chores done, maybe I will do some fishing," I remarked, as the clerk totaled my bill.

"Oughta do just that. Yessir. A man needs his fishin' time," the clerk said, "Fishin' is as important as..." His advice, sage as it was certainly meant to sound, trailed off behind me as I hurried out to the Cutlass. One more stop to buy some dark clothes, and I could go back to the motel in Clearwater, rest up and review my plans for the Chief's breakout.

Driving south on the coastal road, once again I began worrying, only this time about Chief Stonehawk himself. What if the first thing he did after getting cut loose was to hit the bottle? Eyeing the bolt cutters with growing anxiety, I remembered what I'd heard about his uncontrollable habit. It only took a few drinks to set him off, and the wild frenzies that followed were called "destructive" by those who knew him.

I switched on the radio and turned it up to full volume, then kept my eyes on the road ahead. Rock music blared, the lyrics unintelligible. Heat waves rose from the asphalt. The centerline began to waver, soon becoming a writhing, pulsating snake trying to shed its white skin. Fighting the apparition, I slowed the car and pulled onto the shoulder of the road.

Beardslee, if you go through with this plan, you could be judged as having lost your mind again. Can you really believe that cutting an alcoholic out of the asylum could ever be called the actions of a sane man, someone who's supposed to think and act normally? No. In fact, I no longer felt so great, not with the moment of freeing the Chief so close at hand.

But I had a commitment to honor, didn't I? What could be more important than keeping my word? *Aaahhh, promises made in a mental institution probably rarely are kept and are viewed as meaningless once outside,* I rationalized. *Maybe I should do myself a favor and forget about the Chief, throw the bolt cutters into the ditch, check out of the motel, head straight for Michigan, and get started on building a new life for myself.* I sat in the hot car, not moving a muscle, as I thought about my choices.

I gunned the car back onto the road and sped toward the motel. *I'd keep my promise to the Chief and, more important, keep faith in myself. By God, I'd do things my way for once. Call it therapy, my own special therapy, or whatever. I want to feel able to operate with my own rulebook instead of some-body else's.*

Back at the motel, I dialed the all-too-familiar number of the psychiatric hospital, my confidence slowly returning. The soft clicks sounded almost soothing. When I asked for Stonehawk, no questions were asked. The receptionist only gave a rather pleasant, "Just a moment." As expected, the moment ran on for several minutes as they tried to locate him. Then I heard the Chief's voice, sounding tentative and far away, come over the line.

"Who is it?"

"Me."

"Yes?"

"It's Beardslee, Chief, your friend ... and ticket to..."

"Yes, I see."

He sounded very nervous, and I guessed an attendant must be close by, maybe with an ear to the receiver. So, I tried to talk in the code we'd developed during long hours together. "It's a wonderful day out here. I'm ready to go to work."

"You are? What kinda job?"

"The one you and I always talked about, Chief. The big one."

"Huh?"

Clearly, my code talk hadn't gotten through. Did I dare be more explicit? "Stonehawk, can we talk straight out?"

"We can."

"You sure there's no one listening in?"

"I'm sure. The big broad that used to carry you off to solitary was hanging around, but no more."

"I have the tools I need to get you out of there."

Now, came the response I'd expected earlier. Enthusiasm swept away the cobwebs. The dark and dull side of him, brought out by a steady diet of tranquilizers, quickly turned bright and cheery "That's good news, real good news."

"Careful, Chief," I interrupted, remembering how his voice carried when he got excited. "We shouldn't say any more than is necessary. Now, is your recreation time still the same?"

"Yes ... after dark, as usual."

"Good. Then, tonight's the night."

"Tonight...," his voice rose again.

"Stay calm, now. Don't give it all away, Chief," I said, getting that nervous feeling again as thoughts of the possibility that we'd get caught entered my mind again. "Look, Chief, keep the lid on. You're talking loud. Somebody may overhear and screw this up."

"Okay, okay," he said, sounding just as excited as he did before my warning. We hung up.

Lying back on the bed I reviewed in my head the escape plan, a quite simple one that we'd rehearsed over and over in conversations together and then in our minds alone. Every possibility for error had been considered, all chances of getting caught had been reduced to a minimum. I'd park the car in a nearby parking lot used by residents of an apartment complex, then sneak through a few hundred yards of underbrush.

I started laughing, an easy, confident laugh. Funny, how I could visualize exactly what everything around the asylum looked like from the inside, but from the outside, now that was another matter. Nonetheless, I hoped I would enjoy the experience. Yes, if all went well, there'd be plenty to enjoy.

All I needed to do was slink through the bushes to the recreation therapy gate, cut the chain holding the gate in place, then wire the chain loosely back in place so that anything other than a close inspection would indicate the gate as being chained shut. Later, at dark, when Stonehawk and others came out for their exercise, he would pop out of the gate and jump into my rental car.

Stonehawk and I had cooked up a scheme to confuse and embarrass anyone giving chase should the escape be detected right away. Using the two padlocks and wire purchased several days before, the idea was to have me replace the original lock with two new ones, one inside and one outside the fence. The one inside would be locked. The one outside, Stonehawk would lock if he had time. That way, any staff people chasing us would run into big problems unlocking their own gate. Their keys wouldn't fit! In frustration and red-alert panic, they'd probably start screaming at each other about finding the right keys and scratch their hands and arms as they groped through the fence to fit their keys into the second outside lock.

But what if, on the other hand, they gave chase to the Chief before he had time to snap the lock?

"What if? What if? To hell with the what ifs!" I shouted at the empty room, then began getting dressed. Donning the newly purchased clothes — all dark blue, I checked out of the motel.

An inner calmness set in as I drove to the Fort, passed by it and parked in an apartment lot I'd previously staked out. The under-brush looked thicker than I'd guessed and it took the better part of twenty minutes to get near the gate from which the Chief would make his escape. But keeping my bearings proved easy, the loom-ing mental institution acting as a beacon.

Night, hot and humid, would be coming on fast. Sneaking to the ten-foot-high chain-link fence surrounding the recreation area, I could feel my pulse quickening. *So far, so good,* I kept reminding myself, as I studied the asylum grounds, craning my neck from side to side, squinting through the approaching darkness. The night patrolman was nowhere in sight.

Still scanning the perimeter in the hazy gloom, I removed the towel I'd wrapped around the bolt cutters and went to work. Overkill! The bolt cutters sliced through the chain like a knife through hot butter. Kneeling down, I set the substitute locks in place, snapping one shut. The sound of it locking resembled a rifle shot in my ears. Forcing my clammy hands to quit shaking, I then began wiring the chain back together. That done, I eased away from the fence, found a nearby place to crouch and waited for Stonehawk.

I knew it wouldn't be long before he arrived and was escorted into the recreation area. The staff ordinarily kept to a tight sched-ule. I hoped that tonight they would also follow their habit of let-ting inmates wander around unattended.

At the expected time, the floodlights kicked on. To my happy surprise, they cast shadows everywhere totally cloaking me in darkness. I took a deep breath, thinking I needed all the help I could get, then wondering once again if I shouldn't have just left the Chief behind. *Whatever happens,* I told myself, *I can't allow myself to be caught, even if it means sacrificing Stonehawk.*

Patients began filing slowly out of the building. Stonehawk appeared last, and, as called for by our plan, he sat in a wheelchair. He'd masterfully feigned the requirement for one, claiming that his sprained ankle caused him pain. Seated in the chair, he was

assured that the staff would allow him to go to recreational therapy and see him as a minimal escape threat. In fact, his sprained
ankle now approached full mobility and the wheelchair served an
unnecessary purpose.

Slowly, the Chief rolled himself in my direction, never looking
up, moving the wheelchair to and fro as if he didn't care where
he rolled.

Arriving at the gate, he swung around to face the building, his
back to me. Sitting quietly, feigning interest in a one-on-one bas-
ketball game being loudly contested back near the side of the main
building, he might have been just another tranquilized inmate out
for his daily airing. But, when Stonehawk looked over toward me,
and I saw the look of determination, I knew he'd somehow managed to avoid taking his tranquilizers that day.

The next moment, he jumped from the chair and threw his body
against the gate. Nothing happened. "What the hell are you doing?"
I exclaimed in surprise.

I paused before moving or saying anything else, afraid I'd shouted my dismay much too loudly, yet no one seemed to hear, not
even Stonehawk. He sat back down in the wheelchair. *Couldn't he
see that I'd cut the chain, that the only reason the gate hadn't opened came from
one of my new locks, open and with its clasp acting like a hook?* Only now it
had become tangled in the fence.

As loudly as I dared, I told him, "All you have to do is loosen it
a little."

If he heard me, he paid me no mind. As quickly as before, he
sprang out of the chair and charged the gate, hitting it with all his
weight, once, twice. The clanging continued until finally the gate
popped open on the third impact. Stonehawk shot by me without
so much as a word. Realizing no way existed to lock up behind us
now, I followed his crashing progress as best I could. He pulled farther and farther away from me, going off in the wrong direction.

Suddenly I heard a loud crack, and then silence. I found
Stonehawk writhing on the ground, clutching his ankle.

"Damn, I think it's broke."

"Try to stand on it," I urged, pulling him to his feet.

"Hurts like hell."

"But it'll hold your weight, won't it?"

At first, a loud moan sounded his only reply. Then, as the sirens went off and, "RED ALERT ... RED ALERT ... GATE THREE ... GATE THREE," blared from Fort Fumble's speakers, Stonehawk seemed to find an instant cure for his ankle. Grabbing me by the arm, he hissed, "You lead the way. We've got to get to the car."

As sawgrass ripped at my legs and branches whipped my face, I kept telling myself over and over again what I'd told myself before: *You should have left the Chief behind.* The words beat a steady rhythm in my head keeping pace with my struggling breath. Stonehawk limped badly, slowing us down more than I wanted him to, especially since the unmistakable noises of pursuit sounded close behind. My worst fears were coming true. The great escape we'd so carefully planned suddenly had become a three-ring circus, and the tent was threatening to collapse upon us.

We broke out of the brush and onto the road about a hundred-yards from where I thought I'd left the car. "Keep going, Chief. I'll go get the motor running."

"Don't leave me," he demanded

I shouted over my shoulder, "Don't worry," but wondered just how sincere I sounded.

Reaching the car, I jumped in, grabbed the keys from above the visor and jammed them into the ignition switch. The motor quickly roared to life. I reached over to open the passenger door, then flashed on the headlights. In that brief moment of illumination, I saw Stonehawk, only a few painful steps away. Ten yards behind him and closing fast, sprinted the ward attendant. Still, I bet on the Chief. Even if the attendant caught him, the former Green Beret would be hard to hold.

Luckily, the fatigued attendant duplicated the Chief's fall and, by the time he regained his footing, Stonehawk's split-toothed grin greeted me in the car. Jerking the gearshift into drive, I snapped the headlights off and floored the accelerator. The Cutlass lurched ahead, brush banging against it as I blindly tried to find my way onto the road.

"Headlights. Turn on the headlights!" Stonehawk shouted.

"Not on your life. Don't want anyone getting our license number."

Guessing at my position, I made a hard right turn in what I hoped was the direction of the road. The front of the car lurched off the ground and came down with a bone-jarring thud. The engine roared for a moment and then died.

Behind us, I could hear the shouts and footfalls of many pursuers. Slamming the gearshift into park, I tried to restart the car. Over and over it groaned, the sound of protest.

In the rearview mirror, I could make out the forms of several white-coated men about to reach and surround the car, and then pry us out and carry us back to the asylum. *There'd be restraints like straitjackets. And solitary. More time in the padded cells. The single light, out of reach, going on and off with studied monotony, the only sign of when you should sleep or wake.*

I tried the engine again. It caught. I eased the gearshift into drive and carefully accelerated, trying to ignore the shouts outside and the pounding on the trunk, doors and windows.

I switched on the headlights. The way out suddenly became clear. Tires squealing, the car roared away, carrying Stonehawk and me to freedom — at least for the moment.

"Go ... go!" Stonehawk kept shouting.

My initial reaction felt about the same, but it dissipated momentarily. As I drove north on 1-75, wary of police who would probably be responding to an APB by this time, the enormity of what I had just done sank in.

I found it rather simple to explain, or so I thought then. The Chief and I had complimented each other's talents when brought together from a miserable set of circumstances. From there, a bonding had taken place-requiring action on one or the other's part. With my freedom coming first, I was in the barrel. And I owed Stonehawk that. Other than Jonesby, my friends and family left me to my own designs seemingly not caring to help me obtain freedom once again. Stonehawk, on the other hand, had committed to getting me out.

Well after midnight, a "Welcome to Georgia" sign appeared in my headlights, followed by billboards advertising pecans and towels.

"A major milestone," I told Stonehawk. 'We've made it safely out of Florida."

The Chief grunted his satisfaction and quickly asked, "Now can we stop for a drink?" "NO!" I quickly shouted. "Fuck it, Chief. No booze. Sweat it out for a couple of days. You can do it. Goddamn it, you can do it. You did it at the Fort." My forced message seemed to get across as the Chief dropped the subject, saying nothing and then dozing off.

Two hours later, numbed from fatigue and tension, I spotted a motel sign. Waking up Stonehawk, I checked us in for the night.

Nineteen

I AWOKE THE NEXT MORNING TO SEE STONEHAWK SMILING DOWN AT ME, his eyes slightly crossed, face inches from mine; a dangerous looking man. After showering, we sauntered out to the car and once again headed north. After a few miles I looked over at the Chief, who was wadding up his jacket to make a pillow against the window. He stretched his long legs out, crossed his arms over his thick chest and closed his eyes. In a moment his mouth dropped open and he began to snore.

I turned my eyes back to the road, heaved a sigh of resignation and settled down into my seat for the long drive. My mind wandered back to IBM as the road stretched before me.

◆◆◆

January 6, 1979

In the now four-billion-dollar-per-year National Marketing Division, the new industry manager job I held meant trodding familiar ground for me. A key part of the assignment, managing the one hundred ten million-dollar Purchase revenue plan, however, would be new. IBM, traditionally a company that only leased its computers, now had become interested in getting customers to buy them outright. Gaining up-front cash put profits on the books quicker. I had the responsibility of insuring the region's purchase emphasis program looked creative and that our revenue number was met.

Six industry reps reported to me and they looked like an easy-to-manage group; all had been successful sales reps bent on becoming marketing managers. Remembering back to when I had their job, I knew they would do anything I asked. So, while somebody else tugged on my strings, I tugged on theirs.

John Beeman, my new account protegé from Cleveland, had the pleasure of being the region's 5100 microcomputer product manager. Unfortunately for him, the 5100 was IBM's antiquated-from-announcement, cheap (not to be confused with inexpensive) entry to compete with the growing stream of other microcomputer makers; this was to be the last wave of junk before the personal computers. Various internal names were given the 5100, such as "Throwaway" and "Son of Throwaway," but far and away the best handle I ever heard to describe this overpriced and under-functioned little desktop computer came from Bill Kunz.

Kunz, a Family Jewels Division convert, had been a spark plug behind Blaylock's success in Cincinnati, rolling up big numbers selling. As he watched the customary regional announcement take place Kunz could not fathom producing or selling something as small as the System 5100.

After Beeman's half-hour long demonstration, the six-foot Kunz walked up to the 5100, bent over it, sniffed his nose at it, touched the row of flashing lights, stepped back, and thought about what he had digested over the past thirty minutes. From the expression on his face, he obviously had something to say.

"What is it, Bill?" asked a confident Beeman.

"John, Johhnnn, Johhhnnnnn," said Kunz, still searching for the right words to say. "This box ... this box ... this box ... is good for one thing, and one thing only."

Taking the bait, Beeman asked, "What's that, Bill?"

"A night light."

Standing beside him, I cracked up. And so it was that "NiteLite" became the nationwide internal handle for IBM's first microcomputer.

312

Fortunately for Beeman, after a few months of packaging the 5100 as best he could, he moved under Blaylock as the sales planning manager, a position viewed as a sure ticket to branch manager heaven. The three previous chair holders had all gained this job.

I sweated out Fillmore's choice for the 5100's new product manager; Kunz had convinced me of its miserable odds of being successful in the marketplace. Arnie Chance, a fourteen-year veteran of IBM, filled Beeman's vacancy. Coming from Grand Rapids, Chance had been one of the leading marketing managers in the region for the last two years. Popular, nattily dressed and self-confident, he, too, would have his hands full with the slow-selling NiteLite.

Two weeks after Chance arrived in Southfield, I stepped into his office and asked the customary, "How's it goin'?"

Chance, looking tired with purple rings under his reddened eyes and normally groomed hair askew, motioned for me to have a seat. He had just finished a meeting with his boss about how to set up a branch managers meeting. Chance, a normally confident professional, had spent the last couple of hours reviewing the mundane world of gum, cigars, mints, booze, king-sized beds, fruit bowls, and the host of other details that went into Fillmore's meetings. During that meeting, Chance picked up on the spirit of servitude, part and parcel of the Great Lakes Region staff-management team, which sent him damned near into shock.

Chance's shaking hand held several sheets of paper that he gave me to look at. As I read parts of it, I realized they contained Ken Albright's notes on how to handle Fillmore's meetings. The big man had been pleased with Sugar Loaf, so Blaylock, unbeknownst to me, had Albright clone our act for the next one with written notes.

"Max, I can handle the NiteLite stuff, difficult as it is, but why is everybody around here treating Fillmore like a king? The briefing I just attended makes me ill."

We talked for awhile about my experience with the meetings,

but my words fell short of telling Chance how I had made ends meet at the last one; I didn't want to speak about it until I knew him better.

"I spoke with Shepherd about the meeting he ran earlier this year in Boca Raton, and you know what he told me?" Talking fast, Chance continued without waiting for me to answer. "He busted his ass to set up a tennis match at his dad's club down there and got personally stuck with the whole damn bill ... court fees, locker privileges and booze. Seven hundred dollars, I think he said."

Feeling uncomfortable, I just said, "Oh, yeah?" and then changed the subject to the subdivisions nearby that he should consider when buying a new home.

Two weeks later, I was shocked to learn Chance had resigned — and that he had done so loudly. He had written an Open Door to IBM headquarters in Armonk, New York, stating that, in his opinion, playing nursemaid at branch managers meetings was not right. As the region buzzed with speculation as to the contents of Chance's letter, conversely, Chance's boss clammed up while Blaylock also refrained from commenting. The half dozen of us staff managers, all intimate with meeting procedures, speculated about the effect Chance's letter might have. As far as we knew, nothing had come of it, and Chance, a private man in many respects, wasn't talking.

We further argued whether servitude or NiteLites actually caused Chance to resign. With our control strings stretched tight, we were unable to understand that some people in IBM-Land would not compromise themselves to get ahead, a definite blind spot in our vision. I decided Chance didn't like the NiteLite deal, a handy alibi. Still, I felt troubled. After fourteen years, it seemed crazy for Chance to bail out over a temporary job assignment.

By April of 1979, the Great Lakes Region suffered miserable 5100 rankings — sixth out of seven, but none of the other regions would make their quota either. We were merely the worst of the worst.

The downturn in our sales was caused more by outdated technology than by lowered sales ability or effort. While the rest of the world employed disk technology, allowing immediate access to any type of data, the over-priced and under-powered IBM NiteLite only used tape cassettes, allowing for limited and slow sequential processing. In addition, the economy in our manufacturing-dominant region had suffered. Historically, when the economy soured, first-time computer customers targeted for the NiteLite became the first in line to delay a decision.

The next week, I gave a full-blown pitch to Fillmore showing the progress of purchase revenue and industry programs as my part of the regional review meetings the big man customarily held. Our purchase strategy had started to take hold. Fillmore ranked third in the division, an excellent position for a region that historically stuffed a higher percentage of its hardware down customers' throats in December than any other.

I took stock of my progress and chances for promotion. I could perform in the tedium of staff if I had to.

Charlie Samuels, my former branch manager in Indianapolis, took a job in Atlanta. Beeman, ahead of me for promotion, became Fillmore's candidate for the vacated branch manager's job. But Fillmore didn't have the entire say about the job, having to reach agreement with his boss in Atlanta. *If Beeman goes, I'll probably be next,* I consoled myself. Since most staff managers resided in Atlanta, about two of every three branch openings went to head-quarters types as opposed to Fillmore's regional staff managers. Rarely, did more than three branch managers in a region of twelve turn over in one year. With the headquarters guys sucking up over half of those, it left one per year to a regional person. From having six or seven regional players competing for one slot a year, branch-es stayed tough to get.

Beeman's other sweat came from the all-white men's club run-ning Fillmore's branches. Rumor had it that the top execs wanted a black or a female implanted. It didn't happen; Beeman picked up the major promotion.

In turn, Blaylock picked me as the sales planning manager

responsible for tracking all sales measurements, forecasting the future of the region and resolving commission disputes. Only those Fillmore believed should be branch managers got offered the job that was now mine. With Beeman moving up, the last four sales planning managers in a row had made it. *The surest thing to a ticket out,* I thought, while mentally ticking off the previous caretakers of the numbers: Gorman, Sullivan, Gonzo, Beeman ... all went to branch manager heaven.

◆◆◆

August 1, 1979

A feisty, red-headed Irishman named Jim Wahling, with a strong appetite for Tanqueray, approaching retirement and a confidante of Fillmore's, hailed me into my newest job. "Welcome to sales operations, Num's." Now, I would serve under Blaylock, number two in command, and a man on the move. A short-lived celebration.

Beeman left in my hands the biggest ballbuster with which I had ever gotten involved, making my first meeting at Sugar Loaf pale in comparison. My new mentor netted it out.

"We're in lousy shape," Blaylock, a Camel dangling from his lips, began our private meeting in his office. "Fillmore has already, personally, humped the branches with what they have to do in the way of sales. And when they do it, we're gonna treat 'em right with our own brand of recognition."

Blaylock handed me a skinny folder. I read the neatly typed print on the single page it contained: "Mission: Recognize the first-line marketing managers who respond to the second-quarter challenge. Project name: The Great Lakes Region Hall of Fame." The only other information contained on the page were a few notes about the concept.

I knew already what Fillmore needed done. He'd had his staff dissect each of the twelve branches, pointing out their weaknesses in making their sales measurements. Each branch had a sales challenge as a result. What I needed to do was provide everything in the way of meeting rooms, logistics, hotel rooms, rental cars, presentation equipment, recreation and entertainment, guest speakers, and awards for the eventual winners.

Marketing divisions, GSD and Family Jewels installed about a third of their computers during the fourth quarter of the year. Our region had an even greater seasonality; about forty percent was shipped to customers the last ninety days of the year. Two prime factors caused the imbalance. First, the IBM sales reps worked harder and smarter in the fourth quarter since it was their last chance to make quota. Second, to receive the full year depreciation write off and investment tax credit available in the late '70s, a number of businesses accepted equipment late in the year as their last chance for write offs.

Every year Fillmore had to sweat it out, waiting for his usually predictable horses to break from the back of the pack. However, when the first-quarter results showed that we were dead last in business on the books and sixth of seven in equipment already shipped, he figured that this year he needed to get out the whip a little early. Fillmore needed to do something about the eight major sales measurements appearing on his report card where we looked lousy in seven; the exception being purchase revenue, where we held third place.

So for the first time in the region's history, Fillmore chartered an airplane. With the plane handy, he made the rounds of all twelve branches in about five days, hustling his big butt in and out of two plus locations a day, working as hard as I had ever seen him do so. His presentation honed to needle sharpness, pointed to the first-quarter results, the second-quarter target and what each manager had to make happen to qualify for the upcoming recognition event. Losers would attend to hear planned business topics but otherwise would be bystanders.

This campaign served as an excellent example of management through fear, especially with Fillmore delivering the specifics.

Nobody relished the thought of having to hang around Fillmore for three days if they didn't qualify.

Fillmore and Blaylock had settled on King's Island, Ohio, a theme park just outside of Cincinnati and the home of the National Collegiate Athletic Association's Hall of Fame, as the event's location. Each of the forty-five marketing managers and thirty-one systems engineering managers had a custom Fillmore-assigned objective. If you made your "sell objective" or your "install objective," your name was added to the IBM Hall of Fame. If you made both sell and install objectives, your name appeared in a special Double-Whammer category. And, if you didn't meet any of your objectives, you were in the "Hall of Shame."

In my new job, I became the official scorekeeper and head grunt of the whole competition. I mentally added up what Blaylock and Fillmore expected: three days of events for seventy-plus first-line managers followed by two days of events for twelve egotistical branch managers. Sprinkle over the top of all that about two dozen divisional staff types and another twenty-plus out of our own staff.

I knew this much ... I'd have to bust my balls. This time, however, Blaylock insisted on maximum assistance. "Grab anybody you want, Beards'. This has top priority."

Kunz, the guy who coined "NiteLites," a bright, balding, quick-talking, fun-loving heavy drinker possessing boundless energy, became my first recruit. "Bill, can you get me an 'A' in food and transportation?"

"Yup, yup, yup, yup!" Bill delivered his answer in usual machine-gun staccato. "No sweat. No sweat. No sweat."

I had a heavy load of picture taking and slide sets to produce. My weakness. So, I gave all that to Paul Nash, a black, former-marketing manager from Toledo. Nash, quiet, and somewhat sullen, appeared stoical as hell but possessed expert ability at that sort of thing.

With the major tasks farmed out, I needed a grunt's grunt, the lucky winner of this job being the lowest of the low. A slug. Haul people and their luggage to and from the airport. Have pants pressed at midnight. Make unanticipated booze runs, that sort of thing. Not wanting to abuse Albright so soon after Sugar Loaf, Rick Patrick became the unlucky winner. Patrick had been a solid sales rep but hadn't done anything noteworthy on staff. Like others before him, a tough staff assignment would shake him down to see if he could handle pressure under fire. If he could, we would give him a marketing unit. If not, he'd eventually return to the field as a peddler.

I judged Wahling, a ten-year friend of Fillmore's, as the best to write Fillmore's pitches; he agreed to handle all the scripts for Blaylock's presentations as well and to arrange for outside speakers from IBM and private industries.

Preparations went well, initially. Wahling persuaded Lou Holtz, then coach of the Arkansas Razorbacks, to speak, which blended perfectly with our Hall-of-Fame theme. He even persuaded the Indian mascot from the University of Illinois to come in and lay a surprise on Fillmore, who had played college ball there. The agenda took shape.

Beyond Fillmore's first line managers, Lew Gray and two other veeps, a half dozen directors, a dozen or so staff types from Atlanta and a gaggle of staffies from Detroit rounded out the guest list.

Watching the weeks go by, I counted the qualification beans and noted that Fillmore's fear-management strategy was working. Sales had increased dramatically.

As the week of the big event drew closer, arrival packets, rental cars, guest rooms, meeting rooms, special meals, outside speakers, grunts for the guests, press tent, operations room, and the photography set up were coming together. Following the Sugar Loaf success, we put Fillmore in a special set of rooms and everybody else into regular ones. The name of Fillmore's nesting place, carefully concealed from our macho leader, was the "Doris Day Suite."

With Kunz wrapping up a way to have home-made ice cream for dinner, Nash closing the loose ends on his planned video extravaganza, Wahling's script approved, and Patrick's control book even thicker than mine, we invaded Cincinnati. Fillmore's suite had an extra bedroom attached, perfect for the overnight executive guest. Each night, Monday through Friday, Fillmore invited selected people in to the suite, wined 'em, dined 'em, and politicked 'em. Nobody could do it better. Discreetly hustling supplies in and out of his room, I caught parts of it and felt like I was watching a virtuoso play a Stradivarius. In the course of the week, all of the directors, vice presidents, Lou Holtz, and branch managers, wound their way in and out of that suite.

Patrick, Kunz, Nash, and I sweated it out. Up at five-thirty sharp, dropping into the sack after midnight, we handled an overwhelming volume of activity.

Blaylock remained adamant that I personally restock Fillmore's bar, saying, "We don't want Patrick involved. We don't want Fillmore to know that junior staff knows about the booze." This detail seemed to be one of the few effects of Arnie Chance's Open Door, which had since kept everybody higher up on edge about the goings on at meetings.

Every day, three times a day, I personally restocked Fillmore's suite with liquor in pints and quarts, beer, mix, chips, peanuts, fruit, limes, olives, and lemons. Five days of that cost four hundred forty dollars.

On the third day, Fillmore met me outside his suite and placed a massive arm over my shoulder, "You're doing a good job. I don't know what the liquor and munchies cost ... from what I've seen so far, twenty dollars sound about right?"

Whoa, I thought. *What kind of game is this?* But one of my strings was pulled tightly. There was only one answer acceptable: "Yeah, Len. Thanks." As Fillmore walked away to shake another hand, I stood for a moment in disbelief, then shrugged the feeling off. *Well, what the hell,* I figured. *Blaylock and I will figure out the economics of it.*

Later that day, Blaylock ordered me not to collect any money from the arriving branch managers. "We're gonna handle it like they are the regional staff's guests." That meant trouble for me. Twelve times twenty meant another two hundred-forty dollars to be spread among staff managers. Balking at twenty dollars, they'd really heat up over the larger number, if I could get permission from Blaylock to raise it. Well, screw it, I thought. Blaylock would just have to raise it, and they'd just have to pay. No more sweeping stuff under the rug.

From Monday to Wednesday noon, more than eighty first-line managers attended the Hall of Fame. From Wednesday afternoon through Friday, we had twelve branch managers to look forward to. By Wednesday morning, our gang of grunts struggled for a second wind.

Nash ran up one hell of a photography bill, but what a show! He had hired a professional photography studio to help him with action shots of the day and photographs of the award winners.

Back in Detroit, before the meeting Fillmore had decided to order cut-glass wine decanters for the wives of the special award winners, all of whom were male in 1979. We carefully called these decanters water pitchers to avoid any stigma, any question about invoices for a gift used for booze. Lew Gray, vice president of sales out of Atlanta's GSD headquarters, arrived on Tuesday and sat through the awards presentation on Wednesday. During a break, the ever alert Gray walked up to Fillmore and said, "Bubba, where did you get the wine decanters?" intentionally jabbing at Fillmore's previous speech where he called them water pitchers. I quickly glanced away to conceal my broad grin.

After all the decanters had been doled out and Nash's three-screen custom slide show highlighting photographs of the attendees concluded, Fillmore introduced Lou Holtz. Holtz delivered a stirring message about being competitive, concluding with a story about his mother and her advice about the effort required to be a top achiever: "And, Lou, after you've done everything within your ability to play your best game, and you still fall short, then, and only then, can you rightfully say ... *piss on it.*" He brought the house down.

Wahling closed our show with the imported Indian from Fillmore's alma mater in full headdress and body paint, performing a war dance on the stage. Fillmore beamed with pleasure.

With the recognition meeting over, Fillmore held a short meeting with his six principals in the Doris Day Suite and told us how pleased he'd been with the meeting. Later, he privately told me that he heard only one complaint. It concerned using the amusement park's considerable game and ride facilities *"The systems-engineer manager from Evansville ... thought there should have been ... free ... tickets to the park in his packet."*

Watching Fillmore drum his thick fingers on the desk I knew then that the Evansville manager would remain in his job long enough to perform considerable principal reduction on his mortgage.

After his positive review of the Hall of Fame, Fillmore turned to me. "How's the meeting room for the branch managers look?"

The room had previously been reviewed by three others, but I felt embarrassed to have to say, "I don't know, Len ... haven't seen it, but it's the next thing I'll do."

His glare kept me company for quite some time, reminding me of my failure to handle this detail myself. In that room, Fillmore's direct reports would have several hours of data analysis aimed at them in fire-hose fashion — something likely to send anyone into a deep sleep within half an hour. For this reason, Fillmore paid particular attention to the room in which these meetings were held and wanted the setting conducive to attention.

Fillmore liked rooms of masculine nature, dark paneling, rich tapestries and drapes with a "U"-type table arrangement and large captain's chairs. I always placed him at the upper left of the "U" and visiting dignitaries at the upper right. Branch managers were positioned around the rest of the "U" depending on their year-to-date performance. I don't think they realized this, but the ones doing well sat near the front and the ones doing poorly got relegated to the rear.

Grabbing an exhausted Kunz and our hostess at King's Island Inn, we went to check the meeting room. My frazzled, sleep-starved mind couldn't believe it! A cramped room with an eight-foot ceiling and Tinker Toy furniture. After a few minutes of rearranging this and that with Bill trying to console me, I looked King Island's gracious hostess right in the eye and said: "Unacceptable."

The hotel's remaining meeting rooms were booked up, most of them by Delco Battery, a division of General Motors. Our hostess indicated she had a good working relationship with the Delco jocks and, if we wanted one of their rooms, she would see what she could do. Kunz and I looked over the two rooms posing as alternatives. Both were big and barn-like, again falling short of what Fillmore wanted.

Again, I looked her in the eye and said: "Unacceptable."

Only one option remained, getting a facility outside the King's Island complex. I knew moving would gain Fillmore's disfavor, but clearly nothing from King's Island would meet his standards. The overworked hostess, impressed with our seriousness to get the right physical setting, suggested we look at the room used by King's Island for its own Board of Director meetings. "It's located right in the middle of King's Island," she informed us. "I've never seen the place, but I've heard it's deluxe."

As luck would have it, the facility was available. I called Fillmore and told him that rooms currently available were "unacceptable," but I felt we had something that would be perfect and would like him to look it over with me.

Our hotel agent drove the car to the boardroom with Fillmore riding shotgun and Blaylock, Kunz and me jammed in the rear seat, the three of our bodies sweating mightily as they fought against the ninety-five-percent humidity. Despite the former problems, I began to feel that we would pull this off; the room would suit our needs. Filled with relief and gratitude, in front of a startled Blaylock I leaned over and planted a loud kiss on top of Kunz's sweaty, salty head.

Unfolding out of the cramped car and heading for the building I said a silent prayer. This better be good, 'cause I have no other ideas.

As I walked through the doors of the boardroom, my jaw dropped and I let out an audible gasp. I'd never seen anything like it before or since. Two separate rooms, the boardroom with a solid twenty-five-foot long rosewood table, and an anteroom with library and social accommodations, constituted the facility. Space-age audiovisuals were in the ready. Push a button and a viewing screen dropped down; hit another button and the spotlights went on. Luxurious captain's chairs, pewter water pitchers and crystal ashtrays topped off the accommodations. Kunz and I estimated the anteroom held about one hundred grand of furniture including a grand piano. Picture windows overlooked the amusement park, capping a perfect setting.

Wednesday night provided a breather. With all the first-line managers checked out, we had only to contend ourselves with insuring branch managers and staff types from Atlanta arrived okay and getting through a routine dinner. Around eight, we all settled down to a steak fry: Fillmore, Blaylock, branch managers, Atlanta staff, and the four grunts — Kunz, Nash, Patrick, and Beardslee.

Thursday's branch managers' meeting in the boardroom proved uneventful. On Thursday afternoon with just a half day left until the end of the meeting, I enjoyed a break in the schedule by playing a round of golf. However, the high humidity and heat coupled with eighteen-hour days had caught up with me. After eight holes I left the course and walked into the operations room, disdainfully picking up a note saying that Fillmore wanted to see me and review my next day presentation about Purchase revenue ... ASAP.

"You smell like lunch at one of those Greek places in downtown Detroit serving roast goat," said Patrick, who was in the operations room when I arrived.

"Thanks," I said with feigned gratitude. Sweaty, dirty and in clothes mucked up from driving a couple of balls into the woods, I jammed three sticks of liquid-center peppermint gum in my mouth, grabbed my presentation folder and dog-trotted over to the Doris Day suite.

As I walked in, I quickly concluded another half dozen had also been summoned to the mount, giving Fillmore a chance to preview sales messages to be given the following day. While I uncomfortably compared my stained garb to the other suited disciples, Fillmore asked who was ready.

"I am, Len," I volunteered, feeling uncomfortably out of place in the otherwise tidy setting.

"Okay. Let's go."

Fillmore, a fastidious guy, eyed my clothes then looked down at the pad before him on the table; I definitely needed to ditch the gum pronto. I couldn't give an understandable presentation with this wad in my mouth, but where in hell was an ashtray? Fillmore impatiently motioned for me to start. While he glanced the other way, I reached in my mouth, hauled out the big wad and stuck it on the front edge of my cloth covered chair, thinking it a disgusting thing to do but having no other option. I'd remove it when I was done with my presentation.

Fillmore smiled as I showed him projections indicating that we had a shot at finishing first in the division in Purchase revenue. After a few tips on how to improve my message, his eyes signaled I could go. Time to get out of there, down a couple of highballs and get ready for the night's dinner, and I wanted to get out of there fast. I walked out noticing my body odor. Patrick was right. I needed to clean up, take a cold shower and relax, I thought. I won't try taking a nap, though, I'll never get up.

Thirty minutes later, showered and somewhat revived; I worked on a cool gin and tonic and leaned over my second story balcony, gazing down at the Doris Day Suite. Out the door of the suite walked two guys in three-piece, pinstriped suits.

I could see the short one animatedly gesturing about something, but I couldn't hear what he was saying. The tall guy had bent over in what appeared to be laughter. As they came closer, their silhouettes looked familiar. I mused out loud to Patrick, who had now joined me on the balcony: "Christ, that's Rentlow and Hamilton! Wonder what's so funny with Rentlow?"

Then it hit me — *the gum! I forgot the goddamn gum!* From down below, Hamilton offered confirmation.

"Beardslee, you asshole!"

Rentlow, gagging from laughter, toppled over on the grass, three-piece suit and all.

When Rentlow composed himself, he brought Hamilton up to my room and, as I poured them both a drink, told me the story.

As I exited the Doris Day suite, Fillmore had commanded, "Who's next?" Hamilton volunteered and headed for my vacated chair where, for the next twenty minutes, he took Fillmore through his wares. "We're gonna do this, and we're gonna do that." All the time, as my highly energized little buddy wiggled in the chair emphasizing his point of view, each movement ground a little more of the gooey mass from the cloth of the chair to the cloth of his crotch.

Rentlow, with tears in his eyes, wheezed out the conclusion: "And when Dean stood up, the chair came with him. The goddamn front of the chair lifted right off the floor!" Even Hamilton started to laugh. "One foot of gum stretched from his crotch to the chair." Rentlow struggled with another spasm before he continued. "Poor Dean looked down, saw the stuff stuck all over his crotch and began picking away. Len looked it over — Christ, you know Lenny — drummed his fingers on the table, and said, 'Well, who in hell would do a thing like that — leave gum on the chair?' "

Hamilton wrapped up the story by telling me how he had managed to excuse himself, go into the bathroom and remove as much of the goo as he could with ice cubes, all the while cursing me, sure that I must have put the gum there. When he walked out, he thought about mumbling something to that effect to Fillmore, but the big man was already engaged in the next speaker's topic. Despite this diversion from the taffy pull, however, smirks and grins followed Hamilton out the door.

◆◆◆

On the last day, Friday, the morning's presentations went off without a hitch. We had survived. Time to close down the show and to thank the hotel's staff. We had sent their people through hoops for five days getting pants pressed at two in the morning, ordering supplies at a moment's notice, switching meeting rooms, and all the normal last-minute things that always happened at these meetings.

Kunz and I decided to go down to the local florist, buy flowers and deliver them to the hostess with our compliments. I asked for a standard bouquet, and they produced one for about thirty bucks. Kunz looked it over through booze-sodden, sleep-starved eyes.

"Nope, nope, nope, nope, nope ... won't do, won't do, won't do."

With the last "won't do," Kunz disappeared into the back of the shop, humming a tune. Twenty minutes later, he emerged. "Custom, Max. What do you think?"

Too tired to think, I just motioned to him to pay and get out of there. As we delivered the flowers, our hostess acted pleased, giving the both of us a kiss in return. I then told her to add a five-percent tip to the bill — not bad, considering the tab totaled fifty-four thousand dollars and change. Our hard-working hostess exclaimed, "You guys worked harder to make this go off than anybody we've ever had, and thank you, but—"

"But what?" I asked

"IBM never tips."

"We do," Kunz knowingly replied. "IBM is cheap."

With everything else out of the way, only some basic accounting remained. I looked up Blaylock, "The incidentals will run more than twenty dollars per staff manager. How do you want to handle the shortfall — i.e., can I raise the staff manager ante, at least for this one time?"

Blaylock thought about what I asked, his eyes taking on a tired look. "No, goddamn it, I would like to, but keep it at twenty. We'll get Wahling, Kunz, you and me to handle the difference."

"Okay, Tom," I said, shrugging my shoulders, "it'll be done that way."

This time around, I played expenses right by the book. About six hundred dollars of gum, mints, fruit bowls, and booze had been chewed, munched or drank. Forcing every staff manager who attended to belly up twenty bucks, we still fell short about two-hundred-eighty; Blaylock, Wahling, Kunz and I all kicked in seventy-bucks apiece. Clean sailing.

Quite a few of the staff managers attended the meeting for just a few hours, flying in and out the same day, and acted miffed that I dunned them, but I had the pitch down: "You are part of the Great Lakes Region management team, and you helped host the event. Think of yourself as a host — twenty bucks."

Returning home to West Bloomfield the following day, I got on the scale before jumping in the shower. I had lost twelve pounds in the seven days of playing King's Island Coolie. In the past, the mental stress and physical requirements necessary to get through these functions had drained me enormously, but the King's Island event sucked my energy reserves dry. Over the next few weeks I found that I couldn't eat normally, and I was tired much of the time. I endured occassional dizzy spells for two months.

Patrick earned an "A" for surviving the ordeal. In my opinion, although modest in character, Patrick was a damned tough survivor. A few weeks later, Mansfield, Ohio, became his home as IBM's newly promoted marketing manager — a validation of my opinion.

Reflecting on the King's Island experience and others, I felt convinced that IBM's manufacturing and development people, the bulk of the company's population, had no idea what pains sales types went through to insure a top motivational show. I doubted they would care and probably would believe it bordered on the ridiculous. People in sales knew their key trait by necessity had to be the ability to influence others and make things happen. Given the opportunity to run a recognition event, we tried to perform it the best we could, setting a new standard of excellence each time.

While we each had our own level of desire to accomplish the task well, a large part of the drive that kept us up until all hours doing things well beyond the call of our jobs came from the old marionette strings tugging away at us. Fillmore, holding all the strings, wanted us to dance ... and dance we did.

Twenty

CONTINUING NORTH UP I-75, WE DROVE THOUGH THE SMOKY Mountains. Talk was sparse as I continued to wonder about my wisdom in freeing the Chief.

Stonehawk grunted as we passed an interchange with several restaurants dotting the landscape. "Wonder what the Roach Coach is serving up today at the Fort?" he cackled.

"Don't know, Chief. You can bet one thing, though..."

"What's that?" he asked.

"It'll taste bad." More cackling.

As we entered a small town in Tennessee, we decided to stop and call our Fort Fumble friends. To prevent any implication that I might have had something to do with Stonehawk's escape, we decided he should do the talking. Stonehawk hobbled to a pay phone, his ankle obviously hurting from the escape. While he dialed the number, I suggested he ask for Nancy Reston, a nurse who could be expected to shoot straight in the hospital's outlook about the previous night's events.

When the Fort's receptionist answered, Stonehawk said, "Nurse Reston, please."

"Hello."

"Stonehawk here."

I could hear her response: "Thurmond, now you've gone and done it again."

Stonehawk howled with laughter, then replied. "I slicked you guys, good. Went right out the gate."

"Thurmond, we know how you got out," the nurse continued. "Is Max Beardslee with you?"

Stonehawk didn't answer. He just looked at me and I stared back blankly, unsure if she was bluffing.

"If he is, please put him on the phone."

Stonehawk handed it over. I took the receiver feeling apprehensive and said, "Hello."

"Max, the psychiatrists are furious about Thurmond's escape. He's in bad shape medically, being a diabetic with a non-functioning spleen and liver. You need to get him back here, wherever you are. You also were identified as the getaway driver."

I thought about what the nurse, one of the few I had liked at the Fort said. "Nancy, if the Chief requires medical attention, I'll make sure he gets it."

"Okay, but for you, if you're out of Florida, my advice is to stay out. There may be a warrant out for your arrest."

"Okay, Nancy. We'll stay in touch."

An operator came on the line wanting more quarters. While plunking more money in the machine, I thought of my dwindling funds. *The Chief and I might run out of dough before getting to Michigan.* I had to come up with a money-saving idea. We could always drive through the night, thereby saving the cost of a motel, but I didn't want to do that. I was afraid one of us would fall asleep at the wheel. We could sleep in the car, but we would risk having a cop shine his flashlight through the window and asking questions. Or I could come up with someone between Knoxville and Grand Rapids who knew me well enough to offer two beds for the night.

I thought about the latter idea for a few minutes until I remembered that an old IBM friend of mine, Bob Nichols, was a marketing manager in Lexington, Kentucky, just a few hours up the road. I called information and got his number, then placed the call in the hopes of bumming free lodging.

"Hey, Bob. Max Beardslee here," I greeted the familiar voice on the other end of the phone.

"Holy shit, Max." he exclaimed in surprise. "IBM's tie-lines are glowing about you and a deranged Indian war hero escaping from a mental institution. Is that true?"

I chuckled at Nichols' description of the story, initiated by my wife finding out about it and sharing it with one IBMer. Like a fire on a windy, dry prairie, the story spread fast. *Good. Let those bastards on the fourteenth floor know I'm alive and kicking.* "You know how the damn tie-lines are, Bob," I replied to his question. "People always exaggerate." To myself I noted the exaggeration wasn't far off.

"How are you? Where are you?"

Ah ha. My opening ... "It just so happens I'm in southern Tennessee on I-75 and headed your way. I figure I oughta be in Lexington in about three hours, or—," I glanced at my watch, "ten o'clock tonight. I was going to spend the night there."

"Let me meet you somewhere," suggested Nichols. "I'd love to see you." *Not exactly an invitation to bunk in his extra bedroom, but that might come later.* I agreed to meet him at an all-night restaurant near his house.

I rounded up the Chief, who I found walking around looking at animal tracks on the ground. "Been deer in here, a doe and her newborn." I smiled at Stonehawk's unconscious demonstration of his heritage.

"Let's go," I said; we climbed back into the car and turned north once again.

With darkness falling quickly now, Stonehawk almost immediately became bored and fell asleep. I was left alone to my mental musings, which, sparked by my earlier meeting with Samuels and Monahan and my phone call with Nichols, again turned to my IBM career.

◆◆◆

Max Beardslee

September 1979

The Great Lakes Region made its typical yearly uphill second-half run for the roses: Net Install Revenue Increase.

NIRI: IBM's bottom line measurement of business growth, continued to be our bugaboo. However, luckily for us, we sold the Series I, the division's combination analog and digital computer, in sufficient numbers to insure our leadership in that category. Our Purchase revenue, which had been building momentum, had gained us third place. Despite this, by the end of September we ranked only fifth overall coming from dead last before the Hall of Fame rally. I had my hands full in my new job as sales planning manager, especially since my two taskmasters, Blaylock and Fillmore, provided no slack for late or incomplete work. At the age of thirty-nine, for the first time in my life it became a necessity for me to be highly organized.

Resolving sales commission disputes between branches was one of the more unpleasant aspects of my job, because these situations could get nasty at times. Tempers flared over thousands of dollars of commissions and points of quota attainment. Most bickering came down to who got credit for what piece of equipment if it was sold in one state and installed in another or if existing equipment was moved from one territory to another. IBM's forty pages of finely typed sales plan covered every possible equipment dispute, but many of these policies required impartial interpretation. Thus, this part of my job occupied a great deal of my time and patience.

Most of the thirty-to-forty daily phone calls coming in to my office started out with a dissertation on who sold what to whom, which was followed by the problem as they perceived it. A few of my callers had political motives, and asked questions about how Fillmore or Blaylock perceived them. No matter who called, political news always proved to be the most popular topic.

The General Systems Division controlled individual incomes, flagging the big deals and often times raising quotas to hold down windfall dollar gains. As salespeople were paid on percentage of quota attainment, raising their quota reduced the percentage attained and, therefore, their income. A person could be out-producing what his managers thought he could do from their outlook at the beginning of the year. Then, wham — a quota increase — making his performance look just so-so.

Usually, nobody challenged the system, and, if they did, obtaining a victory proved even more rare. Plenty of cursing and stress came out of the distrust developed by the sales force for management because of their fear of potential quota increases. And the stress this type of situation placed on the sales force became obvious when rumors pointed to increased quotas as the reason two salesmen in the region required hospitalization for mental and emotional breakdowns.

IBM measured its business on a monthly basis. Commissions were given monthly, thus month-end accounting resembled a pressure cooker for those in sales. As the end of the month approached, forecasts turned into commitments at every level, and a large amount of paper shuffling and number jockeying took place. Most branch managers carefully massaged their forecast, because they knew sooner or later they would be asked to make a sales commitment that had to stick. Managers made deals to off-load commitments or pick up additional ones with a future IOU attached. The IOU said they could gain relief in a bad month.

On the fifth working day of the month I sent the region's forecast to the division. Two days later, the division's president sent its plate of goods to IBM headquarters. Two weeks of relative peace ensued. Then, two days before the end of the month, the division told the region what it had to have in terms of sales and revenue, forecast be damned.

The regional managers, like Fillmore, in turn, followed the adage of "Crap rolls down hill," and also ignored the branches' forecast. They directed the branches to produce "X" amount of business, no buts allowed, making the last two days a real madhouse.

An internal study revealed that ninety percent of GSD's monthly credited sales occurred during the last five days of the month. Every branch held its cards close to its chest, wanting to make their negotiated commitment, no more no less. Kind of like mess around, mess around, and then press! Fortunately this mind game was played by sales management only; individual sales reps escaped having to play this game.

One creative way our division played the commitment game with the corporation was to keep a couple of cards in our hand, not playing them all when we were supposed to. For example, in late 1979, GSD's new president, and my future nemesis, Bruce P. Hampstead, put out a management newsletter saying that GSD had made its sales objectives for forty-eight months in a row.

Bull roar. The division had a method of withholding excess attainment when it exceeded its monthly objective and applying the excess to other months as needed. Hampstead's financial wizards had built up a "bucket" of surplus sales revenue in 1979, keeping the corporation in the dark about it. Conversely, in the fall, the division missed its monthly sales numbers, but through the use of the bucket gave the illusion of making its sales objective every month. People like me, who saw the real McCoy, knew what was going on, but the corporation, I believe, never did. I learned the other selling division in the United States, Family Jewels, performed much the same game.

In late September of 1979, Blaylock asked me to join him for a drink after work, a rare request; he usually arrived early, and left late, heading straight for home. Over a couple of scotch and sodas Blaylock said, "I thought you'd like to hear how you are doing, Max. Len and I both agree that you should become a branch manager. All we need is an opening. When we have one, you'll be our candidate."

"Ill pick up this tab, Thomas ... with pleasure," I said grinning. We shook hands, and then headed our separate ways out into the night.

The only opening on the immediate horizon, however, came from the possibility of creating a branch in Charleston, West Virginia. We did that, but this time the Men's Club had to move over and make way for the first female branch manager. At her first branch managers meeting, eleven cigars and one rose greeted the attendees.

From knowledge gained in performing the Detroit branch office study, I knew what criteria Fillmore used in formulating his ideas as to whether branches were too big or too small. I had an idea that another study could make logical the off loading of part of Detroit to Lansing, and half of Lansing to Grand Rapids, making Grand Rapids large enough to constitute a new branch. I really liked the idea of controlling my own destiny by perhaps carving out my own branch and approached Blaylock for permission to staff it out.

"Go ahead," he replied matter-of-factly when I told him my plan.

With help from Fillmore's financial types, we ground through all business facets of the new branch, mixing them in with morale expectations and the actual expense to open it up. Some sixty pages of analysis were delivered two weeks later finely honed to Blaylock's demanding satisfaction.

In late October, Blaylock flew to Atlanta and presented the idea to Leo Bracken, IBM's vice president of Field Operations. Bracken didn't appear too excited about the idea nor did he veto it. From there, our plan remained on the shelf, but, fortunately, in early November, Bracken transferred to New York. Lew Gray moved up to Bracken's job.

In November of 1979, Gray visited Fillmore to determine the region's year-end finish. At the end of his meeting, Blaylock escorted Gray to the airport spelling out our reorganization plans on the way. This time, Gray approved them.

When Blaylock told me that our recommendation would be put into effect, a jolt of electricity raced through me. *I would be the region's candidate for the branch.* I would have heavy competition from former marketing managers promoted to the region's headquarters in Atlanta, however.

After reviewing October's final numbers, in November the consensus looked like Fillmore's region could once again shove, push and jam enough business in the fourth quarter to finish respectably. We expected to make every single objective assigned to us in 1979 with the exception of those surrounding the NiteLite. My tall, lanky friend, Rentlow, still had his hands full.

Fillmore perused most of the numbers as he kept his pulse on the business. Staggering amounts of data filtered in and out of his office on a daily basis. Transparencies displayed on a wall-sized screen, darkened with the ink of numbers, were used as the medium. Fillmore's uncanny ability to spot percentages involving seven digits within one percent remained a mystery to those of us who had seen him repeatedly do it. The numbers had to be accurate.

And then there was Rentlow. His transparencies, competing with numbers requiring two commas, carried a lot of white, not much black.

Branch	Systems Sold	Quota	Backlog	Delta To Quota
Columbus	4	3	4	+1
Akron	2	3	2	-1

Not much room for variation here. Rentlow dubbed himself with a new name: "Plus One – Minus One" and it stuck with him for the duration of his NiteLite days.

Launching the usual year-end sales rally, which could be like getting water out of a stone, Fillmore opted for a three-day branch manager's meeting in November. He asked me to pick a special location. The Hyatt Regency in Dearborn became my choice because of its good reputation and proximity to the Detroit Metro airport.

My previous experiences told me that booze alone would exceed the twenty-dollar limitation set for meetings, and by now weary of chipping in, I decided to approach Blaylock about expenses. I walked into his office, where he talked with Chad Russell, who still headed up the Purchase revenue program as he had when I was the industry manager.

I glanced at Russell, decided to broach the subject of money anyway, sat down, and said, "Tom, we've got to raise the twenty dollar limit for meetings. We simply cannot go on handling the overflow ourselves."

Blaylock didn't budge an inch on his position. "Look, damn it, Max," he said, a mean glint in his eye, "we can't raise the limit. Fillmore wants it at twenty dollars; he, frankly, would prefer zero."

I assumed his touchy stance had something to do with the Arnie Chance-sponsored Open Door. Fed up, however, with the constant pressure of having to pay for miscellaneous expenses myself, I pressed it. "Thomas, how about if I have a little talk with Len? I'm getting along with him, and I think I may be able to pull off gently telling him he needs to personally pay his fair share and raise the limit. A lot of people talk about how cheap he is. He needs to fix that."

Blaylock quickly stubbed out a Camel and hunched forward in his chair, his voice turning nasty. "Don't do it, Max. If you bring up the subject of his spending habits to Len ... well ... let me put it this way ... you're history."

Jeesuhs. A really sensitive subject. I got the message. "Okay, Tom, I'll drop it."

Russell followed me out of the office. "Bad news," he acknowledged. "I know this costs you personally every time there's a meeting. What are you gonna do?"

"I don't know," I said. I honestly didn't.

With Fillmore's meeting set for the twentieth, on the nineteenth I took a newly-assigned staff grunt with me and drove to the hotel. I had played it straight since the Sugar Loaf caper, but my mind was made up. *No more personal donations.*

Finalizing the arrangements with the sales department, I shared my dilemma of dealing with champagne tastes on a beer budget with the agent by using a direct approach. "If I need to have cigars, gum or mints called photocopies or slide projector rentals, will you do it?"

After a pause, the hotel's agent replied, "No, Mr. Beardslee we just can't do that." *Fine,* I thought, *can't fault the lady for that. I'll think of something else.*

Running late on meeting day, I bought cigars at the hotel and paid high bucks for doing so. I signed the seventy-seven dollar invoice reflecting that seven was a lucky number. *And a pair ... well ... that should double my luck.*

Before dinner, we had an unattended captain's bar — just help yourself to first-class booze. Drink all you want and divide it up by the number of attendees. *Yeah. Sure.* The branch managers, thinking of big pay checks in November and December, drank more than their fill. Year-end always excited them.

Smoking one of the hotel's long, hand-rolled cigars, Fillmore walked over to me in an unusually good mood. "Let's let 'er go a little longer than planned. The boys and our new lady are having a good time."

"Sounds okay to me, Len," I responded, thinking, *There goes the budget for sure.*

While we enjoyed Crepe Suzettes for desert, the captain's bar was held open for after-dinner liqueur. The Italian headwaiter, a recent immigrant to America, performed a superb job of heating brandy over the rich dessert, flaming each serving individually. Afterwards, with attendees either in the bar or checking into their rooms, I hunted up the flame maker and lauded his performance.

"What do you think the captain's bar ran us?" The Maître de's response put me right at budget sans the cigars. We still had two days to go, which signaled a shortfall of hundreds of dollars.

Hauling out a ten spot, I said, "You remember that invoice I signed for cigars. What about tearing it up and calling it photocopies?"

The waiter replied, "Sure thing. Makes no difference to me." He wrote up a new invoice for the lucky sevens. "C-o-p-p-i-e-s." Noting the spelling error, I signed it.

On the morning of the last day, Fillmore's branch leaders stood up and individually pledged where they would finish the year in terms of Purchase revenue, NIRI and the two emphasized products, the Series 1 and the NiteLite. In another room with four secretaries helping me, I worked on flip charts that summarized the pledges, noxious odors of magic markers filling the room. With the last numbers posted, I rushed the completed charts into the meeting room in time for Fillmore's concluding remarks.

The region would finish with a combined measurement of one-hundred four percent. Purchase revenue would be an excitedly anticipated forty million dollars in December, which Russell had forecast. If the pledges held up, we would finish first in Series 1 sales and first in Purchase — third or fourth overall. Not bad from dead last after the first quarter.

At the meeting's conclusion, once again doing the usual twenty-dollar collection as people shuffled out of the room, all but two people paid me, one being Fillmore. *What the hell,* I thought, weary of the collection effort. *What's another forty dollars?* Including the non-payers, we were short one hundred and fifty dollars. Blaylock and I split it. Back to the trenches for the year-end Tsunami. Fillmore had one more session with Gray about opening the Western Michigan branch, and Gray gave the answer we wanted: "Open it up the first of the year."

Knowing that the job was almost mine kept me going. In a great mood I plowed through my heavy workload with new intensity.

A couple of weeks after the Hyatt meeting, the hotel's invoices showed up. An accounts payable clerk called me into her office, Hyatt invoices spread out on her desk.

"Max, look at this one invoice for seventy-seven dollars. It's marked 'c o p p i e s' and signed by you. What does it mean, photocopies?"

What the hell, I thought. *No sense bullshitting her.* I didn't like her, but I didn't want to lie to her. "No, Martha, they aren't photocopies; they are cigars." I made no other comment and walked out of her office.

About an hour later the region's head administrative manager, Phil Langley, walked into my office and closed the door. Martha worked for Langley. "Max, Martha tells me this invoice is really for cigars. Is it?"

"It sure as hell is, Phil!"

Langley gave me a lecture and concluded by expanding on Paul Beckman's audit-exposure lesson two years earlier. "The best way to recover out of pocket costs is with mileage on your car. Just invent trips up to Flint a couple of times."

I reminded Langley that he, in particular, bitched the loudest about getting dunned the normal twenty bucks per attendee and that wasn't enough. "Blaylock and I usually end up paying the shortfall. It's bullshit!"

"Yeah, it's bullshit, pal. But, look, I don't smoke and I don't drink. I don't like paying anything. You gotta keep Fillmore happy about the meetings; I don't. It's your problem."

I didn't like Langley for that, but I knew he was right about my way of handling the cigars. I whipped out my checkbook and wrote a check to IBM for seventy-seven dollars. "Here, Phil, this oughta make you happy."

Now, other than the long-forgotten Sugar Loaf caper, I should audit cleaner than a doctor's operating room, I told myself as he walked out of my office.

In mid-December, a state of euphoria enshrouded the regional management team. The November commitments pledged at the Hyatt had been fulfilled. I spent December closing down the year through a continuous dialogue between the division and the region and the branches and back. One more time I asked Blaylock for an assistant, pleading that the extra work at year-end more than justified such a hire. This time he agreed.

Russell had done an outstanding job in implementing the Purchase strategy, making a perfect candidate for my needs in this game of numbers. I thought there would be no resistance from Russell; we got along well and Industry Marketing people considered it an honor to come over to Sales Operations. Such a move was perceived as a sure ticket to getting a marketing manager's job in one of the higher potential units. I was, therefore, surprised when at the initial interview Russell showed reluctance.

"Max, I've been traveling on weekends, working seventy-hour weeks. My wife and I have about had it. This is a real honor, but..."

Russell knew taking the job would entail working long hours every day to close the books on year-end. Further conversation showed he had made plans with his wife to visit their families in Louisville over the holidays. Telling Russell, "I'll see what I can do," I covered with Blaylock the salient points of my discussion with Russell.

"No way, Max. We've got to have Russell right through New Year's Eve," came the response.

Hard as it sounded, Blaylock was right. Either Russell or somebody else would have to work through the holidays. I went back to Russell and said, "I'll fix it so you can go back and forth from Louisville for a couple of trips, but we need you to help close out the year."

That night Russell broke the news to his wife. He later told me she cried all night, finding it hard to understand that her talented husband, having already busted his hump for months, had to work the holidays.

Busy climbing IBM's ladder and supporting the corporate string that said, "Do what ever it takes," Blaylock and I found it easy to understand. "Needs of the business."

On New Year's Eve, I delivered the closeout numbers to Fillmore. The big man, desk emptier than a sailor's wallet after shore leave, beamed at me as I walked in. He reviewed my latest projections, which said he was, in fact, going to finish first in Series I installs and Purchase revenue and a surprising third out of seven overall. After completing my pitch and wishing Fillmore a Happy New Year, I went back into my office There would be some last minute jockeying from the field with which I'd have to deal before I could go home.

At about six that evening, Blaylock stuck his head into my office with a big grin on his face. "Have a good cigar available," he said and turned around to walk out, then turned back to me and added, "and brush your hair," he chuckled and then left.

This has to be it, I thought. *Leaving Traverse City in September of 1973 finally has paid off. I'll be a branch manager and assume an operation with one of the highest potentials in the Great Lakes Region – and I'll return to my Genesis, Grand Rapids.* I got out of my seat and paced the floor of my tiny office, wiping my damp hands off on my pants and straightening my tie. *Damned near flunked out of my first IBM class – now, I'll be going back to assume the top job in Western Michigan for one of the world's most outwardly-prestigious corporations,* I told myself.

Fillmore's secretary came in. "Max, Mr. Fillmore would like to see you in ten minutes."

As I impatiently drummed my fingers on the desk and jittered my knee, burning off the nervous energy with which I found myself filled, I reflected on my career thus far. I had gained more confidence the harder the jobs became. Each rung of the ladder had added to my abilities. I knew that my training had been unique. Rather than having jobs in Atlanta with myopic missions, I had broad-based experience in personnel, industry marketing and sales operations. Unique training. Nobody else coming out of Detroit had covered all three bases.

The sky oughta be the limit, I assured myself. *A couple of years in Grand Rapids, and then move on. It would go on forever. Forever. Who knows, I might be the goddamn president of IBM one day,* I told myself while puffing out my chest with anticipated importance.

Knocking on the door of Fillmore's office, I waited nervously for a response. "Come in," came a booming voice. "Have a seat."

Damn, I thought, *the first time in my memory that I'd been invited to sit down in his office.* "You know, Max, I've been reviewing our progress in moving to our new regional headquarters down the street next month."

I knew. I'd been with Fillmore a dozen times at the new location as he perused every detail. A thorough man, he'd left no detail to chance.

"You know what that's going to entail. You are going to have to move all your control books over there ... move all your furniture ... the computer terminals ... all of that has got to be moved."

Fillmore paused and gazed out his window at the cold, wintry Michigan day. He then swiveled around and looked right at me.

"I know you would just kinda view all that as a pain in the ass, so I'll tell you what. Instead of that, how would you like to take over the new Grand Rapids branch?"

I stood up, stunned even though I'd expected this announcement, handed Fillmore a damp cigar from the interior of my suit, and shook his huge hand. For that brief moment in time I was speechless. Whatever I'd thought to say seemed silly.

Then Blaylock came in, all grins, and gave me a hard punch to the shoulder before offering me his hand. The room almost vibrated from the emotion we seemed to collectively exude. I had arrived.

The branch became my reward for having struggled through my job while handling the recognition events, branch manager meetings and guiding Purchase revenue to the top. I had logged several hundred hours in an office whose walls bordered on Fillmore's and Blaylock's. They knew they had put me through my paces, but I had survived this high-exposure task serving the two masters of the three-hundred-fifty-million-dollar annual sales business. I proudly walked out of the office, feeling taller than the six-foot-eight Fleming.

"Hold my calls, kiddo," I shouted at my secretary. "I've got a few calls to make."

I remembered knocking over a cup of stale coffee in my haste to dial our home number. I watched the coffee eat up a perfectly typed header page that Ella had cranked out earlier, but the paper got blurry as my eyes filled with almost as much fluid. Teardrops joined the coffee, tears of relief and emotion.

"Pat, it's done. Grand Rapids is ours!" A flood of emotion came back over the wire.

Fillmore wanted the promotion under wraps over the holidays, but gathered his Detroit Men's Club members for a meeting at the

"Suss." Fillmore, Blaylock, Gonzo, and I downed a few highballs at Fillmore's favorite watering hole and then headed for the suburbs.

Arriving home, Pat looked just as excited as I did. After attending a neighborhood party and announcing the promotion to our subdivision friends, at two that morning we were still raring to go. Knowing Blaylock and his wife, Doris, had hosted a small group at their home that evening and their penchant for partying, I predicted they would still be up.

Planning to crash the party, I rigged a sign for Pat to hang over her neck saying:

I'M A BRANCH MANAGER'S WIFE.
WHO IN THE HELL ARE YOU?

Over to Bloomfield Hills we drove for an enthusiastic reception by the Blaylock's and the Gonzagowski's. My stature had improved with IBM's status string now pulling tightly. We arrived back home by sunup.

Over the weekend I called Russell and gave him the confidential news. "I got the branch, Chad. And, thanks for all your help. Pulling off number-one ranking in Purchase revenue sure helped." Needing to cover a more delicate subject, I added, "Also thanks for your assistance in the year-end close-out under trying circumstances. I know that your wife must be plenty fed up because of your forced change of holiday plans."

Russell sounded far from excited about my promotion, and confided in me why he couldn't yet share in my euphoria. "My wife had a miscarriage," he informed me. "I figure the stress of my work and messed up holidays did it." My excitement quickly fell away, replaced with sympathy.

I had so looked forward to the birth of my children, that I could imagine the disappointment he was feeling now that their first opportunity for a child had ended in tragedy.

As the quiet man told me he strongly was considering resignation because of this event, we had a lengthy conversation about the pluses and minuses of him doing that. I felt like a total ass from picking Russell for the assignment.

After hanging up, I paused to reflect on what I'd become.

Russell, already working hard before I got my hands on him for the year-end pressure cooker, to which I had become accustomed, worked even harder once on my team. Very possibly, his promotion had contributed to him and his wife losing their baby. I thought about the last summer when I had lost twelve pounds at King's Island and the almost unbearable pressure of hosting the meetings. I asked myself, *Is all this really worth it?*

Unlike Russell, I already had become a full-fledged marionette with all the strings in place and tied to the control apparatus. And with my most recent promotion so fresh in my mind, I concluded, *Yep, it is worth it, every last bit of it —especially if you can get to where I'm going.*

Twenty-One

A S WE ENTERED LEXINGTON, I CONCENTRATED ON THE TASK AT HAND
— finding the restaurant at which I told Nichols I would meet
him. As I turned onto the exit ramp, Stonehawk began to stir.
"Hey, Chief, we're in Lexington."

He grunted in reply.

"The restaurant isn't far. Do you think you could act civilly
around my IBM friend, Nichols?"

Stonehawk stared at me blankly.

"Well, if you do, we might get a place to sleep tonight."

Seeing the meeting spot ahead, I slowed down, pulled into the
lot and parked the car. Stonehawk got out of the car slowly, limp-
ing behind me as I walked into the restaurant. I saw Nichols sitting
at a booth, and I walked up to him and gave him a firm handshake.

Nichols' eyes looked right past me, focusing on Stonehawk.
"Sit down here," he said, regaining his composure a bit. He waited for me to slide in so that he could sit on my side. Stonehawk
then sat down.

The waitress took our coffee order as I noticed an uncomfortable
Nichols giving Stonehawk the once over.

As I took a sip of my coffee, Stonehawk said, "My ankle's throb-
bin'. I need to borrow the car to get some aspirin."

He's trying to con me, I thought. *Yeah, but sooner or later I need to trust
him. Might as well make it now rather than in Michigan.* I gave him the

keys without a word.

Nichols and I ordered several refills while we talked about our days together in IBM and waited for Stonehawk to return. After the waitress poured the coffee for the fourth time, he asked, "You're getting worried about your friend, aren't you?" I nodded my head; I had a strong feeling that Stonehawk wouldn't be returning.

Two hours later, my watch showed 1:00 A.M., and I acknowledged to a fidgeting Nichols, "He won't be back."

Clearly I had stupidly misjudged the Chief's booze craving. Wherever he had driven, booze was sure to be nearby. I had given him forty dollars earlier in the day, so that he wouldn't have to feel like he bummed off me for every meal, not that obtaining alcohol, whatever the circumstances, posed much difficulty for the resourceful Indian.

"Well, Linda and I would like you to spend the night with us, Max. Let's get out of here."

"Thanks, Bob, let's go."

With their management's permission, I left a note on the restaurant door telling Stonehawk how to call me in the unlikely event I'd put it together wrong, and then I rode with Nichols to his residence. On the way, he volunteered, "I got about ten more calls today telling me about you and your pal, Stonehawk, heading north, that ... you know ... you helped him escape. If little ol' me got ten, you can imagine how many were made."

"Yeah, but it looks like I screwed up, Bob. I really figured the guy wanted to go straight. I figured wrong."

Once at Nichols' house, we sat in the living room and reminisced about the "good old days" when he worked for me. By the time I headed for his guestroom bed, the sun poked its rays over the horizon. As I lay my head on the soft pillow with the clean-smelling case, I briefly wondered where Stonehawk was spending the night before I fell asleep.

At about ten the following morning, the phone's ring woke me. As I lay lazily in the bed, Nichols poked his head into the doorway.

"I just got a call from an IBM associate," he said with a look that implied I might not like what I was about to hear. "He asked if you were in town, and I said, 'yeah,' but wanted to know how he found out. Well ... he said he had taken a call from the Kentucky State Police this morning telling him that last night they had jailed an individual named Thurmond Stonehawk. Stonehawk told the police he believed Beardslee, his associate, could be found staying with an IBMer in the area."

Shit. What a way to start the day, I thought. As it turned out, Stonehawk and I both got free accommodations but not exactly the way I planned.

"Since my guy at IBM knew about your and my friendship, he immediately called me," Nichols concluded.

"But of course," I replied with a wry grin. "I guess we should call the police."

Nichols dialed the number and inquired about Stonehawk's situation, also asking if they wanted me for anything. With me listening in on another phone, a Kentucky state trooper replied, "No. We don't need Beardslee for anything. He won't be charged."

I let an audible sigh of relief flow from my mouth.

"But, let me tell you," the trooper continued, "this Stonehawk guy gave us quite a go of it last night. He got into a fight in a bar, and, when he left, driving off in this guy Beardslee's rental car, he bounced off half the empty cars in the parking lot."

Oh, my God, I thought. *My rental car ...*

"Then he drove the car out into a hay field, and from there we ran him down on foot," the officer concluded.

Quietly hanging up the other phone and quickly walking into the kitchen where Nichols was on the other extension, I whispered to him, "Ask him what the police are planning to do with Stonehawk?"

Three feet away from the receiver I easily heard the cop's angry reply: "We'll belly-chain him and send his butt back to Florida."

That afternoon, Nichols and I drove to the police compound and examined the Hertz. The front end and right side were caved in and about six inches lower than Olds' intended it to be. From all the

348

weeds and dirt stuck to its tires and underside, it looked like the Chief had given it a real go. After retrieving the orange-handled bolt cutters and my gym bag, Bob drove me to an Avis car rental office. *What Avis didn't know oughta help me get a car,* I figured. Hertz had seen enough of me.

While there, I called Pat with apprehension. She knew I was out, but I hadn't spoken to her, so I had no idea as to what her reaction would be when she heard my voice. Her answering machine greeted me. "Hi, Pat. Hope you and the kids are well. I'm with Nichols in Lexington and should be at your house tomorrow."

So after solemn assurances to Nichols that I had no more planned tomfoolery, his credit card produced another car.

"Thanks, good friend. We'll stay in touch and I'll send you a check as soon as the court attorney will let me." Nichols waved me off. "Don't worry about it. Good luck."

I drove off and stayed behind the wheel of the Avis all night. At six o'clock, one hundred miles from Grand Rapids, the sunrise revealed a cloudless April day. *Just a couple of hours away from my family,* I figured. I felt great. I could even manage the pending divorce without a lot of hassle. *It'll be okay,* I told myself. *Probably for the best.*

As signs for a rest stop passed my window, I decided to stop and call Pat. She answered right away. "Get my message?"

"Yeah, congratulations on getting out, but I heard all about you and your Indian friend from the psychiatrist. How does it feel?"

"Never felt better. Look ... uh, I'll be seeing you and the kids in a couple of hours, that is er ... well, anyway, the Indian is no longer with me."

Pat sounded enthusiastic to hear from me. "Yeah, sure, we're expecting you. The kids are all excited; they've got presents for you. Get on up here."

Steve got on the phone. "Hi, Dad!" Excitedly, he told me, "Mom told us you were coming home. We got a surprise for you."

"Great, Son, I look forward to getting it."

"I knew you weren't sick, Dad. I knew you weren't sick."

"Good for you, Son. I guess for a while only you and I knew that, but you're absolutely right. See you in a couple of hours."

I hung up the phone with a smile on my face and jogged toward the car, eager finally to get home. Reflecting on Steve's prognosis, I believed him right — at least from how I felt. *Probably*, I thought, *I had been grandiose when I arrived in Florida, giving Lucido some reluctant forgiveness for his actions. But, I also thought, remnants of the illness had disappeared in a few days after being stuffed in the Fort. Whacking out Stonehawk, though, should I have? Was that normal behavior? Feeling great and acting normal might be two different sets of propositions,* I thought, as I reviewed the reasons why I had cut the Indian free.

Driving a steady sixty-five miles per hour all the way to Grand Rapids, the two hours went by quickly. Pulling into Pat's condo, the boys spilled out the front door before I could come to a full stop. Quickly stepping out of the car, I was hit with three little guys shouting and clamoring for an arm or a leg of mine. Walking inside, Pat gave me a hug and welcomed me home. A great start.

My three boys climbed all over me while giving me a box wrapped, obviously by them, in bright-colored paper. "Open it, open it!" they all screamed at me. I did, and inside found a V-necked sweater.

"A coming-home present, Dad," said the now-ten-year-old John. With vision clearer from months of being away, I noticed that he looked like me.

"How are John's grades?"

'Straight A's," my wife replied with pride in her voice.

I wasn't surprised. Little Chris, only three, touched the long hairs on my face. "Beard, Daddy." The little guy, all eyes, looked fragile sitting on my lap and happy, his eyes wide with wonder and excitement.

Pat had gotten the job done, our kids looked healthy and well adjusted. There was life after IBM, and a good one it seemed. "Why don't you take the kids to the ball field while I fix dinner?" she suggested. "It's just a block away."

After running around with the kids on the baseball field, an activity I enjoyed more than I'd ever remembered before, we all raced back. Intentionally, I finished last. Back in the condo, I showered and trimmed my beard. Donning a robe, I called downstairs to my wife. "Pat, come on up here, will you? I want to show you something." As she entered the room, I grabbed her and carried her to the bed. Walking to the entranceway, I closed the door and locked it. "We're probably gonna get a divorce, right?" I asked.

"Right," she replied.

"We found out through all this complicated stuff since the firing that we each see life differently than we thought, right?"

"That's about how I see it, yes," she said.

"Well, is it okay to get divorced and still love you as the mother of my children?"

"Sure it is, and thank you for that. I'll need your support in the years to come on that and — by 'that' I mean in ways other than just financial."

"Sure," I said, "I understand..." I hesitated, "Uh, would it be okay if we made love, at least just one more time?"

She didn't hesitate in her reply, her hand moving to the buttons on her blouse and she laughed. "Well, by God, Max, it sure took you a long time to get those words out."

It was to be our last time.

The next day we further defined what divorce would mean to both of us. As she took me through her detailed analysis, it fit with my own. "It's not you just losing your marbles, that's just the tip of our iceberg. You want to write a book, I'm trying to understand that. You don't want to work for a secure company like Steelcase — Roger Martin would have fixed you right up." She took a sip of water before continuing.

"You've got your share of bad habits like staying out late playing IBM, drinking too much, and I'm sure I've got mine."

"Yeah, Pat, you are right. Do you remember the times we used to argue about my job, the travel and all that?" She nodded. "Well, I'm done with all of that. But, you're still a young woman and oughta get married to someone who appreciates you more for what you are: a great mother and a loving and caring person. I don't know what the future holds in store for me and that's one of the reasons our marriage oughta end. Hell, I might want to milk cows in Texas or something. You can't be expected to follow my every whim, and damned if I don't believe I've got a few to flush out."

We ended the conversation on a friendly note; I agreed to move out and lease an apartment a few miles from her and the kids.

The next day I paid a cash deposit and moved into the apartment. After unpacking a few things, I went to find a pay phone, since my phone installation would take a few days. I called Amrose in Detroit.

After talking for awhile about IBM's interest, real or feigned, in hiring me back into the company, Amrose told me what he needed next. "I think we can get IBM to move on this after it's determined that you can represent yourself. Right now, you can't. Your judge in Grand Rapids needs to dissolve your conservatorship and put it in writing, of course."

"Okay, Fred," I enthusiastically replied. "I'll get right on it. Got a few too many attorneys on the payroll, too, as you probably know." I could hear him chuckling as I hung up the phone.

I set my mind to his task, quickly experiencing a new form of entanglement, a legalese one of catch-22 proportions. Still under a court-ordered conservatorship, I had five — count 'em, five — attorneys on the payroll of my very diminished estate. The first two, Amrose and Criswell, previously had been hired by me to take on IBM; a Workers' Compensation attorney Pat had hired to pursue a settlement on mental impairment — if I never made it out of the hospital —occupied the number three position; one court-appointed attorney, Matt White, who was supposed to be conserving my estate, made number four; and the fifth was another attorney Pat hired to process the divorce.

Five attorneys. Unbelievable! A year before that, I wondered why America had six times as many attorneys per capita as Japan.

International Business Marionettes

Back then I was convinced the only lifetime need I had for one would be in drafting a will.

Judge Warwick would not be expected to do me any favors in dissolving the conservatorship, even though I would tell him it had to be done to pursue a settlement with IBM. He had seen me at my worst, babbling about the asylum being a spaceship. Thus, Attorney White, who shuffled his feet on sending me money to get out of the Fort, remained firmly entrenched as the conservator of my estate. However, Amrose still believed that IBM would not want to go further with a settlement until I could legally represent myself, sans the conservatorship. After pondering that predicament, I came up with a solution. Hire lawyer number *six*.

Number six's sole mission was to get rid of White by dissolving my conservatorship. As a start, number six decided that I should go see two shrinks, a psychiatrist and a psychologist, independent of each other and obtain two reports stating that I looked and acted normal.

Concurrently, I read an article about an international organization called MENSA. According to the story, this group's membership represented people who had an I.Q. in the top two percent of adults. I figured getting into their club would be a real coup for me. *Go in and lay on the judge my membership card along with the newspaper article.* The idea appealed to me, I applied for membership. After four hours of playing around with blocks, numbers and spatial relationships, my psychologist-proctor tallied the results: "You have passed." Hot dog!

With two letters from the shrinks, the MENSA membership, and my sixth attorney, I went to court.

Warwick ordered White to pay from my estate any last-minute bills outstanding and ordered the conservatorship dissolved.

The last string was cut.

Out in the hallway, I enthusiastically shook the hand of my sixth attorney, and then executed a friendly firing. He had accomplished all he could. Two down. Four to go.

I met with Amrose and Criswell in Detroit. We agreed to try once again to get an offer from IBM other than just a willingness to put me back on their payroll or filing suit. Gaining needed cash now, as opposed to later, stuck out as the main benefit from such a deal, but not the only one. Legal fees remained a consideration. Amrose felt confident we would win a lawsuit if we needed to go that far; the point of law was clear about forcing an employee to spend his own funds to perform his job. However, I would be forced to settle at some unknown date for some unknown amount with Amrose's law firm gaining forty percent of the settlement. To date I had paid Amrose's law firm by the hour, avoiding a contingency settlement. My family and I could keep the whole settlement, minus a bonus I had in mind for Amrose.

I called Bernard Striker, the Armonk administrative assistant. After filling him in on my return to Grand Rapids and asking him to thank his associate, Kaufman, for sending me badly needed clothing, I brought him up to date on legal matters. "Bernard, I have court clearance papers in hand. The conservatorship has been dissolved. You can settle with me directly if you want to. The alternative is for me to sue IBM."

Striker sounded friendly and amicable as he quickly responded, "Retain counsel. Have them work with our lawyers. They should contact our guy, Raymond Pattinger, and we'll try to settle."

The key words were "retain counsel." Striker would not have me run up a legal tab if he didn't believe things could be worked out.

Great news, if the offer turned out fair, that would be the end of it. "What about a time frame, Bernard? Tell you what I'd like to do," I said before he could answer. "I'd like to fly to New York and meet with you and Kaufman, talk about my Open Door. From there, let's turn it over to the attorneys and see if we can't settle."

"How about mid-June, which makes it about three weeks?" he asked.

"Fine," I replied, encouraged that my normal patience had returned, another sign I'd recovered.

"I'll look forward to the meeting," he said and hung up the phone.

International Business Marionettes

Over lunch, Amrose couldn't get enough of my experiences at the Fort, mixing congenial laughter with a salad. "My stuff is pretty boring compared to yours, but I agree with you; IBM's suggestion that you retain counsel says they'll offer something. The question will be, is it the right something?"

"Yeah, Fred, if it comes to it, how much should I be asking for?" Amrose thought about that for awhile. "Half a million."

I handled that news calmly. "Sounds okay to me. Let's get it."

Back in Grand Rapids, I worked on the manuscript I'd started in the hospital. Gradually an outline took form. Following my natural marketing instincts, I knew it was time to begin figuring out a way to add visibility to my writing project. The answer to my questions of how to accomplish that feat came easily once I named the book, *International Business Marionettes*. I would have constructed a marionette that looked like me. He'd have a three-piece suit and a mug like mine. I'd use him as a marketing tool, perhaps putting him on the book cover or using him on television talk shows. Maybe I'd even bring him to seminars I'd give or signings in bookstores. My mind clicked through the possibilities; I could keep him busy. The anger I still had at how IBM treated me and their slowness in righting their wrong made me also want to use him to point the finger at Big Blue. He could be a busy little fellow.

After several failed attempts in locating somebody who could build a marionette, I hit pay dirt. New York City's directory, available to me in Grand Rapids' public library, contained a listing under "Marionettes" — just one, but it was there. "Bil Baird Studios."

Dialing the number, I was surprised to have the artist's agent on the phone, not him. *Ah,* I thought, *the ways of New York. Everybody probably has an agent.* After learning Baird had brought to life Kukla and Ollie of the "Kukla, Fran and Ollie" show, I agreed to his very high terms — three thousand in cash payable upon delivery. All I needed to do was send several photographs of myself, front and side view, to Baird. I could pick the marionette up when I flew to

New York the next month. Excited about the quality of person I had located to make my marionette, the next three weeks passed quickly.

On Thursday, June 19th, 1981, I flew to New York, and met with Striker and Kaufman, not in Armonk, but in Manhattan at a suite IBM reserved for stockholder relations. My first face-to-face meeting with Kaufman, the poor guy I had made jump through hoops about five months prior. Kaufman looked the executive part — silver haired, tall, firm and cold in his manner and his voice. No warmth left. A man turned marionette, wood and all.

The meeting was not particularly productive. Kaufman reiterated that IBM would be willing to re-hire me with a job in Atlanta, but he specifically stated he would not discuss particulars of my Open Door.

"Why in hell do you think I flew to New York?" I fumed. Kaufman fumed back. "I'm not gonna talk about it. Period."

Striker, who worked in the chairman's office and as part of his job was motivated to prevent lawsuits, calmed us down. "Hold it here, gentlemen, I want us to keep working on a solution, not on this bickering." I couldn't argue with that.

In turn I apologized to Striker for my past "Bungling Bernard" references, assuring him they came purely from the heat of battle.

Striker chuckled. "Aw that's all right," he said. "My wife found out about it, though, and now she occasionally says it." He sighed, palms raised to the ceiling in a feigned gesture of futility. "I'll give you a call, hopefully confirming that we'll try to settle. By the way, say one more time you don't want back into IBM; it'll affect any offer we might make to you."

"Okay," I managed to say through a grin. "I don't want to work another day at IBM — ever. By the way, when will you call? You know I'm hell on missed appointments." I chuckled.

"I remember. Tomorrow, Friday," he replied and smiled.

"Any chance of meeting Mr. Opel?"

"Max, I really doubt it."

Turning to Kaufman I asked, "What about it, Art? Did you check out Operation 30/30? Shouldn't that program get me in to Mr. Opel?"

International Business Marionettes

Kaufman smiled. "I checked it out. The corporation did very well off your program." *Nice praise bought little. That would be it from these two. I wouldn't be meeting John Opel. Well, okay,* I thought. *Enough is enough. Time to move on.*

We shook hands, and I took the long elevator from IBM's stockholder relations' offices in uptown New York to the sidewalk. From there I caught a cab to Baird's workshop in New York's Battery section. After literally going down two blind alleys, I found the one housing Baird's studio.

The artist's second-floor door, a thick steel one, looked formidable and appropriate for the neighborhood. A sharp knock, however, quickly produced the man well known in theatrical circles. The small, elderly gentleman, with a solid gold chain around his time-wrinkled neck, gave me a hearty welcome and a strong-fingered handshake. Walking into the dark studio, light from overhead skylights filtering through dust, I felt like I'd entered a movie studio. Hundreds of marionettes hung neatly from the rafters or sat piled on tables and shelves. Workbenches housed the tools of his trade — saws, drills, chisels, hammers, and a wide assortment of pliers, wrenches and knives. Some of the marionettes appeared several feet in length and were dressed in various garbs representing many periods of time. Pirates, sea captains, ballerinas, animals, and a life-sized owl, its huge eyes peering out at me, filled the man's workshop from floor to ceiling.

This creator must have had several lives worth of memories, I noted as Baird showed me some life-like doll props he'd constructed for the Broadway musicals, *The Sound of Music* and *Peter Pan.*

"The difference between a marionette and a puppet," the artist educated me, "is that a marionette has eleven strings with which to operate it and has oversized hands and feet. Your hand inside controls a puppet. Now, let's look at what I have for you."

With quick hands the craftsman pulled a case off the shelf, unzipped it, reached in, and pulled out my marionette. Its lifelike appearance startled me. Even its eyes glinted from ruby-like sparkling stones Baird had inset in the sockets. And its likeness to me was eerie indeed.

"Perfect, Mr. Baird. Perfect. Can I try it?"

Baird gave me instructions on how to pull the eleven strings individually from a hand-held control stick as I marveled over his construction. Even a string attached through the top of his head made his mouth open and close. "Got a name for the little guy?"

"Yes," I replied, "I do. I'm gonna call him DataBase."

Counting out thirty hundred-dollar bills, I paid the craftsman and carefully packed DataBase into his carrying case. With my mind already picturing how I would use the marionette, I said my goodbyes and took a cab to the airport. From there, my marionette rode with me on the flight back to Grand Rapids.

Mixing a Dewars and soda, I sat back down on the couch at my apartment and stared at the case. After thinking of several ways to put DataBase to work — heaping disfavor on IBM through my book's publicity tact, thus using him as a weapon to fight the behemoth company — I unzipped the case and pulled on the control stick. Out my little pal came, feet dancing and prancing as I gently pulled his strings. For two hours I practiced having DataBase walk, sit, bow, and shake hands. Gingerly, I packed him back in his case while I chuckled about when he would make his first official appearance.

After a good night's sleep, I stayed in the apartment awaiting Striker's call, whiling away the time by practicing with DataBase. I could now put my wooden pal comfortably through the basic moves.

Striker called, in the afternoon, as promised. "We'll try to settle. Our lawyer is flying in to Detroit to meet with yours next week."

"Thanks, Bernard," I said, feeling IBM's stonewalling finally breaking away. "I think we may all get something worked out now. You've been helpful this last go around. Thanks again."

"No problem. And, Max ... good luck."

Calling Amrose, I asked him what he thought about the upcoming meeting. "A very good sign, except for one thing ... IBM's attorney sounded really put out about coming out here."

I described to Amrose my new acquisition, and an idea I had for DataBase's first trial run out of the box. When I had concluded, the serious-natured Amrose gave a rare chuckle. "All right, all right. After all you've endured, you're entitled to a little fun. One thing, though..."

"What's that," I inquired.

"We can't tell my partner about this. He wouldn't go along."

"No problem, Fred. See you next week."

I bought a ten-speed bike and joined a YMCA, two ways to work off the last of the institutional calories during breaks from my work on the manuscript. I also looked forward to the Detroit meeting.

On the appointed day, I put on a dark-blue pinstriped suit and a white button-down shirt. Smoothing down my unruly hair as I looked at myself in the mirror, I thought, *You look pretty damn normal right now, Beardslee.* Grabbing DataBase and driving the two and half-hours to Detroit, I arrived a little early allowing me, through the use of a private office adjacent to the boardroom, to run DataBase through some paces. Satisfied with the results, I placed him back in his case and zipped him up.

Amrose walked in. "We're ready for you." Glancing down at the case he asked, "Is your pal in there?"

I nodded.

"Well, I'm looking forward to whatever you're gonna do with him. The IBM lawyer, a guy named Pattinger, is real tight. He's not admitting anything. Seems aggravated he's here, but what the hell, he flew out here to meet with you. That's a good sign."

Amrose picked up a pitcher sitting on the table and poured himself a glass of water, then took a sip before continuing. "He's got a couple of local lawyers with him. There's three of them plus my partner and me. Presumably, we'll be working with the local lawyers after today, and that's pretty standard."

"Okay, Fred," I said. "Anything you want me to emphasize?"

"Just what we rehearsed on the phone ... that you are determined to see this through. And for you," Amrose said with a grin, "that oughta be easy."

Picking up the case, I followed Amrose. Walking into the mahogany-paneled boardroom, I shook hands with Amrose's partner amicably and nodded to the three lawyers stacked on the other end of the table as they stood up. The middle one, short and overweight, proved to be Pattinger. All three stared at my carrying case, probably wondering if it was full of notes and files and worrying about whether I would want to go through hours of dialogue with them. I merely set the case down on the floor under the other side of the table, where IBM's attorneys couldn't see its contents, unzipped it and placed the control handle outside, ready for quick access.

Amrose opened the discussion. "Gentlemen, since we've pretty much discussed why Mr. Beardslee was fired and why we believe IBM is liable for wrongful dismissal, we thought it would be helpful for you to meet our client and ask him any questions you may have. But first we want Mr. Beardslee to tell you in his own words why he altered an invoice from cigars to photocopies."

Pattinger never looked up as Amrose spoke. He merely examined his well-manicured fingertips and glanced at his expensive-looking watch.

"Thanks, Fred. How much time do I have?"

Pattinger sighed and replied instead, "I have a flight in two hours and the airport is an hour from here."

I sighed back. "Looks like all you feel this trip might do for you is build up your frequent-flyer miles."

Amrose winced.

Pattinger glared.

It felt good.

"Where was I?" I said with heavy sarcasm. "Oh yeah. My firing. Well, Mr. Pattinger, gentlemen, I would have hoped my Open Door simply substantiated two things: one, that non-reimbursable expenditures at meetings under Fillmore's direction ran more than twenty dollars per person, and, two, that I was limited to collecting twenty dollars per person — minus those who chose not to pay anything, of course." I said the latter with a broad grin looking right at Pattinger and enjoying this opportunity immensely, then continued.

"From there I was left to my own resources as to how to balance the pot. On all but two occasions I shelled out my own dough and a guy named Blaylock, my boss at the time, usually also helped cover the shortfall.

"Now about the expense violations ... I called hundreds of dollars of tennis court fees, cigars, gum, and mints 'meeting room rentals' and 'slide projector rentals.' I got ordered to do so by Blaylock."

Turning to Amrose, I summarized: "Those two points, the expenditures and the limits of collection, are easily proven either through my Open Door or a court of law. What I was left with then, meant paying out of my own pocket, or figuring out another way, like invoice alteration, to come out whole."

I paused, then said, "Mr. Amrose, here, says shame on IBM for putting me in that position, because you can't force an employee to spend his own funds for company-ordered functions. It's against the law."

Pattinger, looking agitated, glanced at his watch and asked, "That it?"

Reaching down with my right hand, I grabbed DataBase's control stick and pulled upward.

"No, Mr. Pattinger, not quite." DataBase's oversized feet flipped over my head and came prancing down on the mahogany table. From there he did a bow, walked over, and shook Amrose' hand. Turning him around to face Pattinger, I said, "Gentlemen, meet DataBase."

Pattinger stood up, then sat down, startled over the proceedings. Amrose's partner, a person with a normally even demeanor, also looked strung out as he raised his eyebrows at me, mouth open. The loose flesh around Pattinger's mouth quivered from anger and surprise as he stammered, "What's this got—"

"Relax, Mr. Pattinger," I interrupted. "DataBase, here, won't bite. He's merely a symbol of what I became; I became a puppet, a marionette, to be exact, while in your employ ... not in the early years, but toward the end. See these strings here? Watch what happens when I pull on one of them. The marionette responds to my slightest hand movement. That's what happened to me. IBM wanted me to produce a certain image at its business meetings with an impossible budget, pulling my 'figure-it-out' string to do it. Now, in the middle of my career with IBM, before I got all strung up, I developed a program called Operation 30/30 that is helping pay for your hefty retirement. A retirement denied me."

Five pairs of eyes were riveted on me. Still crazy? they seemed to ask. Well, Amrose believed otherwise; that was enough for me.

"So, DataBase, here, represents thousands of other IBMers out there who either need IBM's strings to hold them up or hate the strings because they hold them back or, like in my case, get entangled in them. DataBase symbolizes an International Business Marionette — an IBMer. A Beemer."

Pattinger glowered at me while he stuffed notes in his briefcase and slammed it shut.

Getting angry as I watched his annoyance at having to get involved in my case at all, I kept going. IBM would hear me out and it would handle the problem I posed to them. "Now, you gentlemen have had several months to ponder my Open Door. From your dour expression, Mr. Pattinger, you either don't believe me or you do believe me and have a 'so-what' attitude about it. Well, after enduring three mental institutions I've learned to be patient. I can wait on a court of law. I know what my witnesses will say."

I stuck my hand in an inner suitcoat pocket, hauled out a cigar, tapped the middle string on DataBase's head and plopped the cigar into his open mouth, releasing the string and watching it clamp down.

"All that's been discussed here, today, is over a box of these." I pointed at the cigar in DataBase's mouth. "Incredible when you think about it."

Setting DataBase down I made my final point. "Having to deal with people like Paulos and Hampstead is one thing. Every company has its so-called saviors like those two portray themselves to be. But having the world's so-called best-managed company, billing itself as a parental corporation, botch up any attempts to right a wrong by dragging this thing out or not wanting to discuss it openly, only says to me I need help making my point. DataBase will help me make my point.

"Well, Mr. Pattinger, you look like you could use a drink. Have a nice day, gentlemen."

With a flip of my wrist I had DataBase sitting on my shoulder as I sauntered out of the boardroom and out to Amrose's typing pool to entertain the secretaries.

Twenty minutes later Amrose found me there. Smiling, he said, "You did well. They don't know what to make of you, and that's probably good. On the way out of the door Pattinger asked for ninety days to receive IBM's final position. I think we'll be getting an offer of settlement. After that it's a question of how much."

Before leaving for Grand Rapids I met "Too Tall" Fleming, the six-foot-eight-incher who ran the manufacturing program for me, and a dozen IBMers at the Golden Mushroom in a suburb of Detroit for a reunion of sorts. DataBase hung from an overhead chandelier acting as a magnet for another dozen of Southfield's fairer sex, all wanting to know who he was and what he represented. I enjoyed repeating the story until well past midnight before turning in at a nearby motel. My cohorts all stayed for the duration, wincing at some of my rhetoric directed at their company, but enjoying the influx of people DataBase attracted.

The next day, arriving in Grand Rapids and placing DataBase safely in a closet, I focused on employment. Almost out of cash, the manuscript would have to wait. Any future job required only that it be with a less-than-tightly-structured organization.

In the next two weeks I lined up some employment interviews gained from ads in the paper and followed up with phone calls and letters. Also I typed up a resume, conveniently listing the time since May in the chronology section as "Self-employed. Writing a book about business."

Pat had an attorney complete a divorce settlement. After amicably reviewing it with her, I thought the conditions appeared fair. She would earn half of any settlement from IBM, and I would pay child support until each boy reached the age of eighteen. A further understanding is that I would fund college.

The worst job hunting experience I had came in September of 1981. From my response to an ad in the newspaper I received an interview with the owner of a car dealership — Western Michigan's largest in both personal girth and dollar volume — that needed a controller. *What the hell,* I figured, *I can do lots of things besides selling. I know the numbers, and maybe it'll lead to something.*

The interview had gone well, including the disclosure of my previous mental illness. The owner had even commented that he knew and liked my father. I happily heard the rotund dealer commit to driving with me to Detroit for a meeting with his accountants in a couple of days. If that went favorably, the job was mine. He gave me his private number, and I left.

In the days that followed, repeated efforts to reach the owner proved fruitless. No meeting, no response, no nothing.

In the weeks to come, three other interviews produced no response. In each of these, the interviewer always appeared eager to follow up despite my disclosure of my mental illness requiring hospitalization. A clear picture was painted for me that Grand Rapids could not be counted on to put a psychiatric hospitalization behind them. Maybe I was overreacting, maybe not. Four interviews were, admittedly, not a lot to form the basis of a case for rejection.

Living away from my family had become an unpleasant reality. I felt Pat would be okay; young and attractive, she surely would find a new mate easily. But three boys being raised without a father, well, that could spell trouble from all I'd read and heard.

Taking John and Steve to a movie, we went to a McDonald's where I brought the subject of divorce up to them. "You know your mother and I are not going to stay married." They nodded, their intensity showing their interest. "Well, the important thing here is that you guys — Chris is too young — understand that you have a mother and a father who both love you and will both take care of you. You will be living with your mother."

John handled the news well but Steve sniffled. "Are you gonna handle this okay, Steve?"

"Yes Dad," he said and then broke into tears.

"Well, come on, let's go back up to the counter and get some ice cream."

With my employment efforts stalemated and enough funds left to wait out the ninety days until I heard from IBM, I rented an office near the apartment and spent more time on the manuscript, my pal DataBase hanging from the ceiling.

In October of 1981, I received a call from Dean Hamilton of "gum on the crotch" fame about a developer he had met in Atlanta who wanted to hire a sales manager. "It's a good deal for him and you. I know the guy pretty well, and you two would get along. He's a good ol' boy with an interesting concept on how to sell real estate tax shelters. But he needs a sales guy to make his dream happen. He wants to build thousands of townhouses."

I had dinner with Pat and the kids, describing this opportunity to them. "It's eight hundred miles away, but it's in a good city ... Atlanta. And the builder is trying to do something new and innovative. It's a lot of financial numbers, so I know I can do it. If the developer wants me, I'll probably take it."

Pat and the boys gave me an enthusiastic send off with a special dinner the night before I left. I arrived in Atlanta on November nineteenth, enjoyed my meeting with the congenial developer and, sans the beard, started the next day.

Every two weeks I got an update about IBM from Amrose. By early December, even though IBM had missed its projected settlement date of three months, he remained positive that an offer would come. "They're showing us income charts, and we're showing them the same. Sooner or later they'll offer something." I remained patient wanting to avoid the only alternative, a lengthy lawsuit, but feeling anger over their snail like pace.

IBM did make an offer — of sorts. In early December, Amrose called again, his voice somber. "IBM has offered to pay fifty-thousand dollars without admitting any wrong-doing on their part."

Taken back at the small number, I quickly replied "Look, Fred, just say, 'no.' Don't even counter. We're too far apart. That's an insult. I could care less what they admit to or don't. It's no longer an ego thing for me, just some bucks." Amrose agreed with my suggested approach. I felt dismayed at the news; a settlement now appeared far on the horizon.

While I enjoyed getting into my new job, which seemed to have positive long-term potential, another two weeks went by before I heard from Amrose again. This time Amrose's voice conveyed excitement. "IBM just offered a quarter of a million in cash," he said, his baritone voice raised half an octave higher than normal.

Yeah, I thought. *We could get this done without a lengthy lawsuit and expensive legal fees.* "What do we need to do to wrap this up, Fred? We aren't quite at the number I have in mind," I replied.

Amrose and I talked about a recent nationally publicized settlement where a Ms. Murray sued IBM in court and won three-hundred-thousand dollars for being unfairly dismissed. The lady, an IBM marketing manager on the West Coast, lived with a salesman whose company competed with hers. IBM viewed their relationship as a conflict of interest, so in their benevolent style, they fired her.

I reminded Amrose that my potential lawsuit would make hers pale in comparison and told him to reject IBM's offer.

Knowing IBM's personnel practices, I predicted to Amrose that we would either get another offer before Christmas, or we would have to sue. "Good news comes before the holidays; bad news after. That's the way they'll play."

Hanging up, I thought, *Amrose can pull it off. IBM wouldn't be too finicky about more dough at this point, and Ms. Murray popped up just in time. Thank you, Ms. Murray.*

At about one in the afternoon on Christmas Eve, as I played backgammon with Chris Jonesby, now back from Germany and living in Atlanta, the phone rang: Amrose. He did not call to wish me a Merry Christmas. He talked and I listened.

As I hung up the phone, Jonesby asked "What? What? What is it?"

I didn't answer immediately. Instead, I picked up my brandy highball — and threw it, glass and all, against the brick fireplace of my condo.

◆◆◆

The month following I went out shopping for a word processor. Finding a Macintosh on sale at a PC store, I marveled at its features and functions versus IBM's personal computers — another clue that IBM would have its hands full in the future. After installing all the software, I sat down to the unfamiliar keyboard and mouse.

Now, let's see ... I oughta begin with DataBase, I concluded. After all, he represented the main point I needed to establish, the one about which I really wanted to write. Pecking away, I glanced at the screen's first line. "At the top of his profession, that's how the old man had been billed..."

Afterword

IN 1981 I MOVED TO ATLANTA AND HAVE HAPPILY REMAINED THERE — MY mental health nightmare never re-occurred. Although I looked like a textbook manic depressive for the better part of a year, I'm not one. Those suffering from manic depressive disorder experience definitive cycles, I've learned, and there's no known cycle as long as twenty years. I can only speculate as to the root cause of the sickness I endured those many years ago.

It's worth considering, however, so, here goes — character is the link here: the link between aspirations and actions. My own character back in the 1970s hadn't sufficient insulation to process what many might conclude to be a reasonable failure. Many sales execs get fired every year for lots of reasons; the job is viewed as high risk and high turnover. My emotional stem, however, was too short, causing the harsh realities of my sacking to leap in unfiltered, overloading and then popping circuits. This overload acted similar to head injury victims, I've come to understand. Somehow I damaged my brain, albeit temporarily.

Over the years I've taken a candid look at this thing called character. And, in my case, I've concluded that many of the negative personality traits like self-centeredness, anger, self pity and denial got compounded through drinking. Booze acts like Miracle Grow in matters of character deficiencies. If character flaws were a category, I'd have won more than my share of blue ribbons at the State Fair.

About ten years ago I quit drinking and began working out in a gym four to five hours per week. The combination has helped me absorb life's experiences on a more even keel basis. It's had the effect of lengthening my emotional stem, affording my brain's circuits to handle life's load.

Gaining relatively high-paying jobs proved pretty easy. I've had four since IBM and all came from someone I knew while at IBM. Ex-IBMers are everywhere! I never had to supply a resumé until after I'd secured the job.

Having been in a mental institution, therefore, proved to be no job barrier at all. I found much less structure at the top in post-IBM jobs. And, by the way, there was no problem in expensing cigars, gum, fruit bowls and even booze, if the business occasion called for them.

I hear Fillmore is in Florida, retired. I miss him. I hear Blaylock enjoyed a few more promotions before getting an "early out" emphasis program IBM employs from time to time. I heard he's running a small bank in Minnesota. I miss him. Lucido and I didn't talk for seven years, but we're now good friends again. Jonesby remains a good friend.

As to the Chief, I have no clue. My guess is the ravages of booze have put him on the wrong side of the sod. I did talk to him once after he'd been belly chained and flown back to Florida. He was at his home and took down my phone number by writing it on the wall. That would be my Chief.

Of the dozens of close friends from the 70s, most left IBM of their own volition. One stuck it out. Thirty-one years. Of solid character including decorations from the Vietnam War, my Irish buddy enjoyed the early years of his career, but the last fifteen or so found him shuffled around quite a bit. In one case he felt used and stepped on by a former friend over a re-assignment. Recently, over a round of golf, he summed up the last five years of his career with this gem: "They piss in your face and tell you it's rainwater."

I entered into a second marriage; it lasted twelve years, identical to my first one in length. Friendly with both ex's, I did make an effort to get back together with Pat, the mother of my children, in the last year. It's not going well for me although I think she enjoyed the chase. At this date it's just "good friends" and she has moved back to Maine after her own second marriage ended in divorce.

Max Beardslee

My sons grew up largely without me nearby, and I have regrets over that. They are doing well, but their formative years came and went without consistent contact with me. There were some unnecessary struggles placed in their paths from my absence, and risking a family livelihood over diddly amounts of dough might seem foolhardy to most readers. After all, a lifetime career at IBM would pay out a couple of million dollars plus retirement. I didn't see it that way at the time, however. My resentment about shelling out any sum of money in the course of running IBM's meetings had built up to a "no mas" level.

I continue to notice that mental health is an uncomfortable subject for most. Whenever I have brought up my circumstances to friends, old or new, most tend to change the subject the first chance they get. Along those lines I've had second thoughts in disclosing to the reading public my mental illness and lapses of character. However, this story would never have evolved without those two ingredients, and I very much wanted the story told in an honest way, the warts on both sides, mine and IBM's, showing.

I wanted the story told because not telling it, or telling it in pieces, proved burdensome. Also, I accepted as a challenge the ability to write something worth reading. For those considering it, getting to an acceptable level of writing can be difficult. When telling a story, one gets to use voice inflection, facial expression and gestures. With writing, however, no such aids exist and without them I really struggled at the start.

And, by the way, getting the story published proved difficult. In 1983, I thought I'd generated a passable manuscript and even gained one publisher's interest based on a query letter I'd sent out. That's as close as I got in the next sixteen years. About ten years ago, I concluded my writing rambled so I hired an editor. She didn't write any text, but she sure as hell coached me, line by line. I felt the outcome was acceptable and to the best of my ability.

Earlier this year I read a book on publishing by Dan Poynter. Deciding to remove the burden of an untold story I initiated activities based on his approach. While contracting for dust cover artistry I literally stumbled into Lucky Press, an up-and-coming publisher based in Ohio specializing in books about people who overcome life-changing experiences. Its owner, Janice Phelps, and I hit it off, Lucky Press offered to publish my book, and the rest is history as they say.

Lastly, let's consider the culturally-driven question of winners. Any winners here? Both sides the way I see it. The Operation 30/30 program clearly made IBM hundreds of millions of extra revenue dollars. My ego basks in the belief that I contributed vastly greater sums to IBM's profits than the personnel guy and divisional president who took me out. I survived, and so I won as well from how I now live my life. I fight my old narcissistic ways by being aware of that kind of thinking and leading a more moderate, balanced life. I sleep better. I got the mid-life crisis over with, and now I can play the back nine of life with a little more grace.